Piaget's Theory of Intelligence

Charles J. Brainerd

University of Western Ontario

Prentice-Hall, Inc., Englewood Cliffs, New Jersey 07632

Library of Congress Cataloging in Publication Data

BRAINERD, CHARLES J
   Piaget's theory of intelligence.

Bibliography: p. 299
   Includes index.
   1. Cognition in children. 2. Piaget, Jean,
1896–   I. Title.
BF723.C5B63   155.4'13'0924   77-20935
ISBN 0-13-675108-3

Back cover photo credit:
1976, Television Center, Faculty of Psychology and Educational Sciences,
University of Geneva, Photograph by Alain Perruchoud

©1978 by Prentice-Hall, Inc., Englewood Cliffs, N.J. 07632

Printed in the United States of America

10 9 8 7 6 5 4 3 2 1

Prentice-Hall International, Inc., *London*
Prentice-Hall of Australia Pty. Limited, *Sydney*
Prentice-Hall of Canada, Ltd., *Toronto*
Prentice-Hall of India Private Limited, *New Delhi*
Prentice-Hall of Japan, Inc., *Tokyo*
Prentice-Hall of Southeast Asia Pte. Ltd., *Singapore*
Whitehall Books Limited, *Wellington, New Zealand*

For Susan and Tereasa

Contents

Contents

v

4

Piaget on Early Childhood:
The Preoperational Stage   95

*The Negative Side of the Preoperational Stage: Mental Operations.
The Positive Side: Illustrative Cognitive Contents. Replication Studies.
Synopsis. Supplementary Readings.*

5

Piaget on Middle Childhood:
The Concrete-Operational Stage   134

*The Transition to Operational Intelligence. Logico-arithmetic Operations.
Spatial Operations. Learning. Replication Studies. Synopsis.
Supplementary Readings.*

6

Piaget on Adolescence:
The Formal-Operational Stage   202

*General Features of Formal-Operational Thought.
Two Categories of Formal Operations. Replication Studies. Synopsis.
Supplementary Readings.*

7

Piaget on Education   270

*Some General Principles of Instruction. Illustrative Piagetian Curricula.
Synopsis. Supplementary Readings.*

Preface

Most introductory textbooks are written because the author thinks he perceives some specific need that is not met by existing works. This book is no exception. For the past five years, I have been attempting to teach Piaget's theory to undergraduates in the social sciences, humanities, and education. I have tried to provide students with a treatment of the theory that is both comprehensive and objective. But I have not found existing secondary sources equal to the task.

In view of the popularity of Piaget's theory (it has been standard fare in introductory courses in psychology and education for some years), one might suppose that a wide variety of textbooks would be available to instructors. Owing perhaps to the theory's complexity, only four have been published in English. Only one of these, Flavell's (1963) classic treatise, meets the twin criteria of objectivity and comprehensiveness. Unfortunately, this is primarily a graduate text and, insofar as Piaget-related research is concerned, it is now somewhat dated. The remaining books, each of which is intended for an undergraduate readership, tend to be rather brief. Although one of them presents a reasonably detailed discussion of the theory, the other two are little more than outlines. All three tend to treat the theory as revealed truth rather than as a set of hypotheses to be submitted to experimental test. One finds, for example, no mention of replication research on the theory conducted by investigators outside Geneva. Since this research is now quite extensive, consisting of hundreds of studies published in several languages, a failure to discuss the key findings seems an unconscionable oversight. Moreover, I believe the student is seriously short-changed when the theory's claims are presented *ex cathedra* and no attempt is made to assess their empirical validity.

From the instructor's point of view, this book would seem to have three important features. First, there are the research summaries that appear in the second half of Chapters 3 and 6. These summaries focus on replication research conducted by investigators outside Geneva, and they contain the major empirical findings on Piaget's four stages. Since this is a textbook rather than a journal article, I have naturally had to be selective in the matter of specific experiments cited. This is especially true of the chapter on the concrete-operational stage. When doubts arose in my mind, I preferred to err on the side of discussing too many experiments instead of discussing too few. Nevertheless, it was sometimes necessary to omit entire research topics that certain readers may consider important (e.g., memory and imagery in Chapter 5). Second, there are the synopses and supplementary reading lists at the end of Chapters 2 through 7. Each synopsis contains a fairly complete reprise of the major points raised in the preceding chapter. Each supplementary reading list provides a source of further material on some of the specific themes covered in the preceding chapter. It is my hope that these lists may be used both as a source of enriched readings for more advanced students and as a source of paper and essay themes.

Third and finally, there is the chapter on education which concludes this book. The desire for information on the instructional implications of Piaget's theory has grown quite remarkably in recent years. Since Piaget himself has been rather vague on this matter, a number of writers outside Geneva have attempted to spell out these implications. We shall see that they have managed to agree on several key points. At the same time, others have been devising and testing experimental preschool curricula that put Piagetian principles to work in the classroom. Both the main instructional ramifications of Piaget's theory and existing Piagetian curricula are reviewed in the last chapter.

One of the most difficult things about textbook writing, at least for me, is the problem of how to avoid writing a book that is tailored to the author's peculiar teaching needs. Inevitably, decisions about whether to include this or that topic are influenced by these needs and corrective feedback from other instructors becomes essential. The present book, despite its remaining inadequacies, benefited greatly from suggestions made by Ruth Ault, Edward Cornell, Dorathea Halpert, Ellen Markman, and Scott Paris. These suggestions are much appreciated and gratefully acknowledged.

Charles J. Brainerd

London, Canada

chapter 1

Introduction

In this book, we shall survey some of the contributions of the Swiss psychologist Jean Piaget to the study of children's intelligence. We shall also consider the findings of selected research conducted by investigators other than Piaget designed to test predictions based on Piaget's views about the development of intelligence. We begin with a brief overview of Piaget's life that draws together biographical facts strewn through his various works. I think that most of these facts are interesting in their own right. More important, however, some of them may serve to illuminate the dark corners of Piaget's theory. We shall discover as we proceed that there are a number of dark corners in need of illumination.

Biographical Sketch

Jean Piaget was born in the small Swiss city of Neuchâtel on August 9, 1896. His father was a medieval classics scholar who taught in the local university and also dabbled in history. Although, as we shall see, Piaget is not one who favors environmentally based explanations of cognitive development, it is nevertheless true that his father was the perfect model for the work Piaget eventually decided to pursue. Thanks to his father's influence, Piaget seems never to have considered the more adventuresome alternatives to scholarly work that captivate other small boys.

At about age 7, Piaget became a serious amateur naturalist. He was especially interested in birds and seashells. At age 10, Piaget wrote his first scientific paper, a short article dealing with an albino sparrow he had discovered in a local park. He submitted the paper to a Neuchâtel natural history journal, *Rameau de Sapin*, whose editor, quite unaware that the paper's author was a 10-year-old boy, accepted it for publication. Following this incident, Piaget became more deeply immersed in the study of natural history. After school, he helped the director of Neuchâtel's Museum of Natural History catalogue an extensive personal collection of mollusk shells. As a reward for his efforts, Piaget was allowed complete access to the museum's fossil collections. The director also gave Piaget several rare shells with which to begin his own collection. His work at the museum continued until the director's death. By this time Piaget was 14 years old.

Between 1911 and 1915 Piaget published a series of papers on mollusks based on his studies at the Neuchâtel museum. These articles made Piaget's name well known in European malacology circles and, eventually, produced conflicts regarding his age. Of these, perhaps the most amusing incident occurred when the director of Geneva's prestigous Museum of Natural History, who knew Piaget only through his published work, wrote to offer him the curatorship of the museum's mollusk collection. Piaget gracefully declined in favor of finishing high school. Piaget's youth also led to less amusing problems. Editors of certain natural history journals in which he had previously published, who were now aware of his age, refused to publish further articles.

At about this time, Piaget began to broaden his interests. While continuing his work on mollusks, he took up the study of philosophy. His early philosophical studies were to have a profound influence on his subsequent investigations of children's intelligence. He read the works of all the popular philosophers of the day—Henri Bergson, William James, Herbert Spencer—and took copious notes. Unfortunately, Piaget's studies soon led to physical and mental exhaustion. (A similar reaction, though considerably less severe, is not unknown among other science students encountering their first readings in philosophy.) The fatigue forced Piaget to withdraw to the Alps for a year of rest and recuperation. Characteristically, he found time to work. He wrote a philosophical novel entitled *Recherche* that was published in 1918.

Piaget received his bachelor's degree from the University of Neuchâtel in 1915 when he was 18—the age when most of us are just beginning our university education. The degree was in biology, and he did no formal course work in what we would recognize as psychology. While still an undergraduate, Piaget spent time reflecting on then-current philosophical controversies. One particular controversy, the so-called *part-whole problem,* haunted his thoughts. The part-whole problem, which had been made fashionable by the German philosopher Hegel, consists of asking whether individual elements (parts) or the classes to which they belong (wholes) are "more real." Philosophically sophisticated readers will recognize this question as a modern version of the medieval debate between the nominalists and the realists. The view of common sense and empirical science is that elements are real and classes are merely names. However, the German idealist school of philosophy, of which Hegel was a member, maintained that classes were more real than their members and thereby precipitated the part-whole controversy.

In any case, Piaget took the part-whole problem very seriously and concluded that it was absolutely fundamental to all areas of scientific investigation. This fact distinguishes Piaget from most psychologists, who consider neither philosophy nor the part-whole problem very relevant to their work. Apart from Piaget's work, Gestalt psychology is the only other influential school of psychology to have viewed the part-whole problem as fundamental. During the course of his undergraduate reflections on the part-whole problem, Piaget formulated a solution that has been embodied in much of his subsequent work. He concluded that all the phenomena that science studies (physical systems, biological systems, social systems, even mathematical systems) are made up of *qualitatively different* "wholes" that impose order and regularity on their "parts." In these systems, there are no parts as such. The parts exist only to the extent that they enter into the structure of the wholes to which they belong. Readers who find this idea somewhat opaque should rest assured that they are not alone. In fact, it may serve to illustrate at the outset an important fact about Piaget's theory: As a rule, the more central an idea is to his theory, the more difficult it is to comprehend. Hence, the would-be Piaget reader must be armed with considerable perseverance. We shall see that the part-whole idea is extremely important to the theory. It is to be hoped that it will become clearer as we go along.

After receiving his bachelor's degree, Piaget enrolled for Ph.D. studies at the University of Neuchâtel. Three years later, in 1918, he completed a dissertation on mollusks and was granted the Ph.D. Once again, he took no formal courses in psychology, a fact that was beginning to bother him. While a doctoral student, he had developed certain psychological hypotheses, mostly concerned with what we would call philosophical questions, that he wished to put to the test of experimentation. Therefore, upon completing his doctoral work Piaget traveled to Zurich intending to work in psychological laboratories there. About a year later, he moved on to Paris for the same purpose. He spent two years in Paris, during which he did course work in psychology at the Sorbonne. To support himself, he took a job as a research assistant in the laboratories of Alfred Binet, the originator of modern intelligence tests. Binet was dead by this time, and the laboratories were being directed by Theodore Simon, Binet's coauthor on the first standardized intelligence test. A British psychologist, Sir Cyril Burt, had devised a new reasoning test based on Aristotelian syllogisms. (Example: Socrates is a man. All men are mortal. Therefore, Socrates is mortal.) The test had recently been translated into French, and Simon assigned Piaget the job of standardizing it on Paris elementary schoolers. Piaget was supposed to find out how many items the average 5-year-old could pass, how many items the average 6-year-old could pass, and so on.

As any good investigator would, Piaget soon struck off on directions of his own. In addition to his assigned task of determining pass-fail norms for French versions of Burt's items, he decided to undertake detailed studies of the reasoning of children who *failed* the items. Whenever a given child answered a given item incorrectly, Piaget would ask probing questions designed to uncover the reasoning strategies the child had employed on that item. Piaget relied on psychiatric interviewing techniques that he had learned at clinics in Zurich and Paris. This psychiatric interview procedure has dominated all of Piaget's subsequent work on cognitive development, and it has come to be called the *clinical method.*[1] The strengths and weakness of the clinical method will be discussed in Chapter 2.

Piaget noticed that the strategies children used on Burt's test were not at all like the strategies adults used. Before long, he reached a important conclusion: Children's thinking processes and adults' thinking processes are *qualitatively different* from each other. He viewed this as preliminary evidence that his undergraduate analysis of the part-whole problem had some empirical merit. The discrepancy between child and adult reasoning also caused Piaget to conclude that cognitive development could be characterized by an invariant succession of qualitatively distinct stages. Piaget has retained this early vision across the years. Later on, we shall see that the notion of qualitative stages remains one of the most basic (and controversial) features of his theory of cognitive development.

During his assistantship with Simon, Piaget decided that his future lay in the study of children's intelligence. He planned a series of investigations of children's language, judgment, and causal philosophies, all of which were eventually conducted in Geneva and Neuchâtel. Piaget's ostensive aim was to show that the basic components of human intelligence are not innate, as most European psychologists of that era supposed, but are acquired gradually as a function of interactions between innate predispositions and experience. This interactionist theme remains central to Piaget's outlook.

Piaget was soon publishing numerous papers in psychological journals. He published one such paper in 1921, two in 1922, and three in 1923. One of these articles was read by Edouard Claparéde, the leading

[1] Recently, some of Piaget's coworkers (Inhelder, Sinclair, and Bovet 1974) have re-named the method calling it the *method of critical exploration.* On the assumption that a rose by any other name smells as sweet, I shall, to avoid confusion, use the older name.

Swiss psychologist of the day. Claparéde was so impressed that he wrote to Piaget and offered him the directorship of research at the Rousseau Institute in Geneva. In the 1920s, the Rousseau Institute was the most prominent French-language center for educational research in the world, and it was no small event for a 24-year-old research assistant to be asked to assume its research directorship. Piaget retained this position until 1925 when he returned to Neuchâtel for a time. Virtually all of the research that we shall be surveying later in this book was conducted at the Rousseau Institute.

Piaget left Paris for Geneva in 1921. He made tentative plans to spend a few years conducting the studies he had designed in Paris. He would then return to philosophy and write a definitive theory of knowledge based on biology and psychology. The latter project took rather longer than he expected. The planned theory, carrying the title *Biology and Knowledge,* was not ready for publication until 1967.

The research that Piaget conducted during his early years at the Rousseau Institute was published in a series of books that appeared in French between 1923 and 1932 and somewhat later in English (Piaget 1926*a*, 1926*b*, 1929, 1930, 1932). These books were concerned more with the social side of child development (e.g., language, moral concepts, philosophies about how the world works) than they were with the logical and mathematical skills that are more commonly associated with Piaget's work. The first of the books, *The Language and Thought of the Child,* brought Piaget instant international notoriety when it was translated in 1926. The book presented an interesting though rather sparsely documented hypothesis about the nature of children's language. According to the hypothesis, language development may be viewed as proceeding from a state in which the main function of language is self-stimulation, which Piaget called *egocentric language,* to a state in which the main function of language is interpersonal communication, which Piaget called *socialized language.* The hypothesis was soon being studied by other researchers with the overall result that investigators outside Geneva did not find as much egocentric language in their children as Piaget did in his. From the 1920s to the present day, the general finding has been that, although egocentric language can be found and seems to decrease with age, socialized language tends to predominate at even the youngest age levels. We shall return to this topic in Chapter 4.

Piaget's research took a new turn during the late 1920s. The earlier studies just mentioned, besides being concerned with social development, had two general features: (*a*) Purely verbal methods were used (i.e., Piaget asked questions and his subjects answered them), and (*b*) the subjects were either preschoolers or elementary schoolers. The new research had neither of these characteristics. Piaget had recently married one of his students at the Rousseau Institute, Valentine Chatenay. They soon had three children —Jacqueline, Lucienne, and Laurent—who, along with Jean-Marc Itard's wild boy and Freud's Anna, are among the most thoroughly investigated offspring in the history of child study. Between 1925 and 1933, while they were infants, Piaget investigated a form of simple problem-solving behavior, which he called *sensorimotor intelligence,* in Jacqueline, Lucienne, and Laurent. His findings and conclusions were published in a series of three books that appeared in French in 1936, 1937, and 1945 but were not translated into English until the early 1950s (Piaget 1951, 1952*b,* 1954). Piaget's work on sensorimotor intelligence, which is the central theme of Chapter 3 of the present book, is notable because it marks the end of his dependence on exclusively verbal research procedures. Although his clinical method remains heavily verbal, it is considerably less so than it was during the early 1920s.

In 1925, Piaget was offered a professorship of philosophy at his alma mater, the University of Neuchâtel. He accepted, and he and his wife left Geneva for Neuchâtel in the same year. Although the studies of sensorimotor intelligence were begun in Neuchâtel in 1925 when their first daughter was born, they were completed in Geneva. In 1929, Piaget, his wife, and two daughters returned to Geneva where he assumed a professorship of scientific history at the University of Geneva and an assistant directorship of the Rousseau Institute. He soon initiated a new line of research on children's intelligence. These new studies were the investigations of children's logical, numerical, and geometric concepts for which Piaget is best known in North America. Much of this work was done in collaboration with Piaget's most famous student, Barbel Inhelder. Among the phenomena they studied were the fascinating conservation concepts. Piaget and Inhelder discovered that, before the age of 6 or 7, children seem not to understand that simple quantitative properties of objects (e.g., number, length, weight) are independent of their visual appearance. For example, the average 5-year-old child who is presented with two identical glasses containing equal amounts of water will assert that the quantities of water are equal. However, as soon as the contents of one glass are poured into a wider or narrower glass, so that the heights of the two quantities are no longer the same, the child asserts that the quantities of water are unequal. The findings of these studies were published in a series of books and papers, too numerous to be cited here, which appeared in French during the 1940s. They were not translated into English until the 1950s and 1960s. This work forms much of the subject matter of Chapter 5.

The studies of children's logical, numerical, and geometric concepts, conducted between 1929 and 1939, are of paramount historical importance in the development of Piaget's thinking. In the resulting data, Piaget believed that he had at last found unequivocal proof of his solution of the part-whole problem. He believed that he had also found definitive proof of his hypothesis that cognitive development consists of an invariant progression of qualitatively different stages. He eventually went on to conclude that there were four stages in all, the first running from birth to roughly age 2, the second running from age 2 to roughly age 7 or 8, the third running from age 7 or 8 to roughly age 11 or 12, and the last running from age 11 or 12 through adulthood. He proposed that each stage is characterized by an underlying set of mental structures that govern intelligent behavior. Each set of structures was viewed as qualitatively different from the others, and this is what presumably makes the stages themselves qualitatively distinct. The underlying structures that govern intelligence during the first stage were deemed to be entirely *motoric*. During the second stage, the governing structures become *mental* for the first time. During the third and fourth stages, mental structures acquire the crucial property of *reversibility*. I shall have much more to say about reversibility later on.

To those who have considered the problem, it is not at all clear that the 1929–39 studies justify Piaget's stage view of cognitive development. Whether these studies show something more than the fact that systematic improvements in logical, numerical, and geometric concepts occur during the preschool and elementary school years has remained a matter of great controversy in the high councils of developmental theory. However, this fact does not dim the historical significance of the studies. Although details subsequently have been filled in, the grand picture of Piaget's stage model of cognitive development has not changed in the more than three decades since these studies were completed.

This brings us to World War II. Being a citizen of a neutral country, Piaget was afforded the great luxury of deciding for himself whether or not to become directly involved in the war. He considered entering military service. However, in view of his advanced age (43 at the time the war broke out), he decided to continue his scholarly work instead. For this we may be thankful. Most of the books and articles reporting the findings of his 1929–39 research were written during and shortly after the war. Piaget's major contribution to the war effort was the presentation of a series of lectures on his new theory of intellectual development at the College of France during 1942. He believed that these lectures would help strengthen the morale of French academicians and encourage them to go on with their work during the German occupation. Piaget, it seems, was one of the very few academicians whom the occupation forces allowed to cross the French border regularly. Moreover, the lectures he delivered were of great historical significance in the development of his theory. They were his first attempt to put forth a general statement of his stages of intelligence. The lectures were published a few years later (Piaget 1950), and they were the only general exposition of the theory by Piaget which existed until the appearance of a very recent book (Piaget and Inhelder 1969).

In 1940, the man who had originally brought Piaget to Geneva, Claparéde, died leaving his professorship of experimental psychology vacant at the University of Geneva. Piaget was soon appointed to fill the vacancy, a post which he retained until his retirement at age 75. At about this time, Piaget undertook a new series of investigations concerned with perceptual development and the relationship between perception and intelligence. The leading European psychological theory of the day, Gestalt psychology, considered perception and intelligence to be one and the same process. However, Piaget concluded that this was not so and that the mental structures he believed he had discovered in his 1929–39 studies could not be reduced to perception. Since the aim of this book is primarily to introduce the reader to Piaget's stages of cognitive development, we shall not consider the perception studies in detail.

Since 1950, there have been three noteworthy developments in Piaget's work. In 1956, he founded a long-planned Institute for Genetic Epistemology at the University of Geneva. This institute has served both to disseminate Piaget's views to those outside the confines of Geneva and to bring together distinguished scholars from a number of areas for purposes of cross-fertilization and the development of their own ideas on the nature of human knowledge. The work of the institute proceeds roughly as follows. Each year, one or more themes relating to knowledge and its development are selected. A group of scholars interested in these themes is then invited to the institute to work on specific problems. At year's end, the results of their work are published as one or more volumes in the continuing monograph series entitled *Studies in Genetic Epistemology.* In the nearly two decades it has been in operation, the institute has served as a meeting ground for psychologists, physical scientists, mathematicians, biologists, and educators to discuss their common problems. Over two dozen monographs in the *Studies in Genetic Epistemology* series have now been published.

A second major post-1950 event has been the publication with Barbel Inhelder of a comprehensive series of studies dealing with adolescent intelligence (Inhelder and Piaget 1958). Piaget's theory, as we saw earlier, proposes four stages corresponding roughly to what we would call infancy, early childhood, childhood, and adolescence. However, the 1929–39 studies that inspired the theory were concerned with children and not with adolescents. To complete the empirical picture, therefore, some investigations of adolescent thinking were imperative. The particular views of adolescent intelligence that stem from these investigations will be taken up in Chapter 6.

The third post-1950 development is a very recent phenomenon. Throughout most of Piaget's career, he has been almost exclusively concerned with intelligence and its development. Moreover, he has tended to stick to a rather narrow behavioral definition of intelligence based on reasoning and problem solving. But what of the many other behavioral capacities that most other psychologists believe are components of intelligence? For example, what about memory, imagery, and learning? How do these capacities relate to intelligence as Piaget conceives it? During the past few years, Piaget and his coworkers have begun to examine these questions. Their general strategy has been to view memory, imagery, and learning in terms of Piaget's stages of intelligence. More specifically, they have tried to show that the stages and mental structures that form the core of the theory place definite constraints on these other capacities. It is proposed, for example, that we can learn or remember or imagine certain things only if we have reached a certain stage of development and possess certain mental structures. So far, books on memory (Piaget and Inhelder 1973), imagery (Piaget and Inhelder 1972), and learning (Inhelder, Sinclair, and Bovet 1974) that echo this theme have been published. More books no doubt are in the offing. Since this work is recent and is indeed still going on, it is impossible to say what its significance ultimately will be. As I write, the jury is still out on the question of whether or not these books will establish a bridge between Piaget's unique vision of intelligence and other psychological theories concerned with such things as memory, imagery, and learning. We shall not be directly concerned with this work in the present book. Instead, we shall concentrate our attention on the theory itself.

Plan of the Book

My aim in what follows is to communicate the central concepts underlying Piaget's theory and to discuss each of his four stages in some detail. I shall also consider the question of the extent to which research by other investigators has borne out Piaget's claims about each of his stages. There is an old maxim in science which says that when one sets out, as Piaget has done, to invent a sweeping theory, it is impossible not to be wrong in major respects. I shall try to say in what major respects the theory most probably is wrong. It is my hope that when the reader has completed this book he or she will have sufficient grounding in Piagetian theory and the research on which it is based to begin reading both original works by Piaget and advanced secondary works (Flavell 1963; Furth 1969) without any further preparation.

In Chapter 2, before taking up the material on the four stages, a number of conceptual issues are discussed. The aim of the chapter is to familiarize the reader with Piagetian language and Piaget's way of looking at intellectual development. For the most part, the chapter deals with issues that are of overriding importance vis-á-vis all four of Piaget's stages. Brief consideration also is given to Piaget's controversial clinical method of conducting research.

Befitting their presumed status as qualitatively distinct entities, Piaget's stages are, in many respects, islands unto themselves. For this reason, it has seemed advisable to devote a separate chapter to each stage. Chapters 3, 4, 5, and 6 deal with Piaget's sensorimotor stage, preoperational stage, concrete-operational stage, and formal-operational stage, respectively. Each of these four chapters follows the same general format. First, any concepts that are crucial to understanding that particular stage are explicated. Second, the various reasoning and problem-solving behaviors that serve as the stage's chief symptoms are considered. Finally, selected experiments designed to examine the validity of the stage are reviewed.

And in Chapter 7, I examine applications of Piaget to education. Piaget's system, like all doctrines about the nature of intelligence, has many implications for the theory and practice of instruction. But Piaget has been reticent about saying exactly what they are. Consequently, the job of isolating the theory's educational implications has fallen to others. Fortunately, most writers have been able to agree that the theory makes at least three types of instructional recommendations; namely, proposals about the sequencing of topics, proposals about curriculum content, and proposals about teaching strategies. In fact, these recommendations have already been put to use in a series of experimental preschool curricula. The discussion of these curricula in Chapter 7 deals chiefly with the work of four people: Celia Lavatelli, David Weikart, Constance Kamii, and Frank Hooper and his associates at the University of Wisconsin.

chapter 2

The Metatheory

My general aim in this chapter is to present an overview of Piaget's rather unique way of looking at cognitive development. I shall review those aspects of his outlook that I believe are essential to subsequent chapters. A few nonessential facts that convey the theory's flavor are also included. First, Piaget's biological emphasis, an emphasis that follows from his early training, is discussed. We shall see in this connection that the word "biological" is somewhat gratuitous. The theory does *not* explain cognitive development by appealing to biological variables.[1] Its use of biological constructs is purely metaphorical. Next, three ideas (structure, function, and content) are examined that are probably the theory's most fundamental concepts. A fourth concept (scheme) is then considered. The generic concept of developmental stage, as opposed to Piaget's specific stages, is also introduced and illustrated. The concept of stage is closely related to the concepts of structure, function, and content. Finally, at the end of this chapter, Piaget's clinical method of studying intelligence is discussed and some of its shortcomings are noted.

Before proceeding further, I think a few remarks on philosophy of science—or, more precisely, the distinction between the vocabularies of science and philosophy—are in order. The languages of science are governed by the rules of *parsimony* and *operationism*. The rule of operationism

[1] This point is critical. Over the years, I have learned that many of my students have heard, from whatever sources, that Piaget's theory is "biological." Of course, this leads them to expect physiological explanations of behavior. Readers who have already adopted this mental set are cautioned to disabuse themselves of it immediately.

says that any concept used in science shall have a precise empirical meaning referring to concrete things that we can measure. The second rule, parsimony, says that the language of any science should be a *minimum vocabulary*. This means that we should restrict ourselves to the smallest possible number of concepts required to describe the things that we are studying.

Philosophical languages, on the other hand, are not necessarily governed by either operationism or parsimony. Most classical philosophical systems make use of imprecisely defined ideas whose concrete meanings (if any) are unclear. Philosophical languages also tend toward redundancy and repetitiveness. Therefore, we have, at one extreme, scientific vocabularies consisting of small numbers of rather precisely defined concepts and, at the other extreme, philosophical vocabularies consisting of large numbers of somewhat vague concepts that tend to overlap with each other. This brings me to the concepts we shall be examining later on in this chapter. I believe it is fair to say that they fall somewhere between the extremes of science and philosophy as I have described them. (This is not to say that anyone, particularly philosophers, would agree with my description!) Piaget clearly intends that his theory should be considered a scientific rather than a philosophical doctrine. However, it is also true that the theory is not rigidly constrained by the canons of parsimony and operationism. Piaget does not hesitate to introduce ideas whose empirical meanings are less than clear. Nor is he averse to introducing more concepts than the minimum needed to describe the phenomena he studies. Consequently, many of the ideas we shall be examining have meanings that are essentially intuitive. For this reason, I have tried to make my illustrations as elementary as possible. But in view of the intrinsic difficulty of many Piagetian concepts, some illustrations will undoubtedly fail to instill clarity.

In science, lack of precise operational definitions usually poses more severe problems than lack of parsimony. The worst of these problems is that, when we do not know the exact empirical meaning of a certain idea, there is always the possibility that it refers to nothing at all. This possibility rarely arises with the concepts of the more advanced sciences. Consider the physicist's concept of gravity, for example. Although physicists may disagree about the laws which govern gravity, they do not disagree about whether there *is* such a thing as gravity. This is because they all know the empirical phenomenon that the word "gravity" refers to, namely, the attraction between two masses. We shall see that, to a certain extent, the question of whether given ideas refer to anything at all arises with Piaget's theory. Some of the most important concepts that the theory uses to explain cognitive development are sufficiently murky that some people have been led to wonder whether they refer to anything tangible. A case in point is the *stage* construct. The theory says that cognitive development consists of an invariant sequence of qualitatively distinct stages. Age-related changes in intelligence are always described in terms of stages. However, the theory does not tell us exactly what a stage is or, more important, how to recognize a stage when we see one. This fact has led some investigators to claim that Piaget's stages do not exist. Throughout this book we shall see that this *existence criticism* is frequently raised in conjunction with Piagetian theory. A major theoretical dispute that will concern us in Chapters 3 through 6, the *performance-competence* debate, hinges on an existence criticism of another Piagetian concept, cognitive structure.

General Background

Piaget's biological orientation

In psychology, we are used to theories that place heavy emphasis on learning and explain behavior in the language of stimuli and responses. Hence, the most striking thing about Piaget's system is that it does not have these characteristics. Instead, it has a distinctly biological flavor. This flavor is usually attributed to the fact that Piaget is a biologist by training. Whatever the reasons, the biological orientation shows up in six important features of the theory. First, Piaget has borrowed some well-known descriptive principles of biological growth (in particular, *organization* and *adaption*) and has used them to describe the development of human intelligence. Unlike many psychologists, Piaget believes that biological principles are directly applicable to the study of intellectual development. Specifically, he maintains that (*a*) the growth of intelligence is a special case of growth in general, (*b*) we must understand biological development if we are to understand intelligence, and (*c*) the study of intellectual development is rightfully a branch of embryology (Piaget 1967*b*, 1970*b*). The connection between biology and intelligence is, therefore, assumed to be intimate.

A second fact reflecting the theory's biological leanings is the general tone and style of Piaget's writing. The manner in which he sets about explaining the development of this or that cognitive skill always is reminiscent of the way Darwin or Wallace might have explained the origin of the species. To illustrate, one of Piaget's most strongly held beliefs is that higher cognitive processes in adults "evolve" from the consolidation and generalization of the more primitive cognitive processes that are present during infancy and childhood. Piaget also believes that the intellectual adaptions that occur during the course of development are always meaningful and are never the result of chance or trial and error. A final illustration is provided by Piaget's belief that intellectual development is governed by sets of *cognitive structures* that simultaneously adapt themselves to the demands of the environment and alter these demands in lawful ways. (This particular illustration is reminiscent of the biological process of digestion.)

As I noted in Chapter 1, Piaget's cognitive structures undergo *qualitative* change during development—i.e., the structures which govern the intelligence of adults are something more than mere beefed-up and fleshed-out versions of the structures which govern the intelligence of infants and children.

The third unmistakable sign of Piaget's biological orientation is the strong emphasis he places on the role of children in determining the course of their own cognitive development. In the language of psychology textbooks, Piaget believes that the child must be viewed as an *independent variable* (a causative factor) with respect to her own development. This is just another way of saying that children exert as much control over their development as do factors located in the children's environment (parents, schools, churches, etc.). Piaget's organism-centered approach stands in sharp contrast to the learning interpretations of intellectual development that have been popular in North America for most of this century. In a learning approach, children are primarily assigned a *dependent variable* status, and reinforcement contingencies located in the environment are the causative factors. That is, children are not assigned a crucial role in determining their own cognitive development. Instead, intellectual development is seen as a process by virtue of which factors located in the environment make impressions on the "wax tablet" of the child's mind. Cognitive development becomes synonymous with cumulative experience. In contrast, Piaget believes that children are capable of altering the forces in their environment as well as being altered by them. Hence, both children and their environment are necessary parts of Piaget's formulation, whereas only the environment is essential in the traditional learning approach.

Fourth, Piaget has been concerned almost exclusively with cognitive development in situ as it were. Like modern ethologists, he has placed strong emphasis on "natural" development and has tended to look with disfavor on training experiments and other forms of manipulative research that North American psychologists use to study intelligence. Piaget does not believe that such research is very useful because it constitutes an artificial disruption of normal cognitive growth and, therefore, may produce a false or perverted picture of intellectual development. In a recent interview (Piaget, 1970*d*), Piaget also admitted harboring some fears about the ultimate consequences of manipulative research for the children who serve as subjects in the experiments. Piaget's view is that we do not know nearly enough about the fine details of spontaneous cognitive growth to make rational decisions about the consequences of such research. This leads him to conclude that psychologists ought to be more willing to let nature take its course.

A fifth example of Piaget's biological orientation is his belief that the *direction* that intellectual growth takes is always from simpler to more complex levels of functioning. The assumption that cognitive development is an intrinsically directional process lends an air of purposiveness or "teleology" to Piaget's child psychology that is not uncommon in biological theories but is generally rare in modern psychology. The particular direction of change, from simple to complex, that Piaget imputes to cognitive development has been a part of evolutionary thinking since Darwin. Piaget's directional assumption is also intended to provide an answer to the question "What motivates cognitive development?" While learning-oriented psychologists attempt to answer this question by teasing out sources of motivation from reinforcement contingencies specified by the environment, Piaget maintains that cognitive development is inherently *self-motivating* because it is directional. In other words, we do not have to look around in the environment for motivation; it is built into the child to begin with.

A final illustration of Piaget's biological perspective is his belief in the unity of cognitive development and physical maturation. This particular view is most evident in the 1925–29 studies of infancy mentioned in Chapter 1. In these studies, Piaget was guided by the hypothesis that the keys to understanding mental growth may be found in the principles that govern physical maturation. Although, as we shall see in the next chapter, the behaviors that Piaget calls "physical" have a decidedly more mental air about them than the behaviors that pediatricians might put in this category, it is fair to say that Piaget holds that cognitive development (especially during infancy) is related to maturational changes in the physique and the nervous system. In a recent book (Piaget and Inhelder 1969), he discusses three explicit physical-maturational factors that control early cognitive development: maturation of the system of endocrine glands, embryology of the fetus, and myelination of the nerve fibers. Needless to say, the assumption that mental and physical growth are closely linked has not been very influential in the traditional learning view of cognitive development. According to the learning view, physical maturation only sets some very broad constraints ("floors" and "ceilings") within which environmental influences have free reign.

some other interesting features
of Piaget's orientation

There are three other features of Piaget's system that are unusual when viewed from the standpoint of North American psychology but which cannot easily be charged off to Piaget's biological outlook. In the order of their general importance, they are: (*a*) an almost exclusive emphasis on developmental changes in cognition that are *qualitative rather than quantitative* (i.e., changes of "kind" rather than "amount"); (*b*) a recurring emphasis on relating the findings of studies of cognitive development to some of the broad issues of philosophy, especially philosophy of science, general epistemology, and epistemology of mathematics; and (*c*) lengthy, repetitive, and often somewhat pedantic theoretical analyses of virtually every scrap of data derived from his empirical research.

Concerning (*a*), the approach that has long dominated research on cognitive development is the mental testing tradition. This tradition, which focuses on IQ test data, has been largely concerned with quantitative questions. Among them are questions such as age-related improvements in mental test performance and the extent to which mental test performance predicts external criteria such as school achievement. One such question, which has precipitated an enormous amount of research and controversy, concerns whether performance on mental tests administered during infancy can predict performance on mental tests administered during the preschool and childhood years. Piaget has not concerned himself with problems of this sort. Instead, he has been occupied almost exclusively with the qualitative issues mentioned earlier, namely, the nature of the cognitive structures that underlie intelligent behavior and the discrete stages through which intelligence passes during the course of its development. Hence, Piaget's theory of cognitive development deals primarily with the developmental progression of cognitive stages and the mechanisms whereby the mental processes of one stage are transformed into those of the next stage. In contrast, the chief concern of the mental test movement has been to say "how much" of any given intellectual skill is possessed by children of any given age. The closest Piaget ever comes to posing such a question is when he establishes broad age norms for his four global stages. However, he repeatedly warns us that age and cognitive development are not related in any simple manner and that, hence, we must not take the age norms for his stages too seriously.

Concerning (*b*), Piaget is fond of relating both his theory and his research to basic epistemological problems that philosophers have debated since the dawn of recorded history. In Chapter 1, we saw that Piaget's undergraduate hope of resolving a famous philosophical controversy, the part-whole problem, is what led him into psychology in the first place. Piaget's emphasis on the philosophical implications of his theory is so pronounced that many psychologists are convinced that his work is motivated by the desire to resolve ancient philosophical debates rather than the desire to illuminate cognitive development. Piaget does very little to discourage this interpretation of his work. He even has coined a label for his approach to the study of cognitive development with an eye toward resolving philosophical controversies: *genetic epistemology*. The word "genetic," as Piaget uses it, is a nineteenth-century term referring to any sort of research dealing with ontogenetic or phylogenetic development. Perhaps the most obvious indication of Piaget's continuing devotion to mixing philosophical issues and developmental research is his Institute for Genetic Epistemology.

Concerning (*c*), one of the most striking things about Piaget's writings is the large number of pages that he devotes to theoretical analysis. The author of the most important advanced text on Piaget's system, John H. Flavell, issued careful warnings to would-be Piaget readers about the lengthiness of Piagetian theoretical analyses. Flavell pointed out that what would be short papers in a technical journal for most psychologists become books for Piaget. This particular aspect of Piaget's work grows out of the fact that, for whatever reasons, he feels it is his duty to trace even the most indirect implications of his research. This style of exposition stands in sharp contrast to the standards of scientific communication in most areas of psychological research. A reader browsing a current issue of most psychological journals would find that the space devoted to theoretical analysis in the Introduction and Discussion sections of such papers typically accounts for much less than half of their overall length. More than half the space in such papers usually is devoted to describing the precise methods employed in the research and the quantitative findings. In most cases, the authors will restrict their theoretical analysis to the most direct and obvious implications of their findings. In contrast, Piaget routinely gives the methods and quantitative results of his research very brief (and sometimes cavalier) treatment while he concentrates on theoretical interpretation. One of Piaget's more popular works, *The Growth of Logical Thinking from Childhood to Adolescence,* provides a prime example of how lengthy, relative to the research on which they are based, these interpretations can sometimes be.

Three Key Piagetian Concepts:
Structure, Function, and Content

At the heart of Piaget's theory lies a distinction between three concepts: cognitive *structure*, cognitive *function*, and cognitive *content*. Although these ideas will be discussed more thoroughly later on, we may say the following preliminary things about each. *Cognitive structure* refers to the *form* (or shape or pattern) that cognition takes during each of Piaget's stages of mental growth. Piaget believes that we may discern abstract organizational patterns (i.e., structures) that underlie cognition and that may be said to *control* it. Piaget also believes each level or stage of cognitive development is characterized by its own unique set of governing structures.[2]

[2] I cannot emphasize too strongly that Piaget sincerely believes his structures are "real." That is, he believes they are "really there" controlling intelligence in the same sense that a pilot is "really there" controlling his aircraft. This view, which philosophers call *naive realism,* is more common in European psychology than it is in North America. Here, the standard view, which philosophers call *conventionalism,* is that theoretical constructs such as cognitive structure are just that—constructs—and have no tangible existence. This is definitely not Piaget's view.

Cognitive functions, as their name suggests, are *purposes* or *goals* that express where cognitive development is going. In other words, they are statements of direction. The simple-to-complex principle mentioned earlier is a case in point. Generally speaking, Piaget maintains that intellectual skills which characterize each stage of mental growth should be viewed as helping the organism to attain certain goals or end states that are part of the organism's hereditary endowment. Thus, the cognitive functions that we shall discuss are what Piaget assumes intelligence is actively striving for at every stage of development. *Cognitive contents* are the specific intellectual acts that comprise intelligence at any given stage of development. Such things as a visual image, an auditory image, a mathematical concept, and an abstract symbol all are examples of cognitive contents. All of the problem-solving and reasoning skills that we shall consider in later chapters (e.g., object permanence, conservation, transitivity) are cognitive contents. Of the three concepts, structure, function, and content, cognitive contents are the only things that can be directly measured. Both structures and functions are inferred from the measurement of content.

cognitive structure

The notion of cognitive structure has received far more attention in Piaget's writing than either function or content. It pervades all of Piaget's research and theory. In a recent book, he has indicated that cognitive structure probably is the single most important concept in his system (Piaget 1970a). It is easy to see that this emphasis reflects his interest in the part-whole problem.

The abstract nature of Piaget's structures. Perhaps the most striking fact about Piaget's cognitive structures is that they are very abstract ideas by comparison with structural concepts common to other sciences. There are many disciplines, scientific and nonscientific, that deal primarily in structural ideas. In the building industry, for example, architects create the form or structure of buildings while plumbers, electricians, carpenters, etc., fill in the contents. Similarly, there is a special branch of biology, anatomy, that is devoted to describing bodily structures (the skeleton, the circulatory system, the digestive system, etc.) as precisely as possible. Other branches of biology, such as physiology, fill in the functions and contents of these structures. Similar to the roles of architecture in building and anatomy in biology, there is a branch of engineering called structural engineering. There are many other examples of this sort. The general point for the reader to bear in mind is that structures are usually *tangible* entities (buildings, lungs, automobiles, etc.) that can be seen, heard, felt, tasted, and smelled. Not so with Piaget. His cognitive structures are completely abstract, and they cannot be directly measured. Although they are "real," they cannot be directly observed the way a tooth or brain cell can. This no doubt leads some readers to wonder whether these structures are simply rhetorical devices akin to Plato's ideal forms or Kant's synthetic a priori. Perhaps, just perhaps, they are more than rhetorical. Piaget claims we can infer the presence of his structures from what the various cognitive contents specific to a given stage of development have in common. From the standpoint of measurement, this is what Piaget's cognitive structures are—the common properties of the intelligent acts of a given stage of mental growth. If this is true, then cognitive structure is just as good a scientific construct as, say, "electron" or "gene." No one has ever seen or directly measured either an electron or a gene. We infer their presence by measuring other things—notably the effects that they have on physical and biological systems. The presence of Piaget's cognitive structures is supposed to be inferred in the same way. But let us consider a brief example.

Consider the sentence "Jim pushed John." We may describe the concrete structure of this sentence as follows. It consists of a specific subject (Jim), a specific verb (pushed), and a specific object (John). Now, consider three other simple sentences, "Fido bit Mary," "Mother spanked Tom," and "Teacher praised Dick." Each of these latter sentences has a concrete structure that we can exhibit in the same manner as we exhibited the structure of "Jim pushed John." Notice that because none of the four sentences share even a single word in common, the concrete structure of each is completely different from the concrete structure of the others. Notice also, however, that although the concrete structure of each sentence differs from the concrete structure of the remaining sentences, all four sentences share a common abstract structure. We might describe this common abstract structure somewhat informally as "an unmodified subject followed by a past tense verb followed by an unmodified object." Note that this structure is truly "abstract" in the sense that, first, it is shared by all four sentences and, second, it is shared by literally an infinite number of other sentences that we could construct. Astronomy is another field that provides some fairly common examples of abstract structure. For example, consider the structure of our particular solar system. It may be described as consisting of nine specific planets revolving about a specific star in nine specific eliptical orbits. However, in view of the indefinitely large number of solar systems in this and other galaxies, there probably are many others comprised of nine planets revolving about a single star in eliptical orbits. Although none of these planets, stars, and orbits are precisely the same as those of our own solar system, they all share the same abstract structure.

It is abstract structures of the preceding sort that Piaget is interested in. The only essential difference between Piaget's cognitive structures and the preceding examples lies in where the structures are to be found. Whereas abstract linguistic structures are to be found in language behavior and abstract spatial structures are to be found by looking at solar systems, Piaget finds his abstract cognitive structures in the reasoning and problem-solving behavior of infants, children, and adolescents. Moreover, if we accept the idea of abstract linguistic structures, abstract astronomical structures, etc., I fail to see why we should be bothered by abstract cognitive structures.

Structural change. A second fact that Piaget stresses about cognitive structures is that they are neither innate nor static. Instead, they grow and change during the course of development. Although they are not always precisely formulated, each of the four Piagetian epochs of development that we shall consider in subsequent chapters is supposed to be characterized by its own unique complement of cognitive structures. In fact, Piaget believes that the key differences between successive stages are structural. He believes this even though the most obvious differences are in cognitive content. For example, Piaget describes the intelligence of infancy (sensorimotor stage) in terms of underlying organizational patterns which are crude and inflexible, while he describes adolescent intelligence (formal-operational stage) in terms of structures that are sophisticated and flexible. The contents from which he infers these descriptions are strictly secondary. Because Piaget's theory emphasizes qualitative reorganizations of the structures that govern intelligence rather than incremental changes in cognitive content, it is usually called a *discontinuity theory*. Theories derived from the mental test tradition, which emphasize age changes in cognitive content, are called *continuity theories*. Continuity theories assume that the underlying organization of intelligence is innate and remains constant throughout life. Piaget does not.

Piaget's cognitive structures are said to grow and change as a function of two immutable laws of development: organization and adaption. These two laws, which Piaget calls *functional invariants,* will be discussed in detail in the upcoming section on cognitive functions. The actual process whereby structural change takes place is called *equilibration.* This process may be described as consisting of the following four steps. First, we have some given level of intelligence (e.g., one of the six substages of sensorimotor intelligence that we shall discuss in the next chapter) and the cognitive structures that govern that level. The range of situations demanding intelligent behavior that these structures can handle is limited (e.g., we shall see that the cognitive structures of infancy can handle only simple concrete information). Second, the organism encounters new information that calls for intelligent behaviors that lie beyond the scope of its present level of cognitive structure. Third, these encounters produce a state of *disequilibrium* in the cognitive structures. Fourth, the state of disequilibrium induces the cognitive structures to change or "accommodate" themselves in a manner that will allow them to handle the information that is currently beyond their scope. This new level of structure is said to be *more stable* than the preceding level. This simply means that there are fewer situations that will throw the new structures into disequilibrium because their scope has broadened.

This process of structural change can be illustrated by returning to our earlier example of abstract sentence structure. Suppose at some point during development our language structure corresponds to "unmodified subject followed by verb followed by unmodified object." The only sentences we can understand are sentences which have this abstract structure or a simpler one. Suppose we encounter sentences such as, "Father thanked grandmother sincerely" or "Susan paints pictures rapidly." On the basis of our current level of structuration, we cannot understand or interpret either sentence. We cannot tell the first one from "Father thanked grandmother," and we cannot tell the second one from "Susan paints pictures." But in each case there is an important difference between the two, a difference that we must grasp if we are going to get on in the world. Disequilibrium ensues. Eventually, after encountering many more such examples, our abstract structure changes to "unmodified subject followed by verb followed by object with or without adverb modifier." As we introduce still other complications (adjectives, altering the order of the components, etc.) more disequilibrium ensues and further broadening of the abstract structure results. According to Piaget this process of equilibrating (or, more simply, broadening the scope of) cognitive structures is constantly taking place between birth and late adolescence. From late adolescence through maturity very little broadening is believed to occur. There has been some recent speculation that during old age the equilibration process may begin to operate again *in reverse.*

What we have said about Piaget's cognitive structures up to this point should suggest to the reader that they are not measurable in the sense that buildings and cardboard boxes are. In point of fact, Piaget's structures cannot be directly measured at all. Remember that we never *directly* encountered or measured the subject-predicate-object structure or celestial structure mentioned in our earlier examples. In both cases, we inferred an abstract structure shared by a class of concrete and tangible structures. The same thing is true of Piaget's cognitive structures. Each one is inferred from a class of behaviors whose members, like our four sentences, may be shown to share an abstract structure. For psychologists of a strongly empirical turn of mind, all this is, to say the least, rather difficult to countenance. To them, the really important variables in cognitive growth are those that can be directly measured. In contrast, Piaget maintains that the most important factors, factors that are said to control intelligence within any given stage, are things that cannot be directly measured at all. He is, in effect, challenging us to look behind the phenomena we study to find deeper underlying communalities. All this seems a bit far-fetched to many measurement-oriented psychologists.

Piaget's structural models. The final and most difficult aspect of cognitive structure concerns the specific types of structural models on which

Piaget relies. We have already examined illustrations of biological, linguistic, and celestial structures. But these are not the sort of models Piaget uses. His structures are borrowed primarily from mathematics. There is a branch of higher mathematics known as abstract algebra that deals with the underlying structure of things. Abstract algebra originally evolved as a tool for formulating the structure of familiar mathematical entities such as the elementary number systems (integers, rational numbers, irrational numbers, etc.). Several devices for analyzing and classifying structure have been developed. By far the most important of these is *group theory*. Group theory is so powerful that it can be used to analyze the structure of nonmathematical systems as well as mathematical ones. During the past few decades, group theory has been extensively used in sciences such as physics, engineering, and chemistry. Our modern picture of the atom, for example, has been created by applying group theory to a few simple facts about the behavior of elementary particles. Moreover, it turns out that group structures show up all the time in everyday life—especially in the simple problem-solving situations that Piaget uses to study intellectual behavior. Consequently, group theory may be used to elaborate their structure. In Chapter 6, where group theory is more fully discussed and some examples of group structures in everyday life are given, I shall show precisely how it is possible to do this. For now, the point I wish to make is that Piaget relies almost exclusively on abstract algebra to provide models for his cognitive structures. Moreover, most of these models come from that particular branch of abstract algebra called group theory.

Piaget's use of the tools of abstract algebra tends to be less precise and more metaphorical than, say, the manner in which a physicist or a chemist would use the same tools. When physicists claim, for example, that the spectrum of visible colors has a certain kind of group structure, they are required to give a formal proof of this fact that is akin to mathematical proofs. As a rule, Piaget does not give such proofs. When he claims that the cognitive contents associated with some given stage share a certain abstract structure, he rarely offers a formal demonstration. Consequently, much of the follow-up work on Piaget's theory done by his more mathematically inclined collaborators has focused on proof construction.[3]

cognitive functions

Piaget believes that cognitive functions, unlike structures, remain *constant* during the course of development. Because cognitive functions do not change with age, Piaget also refers to them as functional *invariants*. He

[3] This section has provided only a very global introduction to the important concept of cognitive structure. The question of what things a cognitive structure consists of remains to be discussed. This question is dealt with in Chapter 4 where the concept of mental operation is introduced and defined.

has proposed that two functional invariants guide cognitive activity during all stages of development: *organization* and *adaption.*

In their most general sense, Piaget's cognitive functional invariants are broad principles of intelligent behavior that characterize all human beings regardless of age. Moreover, they can be stretched to fit many forms of behavior other than cognition. In fact, he maintains that functional invariants are characteristics of all biological activity. This belief leads to two important maxims of Piaget's system: (*a*) Cognitive functioning is just a special case of biological functioning; and (*b*) the two functional invariants (organization and adaption) are as relevant to biological and physical growth as they are to intellectual development.

Broadly speaking, organization and adaption are complementary. The organization principle presumably is responsible for the organism's cognitive continuity across short or long periods of time. That is, cognitive organization accounts for the fact that there is some degree of sameness in intelligence across time. In contrast, the adaptive side of intelligence presumably is the chief instrument of discontinuity. The equilibration process is an example of adaption at work. The crucial fact that Piaget's adaption principle is intended to embody is that experience does not leave cognition unaffected; our cognitive processes change and develop by virtue of our contacts with reality. Neither do we leave our intellectual environment unchanged; the manner in which intelligence sets about interpreting reality leaves reality forever altered.

Piaget believes that the organizational function of intelligence can be inferred from the fact that intelligent behavior does not seem to be a random or trial-and-error process. It is characterized by forethought and planning. In Piaget's language, it is organized into coherent and discernible patterns. These "coherent and discernible patterns" are the abstract structures discussed in the preceding section. Thus, Piaget's cognitive structures are the primary manifestations of the organizational function of intelligence. This makes organization an even more abstract and unmeasureable idea than cognitive structure is. The really important thing about Piaget's organization principle is that it is used to justify a doctrine about the nature of intelligence that is peculiar to his theory: the doctrine of *holism.* According to this doctrine, every act of intelligence is related to every other act of intelligence. More explicitly, Piaget describes intelligent behavior at every stage of cognitive development as *integrated totalities* and *systems of relationships among elements.* There is an obvious relationship between this doctrine and Piaget's early views on the part-whole dilemma.

The principle of organization may be contrasted with another principle that shows up regularly in learning-oriented accounts of cognitive growth (e.g., Mowrer 1960). In learning approaches, it is traditionally assumed that intelligent behavior starts out as a random and unorganized affair. Whatever organization eventually characterizes adult intelligence is thought to be gradually built up through the medium of infant and childhood learning experiences. The random, trial-and-error learning in the operant conditioning paradigm made famous by B. F. Skinner (e.g., 1938) is offered as an approximate model of cognitive growth. In this view, a crucial fact about intelligence is that its organizational capabilities must be acquired. For Piaget, on the other hand, organization is a guiding force from the beginning and, therefore, presumably is an innate feature of intelligence. One might summarize the differences between the Piaget and learning views by saying that while learning accounts postulate that organization gradually is imposed on intelligence by the environment, Piaget believes that organization always is present, although the specific structures through which it is manifest change.

Piaget's second functional invariant is adaption. Adaption is the principle whereby the various levels of cognitive structure are layed in. It is adaption that presumably is responsible for the discontinuities in our cognitive processes that occur as development proceeds. Piaget divides adaption into two complementary aspects: *assimilation* and *accomodation.* Assimilation refers to the fact that intelligent behavior always involves an underlying process whereby the organism interprets or "adjusts" incoming information in a manner that is congruent with its current level of cognitive structure. Information is assimilated into cognitive structures in roughly the same way a piece of food is assimilated by digestive structures. How thoroughly we assimilate information depends on our level of cognitive structures in roughly the same manner as how well we assimilate sugar depends on our insulin level. Perhaps the best way to think of Piaget's cognitive assimilation is as an *interpretation* of information that is made by the individual. The individual simply attempts to "make some sense of" or derive some meaning from information received. As is always the case with interpretation, the sophistication and accuracy of the interpretation depends on the individual's current level of mental sophistication (structure). The more mentally sophisticated the individual is, the more sense will be made from incoming information.

Cognitive accomodation is the complement of cognitive assimilation. While assimilation involves changing incoming information, accomodation involves changing the structures used to assimilate information. Cognitive structures accomodate in the special manner, called equilibration, outlined earlier. Their scope broadens so that the organism may correctly interpret a larger and larger range of information. During each of Piaget's four stages of cognitive development, as we shall see, there are definite limits on the extent to which information can be assimilated, or poured into the molds provided by the cognitive structures. When this limit is reached, disequilibrium ensues and some change in the structures is in order. Piaget calls this change accommodation.

I should also note that assimilation and accommodation are inseparable in Piaget's scheme of things. He maintains that the two faces of adaption may be separated for purposes of discussion but not in actual fact. They simply are not, he believes, distinct processes, but two sides of a single process. For Piaget, the occurrence of one aspect of adaption without the other is just unthinkable. This does not mean that one cannot discover forms of intelligent behavior (contents) in which there is a *relative predominance* of one or the other. For example, we shall see in Chapter 3 that Piaget believes play is characterized by a relative predominance of assimilation and that imitation is characterized by a relative predominance of accommodation.

cognitive content

We turn now to cognitive contents. Of the three concepts considered in the present section, this particular notion is by far the easiest to understand and requires the fewest words to explicate. Cognitive contents simply refer to the raw and observable behaviors which we call intelligence. It is cognitive contents that form the empirical base of the theory. It is the contents that are measured and from these measurements, the functional invariants and the cognitive structures are inferred.

Piaget argues that cognitive contents, like cognitive structures, change with age as a function of experience and structural reorganizations. Actually, no "argument" is needed. This is what the data show. If the child's cognitive structures develop in the direction of more accurate interpretations of reality, then it seems reasonable to suppose that the child's overt intellectual behaviors should reflect the change toward broader and more accurate interpretations of reality. Piaget employs the data of several ingenious experiments to make this very point. To use a cognitive content that will be considered in the next chapter, Piaget interprets certain behaviors of infants as indicating that they do not share the adult belief that objects and their properties continue to exist when no one is directly perceiving them. Piaget calls this belief *conservation of the object* (or simply object permanence). To assess the presence of this concept, Piaget first shows an infant a desired object (say a ball) and then hides the object under something (say a pillow). The specific cognitive content that Piaget is interested in is the searching behavior that should occur once the object is hidden. If the infant proceeds to search for the hidden object, then Piaget infers that object permanence is present. If the infant does not search, then Piaget infers that the infant does not possess object permanence.

The main fact that distinguishes cognitive contents from the structures and functions of cognition is that only cognitive contents are directly observable. Cognitive contents may be observed and measured in conventional ways. On the other hand, we have seen already that neither cognitive structures nor cognitive functions can be observed or measured directly. Hence, although structure and function may receive considerably more attention in Piaget's writings, the raw contents of cognition are still the hard empirical facts without which the notions of structure and function would have no meaning.

Schemes

We turn now to an idea that is particularly central to Piaget's views on early development: the concept of *scheme*. This concept is crucial to what I shall have to say about infant intelligence in Chapter 3. Readers who are familiar with other secondary sources or translations of Piaget may be aware of another label that is frequently applied to the present concept: *schema*. Piaget's writings always appear first in French and then are translated into English. Over the years most translators have chosen to translate the idea under consideration here as "schema," rather than as "scheme." In a recent work (Piaget and Inhelder 1969), Piaget has noted that this is a mistranslation. In Piaget's terminology, a scheme and a schema differ in that the former is a very active organizational principle while the latter refers to more or less passive modes of organization. Although this may seem like an inconsequential point to most readers, Piaget sees it as fundamental because it is related to his desire to maximize the role of the organism in its own cognitive development. In our discussion of schemes, we shall respect Piaget's preference and substitute scheme for schema.

general definition

In their most important sense, schemes are *examples of the abstract cognitive structures* by which the organism assimilates information; they are the basic units of cognitive structure. Therefore, all of the earlier comments about structures may be applied to schemes. However, although all cognitive structures are schemes, the reverse is not true. That is, scheme is a broader and more inclusive idea than cognitive structure. For example, we shall see in Chapter 3 that Piaget describes infant intelligence in terms of "sensorimotor schemes" but he believes that true cognitive structures are absent during infancy. Because scheme is a more inclusive concept than cognitive structure, it is characterized by certain properties that are not true in general for cognitive structures. It is these properties that we shall focus on.

First, we may say that a scheme is always a series of *related cognitive contents* that are tightly knit and tend to trigger each other. For example, in Piaget's account of infant development, the "scheme of grasping" is defined as certain sequences of highly similar motor behaviors involving the hand and arm that occur when the infant tries to grasp a desired object. In its simplest form, very early in infancy, a scheme seems to be nothing more than a predictable sequence of responses to a given stimulus. Further, the coordinated sequences of infant behaviors that Piaget chooses to call schemes also seem to involve the attainment of some important or interesting goal (e.g., reaching, seeing, grasping, or tasting a desired object). As cognitive development proceeds, schemes evolve into abstract cognitive structures of the type we discussed earlier.

Like their relatives, the cognitive structures, schemes are *structural mediators* that both control the expression of specific cognitive contents and allow the functional invariants to be expressed. Also like cognitive structures, schemes presumably change and develop with age in the direction of more accurate interpretations of incoming information.

Although the scheme concept has other uses in Piaget's thinking, we may say that for practical purposes schemes come in just two forms: *sensorimotor* and *cognitive*. Schemes falling in the second category are simply cognitive structures. However, schemes falling in the first category have not been considered up to this point. As we shall see in Chapter 3, sensorimotor schemes underlie Piaget's views about intelligence during the first two years of life. Their most important feature, the feature that distinguishes them from the schemes of later life, is that they are believed to be *entirely overt*. Unlike cognitive schemes, sensorimotor schemes are not "in the mind." Instead, they are "in the action" of the infant. When Piaget speaks of a sensorimotor scheme, he still is talking about an inferred organization of overt behavior; however, he is not assuming that the inferred organization is in any way mental. Rather, the inferred organization is *motoric*. More simply, the organization is in the peripheral nervous system rather than in the brain. This assumption about where sensorimotor schemes are located stands in sharp contrast to Piaget's assumption about cognitive schemes. These latter schemes are "in the mind." That is, they are located in the central nervous system rather than in the peripheral nervous system. It may be useful for the reader to think of sensorimotor schemes as roughly synonymous with "motor skill" and to think of cognitive schemes as roughly synonymous with "thought." To me, this distinction seems appropriate, but I should not be so rash as to maintain that is exactly what Piaget has in mind.

Another important aspect of schemes is their *mobility*. This refers to a fact hinted at in the brief discussion of the scheme-schema distinction: Schemes are not to be thought of as rigid molds into which reality is poured. A scheme is to be viewed as a flexible framework that can be "stretched" to fit a variety of cognitive contents. Piaget also argues that, at any given point in life, certain schemes are less rigid (i.e., more mobile) than others. The relative mobility of a scheme is said to depend on its *instrumentality* or *goal-directedness*. Other things being equal, those schemes that organize behaviors involved in the pursuit of much-desired goals are more flexible than schemes underlying less instrumental behavior sequences. The mobility aspect of schemes is said to apply to both sensorimotor and cognitive schemes. Both types of schemes supposedly illustrate an absolutely fundamental Piagetian theme: *Human intelligence is active and constructive.* (Educators who support learning-by-doing find considerable face validity in this particular Piagetian theme.) The idea of scheme mobility is presumably made necessary by two well-known facts about intelligent behavior. First, specific behavior sequences never occur twice in precisely the same manner and, second, successive situations to which a given behavior sequence is applied are never twice the same. Although schemes are mobile, this does not suggest lack of developmental change to Piaget. Even the most mobile schemes cannot be stretched indefinitely. When their limits have been reached, equilibration takes over.

how schemes develop

Some things remain to be said about how schemes change during cognitive growth. In the earlier section on cognitive structure we gave a very brief description of the so-called equilibration process by which narrower and less mature levels of cognitive structure evolve into more inclusive and sophisticated levels of cognitive structure. The present remarks are an expansion of this earlier discussion. We begin by discussing the general mechanisms of structural development that Piaget feels are important and then consider a series of specific steps that occur during scheme change. It is important to note that because Piaget's idea of "cognition" at any given stage of development is more or less synonymous with a certain set of cognitive structures, this series of steps is the very essence of cognitive growth in the Piagetian framework.

To begin with, Piaget maintains that all schemes—both sensorimotor and cognitive—tend to be spontaneously applied or "exercised." This provides the starting point for change—schemes will never change if they do not come in contact with new information. Their spontaneous repetition, therefore, insures change. Piaget makes such repetition the sine qua non for inferring a scheme from overt behavior. If a behavior sequence does not occur repeatedly, then Piaget does not see fit to infer a scheme underlying it. This, in turn, insures that every scheme is characterized by the minimum basis for change, namely, repeated spontaneous application. This tendency toward repetition is called the *functional-reproductive* property of schemes.

As we shall see in Chapter 3, the functional-reproductive property of schemes is used to define an important cognitive content of infancy: the so-called circular reaction.

As a scheme is repeatedly applied to incoming information, it is refined in two fundamental ways: (*a*) It *generalizes* to incorporate more diverse forms of information, and (*b*) it becomes internally discriminated or differentiated from other related but not identical schemes. The development of the scheme of grasping serves to illustrate the first aspect of scheme change. Early in life, grasping is said to involve a rigid and reflexive scheme that can only be triggered by a small number of relatively similar objects that will fit into the infant's palm. By eight or nine months, however, the grasping scheme is applied to a large number of dissimilar objects that do not fit into the palm (e.g., bottles, balls, doorknobs). The second aspect of scheme change also may be illustrated by the grasping scheme. Early in life, grasping is a crude scheme that is applied in more or less the same way to all graspable objects. By the end of the first year of life, however, grasping reactions toward different graspable objects have changed significantly. Some items are clutched tightly, while others are grasped lightly with only the tips of the fingers. The second aspect of scheme change is viewed by Piaget as a sort of ultimate proof that new schemes emerge as development proceeds. When two behavioral sequences become sufficiently differentiated, this is taken as evidence that a new scheme has evolved from the original one.

It might be thought that the fact that more and more schemes evolve during the course of cognitive development would tend to imply that schemes become isolated and compartmentalized with time. Not in Piaget's view. Piaget believes that even though schemes proliferate with age, they become *more* tightly integrated and interdependent as cognitive development proceeds. Piaget's schemes begin as "isolated islands" of intelligence but gradually become subordinated to a grand superstructure. This leaves us with a somewhat paradoxical contrast between the infant with a small number of independent schemes and the adult with a large number of interdependent schemes. Obviously, one needs some sort of process to account for the development of this mutual interdependence among different schemes. As a rule, the process is called *reciprocal assimilation.*

The following five-step model summarizes the points we have just covered. First, spontaneous repetition provides the basic precondition for scheme change. Whenever a scheme is applied to incoming information that it cannot completely handle, the stage is set for some sort of structural change. Second, the scheme generalizes in such a way that the range of objects and events to which it may be applied is expanded. Third, the scheme differentiates in such a way that new and more precise schemes are created from their narrower and more primitive predecessors. These new schemes are more easily applied and they are more attuned to the demands of a wider variety of situations. Fourth, the process of reciprocal assimilation insures that newly created schemes do not become isolated from each other. As schemes are created, reciprocal assimilation integrates individual schemes into complex patterns as constituent elements of the patterns. Fifth, the functional-reproductive aspect takes over once again. Through repetition the new gains derived from the alteration of existing schemes or the creation of new schemes are consolidated and stabilized.

We shall encounter several examples of scheme change in Chapter 3 that, hopefully, will flesh out the above remarks.

The Concept of Stage

I already have noted that Piaget's system is what psychologists call a discontinuity theory of development. The general process of cognitive growth is not seen merely as a matter of continuous and quantitative improvements in processes that remain qualitatively constant throughout the life span. Piaget speaks of qualitative changes in the underlying processes themselves as a fundamental fact of mental growth. He groups these qualitative changes into a succession of four global stages that are sometimes also called "periods." We shall take up each stage in a separate chapter. For the present, let us consider the key properties of the stage concept itself.

The first important feature is that Piaget believes his stages are *real and not arbitrary*. Stages are real in the sense that they are believed to comprise what I call "natural groupings" of cognitive contents that occur at specified points during development. Piaget's assumption that his stages are real and natural entities sets his theory apart from other approaches to cognitive development. Other investigators, who do not believe qualitative changes occur during mental development, frequently speak of stages. But their stages are quite different entities. Explicitly, they are *purely arbitrary* methods of slicing up development, are employed for *practical reasons* only, and imply no *specific position* on the qualitative change issue (Kessen 1962). For example, the arbitrarily chosen 0–2 years age range is widely referred by psychologists to as the "stage" of infancy. Other arbitrarily selected age ranges are called the "stages" of early childhood (2–5), middle childhood (5–11), adolescence (11–18), and adulthood (18 and up). In contrast, Piaget believes that his stages reflect actual qualitative changes in cognitive content; hence, the stages are not arbitrary at all.

In its most general sense, Piaget's stage concept is a means of grouping together qualitative changes in schemes. It will be recalled that scheme changes come in two varieties: broadening a given scheme to include a wider range of situations, and differentiation of new schemes from old ones.

When the second type of scheme change occurs, the child passes from one stage of cognitive functioning into the next higher stage. Here, it is absolutely essential to remember that Piaget's stages of cognitive development are totally dependent on his ideas of scheme and scheme change. To say that a child is "at" a particular stage of cognitive development is to say that a certain set of sensorimotor or cognitive structures is present. To say that a child has entered a new stage of cognitive development is to say that qualitative changes in sensorimotor or cognitive structures have occurred.

With these general remarks as a preface, we shall now review some of the finer detail of Piaget's stage concept. We begin by discussing and illustrating four general criteria for stages. Second, we shall examine two important characteristics of Piaget's stages which are not strict defining requirements. Third, as a prelude to later chapters, we shall summarize Piaget's four major stages of cognitive development.

stage criteria

According to Piaget, each of his stages must satisfy a certain set of criteria. Discussions of these criteria are scattered throughout Piaget's writings (see especially Piaget 1960). The exact number of criteria given in different writings varies between three and five. The most important ones seem to be the following four: (*a*) *qualitative change* in cognitive contents, (*b*) a *culturally universal invariant sequence* in the overall progression of stages, (*c*) inclusion of the cognitive structures of each preceding stage in each subsequent stage (usually called the *hierarchization* principle), and (*d*) an *overall integration* of the structures of each stage (usually called the *structures d'ensemble* principle).

Concerning requirement (*a*), it is not enough to find significant quantitative improvements in intelligence. Qualitative "leaps" must also occur. Requirement (*a*) is Piaget's way of insuring that each stage will have qualitatively different cognitive structures. It will be recalled that structures are not directly measured but, rather, are inferred from overt behavior. Unless there are qualitative changes in overt behavior, there is no reason to infer qualitative changes in underlying organization. (I should point out that even when qualitative changes in behavior are observed, this does not guarantee qualitative changes in structure have occurred.) Requirement (*a*) may be illustrated by an apparently qualitative behavioral change which takes place during infancy. It is well known that there are progressive quantitative improvements in grasping and looking behavior during infancy. However, another change occurs which looks qualitative, namely, the two behaviors become tightly coordinated. In addition to the separate incremental improvements in looking and grasping, the behaviors eventually become subordinated to a single system that psychologists sometimes call the *eye-hand scheme.* The concept of transitivity, which we shall consider in Chapter 5, provides another case of qualitative-looking changes in cognitive content. Suppose we show a child three sticks (*X, Y,* and *Z*) that appear to be the same length but actually differ by very small amounts. Suppose that we show the child the relative lengths of the first two sticks (e.g., *X* is shorter than *Y*) and the relative lengths of the second two sticks (e.g., *Y* is shorter than *Z*). Suppose that we now ask the child about the relative lengths of the remaining pair of sticks. Preschool children will almost always say that *X* and *Z* are the same because they look to be the same length. About age 5, however, children reverse themselves and maintain that *Z* must be longer than *X.* This shift from perception-based reasoning to internal deduction looks suspiciously like a qualitative change—or at least so Piaget and others (e.g., Flavell 1971) have argued.

According to stage requirement (*b*), every child passes through Piaget's stages in exactly the same order. The first stage (sensorimotor intelligence) must precede the second stage (preoperations) invariably—*not just on the average.* The same thing holds true for the relationship between the second stage and the third stage (concrete operations) and the third stage and the fourth stage (formal operations). The invariant sequence of Piaget's stages is referred to as their *natural acquisition order.* According to Piaget, there must be an invariant order in the emergence of his stages for the good and sufficient reason that the underlying structures of a preceding stage are always incorporated by the structures of the subsequent stages. The sort of invariant progression that Piaget is talking about is usually called a *logically guaranteed progression.* Invariant sequences of this sort are very common. For example, consider elementary school children who are being taught to add and multiply in their arithmetic class. When addition and multiplication are taught in the usual manner, there must be an invariant sequence such that the children learn how to multiply *after* they have learned how to add, but never the reverse. We cannot hope to change this fact because multiplication is always defined for children as a process whereby a given number is added to itself so many times (e.g., 10×5 is defined as adding 10 to itself five times). Thus, children must understand how to add before they can understand how to multiply because adding is a necessary component of multiplying. Logically guaranteed sequences of this sort also abound in the six sensorimotor substages that we shall consider in the next chapter. In the sensorimotor substages, the cognitive contents that characterize each substage always consist of improved versions of the behaviors of the previous substage plus some new acquisitions. Within the general context of requirement (*b*), the reader should bear in mind an important point that we touched on earlier. The notion of invariance of stages refers *only* to the general order in which the stages emerge. It does not refer to the specific ages at which they appear. In Piaget's view, the ages at which the stages appear may vary widely as a function of both maturational and environmental influences.

Stage requirement (c), the *hierarchization* requirement, is closely related to the invariant sequence requirement. In fact, the hierarchization requirement is one way of insuring an invariant progression of stages. The central idea expressed by requirement (c) is that earlier and more primitive cognitive structures do not simply "drop out" during mental growth. Instead, more primitive structures form the foundations on which more advanced levels of structure are built. The emergence of the eye-hand scheme again serves to illustrate this point. According to Piaget, there is a separate grasping scheme and a separate looking scheme before the eye-hand scheme emerges. When the eye-hand scheme finally appears, the grasping and looking schemes do not simply disappear in favor of the more sophisticated eye-hand scheme. They are coordinated and the eye-hand scheme emerges from this coordination. In effect, the eye-hand scheme turns out to be the grasping scheme plus the looking scheme plus some other things that were not possible with either scheme by itself.

Concerning requirement (d), Piaget maintains that the various structures that characterize a given stage must be consolidated into a uniform whole before a new stage is declared. Piaget uses the phrase *structures d'ensemble* (structures of the whole) when referring to requirement (d). Requirement (d) follows the first three both logically and developmentally. While (a), (b), and (c) are all necessary conditions for a stage, only (d) is sufficient. When requirements (a), (b), and (c) each have been met, it still remains for the newly acquired cognitive structures to be integrated into a functional whole before the child is said to have achieved a new stage. The process of reciprocal assimilation, which was discussed in the section on scheme change, is believed to be responsible for establishing the close interdependencies among the structures that characterize a given stage. It is useful to contrast requirement (d) with requirement (b). The latter specifies that the stages defined by each level of structure must emerge in a definite order. In contrast, the *structures d'ensemble* criterion specifies that the individual members of the set of cognitive structures that characterize a particular stage *shall not emerge in any fixed sequence*. Instead, they should emerge more or less in unison. Empirically, this means that if we were to study two cognitive contents indigenous to a particular Piagetian stage that are believed to reflect distinct cognitive structures, both behaviors should appear in children's thinking at about the same time (on the average). We shall see in Chapter 5 that Piaget's stage philosophy of cognitive development appears to be on rather insecure ground with regard to requirement (d).

Although each of the four stage criteria I have mentioned are equally important to Piaget, they are not equally important when one gets down to the business of doing empirical research on the stages. Like Piaget's cognitive structures, requirements (*a*) and (*c*) are several steps removed from the world of behavioral measurement. With criterion (*a*), one can always get into an argument about exactly how big a cognitive content change must be before we can call it qualitative rather than quantitative. This is called "the how much more is different" dilemma (e.g., Anderson 1972; Brainerd 1976*a*). One encounters even more severe problems attempting to visualize exactly how to go about measuring the hierarchization criterion. In contrast with (*a*) and (*c*), the remaining two requirements seem reasonably amenable to direct study. To assess (*b*), one simply measures several cognitive contents that are believed to result from the structures of some earlier stage and several other contents believed to result from the structures of some later stage. By requirement (*b*), all the behaviors in the first group should appear earlier in cognitive development than any of the behaviors in the second group. Suppose, for example, that we were to take a sample of the preoperational contents to be discussed in Chapter 4 and the concrete-operational contents to be discussed in Chapter 5. Suppose that we then tested a group of preschoolers and elementary schoolers for these behaviors. We should find that all of the behaviors drawn from Chapter 4 appear earlier in life than any of the behaviors drawn from Chapter 5. Requirement (*d*) can be studied directly in much the same manner as requirement (*b*). The only difference is that all of the contents we measure would have to be drawn from the same stage. For example, if we measured only a sample of concrete-operational behaviors drawn from Chapter 5 we should find that all of these behaviors appear at about the same time on the average.

two other features of Piaget's stages

There are two additional characteristics of Piaget's stages that, although they are not formal criteria, nevertheless are important enough to merit discussion. These features are the notion of *preparation and achievement phases* for each stage and the notion of *décalages* within and between stages.

The distinction between the preparatory and achievement phases of a stage appears to be simply Piaget's way of saying that a new stage never materializes full blown at some given instant in time. Piaget maintains that *quantitative* improvements in both the structure and content of cognition occur during the course of each stage. In view of the fact that acquisition of new structures only occurs between stages, the sort of structural change that occurs during the preparatory phase of a Piagetian stage must be the first of the two types we discussed earlier (i.e., broadening of structures to include a wider range of information and situations). Because cognitive content always presupposes underlying structure in Piaget's theory, cognitive content also will change as a function of the quantitative structural changes taking place during a preparatory phase. The chief feature of the preparatory phase of any stage is that the contents characteristic of that stage are unstable. Sometimes children's behavior makes it seem as though they are "in" that stage, while at other times, their behavior makes it seem as though they are "out" of that stage. Let us consider a simple example, namely, the concept of transitivity (if we know X is shorter than Y and Y is shorter than Z, then we conclude that X also is shorter than Z) that we used earlier to illustrate the qualitative change criterion. Transitivity is one of Piaget's chief indexes of the third of his four stages of cognitive development. Now, if one follows the development of transitivity from the preschool years through the elementary school years, one finds the two characteristic response patterns mentioned above, i.e., the youngest children always fail transitivity problems, while the oldest children always pass them. However, one also finds a third response pattern "in between" the other two. This pattern may be described as follows. If we administer a large number of different transitivity problems (say ten or fifteen), we will find that some of the children will answer correctly about half the time and incorrectly about half the time. Transitivity is an unstable cognitive content in these children; it shows up in some of the situations where it should show up but not in others. This fact is taken to indicate that such children are in the preparatory phase of the stage for which transitivity is a cognitive content.

When instabilities of the preceding sort have largely disappeared from the cognitive contents characteristic of a given stage, Piaget says that the achievement phase has been attained. During the achievement phase, the relevant structures presumably are functioning as a well-integrated whole, rather than in comparative isolation. In Piaget's terminology, the relevant structures are in a state of *equilibrium* during the achievement phase.

A final interesting fact about the preparation-achievement distinction is the motivation that apparently underlies it. It seems to be motivated by the old nativism-empiricism controversy. Piaget wisely wishes to avoid being caught on the horns of this dilemma. Therefore, he has argued that cognitive development must be treated as an outcome of the *interaction* of hereditary and environmental factors. Others who have studied Piaget's writings on this subject disagree and say that his is a strongly hereditarian theory of development (e.g., Beilin 1971*a*). Developmental psychologists use two criteria to judge the extent to which the emergence of any given type of behavior (in this case cognition) results from hereditary or environmental factors. The first of these is the extent to which the behavior tends to develop in a *stereotyped manner*. A classic illustration of stereotyped development is when behaviors appear one after the other in a fixed invariant sequence. Other things being equal, behaviors that emerge in fixed invariant sequences are viewed as under more direct hereditary control than behaviors that do not. The second criterion is the *rapidity* with which behavior changes as a function of age. Other things being equal, we assume that forms of behavior that appear more or less full blown are under more direct hereditary control than behaviors that develop gradually. The point is that, by virtue of the distinction between preparatory and achievement phases, Piaget's theory seems to straddle the nativism-empiricism controversy successfully. While it is true that the theory leans toward stereotyped emergence, the provision of a preparatory phase for each stage allows the theory to lean away from rapid emergence.

A second informal feature of Piaget's stages is the notion of *décalages* within and between stages. In its most basic sense, *décalage* is simply a name for *any invariant sequence between cognitive contents* such that one content always appears earlier than the other. Now, we already have discussed the idea of an invariant sequence or progression in conjunction with stage requirement (*b*). However, requirement (*b*) refers to an invariant progression of the stages themselves or, more precisely, an invariant progression of the structures which characterize each stage. In contrast, the notion of *décalage* refers to invariant progressions of the measurable cognitive behaviors from which structures and stages are inferred. They come in two varieties. First, there are the so-called "horizontal" *décalages*. These occur *within* stages. Specifically, they refer to invariant sequences in *two or more versions of a single cognitive content*. To illustrate, consider a cognitive content from Piaget's third stage that was mentioned in Chapter 1, namely, conservation. It will be recalled that conservation refers to children's understanding that the quantitative relationship between two objects remains constant across irrelevant perceptual alterations of one of the objects. But there are many specific quantitative relationships that are "conserved" (mass, weight, number, length, etc.). It may be that children always learn to conserve some of these relationships before they learn to conserve others. If they do, then this is what Piaget calls a horizontal *décalage*. It is important to note that requirement (*d*) permits invariant sequences of this sort between different versions of the same cognitive content. Thus, finding that children conserve number before weight does not violate requirement (*d*). The type of within-stage invariant sequence that (*d*) prohibits is *between the same version of two different cognitive contents*. Thus, finding that children always learn transitivity of length before conservation of length, transitivity of weight before conservation of weight, and so on is a violation of requirement (*d*). I shall have more to say on this subject in Chapter 5.

The second form of *décalage* is called "vertical." These occur *between* stages. When there is an invariant sequence between two different contents and the contents belong to different stages, we have a vertical *décalage*. We may return to conservation concepts for a brief illustration. Conservation concepts emerge during Piaget's third stage. Hence, if we compare them with contents from Piaget's second and fourth stages, conservation should emerge before the latter and after the former.

Two further points should be mentioned about horizontal and vertical *décalages*. First, in view of the fact that horizontal *décalages* are within-stage and vertical *décalages* are between stages, it is obvious that the two must result from different types of changes in the underlying structures. Explicitly, horizontal *décalages* must be caused by quantitative structural changes, while vertical *décalages* must be caused by qualitative structural changes. Second, the distinction between horizontal and vertical *décalages* is related to the distinction between preparatory and achievement phases of stages. Horizontal *décalages* presumably occur during the preparatory phase of each stage, because this is when quantitative structural changes occur. In contrast, vertical *décalages* would be most apparent if one were comparing groups of subjects in the achievement phases of different stages.

the four stages

To conclude this section on the stage concept, I shall briefly outline the general outcome of Piaget's stage viewpoint, namely, his four global stages of cognitive development. Since they are dealt with individually in the subsequent four chapters, I shall make only a few brief comments about each here. I wish only to make the reader aware of the names of the four stages, the order of their presumed appearance, and the most general features of each.

In the order of their appearance, Piaget's four stages are: the *sensorimotor* stage, the *preoperational* stage, the *concrete-operational* stage, and the *formal-operational* stage. The first of these, the sensorimotor stage, will be considered in detail in Chapter 3. The sensorimotor stage spans roughly the age range that most psychologists call infancy—i.e., from birth to about age 2. According to Piaget, the salient feature of this first stage is that internalized thinking processes are absent. In other words, infants cannot carry out many activities "inside their heads." Infants are said to be capable of only those processes that, somehow, can be manifest in overt behavior. To paraphrase an old revolutionary war slogan, there is action without representation.

During the second or preoperational stage, Piaget believes that children acquire the internalized thought processes that they lacked as infants. These processes are said to originate in the child's internalization of the overt action schemes that dominate the sensorimotor stage. Hence, in Piaget's system the early precursors of what subsequently will be called "thought" are internal representation of overt actions. Although preoperational children have acquired "thought" in a broad sense, their thinking remains relatively unsophisticated by adult standards. As we shall see in

Chapter 4, Piaget has concluded that the preoperational child's thought is best described as intuitive—i.e., as lacking the rigorous, logical, and deductive properties characteristic of the two remaining stages. Piaget's age ranges for the preoperational stage are roughly age 2 to age 7.

The third or concrete-operational stage is said to begin at about age 7 and end at about age 11. The major feature of this period is that children's thought processes lose their intuitive character and become rigorous and logical. Children can now "figure things out"; they can reason. For example, children acquire several of the previously mentioned conservation concepts. When thought processes acquire this flexible and rigorous (but not rigid) character, Piaget calls them *operational*. This latter notion is a central concept of Piaget's system and I shall have much more to say about it in Chapters 4 and 5. Even with their new-found sophistication, concrete-operational cognitive processes fall short of adult intelligence in one significant respect. They produce rigorous, logical thinking *only* when applied to concrete informational inputs. In short, concrete-operational thought is not sufficiently abstract. This latter fact obviously is responsible for the label "concrete."

The final or formal-operational stage begins around age 11 and continues through the remainder of mature life. During this stage, the remaining refinements of adult thought are acquired. The thinking processes are said to be fully abstract. They no longer must depend on observed data. Thought operations now can be carried out on hypothetical information or situations that may never occur in reality. For example, physicists are able to reason about atomic isotopes or nuclear interactions that may never have occurred in nature, but nonetheless are predictable from some mathematical formula. By the time the achievement phase of the formal-operational stage is attained (about age 15), Piaget believes intelligence has arrived at its ultimate equilibrium and no further qualitative structural improvements will occur.

Piaget's Research Techniques

To close this chapter, let us consider Piaget's unique method of conducting research on cognitive development. His clinical method is, to say the least, somewhat unorthodox by traditional psychological standards. We shall begin by examining some general facts about the method. We conclude by examining its most obvious dangers.

Several years ago, Flavell (1963) noted that the clinical method may be described as consisting of three general steps. First, the subject is presented with a problem-solving situation of some sort. Second, several variations of the same problem-solving situation are presented to probe the limits of the subject's ability. Third, the response that the subject gives on each variation of the situation determines what variation will be introduced next. With these general remarks of Flavell's as background, I should like to make several observations about the clinical method and how it relates to more traditional research procedures.

Most psychologists distinguish two general methods of conducting research: the *experimental* method and the *survey* method. This distinction, which was originally proposed by the psychometrician Lee J. Cronbach in 1957, runs roughly as follows: In an experiment, we manipulate a causative agent (called a "treatment") and then determine its effects on behavior. For example, we administer various drugs to subjects and assess their effects on automobile driving. In a survey, we simply measure various behaviors and determine which ones correlate with each other. For example, we measure baseball throwing and football throwing to determine whether people who can throw baseballs accurately also tend to throw footballs accurately. The difference between the two methods, then, is that in experiments we always manipulate a causative variable and in surveys we never do. The first general point I should like to make about Piaget's clinical method is that it falls somewhere between these manipulative and nonmanipulative extremes. In some cases, the method is used mainly for observation, while in others it is used in a very manipulative manner. Usually, the method tends to be more manipulative and interventionist when older children are being studied than when the subjects are infants. However, even when infants are being studied, the method can be very manipulative at times:

> *Observation 95.*—Luciene, at 0;4 (27) is lying in her bassinet. I hand a doll over her feet which immediately sets in motion the schema of shakes (see the foregoing observations). But her feet reach the doll right away and give it a violent movement which Luciene surveys with delight. Afterward she looks at her motionless foot for a second, then recommences. There is no visual control of the foot for the movements are the same when Luciene only looks at the doll or when I place the doll over her head. On the other hand, the tactile control of the foot is apparent: as though to grasp and explore. For instance, when she tries to kick the doll and misses her aim, she begins again very slowly until she succeeds (without seeing her feet). In the same way I cover Luciene's face or distract her attention for a moment in another direction: she nevertheless continues to hit the doll and control its movements. [Piaget 1952b, p. 159][4]

A second general feature of the clinical method is that very small numbers of subjects are used. This is particularly true of the infancy studies we shall take up in the next chapter in which only three babies were studied. Unlike Piaget, most psychologists prefer to use large numbers of subjects in their research. Hence, Piaget's research qualifies as little more than pilot

[4] Reprinted from *The Origins of Intelligence in Children* by Jean Piaget. By permission of International Universities Press, Inc. Copyright 1952 by International Universities Press, Inc. Reprinted with permission of Editions Delachaux and Niestlé, Switzerland.

data by most psychologists' standards. Perhaps Piaget's biological perspective is what causes him to have confidence in findings from small subject samples. He certainly believes that his cognitive structures are the same for all normal members of the human species. Whatever his reasons are, the fact that Piaget studies very small numbers of subjects means that skepticism is often the first reaction that his findings provoke. Most psychologists are not willing to accept his findings until they have been able to verify them with larger groups of subjects.

Third, for any given group of subjects exposed to a particular problem-solving situation, the exact procedure varies widely from one subject to another. Different subjects will respond differently to the same situation. Since the variations that are presented are determined by the subject's responses, it follows that subjects who respond differently will not receive the same tasks. In short, the testing procedures are not what we call *standardized*. Consequently, the use of the clinical method is heavily dependent on the skills and sophistication of the experimenter. Ultimately, only those who have trained several years in Geneva can hope to use the method properly. To those for whom the essence of scientific research is its impersonalness and public communicability, this fact inevitably smacks of priestcraft and obscurantism.

A fourth and final point that I should like to make about the clinical method is that it is a *conservative* diagnostic procedure. To test for the presence of a particular cognitive content, several variations of a given problem-solving situation are administered. The cognitive content in question is said to be present only if the subject solves the problem in all or nearly all the situations. This means that many of the subjects who are classified as not having a particular cognitive content are what psychologists call Type II errors. A Type II error is a *false negative error*—i.e., we say that subjects do not possess a certain property that they really do possess. The clinical method's potential for diagnosing subjects as not having a cognitive content that they actually do have causes some serious problems that are briefly noted below and that crop up again and again in the next four chapters.

The third and fourth characteristics of the clinical method produce some problematical consequences. The third characteristic entails that subjective attributes of the experimenter—such as empathy, objectivity, and perceptiveness—are absolutely critical. Unfortunately, as any clinical psychologist knows only too well, a person's subjective attributes are very difficult "conditions" to replicate. Because one of the central goals of any science is replicability, Piaget's clinical method provokes strenuous objections. Whenever one reads the results of any of Piaget's investigations, one must place complete faith in the astuteness and honesty of the experimenter. Most psychologists would prefer not to place such faith in any experimenter. Experimenters, being human, will entertain certain hypotheses about what is "going on" in the studies they are conducting. Standardized research procedures are designed to protect us from the most blatant effects of prejudicial hypotheses. The clinical method affords no such protection.

The fourth characteristic entails that the clinical method normally will overestimate the age at which a given cognitive content appears. This has never bothered Piaget very much because he is concerned primarily with the order in which his stages are acquired and not with age norms. Other investigators believe that the consequences of consistently overestimating age norms are more serious than Piaget believes.

Given these difficulties with the clinical method, one may reasonably ask why Piaget continues to use and remains adamant in the face of criticism. The perplexity deepens when one realizes that Piaget both understands and sympathizes with the views of his critics (e.g., see Piaget's introduction to Almy, Chittenden, and Miller 1966). Piaget believes that his methods are vital to the study of cognitive development because he feels cognitive structures are just too complex to be revealed by less flexible, standardized research techniques. Piaget seems to think that his techniques "get the most for the least." He also argues that one must avoid constricting children's behavior and thereby perhaps producing findings that are either trivial or, worse yet, artificial. Here, Piaget is saying that investigators should not see themselves as manipulators but as interpreters who chase after childen's thoughts as they go wandering where they may.

Synopsis

Piaget attempts to explain cognitive development by appealing to certain concepts that are not very familiar to most psychological readers. Although his theory is intended to be a scientific doctrine, many of its ideas have a distinctly philosophical aura. Explicitly, they tend to violate the rules of operationism and parsimony. Concerning operationism, the precise empirical meaning of several key concepts is less than clear. Cases in point mentioned in this chapter include stage, structure, and function. It is not completely clear how one goes about recognizing a Piagetian stage when one sees it. Structures and functions apparently cannot be recognized at all—at least not in the narrow sense of being measurable directly. Structures and functions must both be inferred from behavior. Concerning parsimony, Piagetian concepts tend toward redundancy. Scheme and structure are illustrations of notions that overlap considerably.

Compared to other approaches to the study of intelligence, the most striking feature of Piaget's theory is its reliance on biological terminology. Descriptive principles of biological growth, such as organization and adaption, are used to describe cognitive development. Evolutionary analogies are fairly common. The role of the organism in determining its own development is strongly emphasized. Like modern ethologists, Piaget prefers to base his conclusions on the study of intelligence in its "natural habitat" rather than on carefully controlled laboratory experiments. Cognitive development, like physical maturation, is viewed as an intrinsically self-directed and self-motivating process. On the whole, cognitive development and physical maturation are treated as complementary aspects of a single process—development. Despite these leanings, the use of biological concepts in Piaget's theory is almost entirely metaphorical. There is no attempt to spell out the connection between biological and intellectual development. Since the latter obviously is related to the maturation of the brain and other areas of the nervous system, one might reasonably suppose that a biologically oriented theory would rely on well-known principles of neurophysiological development such as myelination of cortical centers or lateralization of hemispheric function. However, no attempt has been made to incorporate such variables into the theory.

The three most important concepts that Piaget uses to explain cognitive development are, in their order of importance, cognitive structure, cognitive function, and cognitive content. Cognitive structures undergo both quantitative ("stretching") and qualitative ("reorganization") change during development. Actually, cognitive development is essentially synonymous with changes in cognitive structure. By comparison with other familiar structures (the skeleton, the circulatory system, the nervous system, etc.), cognitive structures are very abstract and cannot be directly measured. They are somewhat like the grammatical structures that are said to underlie language. Since cognitive structures cannot be directly measured, we are confined to constructing "models" of them. Piaget has preferred to use models borrowed from logic and higher mathematics. Cognitive structures are the underlying variables that control intelligence at any given level of development. Piaget's theory is normally classified as a discontinuity theory because these structures are said to change with development. The mechanism whereby structure change takes place is called the equilibration process. Equilibration produces new structures that are more general in scope and more stable than previous ones.

Piaget's two cognitive functions are organization and adaption. These two principles operate in the same manner throughout the life span and, hence, they are called functional invariants. Organization and adaption are complementary processes. Organization is responsible for the organism's cognitive continuity across time, whereas adaption is responsible for cognitive change. Perhaps the most important thing about organization is that, for Piaget at any rate, it implies that intelligence is an integrated whole rather than a collection of isolated behaviors. The adaption principle really comprises two principles, assimilation and accomodation. Cognitive assimilation and accommodation are analogous to digestive assimilation and accommodation. Cognitive assimilation is a process whereby incoming information is broken down to fit the organism's current level of cognitive organization. Cognitive accommodation is a process whereby structures change in a manner that permits them to assimilate new forms of information.

Cognitive contents are the specific acts of intelligence that characterize given stages of development. Concepts such as object permanence (sensorimotor stage), animism (preoperational stage), classification (concrete-operational stage), and numerical proportion (formal-operational stage) are all cognitive contents. Although contents are less central to the theory than structures or functions, it is not possible for the theory to get along without them. Since neither structures nor functions are amenable to measurement, their presence must be inferred from the presence of cognitive contents.

The concept of scheme overlaps with the concept of structure. Technically speaking, cognitive structures are advanced types of schemes that appear during the later phases of cognitive development. Schemes are organizational variables controlling the expression of the cognitive contents of the early stages of development—especially during infancy. Unlike structures, schemes do not necessarily involve mental representation. They may be entirely motoric. Schemes undergo developmental change via the equilibration process. An important feature of schemes is that organisms tend to apply them repetitively—in effect, to rehearse them. Through the mechanism of reciprocal assimilation, schemes become internally differentiated and more tightly coordinated with each other as development proceeds.

Piaget always describes age-related changes in cognitive contents in terms of stages. Importantly, he believes that his stages are real and not merely convenient headings under which to group a wide variety of behaviors. This particular use of the stage concept creates several problems. Chief among them is the question of how we should go about verifying the actual existence of these stages. Piaget offers some criteria whereby the existence of stages might be established. The most important ones seem to be qualitative changes in cognitive contents, culturally universal stage sequences, hierarchical organization of the structures of earlier and later stages, and integration of the structures of individual stages. To those who have studied the problem, it is not at all clear whether such criteria suffice to confirm the existence of stages. Some of them seem to be more philosophical than empirical. Although other criteria generate clear empirical predictions, these predictions may not be unambiguous consequences of stages. Each of Piaget's stages is said to be characterized by a preparation phase and an achievement phase. The new structures indigenous to a given stage appear during the preparation phase and are eventually consolidated during the achievement phase. The achievement phase of any given stage is the preparation phase of the next stage. The cognitive contents of a given stage do not appear full blown at the outset. Some contents emerge sequentially during the course of the stage. These sequences are known as horizontal *décalages*. The sequential emergence of contents belonging to different stages are called vertical *décalages*.

Finally, Piaget uses a unique research procedure that he calls the clinical method. As its name suggests, the clinical method resembles psychiatric interviewing techniques more than the standardized measurement procedures favored by modern experimental psychologists. The clinical method has provoked a good deal of criticism of Piaget. Most of this criticism centers on the fact that the clinical method does not lend itself to precise replication. Each subsequent question posed during a clinical interview is determined by how the subject answers previous questions. Therefore, the exact details of such an interview vary widely from subject to subject. This fact inevitably generates skepticism about the data reported by Piaget and his coworkers. When an investigator reports certain findings using standardized procedures, the scientific community tends to accept them at face value. With Piaget's findings, on the other hand, the scientific community tends not to accept them unless they can be replicated under controlled conditions. Piaget defends his continued use of the clinical method on the ground that other procedures are too inflexible to get at the phenomena he wishes to study.

Supplementary Readings

The following seven books and papers offer advanced treatments of selected topics covered in the present chapter. The list is not exhaustive, but all of the theoretical concepts examined earlier in this chapter are discussed in some detail in these readings.

BRAINERD, " 'Stage,' 'Structure,' and Developmental Theory" (1976a). Deals with the concepts of stage and structure.

FLAVELL, "Stage-related Properties of Cognitive Development" (1971). Examines questions related to the empirical verification of stages.

PIAGET, *The Psychology of Intelligence* (1950). A general introduction to the theory including the main epochs of development and the major cognitive contents.

PIAGET, *The Origins of Intelligence in Children* (1952b). This is probably the single most important reference for the concept of scheme and the mechanisms of scheme change.

PIAGET, "The General Problems of Psychobiological Development in Children" (1960). This paper provides a wealth of information, in fairly readable prose, about the concepts of stage and structure. It is widely regarded as the best source of facts about the principle of equilibration.

PIAGET, *Biology and Knowledge* (1967b). The most comprehensive discussion of the theory's biological roots appears in this text. The concepts of structure, function, scheme, and stage are all discussed with reference to species other than man.

PIAGET, *Structuralism* (1970*a*). This is the most important reference for Piaget's concept of cognitive structure. A general definition of this notion is presented, and the connection between stages and structures is formulated.

chapter 3

Piaget on Infancy:
The Sensorimotor Stage

We turn now to Piaget's account of cognitive development during infancy. In Chapter 1, we saw that Piaget's studies of infant intelligence were conducted in Neuchâtel and Geneva a half century ago. The great bulk of this research, with Piaget's accompanying interpretations of the findings, may be found in three main works: *The Origins of Intelligence in Children* (1952b); *The Construction of Reality in the Child* (1954); and *Play, Dreams, and Imitation in Childhood* (1951). It will be recalled that Piaget's infancy research consisted of a series of investigations that he conducted using his own three children—Jacqueline, Laurent, and Lucienne—as subjects. Some of the investigations were purely observational with Piaget simply recording the behaviors spontaneously emitted by his children. Other investigations were more experimental with Piaget repeatedly intervening and attempting to influence his children's behavior through his own actions.

We saw in Chapter 2 that Piaget believes the central task of cognitive development during infancy is the acquisition of a rudimentary capacity for internal thought. If there is a single thread that unites the diverse forms of infant cognitive content considered in this chapter, contents which Piaget collectively calls *sensorimotor intelligence,* it is this emphasis on infancy as the time of transition from completely overt content to internalized (representational) content. In his six levels of sensorimotor intelligence, Piaget describes this transition in terms of a succession of concepts, skills, and strategies that make their appearance during the first two years of life. A second uniting theme that is worth mentioning is what I shall call the *development of objectivity*. As we shall see, Piaget believes that newborns live in a world in which there is no clear distinction between their own bodies, on the one hand, and the people and things in their environment, on the other. In the language of philosophy, there is no distinction between the *subject* and the *object* for the newborn. During the first two years of life, infants gradually learn to distinguish themselves from the objects in their environment. They also learn to distinguish the objects in their environment from the actions they perform on them. In effect, infants discover that there are objects other than themselves in the environment and they discover that the existence of these objects does not depend on their own existence. This is what I mean by the development of objectivity. We shall see that Piaget infers the evolution of the distinction between subject and object from changes in six specific cognitive contents that occur during the sensorimotor stage.

In Chapter 2, I noted that Piaget's theory tends to be more concerned with abstract structures than with tangible cognitive contents. However, this emphasis on structure rather than content is more pronounced for some stages of development than others. It is least evident with the sensorimotor stage. Perhaps this is because Piaget's infancy research was conducted very early in his career when he was less interested in structures. Perhaps it also is because infancy is a time of sensorimotor schemes—schemes that do not involve much if any internal representation. Whatever the reasons, Piaget's account of infant cognitive development is more closely connected with measurable behavior than are his accounts of subsequent stages.

In the broadest sense, Piaget's sensorimotor stage is a step-by-step account of the infant's progress from cognitive contents that are reflexive, self-centered, and disorganized to cognitive contents that are instrumental, adapted to the demands of the environment, and well organized. Sensorimotor schemes, like the structures of every stage, are said to begin as narrow and rigid affairs and to evolve in the direction of increased comprehensiveness and flexibility. Another very general aspect of the sensorimotor stage is that our familiar perceptual and sensory systems (vision, smell, hearing, etc.) are said to become coordinated during this stage. Piaget believes that infants begin life with perceptual and sensory systems that function in relative isolation from each other. For example, auditory information cannot be used to localize an object in visual space and vice versa. This condition stands in contrast to the marked overlap observed between adult perceptual systems. An adult, for example, will look in the direction of something that has just been heard. Piaget uses the progressive coordination of perceptual systems as one of his main indexes of sensorimotor intelligence.

Piaget describes cognitive development during infancy in terms of a succession of six distinct levels or substages. Each of these substages is defined by the most sophisticated cognitive content found within it. In fact, we shall see that Piaget's name for each substage is simply the name of a certain cognitive content. Within each substage, Piaget explains and catalogues each new content by appealing to contents that immediately precede it. Piaget's sensorimotor substages focus primarily on six forms of cognitive content: (*a*) imitation, (*b*) circular reactions, (*c*) time reactions, (*d*) the object concept, (*e*) the causality concept, and (*f*) the space concept. In Piaget's view, the key to understanding how internalized thought develops during infancy lies in the study of these six contents. We shall consider each of them separately. After the contents have been discussed and illustrated, Piaget's six substages of sensorimotor intelligence will be examined. In the concluding section of this chapter, we shall review some of the most recent research on the sensorimotor stage. All of this research was conducted by investigators outside Geneva and it focuses on the replicability of Piaget's research on infants.

Sensorimotor Cognitive Contents

imitation

Psychologists sometimes call the ability to imitate another's behavior *matched-dependent behavior* (e.g., Miller and Dollard 1941) or *observational learning* (e.g., Bandura and Walters 1963). Imitation also is the first of Piaget's indexes of sensorimotor intelligence. Even if it did not play a role in Piaget's theory, the relevance of imitation to the development of mental representation seems obvious to common sense. To mimic the behavior of others, one must, at the very least, (*a*) make some rather complex observations and (*b*) represent these observations either via overt mediational behaviors or via internal symbolic processes. Thus, there seems to be a very close intuitive connection between imitation and mental representation.

Another important fact about sensorimotor imitation relates to the adaption principle discussed in Chapter 2. It will be recalled that there are two sides to adaption, namely, assimilation and accommodation. It will also be recalled that although Piaget believes that assimilation and accommodation can never be completely separated, he also believes that it is possible to find contents in which one or the other predominates. Imitation is one such content. It is supposed to be a content in which accommodation predominates over assimilation. Given our earlier definition of accommodation as a change in the organism (rather than a change in the environment) and our common sense understanding of imitation as changing our behavior to match the behavior of another, this description of imitation as a predominantly accommodative content seems very reasonable.

The imitative behavior of infants is, of course, more crude than that of children or adults. Obviously, imitation (and any other form of behavior for that matter) will be limited by the infant's lack of fine motor coordination. If Piaget is correct in maintaining that the sensorimotor stage is a time of little or no mental representation, then this should also restrict imitation. Imitation, as we just saw, in some sense presupposes the capacity to represent the behaviors one observes in others. Despite these difficulties, Piaget reports considerable evidence of imitative behavior in infants. He also reports that the ability to imitate shows marked improvement between birth and about age 2. More particularly, the infant is said to progress all the way from immediate reflexive imitations to imitations that are instrumental in satisfying desires and that may not occur until several days after a behavior was originally observed.

During the earliest substages of the sensorimotor stage, Piaget views imitation primarily as a mechanism whereby one of the forms of adaption, *reproductive assimilation*, takes place. We saw in Chapter 2 that Piaget believes that in order for schemes to develop they must be repeatedly exercised. It is imitation that, at least during the first few months of life, is supposed to provide the chief means of accomplishing the repeated exercise necessary for the differentiation, coordination, and generalization of schemes. The reflexive action schemes of the newborn may be activated by observing the behavior of others (usually adults). These early imitations are rigid and stereotyped, like any other reflex. By the end of the first year of life, imitation is said to become both more flexible and more instrumental. Instead of immediately imitating any behavior of which they are capable, infants selectively imitate behaviors that are either especially interesting to them or that will help satisfy their needs. By the latter half of the second year of life, Piaget claims that infants are able to imitate behaviors involving parts of the body that cannot be directly observed—e.g., imitating facial expressions or eye movements. Somewhat younger infants can only imitate behaviors involving parts of the body that they can see (e.g., hands or feet). Piaget attributes the ability to imitate behaviors involving unobservable parts of the body to increased scheme mobility, increased coordination of different perceptual systems, and, of ourse, the acquisition of mental representation.

During the sensorimotor stage, as I just mentioned, Piaget sees imitation as a vehicle for reproductive assimilation. By the end of the sensorimotor stage (about age 2), however, imitation begins to fulfill a quite different function. Now, it serves primarily as a device whereby new behaviors are added to the infant's repertoire. This new function of imitation contrasts sharply with its earlier function of reproductive assimilation. Recalling the definition in Chapter 2, reproductive assimilation consists of imitating behaviors that the infant *already possesses*.

Piaget reports that by the end of the second year of life two especially interesting improvements in imitation have taken place. The infant becomes capable of delaying the imitation of a behavior until several days after it was first observed. At about the same time, the infant begins to show signs of imitating the movements of inanimate objects as well as the behavior of people. Piaget interprets the first of these advances as a clear indication that mental representation has been acquired. His reasoning on this point runs roughly as follows: Although it may be possible to postpone imitation for a short time (e.g., a few minutes) by mediating a behavior overtly, it seems inconceivable that imitation could be postponed for *days* without the aid of some internal symbolic device for representing the behavior.

circular reactions

Generally speaking, this second type of sensorimotor cognitive content may be defined as cyclic behavior sequences that permit various action patterns to be refined into well-formed schemes. Here, the process of refining action patterns into schemes involves the principles of both consolidation and generalization discussed in Chapter 2. In Piaget's view, circular reactions are the infant's chief method of consolidating and generalizing schemes. Piaget describes a circular reaction as any action sequence that *tends to be repeated because the actions produce forms of stimulation that lead to repetition of the actions.* The action sequence is, in a word, circular.

Piaget's standard illustration of a circular reaction is the infant's suckling behavior. Stimulation of the infant's lips by the mother's nipple produces a sequence of behaviors consisting of lip, jaw, and neck movements which we call suckling. In most cases, this sequence of behaviors results in milk in the infant's mouth. This in turn produces the muscular contractions associated with getting the milk into the infant's stomach. But the behavior sequence does not end there. The muscular contractions involved in swallowing the milk produce internal stimuli which cause the infant to continue suckling. Thus, although an external stimulus (the nipple) was required to trigger the behavior sequence in the first place, the sequence is self-sustaining once initiated. It is in this sense that suckling, and other behavior sequences, are said to be circular.

A thorny and somewhat philosophical question arises concerning what motivates circular reactions. We saw in Chapter 2 that Piaget does not speak of motivation in the same way that most psychologists do. In particular, we saw that Piaget is not very much concerned with motives such as hunger, thirst, fear, etc., that are under the direct control of *external stimuli.* Such motives are subject to what learning psychologists call *contingencies of reinforcement.* That is, behavior can be changed through the selective application of the external stimuli that control the motives—e.g., a thirsty rat will learn to press a bar to obtain water. Piaget uses a quite different motivational language in which certain forms of behavior are said to be *intrinsically motivating*. That is, Piaget frequently speaks of behaviors that are motivating in their own right and do not require additional pushes or pulls. He views circular reactions in this way—i.e., he maintains that self-sustaining behavior sequences such as suckling are also self-motivating. This statement does not satisfy most psychologists because it appears circular. It seems to say, "A circular reaction occurs because it occurs." If this is true, then "intrinsic motivation" is not really any explanation of why circular reactions (or any other behavior) take place.

Although it is not at all clear what motivates circular reactions, it is clear *when* they are supposed to occur. A circular reaction is most likely to occur (is most highly motivated) when the infant is in a *moderately* familiar stimulus situation. That is, the stimuli the infant is experiencing are not entirely new but they are not familiar either. In Piaget's language, any given circular reaction occurs with the greatest frequency when the amounts of scheme generalization and consolidation associated with it are moderate. Behind Piaget's language is a very simple idea. When presented with an entirely new stimulus, the infant may not know how to react to it and may even fear it. When presented with a thoroughly familiar stimulus, the infant has learned how to react to it but the stimulus and the behaviors are so familiar that they no longer are interesting. Between these two extremes are stimuli that are sufficiently familiar that the infant knows how to react to them but are not so familiar that they are uninteresting.

Piaget's circular reactions come in three varieties: *primary* circular reactions, *secondary* circular reactions, and *tertiary* circular reactions. As the names suggest, the three forms of circular reaction are supposed to represent increasing levels of sophistication. In *The Origins of Intelligence in Children*, Piaget distinguishes the three categories in terms of the function and content of each. Each form of circular reaction is instrumental in achieving somewhat different goals and the topography of the actual responses is somewhat different.

Primary circular reactions are supposed to appear during the second substage of sensorimotor intelligence (about the first to the fourth months of life). They are more like reflexes than like voluntary behavior. They consist of behavior sequences that are directed at the infant's own body. Secondary circular reactions are supposed to appear during the third sensorimotor substage (about the fourth to eighth months). They are less reflexive than primary circular reactions. They consist of behavior sequences that the infant has discovered more or less by chance (in Piaget's language: *nonsystematic adaptions*). Most of Piaget's illustrations of secondary circular reactions are concerned with repetitious looking and listening behavior. We shall consider some examples when we discuss the sensorimotor substages. Tertiary circular reactions make their appearance during the fifth sensorimotor substage (about the first half of the second year of life). Like secondary circular reactions, they are voluntary rather than reflexive and they involve behavior sequences that the infant has happened on by accident. The distinguishing feature of tertiary circular reactions is that the infant engages in *systematic variations* of the specific behavior sequences. Tertiary circular reactions are a sort of action-based scientific method: The infant is familiar with the outcome of a given behavior sequence and, therefore, makes small changes in the components of the sequence to see what changes occur in the outcome. Another difference between secondary and tertiary circular reactions is that the former are principally concerned with scheme consolidation whereas the latter are principally concerned with scheme generalization. In effect, secondary circular reactions polish the behavior sequence and tertiary circular reactions discover how many different situations the sequence can be stretched to fit.

time

According to Piaget, the infant does not have any real sense of duration at the beginning of life. Time is not a *concept* in the sense that it is for children and adults. The infant simply is not aware of time as an objective "thing." Piaget believes that the fact that behaviors that comprise certain reflexes invariably occur in the same fixed order is about the only evidence that time has any relevance for the newborn. Presumably, it is from this fact the infant's primitive concept of duration evolves. By the middle of the first year of life, Piaget believes, a rudimentary grasp of duration is present. In fact, he thinks that it is responsible for the appearance of secondary circular reactions. The shortcoming of the infant's sense of time at this age is that time is an entirely subjective phenomenon. It is something that applies to the private world of the infant's own behavior but not to the external world. Intervals of time are defined only as intervals between the infant's actions. By the end of the first year of life, Piaget believes, infants are beginning to free themselves from this personal concept of time and time is beginning to take on an objective existence of its own. Piaget infers that time is becoming objective from the fact that infants can now establish temporal relations between events in which they did not directly participate—e.g., between events they have only seen or heard. Hence, time intervals are no longer restricted to the intervals between the infant's own actions.

Another important advance in the infant's sense of time is supposed to occur during the second half of the second year of life, the time when internal representation finally appears. Representation gives a considerable boost to the time concept. The infant now can recall events of long ago as well as those that occurred in the immediate past. At this point time comes to be perceived as a very general concept that applies to all people and events. Time is conceived as a dimension in which events occur, not just as a by-product of behavior.

the object concept

Perhaps the most intriguing aspect of Piaget's 1925–29 infancy studies was that a particular portion of the research was concerned with sorting out the gradual development of the so-called object concept. The object concept refers to our general belief that people, places, and things continue to exist when we are no longer in direct perceptual contact with them. The old philosophical conundrum of whether there is a sound when a tree falls and there is no one there to hear it amounts to doubting the validity of the object concept.

For Piaget, the *mature* object concept consists of the belief that the existence of people, places, and things is independent of our own behavior. To put it another way, the existence of things outside us is not contingent on what we do to them. At its most sophisticated level, the object concept also consists of the belief that one's self is merely another object having properties in common with other external objects. Piaget's central thesis about the object concept is that newborns and infants do not possess the beliefs just described. Piaget claims that these beliefs evolve gradually during infancy and that a mature object concept is not present until the end of the sensorimotor stage. Newborns, unlike children or adults, simply do not discriminate between external objects and the actions they perform on those objects. The existence of objects is contingent upon seeing them, hearing them, and touching them. Infants, if they could speak, presumably would tell us that there could not possibly be a sound when a tree falls and there is no one around to hear it. If there is no one around, then there is no tree!

Piaget's claim that the world of stable objects has to be gradually constructed seems to imply that the infant's first perceptions are of the sensory feedback that accompanies motor activity rather than of objects per se. According to this view, infants are not aware that either their bodies or external objects have sharp boundaries. This interpretation of the newborn's perceptual experience was very popular at the time Piaget conducted his infancy studies. Freud had described the infant's perceptual experiences as "oceanic," and William James had described them as "blooming, buzzing confusion." This interpretation, though popular when Piaget was young, is now believed to be incorrect. In the 1920s, almost nothing was known about the infant's perceptual capacities. In fact, almost nothing was known until very recently. During the late 1950s and early 1960s, several investigators set out to determine just how perceptually skilled infants are. The results of this research (e.g., Bower 1966, 1971; Fantz 1961; Gibson and Walk 1960) consistently showed that infants are perceptually very sophisticated. Newborns, for example, are capable of percepts such as depth, three-dimensionality, size constancy, color, and shape constancy. The general opinion among infancy researchers now appears to be that the differences between how infants and adults perceive the world are quantitative rather than qualitative.

During the middle of the first year of life, infants evince certain behaviors that Piaget interprets as the first signs that the object concept is beginning to evolve. When an interesting object (e.g., a toy) is taken away, the infant will make some effort to recover it. These recovery attempts typically involve repeating whatever behavior sequences took place when the object was present. Obviously, such behaviors are not always appropriate to the task of recovering the desired object. They may be thought of as magic of a sort. Despite their limitations, these first attempts at recovery are an advance over the behavior of the newborn. The newborn simply gives up when objects are taken away. By the end of the first year of life, Piaget reports further improvements in the object concept. Infants begin to show some signs of *searching behaviors* that are appropriate to the task of recovering a desired object. But infants' searching is still limited by their own actions at the time the object is removed: Piaget has observed that 1-year-olds will attempt to recover an object that is removed and hidden *only if they are moving in the direction of the hiding place at the time the object is hidden.* Otherwise, they simply will not search.

New behaviors appear during the first half of the second year of life that Piaget interprets as evidence of further advances in the object concept. The behaviors are also concerned with the search for removed and hidden objects. Infants are no longer restricted by their own actions at the time an object is hidden. They now direct their search activities toward places where they have *seen* an object hidden and *only* toward such places. Thus, according to Piaget, it takes infants roughly a year and a half to learn how to use rather simple (for children and adults) perceptual information about objects in what we would call an intelligent manner. Moreover, the behavior of infants with regard to objects still is limited by the fact that they must observe all hidings *directly,* if they are to find a given object. If, for example, one hides a toy under a cloth, hides the toy and the cloth under a pillow, and then removes the cloth from under the pillow leaving the toy, the infant will search under the cloth rather than under the pillow!

Finally, during the second half of the first year of life, certain behaviors appear that Piaget interprets as evidence of a mature object concept. In particular, the unobservable hidings just described which baffle younger infants are no longer a problem. The 2-year-old searches under the pillow rather than the cloth. When behaviors of this sort appear, Piaget concludes that the infant at last possesses the object concept. As is the case for the time concept, Piaget believes that the appearance of internal representation is responsible for the final advances in the object concept that occur at the end of the sensorimotor stage.

causality

The most important fact to note about the sensorimotor concept of causality is that even by the end of this stage the infant's understanding of cause-effect relations is quite unlike that of children or adults. By "causality," Piaget means, at most, the relatively simply capacity to anticipate what consequences will follow from a certain cause or what cause probably produced a particular result. We saw earlier that this conception of causality is part of secondary and tertiary circular reactions. Although it is a primitive type of causality by adult standards, Piaget believes that it takes a long time to acquire. Like the object concept, the causality concept develops slowly over the first two years of life.

Piaget maintains that the mature causality concept of adults consists of two separable aspects: *psychological* causality and *physical* causality. Psychological causality refers to what we commonly call "volition" or "will." That is, it refers to the belief that one's actions are guided by one's wishes and desires. Physical causality refers to more objective cause-effect relations. A bat meets a ball (cause), and the ball is propelled several hundred feet (effect). Although these two aspects of causality are adult concepts, Piaget argues the primitive precursors of both may be found in the sensorimotor stage. The sensorimotor precursor of psychological causality is what Piaget calls *dynamism*. The sensorimotor precursor of physical causality is what Piaget calls *phenomenalism*. Dynamism refers to the infant's understanding that internal feelings (hunger, cold, wetness, etc.) somehow produce external behaviors (e.g., crying, arm flailing, leg flailing). Piaget's description of phenomenalism is almost the same as Webster's definition: the primitive belief that any two events that occur closely in time must be causally linked—i.e., the first event must have "caused" the second.

Piaget believes that dynamism and phenomenalism are undifferentiated at birth. Therefore, the main task of causal development during infancy is to develop a dual system of causality by separating dynamism from phenomenalism. Since phenomenalism and dynamism are undifferentiated at birth, Piaget maintains that the newborn's causal experiences are radically different from those of children and adults. In particular, the first days of life are said to be a time of "magic"—i.e., a time when physical cause-effect relations are believed to be produced by internal psychological processes. In the same way that spirtualists or mentalists believe that they can cause people or objects to do certain things merely by willing them to do so, infants believe that their personal desires affect the behavior of objects in the external world.

The first movement toward differentiation of dynamism and phenomenalism occurs around the middle of the first year of life. With the development of secondary circular reactions, some differentiation of the two forms of causality is possible. Thanks to secondary circular reactions infants can now observe their actions and the consequences of these actions in a detached and objective manner and, as a result, they no longer associate them with feelings or states of mind. Further differentiation of dynamism and phenomenalism occurs near the end of the first year of life. The 1-year-old appears to be capable of classifying various behavioral sequences in terms of the consequences that they produce. Piaget infers the presence of this classification capacity from the fact that the infant will emit only a limited range of behaviors to gain a desired goal. Also, the 1-year-old seems to be able to classify at least some of the behaviors of other people in terms of the consequences they produce.

Causal development receives a further boost during the first half of the second year of life with the appearance of tertiary circular reactions. Tertiary circular reactions help make infants aware that there are many cause-effect relations that have nothing whatsoever to do with the infants' own wishes and desires. Like time, causality is beginning to become an objective "thing" rather than an intensely personal construct. By comparison, Piaget says that 1-year-olds are only aware of causal relations that have some personal consequences for them. However, eighteen-month-olds are aware of causal relations that do not affect them in any direct way. These impersonal causal relations include those that infants observe between people and objects in their surrounding environment. This new-found objectivity means that infants no longer view their own behavior exclusively in terms of its causal effects. Infants now realize that their behavior can be affected by people and things in their environment. In other words, infants now view their behavior as both causing other things and being caused by other things. Prior to the appearance of tertiary circular reactions, Piaget maintains that infants are restricted to the former interpretation of their behavior.

space

Space is the last of the six sensorimotor cognitive contents. Piaget's treatment of infant spatial constructs differs markedly from the approach of most other psychologists. Piaget thinks of space as a *concept,* whereas most other psychologists think of it as a *percept.* That is, Piaget treats space as though it were an abstraction that is gradually constructed by applying mental processes to the data of perception. But most other psychologists treat space as though it were part of the data of perception and does not require the application of mental processes. Piaget argues that the fact that spatial development is a lengthy process, spanning the first fourteen or fifteen years of life, suggests that space is more conceptual than it is perceptual. Piaget's idea of what constitutes a mature concept of space leans heavily on geometry. He believes that this mature concept of space probably is not attained before age 14 or 15. Hence, what I shall have to say here about sensorimotor development in the spatial domain will not end the matter. We shall take up spatial development again later, especially in Chapter 5.

In general, Piaget sees infants as progressing from a disorganized series of spatial collages at birth to an internalized and differentiated conceptualization of space by age 2. By the end of the sensorimotor stage, infants view both themselves and other people and things in terms of an internal system of spatial coordinates. Newborns, on the other hand, have great difficulty distinguishing the relative spatial positions of their own bodies and the people and things in their environment. In the newborn's world, Piaget says, things do not occupy stable spatial coordinates. We noted earlier that Piaget believes that newborns do not differentiate between themselves and the people and things in their environment. That is, objects (including the infant) do not have definite boundaries in the newborn's world. If objects do not have boundaries, this would seem to guarantee that they do not occupy stable spatial coordinates. Since objects are not clearly distinguished from each other, it follows that they cannot be unambiguously related to each other in space. On this point, one of Piaget's most intriguing suggestions is that newborns possess a series of unrelated spaces, each of which is specific to one of their perceptual systems (a visual space, an auditory space, an olfactory space). Gradually, during the sensorimotor stage, a single objective space is constructed from these unrelated spaces.

Unfortunately, Piaget's suggestions that, first, newborns live in a fuzzy world without boundaries and, second, they possess a series of unrelated spaces do not square with the known facts of infant spatial perception. An excellent and eminently readable discussion of the spatial capabilities of infants may be found in a recent book by T. G. R. Bower (1974). Since my aim in this section is to report what Piaget has to say about space and not necessarily to report on the other, conflicting findings, I shall not discuss the findings that Bower reviews. Suffice it to say that the newborn's spatial skills in at least two domains, vision and hearing, suggest that the two assumptions just mentioned probably are incorrect. Infants can localize objects very well in either visual or auditory space. Moreover, they can localize an object in one space that has been presented in another space. For example, a newborn who hears a sound coming from a certain direction will immediately look in that direction. These facts suggest that, contrary to Piaget's assumptions, the newborn lives in a world in which objects have definite boundaries and the spaces associated with different perceptual systems are coordinated with each other. Therefore, in the discussion of sensorimotor spatial development that follows, the reader should bear in mind that the two assumptions which serve as the points of departure for Piaget's account are probably incorrect.

According to Piaget, the infant begins life without any conception that objects occupy stable spatial coordinates. The first important advance in spatial development is said to occur with the appearance of secondary circular reactions. Secondary circular reactions aid spatial development in the same manner that they aid causal and temporal development. The repeated manipulations of objects in the environment (scheme coordination) that characterize secondary circular reactions make infants aware of their own behavior as something that acts upon distinct objects. Since objects can now be distinguished by virtue of the different types of actions performed on them, infants can begin to relate them spatially. Infants still have a long way to go, however. They have not yet developed the capacity for separating objects spatially, independent of the actions they perform on them. Hence, while the spatial coordinates of objects are beginning to stabilize, space is still a personal construct and has not yet become "objective." We saw earlier that the same thing is supposedly true of the 6-month-old's time and causality concepts.

By the end of the first year of life, infants have begun to differentiate objects from the actions they perform on them. This produces a corresponding improvement in the space concept. Piaget uses his experiments on object permanence to support the conclusion that 1-year-olds have developed a system of spatial coordinates that no longer includes their own actions. To Piaget, the fact that the 1-year-olds will search for and find hidden objects suggests that they must assign objects spatial locations that are independent of their own behavior. Piaget also maintains that the 1-year-olds are capable of relating their own position in space to the positions of objects.

During the first half of the second year of life, spatial awareness is further refined and objectified. Eighteen-month-olds can place two objects in space without regard to the spatial relationships between their bodies and the objects. Piaget says that 1-year-olds cannot. Once again, object concept experiments are used to support this contention. It will be recalled that 18-month-olds will search for and find an object following a series of hidings in which they did not observe all of the hidings. To Piaget, the fact that 18-month-olds can infer some unseen hidings from others they have seen suggests that they can now conceptualize spatial relations among objects without regard to their own experience. More particularly, the infant can now grasp the spatial relationship between two objects directly without having to interpose the spatial relationship between her body and the second object.

The emergence of internal representation at the end of the second year of life brings a final advance in the sensorimotor space concept. The infant is now potentially capable of relating objects to each other via a completely internal system of spatial coordinates. At this point, according to Piaget, the spatial system is at last released from any dependence on the infant's own behavior and has become truly "objective." As I mentioned earlier, all representation is supposed to be via overt behavior before the advent of internal representation. Obviously, the system of spatial coordinates associated with such overt representation cannot be said to be entirely free of the infant's behavior.

The Six Sensorimotor Substages

We turn now to the six substages of sensorimotor intelligence. These substages are the heart of Piaget's theory of intellectual development during infancy. The six cognitive contents we have just reviewed will be used to explicate the stages.

the first substage (birth to 1 month):
use of reflexes

Understandably, the newborn's behavior consists almost entirely of inherited action patterns. The hallmark of these behaviors is their rigid, reflexive, and stereotyped quality. Piaget provides the following observations, which serve to illustrate the individual differences between newborns' responsiveness to stimuli as well as their rigidity and inflexibility:

Observation 1.—From birth suckling-like movements may be observed: impulsive movement and protrusion of the lips accompanied by displacements of the tongue, while the arms engage in unruly and more or less rhythmical gestures and the head moves laterally, etc.

As soon as the hands rub the lips the suckling reflex is released. The child sucks his fingers for a moment but of course does not know either how to keep them in his mouth or pursue them with his lips. Lucienne and Laurent, a quarter of an hour and a half hour after birth, respectively, had already sucked their hand like this: Lucienne, whose hand had been immobilized due to its position, sucked her fingers for more than ten minutes.

A few hours after birth, first nippleful of collostrum. It is known how greatly children differ from each other with respect to adaption to this first meal. For some children like Lucienne and Laurent, contact of the lips and probably the tongue with the nipple suffices to produce sucking and swallowing. Other children, such as Jacqueline, have slower coordination: the child lets go of the breast every moment without taking it back again by himself or applying himself to it as vigorously when the nipple is replaced in his mouth. There are some children, finally, who need real forcing: holding their head, forcibly putting the nipple between the lips and in contact with the tongue, etc. [Piaget 1952*b*, p. 25][1]

As rigid and predictable as they may seem, however, Piaget believes that at least some Substage I reflexes show change as a function of experience. Among the most adaptive reflexes are hearing, suckling, grasping, visual accomodations, eye movements, and vocalizations. These particular reflexes are said to be most adaptive because they have a high degree of circularity built into them. This built-in circularity allows the large numbers of repetitions that are necessary for the differentiation of one reflex from another—Piaget's primary index of reflex adaption. These reflexes stabilize during Substage I and form the basis for the acquisition of related schemes during the subsequent sensorimotor substages. More primitive and less adaptive reflexes "drop out" during the first month of life because their degrees of built-in circularity are insufficient to insure the constant repetition necessary for reflex adaption. Of the six reflexes mentioned in the preceding observation, Piaget gives by far the most extensive consideration to the movements associated with suckling. As many readers are aware, this concern with the oral behavior of newborns also is characteristic of Freudian theory.

The behaviors of Substage I differ from the behaviors that dominate subsequent stages in that they are almost entirely innate. This is not to say that Substage I reflexes cannot be affected by experience. The term "innate" simply means that infants begin life with these capacities; that they do not acquire them. The fact that a behavior has been inherited does not imply that its topography cannot be changed by experience. If a subject plunges his hand into a container of ice water, his immediate response is to withdraw his hand. This response, insofar as we know, is innate. That is, it is inherited rather than learned. But experience can alter the response. After a few exposures to the ice water, the subject can begin to inhibit reflexive hand withdrawal. After several exposures, some subjects will be able to inhibit reflexive hand withdrawal completely. Experience has had a marked influence on an otherwise reflexive behavior. The same may be said of Substage I infants, or at least so Piaget argues.

Finally, Piaget believes that Substage I infants are not yet capable of distinguishing their *needs* from their *actions*. This lack of differentiation between need and act is thought to be implied by the newborn's lack of differentiation between subjective causality (dynamism) and objective causality (phenomenalism). If Piaget is right about this need-act confusion, then it is clear that we cannot speak of *intentionality* (or will or volition) as being a trait of Substage I behavior. Intentionality suggests an overt action being initiated by a reasonably well-defined internal need.

[1] Reprinted from *The Origins of Intelligence in Children* by Jean Piaget. By permission of International Universities Press, Inc. Copyright 1952 by International Universities Press, Inc. Reprinted with permission of Editions Delachaux and Niestlé, Switzerland.

the second substage (1 to 4 months):
the first acquired adaptions
and the primary circular reaction

The main advance of Substage II is that the infant now is capable of *learning* in the usual sense of the term. In other words, experience now plays a *formative* role in the infant's behavior. During Substage I, the effects of experience are confined to modifying inherited reflexes. True learning effects are precluded by the Substage I infant's lack of basic structures (sensorimotor schemes) for incorporating formative experiences. A related advance of Substage II is a new-found ability to initiate behaviors that will produce and/or cause to be repeated interesting or novel situations. This sort of behavior leads Piaget to conclude that the first sensorimotor schemes (acquired adaptions) appear during Substage II.

The preceding characteristics of Substage II imply some rudimentary differentiation of need from act. To illustrate, Piaget believes that the need for nourishment and the suckling activity are inseparable during Substage I. By Substage II, however, the infant's frequent displays of nonnutritive suckling lead Piaget to conclude that the need for nourishment and the act of suckling have been differentiated from each other. Thus, although suckling behavior originally is innate and reflexive, Piaget feels that there is little doubt that it has been altered by experience by Substage II.

The key advance of Substage II is the infant's acquisition of *primary circular reactions.* We now can offer a more concrete definition of primary circular reactions than was possible in the preceding section on sensorimotor cognitive contents. Of the three forms of circular response (primary, secondary, tertiary), primary circular reactions are the only ones composed of innate reflexive responses. In other words, the actual behaviors are part of the infant's inborn repertoire of actions. The fact that both Substage I reflexes and primary circular reactions involve unlearned behaviors leads to the question of what the basis is for separating the two. Piaget appeals to the notion of intentionality. He says that the primary circular reactions show signs of minimum intentionality on the part of the infant, but the reflexes of Substage I do not. This brings us back to the problem of the differentiation of need from act. Some of Piaget's observations will serve to clarify the distinction between reflexes and primary circular reactions:

> *Observation 11.*—Laurent at 0; 0 (30) stays awake crying, gazing ahead with wide open eyes. He makes suckling-like movements almost continually, opening and closing his mouth in slow rhythm, his tongue constantly moving. At certain moments his tongue, instead of remaining inside his lips, licks the lower lip; the sucking recommences with renewed ardor.
>
> Two interpretations are possible. Either at such times there is searching for food and then the protrusion of the tongue is merely a reflex inherent in the mechanism of sucking and swallowing, or else this marks the beginning of

circular reaction. It seems, for the time being, that both are present. Some-times protrusion of the tongue is accompanied by disordered movements of the arms and leads to impatience and anger. In such a case there is obviously a seeking to suck, and disappointment. Sometimes, on the other hand, pro-trusion of the tongue is accompanied by slow, rhythmical movements of the arms and an expression of contentment. In this case the tongue comes into play though circular reaction. [Piaget 1952*b*, p. 50][2]

Piaget discusses primary circular reactions primarily with regard to sucking, vision, verbalization, hearing, and grasping. The latter receives by far the most extensive coverage in Piaget's treatment of Substage II. Even if one takes Piaget's description of primary circular reactions as completely accurate, an important question still remains: What does the concept of primary circular reaction *do* for us; how does it help us explain infant intel-ligence? The chief advantage seems to be that if one believes what Piaget says about the advent of primary circular reactions, then one is permitted to refer to inherited sequences of visual behavior as "looking," to inherited sequences of auditory behavior as "hearing," etc. That is, we may view these behaviors as self-initiated and self-controlled, rather than as simply reflexive.

Piaget's discussion of Substage II includes two final points: (*a*) He reports some evidence that the infant's sensory systems (e.g., vision, grasp-ing) are becoming coordinated. The Substage II infant is said to be able to employ information from one sense modality as a basis for action in an-other modality (e.g., using vision as a basis for grasping). (*b*) The Substage II infant evidences some rudimentary differentiation of the two forms of adaption, assimilation and accommodation.

the third substage (4 to 8 months): the secondary circular reactions and the procedures destined to make interesting sights last

Substage III heralds an advance in infant circular reactions; they are now called "secondary." Unlike primary circular reactions, the action se-quences that compose secondary circular reactions are not inherited reflexes; instead, they are viewed as acquired adaptions—behaviors that infants have learned on their own. The following example serves to contrast secondary circular reactions with the primary circular reactions of Substage II.

Observation 94.—At 0;3 (5) Lucienne shakes her bassinet by moving her legs violently (bending and unbending them, etc.), which makes the cloth dolls swing from the hood. Lucienne looks at them, smiling, and recommences at once. These movements are simply the concomitants of joy. When she experi-ences great pleasure Lucienne externalizes it in a total reaction including leg movements. As she often smiles at her knick-knacks she caused them to swing.

[2] Ibid.

But does she keep this up through consciously coordinated circular reaction or is it pleasure constantly springing up again that explains her behavior?

That evening, when Lucienne is quiet, I gently swing her dolls. The morning's reaction starts up again, but both interpretations remain possible.

The next day 0;3 (6) I present the dolls: Lucienne immediately moves, shakes her legs, but this time without smiling. Her interest is intense and sustained and there also seems to be an intentional circular reaction.

At 0;3 (8) I again find Lucienne swinging her dolls. An hour later I make them move slightly: Lucienne looks at them, smiles, stirs a little, then resumes looking at her hands as she was doing shortly before. A chance movement disturbs the dolls: Lucienne again looks at them and this time shakes herself with regularity. She stares at the dolls, barely smiles and moves her legs vigorously and thoroughly. At each moment she is distracted by her hands which pass again into the visual field: she examines them for a moment and then returns to the dolls. This time there is definite circular reaction.

At 0;3 (13) Lucienne looks at her hand with more coordination than usually (see Obs. 67). In her joy at seeing her hand come and go between her face and the pillow, she shakes herself in front of this hand as when faced by the dolls. Now this reaction of shaking reminds her of the dolls which she looks at immediately after as though she foresaw their movement. At certain times her glance oscillates between her hand, the hood, and the dolls. Then her attention attaches itself to the dolls which she then shakes with regularity.

At 0;3 (16) as soon as I suspend the dolls she immediately shakes them without smiling, with precise and rhythmical movements with quite an interval between shakes, as though she were studying the phenomenon. Success gradually causes her to smile. This time the circular reaction is indisputable. Same reaction at 0;3 (24). Same observations during succeeding months and until 0;6 (10) and 0;7 (27) at sight of a puppet and at 0;6 (13) with a celluloid bird, etc. [Piaget 1952*b*, pp. 157–58][3]

An additional feature of secondary circular reactions is that they are *reinforced by external events* (e.g., seeing cloth dolls move above one's bassinet). In the language of learning theory, secondary circular reactions are subject to contingencies of reinforcement. Piaget does not believe that primary circular reactions are externally reinforced. He sees such reactions as *inherently* reinforcing. For Piaget, these features of the secondary circular reaction lead to the important conclusion that the Substage III infant is capable of acquiring many more sensorimotor schemes than the Substage II infant. If behavior is subject to environmental constraints, then adaption should proceed at a much faster pace. With reference to differentiation of need and act, the fact that secondary circular reactions are externally reinforced suggests that during Substage III needs normally precede the instrumental acts which gratify them. The fact that such behaviors are reinforced externally implies a functional differentiation of need and act in which the need becomes associated with the external gratification as distinct from the instrumental activities leading to gratification.

As the second half of Piaget's label for Substage III indicates, the infant's behavior suggests the presence of schemes capable of producing

[3] Ibid.

results which the infant finds novel or interesting. The acquisition of such schemes should be related to the development of secondary circular reactions, because novel or interesting events constitute external reinforcers. This new capacity for evoking interesting results is illustrated by one of Piaget's observations:

> *Observation 105.*—Laurent, from 0;4 (19) as has been seen (Obs. 103) knows how to strike hanging objects intentionally with his hand. At 0;4 (22) he holds a stick; he does not know what to do with it and slowly passes it from hand to hand. The stick then happens to strike a toy hanging from the bassinet hood. Laurent, immediately interested by this unexpected result, keeps the stick raised in the same position, then brings it noticeably nearer to the toy. He strikes it a second time. Then he draws the stick back but moving it as little as possible as though trying to conserve the favorable position, then he brings it nearer to the toy, and so on, more and more rapidly.
>
> The dual character of this accommodation may be seen. On the one hand, the new phenomenon makes its appearance by simple fortuitous insertion in an already formed scheme and hence differentiates it. But, on the other hand, the child, intentionally and systematically, applies himself to rediscovering the conditions which led him to this unexpected result.
>
> It goes without saying that the use of the stick described in this example was only episodical: it has nothing to do with the "behavior pattern of the stick" which we shall describe in connection with the fifth stage. [Piaget 1952*b*, p. 176][4]

It is during Substage III that Piaget reports the first evidence of actions directed toward the recovery of lost or hidden objects. But these actions still are quite limited and are not persistent enough to suggest the presence of a stable object concept. In particular, Substage III infants will find a hidden object only if they are moving in the direction of the hiding place at the time of hiding. Although limited in this manner, Substage III object search behaviors represent a clear advance over Substage II, and Piaget refers to them as the *ability to prolong accommodations* already occurring at the time of hiding. Finally, Piaget reports further advances in the coordination of the various sensory systems during Substage III. He makes specific reference to increased coordination of hand and eye.

To summarize, Piaget notes three general advances in the Substage III infant's behavior: (*a*) the acquisition of many new schemes via the secondary circular reaction, (*b*) the capacity for prolonging certain accomodations, and (*c*) increased coordination of looking and grasping.

the fourth substage (8 to 12 months): the coordination of the secondary schemes and their application to new situations

Substage IV is a time of consolidation; a time when the advances of the preceding stages are reconciled with each other before proceeding onward to the second year of life. Thus, unlike Substage III, this is not a

[4] Ibid.

time of rapid acquisition of new schemes. On the contrary, it is a time when previously acquired schemes are broadened to cover new situations. Secondary circular reactions are coordinated to yield schemes that are at once more adaptive and more intentionally controlled than those of Substage III. These latter schemes now are referred to as "derived" secondary circular reactions.

Notable improvements in the infant's imitative abilities are observed and are said to result from increased scheme generality. Piaget believes that any of the infant's schemes now can be brought to bear on the task of imitating an observed event. Infants who have facial movement schemes, can now imitate a model's facial expressions. Prior to this time, Piaget claims, infants can imitate only those actions of a model that they have seen themselves perform (e.g., hand movements, leg movements). The following observation illustrates the nature of this advance:

> *Observation 35.*—0;11 (0) J. was sitting in front of me, her feet free. I alternately bent forward and straightened my head and trunk. J. reacted three times in succession with a wave of the hand, and then imitated my movement correctly.
>
> At 0;11 (1) she was seated and I was half-lying in front of her. I raised my right leg and swung it up and down. She first reacted by bending and straightening her whole trunk (as she had done the day before), and then by waving her hand. This goodbye gesture was roughly similar to that of my leg, but was made with the arm and the hand.
>
> At 0;11 (11) the same model produced the following reactions. J. began by waving goodbye, as before (this had been her response to my action during the preceding days). Then, a few moments later, she moved her feet, slightly raising her leg. Finally she definitely raised her right foot, keeping her eyes on mine.
>
> At 1;0 (2), when I resumed the experiment, she immediately imitated me. [Piaget 1951, p. 48]

During Substage IV, Piaget finds the first evidence of an *internalized* conception of objects. Infants now will search for and find a hidden object, even though they were not moving in the direction of the hiding place at the time the object was hidden. However, the object concept is far from complete. The Substage IV infant does not behave appropriately when an object is successively hidden under more than two other objects. Thus, a rattle will be found if it is hidden under a single book, but it probably will not be found if the book in turn is hidden under a pillow. This may indicate that the infant is not searching for an object per se, but is merely repeating previous patterns of instrumental behavior. Such behavior may be analogous to the superstitious behaviors that adults are frequently known to engage in.

In general, one can characterize Piaget's Substage IV infants as very active little problem solvers. Since their schemes have become more and more instrumental, they are capable of handling many problem-solving situations. Infants' problem-solving capabilities undoubtedly are aided by the fact that, by now, infants no longer seek to produce novel events for their curiosity value alone. During Substage IV, the capacity for evoking novel events comes to be employed as a vehicle for obtaining other desired goals. Thus, while the evocation of novel events was an end in itself during previous substages, it becomes an instrumental form of behavior during Substage IV.

the fifth substage (12 to 18 months): the tertiary circular reaction and the discovery of new means through active experimentation

The key advance of Substage V is concerned with schemes related to situations the infant finds novel or interesting. During Substage V, the infant acquires the capacity *to create entirely new sequences of behaviors* to deal with novel situations. Piaget therefore speaks of Substage V behavior as creative in a broad sense. In large part, this capacity for creativity stems from the emergence of Piaget's *tertiary* circular reactions.

As was the case for the primary and secondary forms of circular response, tertiary circular reactions involve repetitions of actions that the infant finds interesting. Unlike earlier circular responses, however, Piaget contends that Substage V circular responses involve slight but definite variations in the relevant action sequences. Piaget feels that these variations are *systematic* in that they are intentional adaptions to specific situations. In other words, the variations observed in circular action sequences during Substage V are not merely random fluctuations; they are "intelligent." The following observation serves to clarify tertiary circular reactions and to distinguish them from previous circular reactions.

> *Observation 141.*—This first example will make us understand the transition between secondary and "tertiary" reactions: that of the well-known behavior pattern by means of which the child explores distant space and constructs his representation of movement, the behavior pattern of letting go or throwing objects in order subsequently to pick them up.
>
> One recalls (Obs. 140) how, at 0;10 (2) Laurent discovered in "exploring" a case of soap, the possibility of throwing this object and letting it fall. Now, what interested him at first was not the objective phenomenon of the fall—that is to say, the object's trajectory—but the very act of letting go. He therefore limited himself, at the beginning, merely to reproducing the result observed fortuitously, which still constitutes a "secondary" reaction, "derived," it is true, but of typical structure.
>
> On the other hand, at 0;10 (10) the reaction changes and becomes "tertiary." That day Laurent manipulates a small piece of bread (without any alimentary interest: he has never eaten any and has no thought of tasting it) and lets it go continually. He even breaks off fragments which he lets drop. Now, in contradistinction to what has happened on the preceding days, he pays no attention to the act of letting go whereas he watches with great interest the body in motion; in particular, he looks at it for a long time when it has fallen, and picks it up when he can.

At 0;10 (11) Laurent is lying on his back but nevertheless resumes his experiments of the day before. He grasps in succession a celluloid swan, a box, etc., stretches out his arm and lets them fall. He distinctly varies the position of the fall. Sometimes he stretches out his arm vertically, sometimes he holds it obliquely, in front of or behind his eyes, etc. When the object falls in a new position (for example on his pillow), he lets it fall two or three times more on the same place, as though to study the spatial relation: then he modifies the situation. At a certain moment the swan falls near his mouth: now, he does not suck it (even though this object habitually serves this purpose), but drops it three times more while merely making the gesture of opening his mouth.

At 0;10 (12) likewise, Laurent lets go of a series of objects while varying the conditions in order to study their fall. He is seated in an oval basket and lets the object fall over the edge, sometimes to the right, sometimes to the left, in different positions. Each time he tries to recapture it, leaning over and twisting himself around, even when the object falls 40 or 50 cm. away from him. He especially tries to find the object again when it rolls under the edge of the basket and hence cannot be seen. [Piaget 1952*b*, pp. 268-69][5]

An additional observation illustrates the manner in which tertiary circular reactions promote the "creative" acquisition of new schemes:

Observation 149.—As early as 0;9 (3), Jacqueline discovers by chance the possibility of bringing a toy to herself by pulling the coverlet on which it is placed. She is seated on this coverlet and holds out her hand to grasp her celluloid duck. After several failures she grasps the coverlet abruptly, which shakes the duck; seeing that she immediately grasps the coverlet again and pulls it until she can attain the objective directly—two interpretations are possible. Either she perceives the duck and the coverlet as a solidified whole (like a single object or a complex of connected objects) or else she simply satisfies her need to grasp the duck by grasping no matter what and so discovering by chance the possible role of the coverlet.

Until 0;11 Jacqueline has not again revealed analogous behavior. At 0;11 (7), on the other hand, she is lying on her stomach on another coverlet and again tries to grasp her duck. In the course of the movements she makes to catch the object she accidentally moves the coverlet which shakes the duck. She immediately understands the connection and pulls the coverlet until she is able to grasp the duck.

During the weeks that follow Jacqueline frequently utilizes the schema thus acquired but too rapidly to enable me to analyze her behavior. At 1;0 (19) on the other hand, I seat her on a shawl and place a series of objects a meter away from her. Each time she tries to reach them directly and each time she subsequently grasps the shawl in order to draw the toy toward herself. The behavior pattern has consequently become systematic; but it seems that it does not yet involve conscious foresight of the relationship since Jacqueline only utilizes this schema after having attempted direct prehension of the object. [Piaget 1952*b*, p. 285][6]

Thus, Piaget views the 18-month-old as a designer of spontaneous ad hoc action sequences which appear to vary around some purpose in a sur-

[5] Ibid.
[6] Ibid.

prisingly systematic manner. Obviously, this ability should prove enormously useful in the task of problem solving. This fact also suggests that Substage V may mark the first appearance of the trial-and-error learning that plays such a central role in traditional learning approaches to cognitive development (e.g., Skinner 1974). In trial-and-error learning, problems which cannot be solved a priori via logical analysis are solved on the basis of a hit-or-miss strategy. This form of learning always involves a certain amount of experimentation, where "experimentation" is taken to mean that systematic variations in behavior are introduced as a means of maximizing the "hits" and minimizing the "misses." If tertiary circular reactions are not acquired until Substage V, then such experimentation should be largely absent from the infant's behavior during the first year of life. Although some variations in circular reactions are noted during earlier stages, Piaget reports that they are not sufficiently *systematic* to justify the label "experimentation."

During Substage V, infants make further progress toward an internalized and stable conception of external objects. Unlike Substage IV infants, Substage V infants will find a hidden object even though it has been hidden under several successive objects. This capacity is definitely absent during Substage IV. The internalized conception of objects still is not complete, however. Infants fail to take into account the possibility of *nonobservable* movements of objects—they only look for an object *where they have seen it hidden,* and if they do not find it there they fail to suspect that it could have moved elsewhere covertly. For example, suppose that after an object is visibly hidden under a pillow it is surreptitiously hidden under a blanket. Naturally, infants search first under the pillow. However, when they fail to find the object under the pillow, they do not guess that it must be under the blanket.

By the end of Substage V all indications are that infants are very close to the major goal of sensorimotor development—the acquisition of internal mental representation. The increasingly sophisticated object concept, the "experimental" nature of circular reactions, the instrumental character of behavior in general, and the advances in all the other cognitive contents point to the nearness of internal thought. Piaget believes that Substage V infants are not quite there, however, and reserves this ultimate acquisition for Substage VI.

To summarize, the most important single feature of Substage V is the acquisition of tertiary circular reactions. From the standpoint of general cognitive development, these circular reactions are vital because they bring with them (*a*) the ability to acquire new schemes by retaining chance adaptions, and (*b*) the ability to coordinate schemes with one another so that the evocation of novel situations can serve as a means of obtaining further goals, as well as an end in itself.

the sixth substage (18 to 24 months):
the invention of new means
through mental combinations

The infant at last becomes capable of mental representation during Substage VI. Infants can now represent both their own actions and external events *internally*. That is, they possess a mental symbol system of some sort whereby symbols can be used to stand for things. By virtue of this symbol system, infants presumably can deal with their environment subjectively and are not solely dependent upon overt actions. Piaget infers the presence of mental representation from two key forms of behavior observed in Substage VI infants: (*a*) the ability to solve problems without overt trial-and-error behavior, and (*b*) the ability to defer imitation of an observed event until some later time.

The ability to solve problems without overt trial and error is what Piaget means by the phrase "the invention of new means through mental combinations." As was the case for tertiary circular reactions, Piaget says that the need for inventing new means via mental combinations arises in problem-solving situations whenever the infant possesses no available scheme for obtaining a desired goal. This fact presumably forces the infant to create a new sequence of instrumental behaviors. During Substage V, new instrumental sequences are acquired through a systematic trial-and-error technique. During Substage VI, however, Piaget believes that infants can invent entirely new schemes by representing problems in their mental symbol systems and solving them through mental combinations of the symbols. The necessity of overt trial-and-error behavior thereby is eliminated in many problem-solving situations. Here are some observations that Piaget uses to demonstrate the Substage VI capacity for inventing new instrumental schemes.

Observation 178.—We recall Jacqueline's groping's at 1;3 (12) when confronted by a stick to be brought through the bars of her playpen (Obs. 162). Now it happens that the same problem presented to Lucienne at 1;1 (18) gives rise to an almost immediate solution in which invention surpasses groping. Lucienne is seated in front of the bars and I place against them, horizontally and parallel to the bars (half way up them) the stick of Observation 162. Lucienne grasps it at the middle and merely pulls it. Noticing her failure, she withdraws the stick, tilts it up and brings it through easily.

I then place the stick on the floor. Instead of raising it to pull directly, she grasps it by the middle, tilts it up beforehand and presses it. Or else she grasps it by one end and brings it in easily.

I start all over again with a longer stick (30 cm. long). Either she grasps it by the middle and tilts it up before pulling it, or else she brings it in by pulling on one end.

Same experiment with a stick 50 cm. long. The procedure is obviously the same but, when the stick gets caught, she pulls it away briefly, then lets it go with a groan and begins again in a better way.

The next day, at 1;1 (19), same experiments. Lucienne begins by merely pulling (once), then tilts up the stick and so rediscovers the procedures of the day before. At 1;2 (7) I resume the observation. This time Lucienne tilts up the stick before it touches the bars.

It may thus be seen how these attempts are reminiscent of Jacqueline's, taking place through groping and apprenticeship. Lucienne begins by merely pulling the stick and repeats this once the next day. But, in contrast to her sister's prolonged efforts, Lucienne at once profits from her failure and uses a procedure which she invents right away through simple representation. [Piaget 1952*b*, p. 336][7]

Turning to the Substage VI infant's capacity for delayed imitation of observed events, Piaget believes that this particular ability is what makes the mental symbol system possible. Simply put, mental symbols are seen as internalized imitations that may be recalled for use after long intervals. Thus, Substage VI witnesses the emergence of both the process by which thought itself becomes possible (mental representation) and the capacity (delayed imitation) that makes the acquisition of the contents of thought (symbols) possible. Taken together, Piaget believes that these two advances prepare the way for the major advance of the next stage of cognitive development, the acquisition of language.

The full-blown object concept also appears during Substage VI. Infants now can take account of invisible as well as visible displacements of an object for which they are searching. They will search in all probable places where the object may have been hidden. This represents a clear advance over Substage V infants, who search only where they actually have seen objects hidden.

Finally, the acquisition of mental representation introduces the possibility that infants may guide their behavior via internal hypotheses or "hunches." In some primitive sense, infants may now be capable of reflecting before they act. During preceding substages, hunches and actions were one in the same. Certainly the first observation cited above suggests that Stage VI infants may be entertaining internal hunches.

summary

We have seen that Piaget's model of sensorimotor development may be divided into two parts: (*a*) the six sensorimotor cognitive contents, and (*b*) the six substages of sensorimotor development. The notion of developmental substages is used to give order and structure to the sensorimotor contents. The contents, in turn, are used to make the notion of developmental substages real and tangible. In fact, the cognitive contents *are* the substages for all practical purposes. They are what we measure to determine an infant's substage.

[7] Ibid.

Replication Studies

During the early 1960s, many developmental psychologists outside Geneva became interested in conducting research on the sensorimotor stage. As I noted in Chapter 2, the idiosyncracies of Piaget's clinical method of doing research (nonstandardized testing methods, small numbers of subjects, etc.) make it difficult for other psychologists to accept his findings without first verifying them in their own laboratories. In science, such verifications are called *replication studies.*

Many replication studies dealing with sensorimotor cognitive contents have been published during the past decade and a half. For the most part, these studies fall into one or more of three categories: (*a*) test construction studies, (*b*) stage sequence studies, and (*c*) object permanence studies. Category (*a*) is the most basic of the three in that studies falling in the other two categories cannot be conducted without first conducting category (*a*) studies. Test construction studies have sought to determine whether it is possible to devise standardized tests of sensorimotor cognitive contents. The principal aims are to construct tests that are *valid* (i.e., that actually measure one or more of six contents) and *reliable* (i.e., that give stable results across several administrations of the same test to the same subjects). As many readers are aware, most psychologists believe that validity and reliability are absolutely essential characteristics of any good psychological test. A secondary aim of test construction studies is to devise tests that can be administered easily by any examiner.

Category (*b*) studies are concerned to discover whether infants tend to pass through the sensorimotor substages in an invariant order. As we saw earlier, Piaget firmly believes that his six substages form a fixed and immutable sequence. To get to, say, Substage IV, it is essential for the infant to pass through Substages I, II, and III first. In other words, the contents observed during Substages I, II, and III are absolutely necessary prerequisites for the contents observed during Substage IV (and Substages V and VI as well). Since the contents are what we measure to discover an infant's sensorimotor stage, we cannot determine whether infants pass through the substages in an invariant order until we have devised valid and reliable tests of at least one of the six contents.

Category (*c*) studies are concerned to discover whether infants do or do not possess the concept of object permanence. Despite the evidence reviewed above, many developmental psychologists believe that the infant's failure to search for hidden objects may not result from the absence of object permanence. Instead, they believe that infantile search failures are best explained by appealing to other factors, such as performance abilities, as we shall discuss later. For now, I wish only to observe that category (*c*) studies, like category (*b*) studies, presuppose that we have valid and reliable tests of the contents that Piaget associates with object permanence.

test construction studies

There have been many small-scale attempts to develop valid and reliable tests of sensorimotor cognitive contents. Such projects have usually preceded stage sequence and object permanence studies (e.g., Gratch et al. 1974; Gratch and Landers 1971; Harris 1971). Most of these small-scale attempts at test construction have been confined to one content (e.g., object permanence) and two substages (e.g., IV and V). Fortunately, there have also been two large-scale projects in which the investigators have formulated tests of more than one content that span all six substages. The principal investigators in these large-scale projects were Sybille Escalona (e.g., Corman and Escolona 1969) and Ina C. Uzgiris and J. McV. Hunt (e.g., 1974). Of the two projects, the work of Uzgiris and Hunt is far and away the more impressive. The tests that they have evolved are more comprehensive—i.e., they tap a broader range of sensorimotor content. Also, their test administration procedures and reliability evidence are reported in greater detail. Recently, Uzgiris and Hunt published a book, *Toward Ordinal Scales of Psychological Development in Infancy* (1974), that documents the history of their project, the project's aims, the tests they constructed, statistical data on the tests, and procedures for administering the tests. In the remainder of this section, I shall summarize the Uzgiris and Hunt project.

The Uzgiris-Hunt project began at the University of Illinois during the early 1960s while Uzgiris was completing her doctoral studies under Hunt's direction. The project, as they originally planned it, was to involve six steps. First, they carefully examined Piaget's three books on sensorimotor intelligence (Piaget 1951, 1952b, 1954) and culled a long list of cognitive contents associated with the six substages. Second, they devised procedures for measuring these contents in infant subjects. Third, they administered their measurement procedures to a large sample of infants to determine whether they actually evidence the contents being measured. Fourth, a new examiner was trained to administer the test, and the test was administered over again to another large sample of infants. Fifth, the test was used in a longitudinal investigation—i.e., it was administered to the same group of infants at various points during the first two years of life. From the longitudinal data and the comparison of the test results obtained from different examiners, Uzgiris and Hunt hoped to determine whether or not their test was reliable.

The test that Uzgiris and Hunt finally arrived at consisted of sixty-three items spanning all six substages and tapping five of the six cognitive contents discussed earlier (space, object permanence, circular reactions, imitation and causality). Since, as we have seen, Piaget uses behavioral evidence in the causality area to infer things about the infantile time concept, the Uzgiris-Hunt test actually measures all six sensorimotor contents.

Uzgiris and Hunt's test definitely is a valid one. Not only did they draw their items from Piaget's original books on sensorimotor intelligence but, moreover, when one independently compares their sixty-three items with Piaget's examples of infantile behaviors in the space, object permanence, circular reaction, imitation, and causality areas, it is clear that Uzgiris and Hunt are measuring the same things that Piaget tested his own three children for. For example, most of the sensorimotor behaviors mentioned earlier in this chapter appear on Uzgiris and Hunt's test. Thus, there appears to be little doubt that this particular test measures what Piaget would call sensorimotor intelligence.

Now, let us turn to the question of reliability. Uzgiris and Hunt used two methods to evaluate the reliability of their instrument: *interexaminer agreement* and *test-retest stability*. The first method is concerned with whether two examiners administering the same test to the same subjects tend to obtain the same results. Uzgiris and Hunt found that different examiners did, in fact, tend to obtain the same results with their test. Over all the items on the test, they found that interexaminer agreement ranged from a low of 93% with younger infants to a high of 97% with older subjects. That is, over all sixty-three items on the test, different examiners agreed more than 90% of the time, on the average, on how given items should be scored. The second method of evaluating reliability is concerned with whether successive administrations of the same test (by the same or different examiners) to the same subjects tend to produce similar findings. To answer this question, Uzgiris and Hunt had different examiners independently administer their test to the same sample of infants. The two administrations of the test were forty-eight hours apart. The results of the first administration then were compared to the results of the second administration. For the sixty-three items on the test, Uzgiris and Hunt found that the amount of agreement between the two administrations ranged from a low of 50% to a high of 100%. In other words, (*a*) on the worst items about half the subjects gave the same response on the second administration as on the first and (*b*) on the best items all the subjects gave the same response on both administrations. Further, the average agreement between the two administrations was 80%. This means that over all the different items on the test, roughly 80% of the subjects showed the same response on the second administration of a given item as on the first.

To summarize, the Uzgiris-Hunt project provides ample evidence that it is possible to devise a valid and reliable test of the sensorimotor contents reviewed earlier in this chapter. Concerning validity, Uzgiris and Hunt's work reveals that the various sensorimotor behaviors that Piaget observed in his own three children also are found in most other children between birth and age 2. Concerning reliability, Uzgiris and Hunt's work reveals that it is possible to devise a sensorimotor test that is characterized by high interexaminer agreement and that yields very stable findings when it is administered repeatedly to the same group of infants. In fact, the 90% plus interexaminer agreement and 80% test-retest correlation observed with this test are tolerably high by the standards of most other psychological tests.

I should add, in closing, that Uzgiris and Hunt's project had other aims in addition to constructing a valid and reliable test. In particular, the project was designed to determine whether infants pass through the sensorimotor substages in an invariant order. This aspect of Uzgiris and Hunt's work will be discussed in the following section. For now, it is sufficient to note that their research confirms that Piaget's original data on the sensorimotor stage are not the result of either the idiosyncracies of his clinical method of doing research or the idiosyncracies of the three infants he investigated.

stage sequence studies

Design of stage sequence studies. The purpose of any stage sequence study is to decide whether subjects pass through two or more Piagetian stages in a fixed order. Sensorimotor stage sequence studies are of two sorts: *micro studies* and *macro studies.* The former are designed to deal with only two or three sensorimotor substages. The tests administered in micro studies deal with only one cognitive content. The aim of most micro studies is to determine whether *two or three selected substages* are acquired in an invariant order. For example, Gerald Gratch and his associates at the University of Houston have conducted studies concerned with only Substage IV and Substage V (Evans and Gratch 1972; Gratch et al. 1974; Gratch and Landers 1971) with object permanence as the only content. Macro studies, on the other hand, deal with all or nearly all of Piaget's sensorimotor substages. Some macro studies focus on only one cognitive content (e.g., object permanence), but others focus on at least two contents. Both of the large-scale test construction projects mentioned in the preceding section (Corman and Escalona 1969; Uzgiris and Hunt 1974) were also macro stage sequence studies.

Before reviewing what stage sequence studies have found, I should like to make some observations about the underlying logic of such studies and how they are conducted. In the first place, researching *any* prediction about Piagetian stages or substages poses some logical problems. We saw in Chapter 2 that Piaget's stages are, to say the least, not among psychology's most clearly defined concepts. It is true that Piaget has formulated some "recognition criteria." We reviewed four of these criteria in Chapter 2. However, we saw that the criteria themselves are not very clear. The result, some scholars (e.g., Flavell and Wohlwill 1969) have commented, is that we do not really know how to recognize a Piagetian stage when we see one. The only one of the four recognition criteria discussed in Chapter 2 that seems to lend itself readily to research is the *invariant sequence* criterion. According to this criterion, if we are given any two stages (or substages) X and Y such that X is an earlier stage than Y, then we should find that children invariably acquire the cognitive contents associated with Stage X before they acquire those associated with Stage Y. In theory, of course, the other recognition criteria mentioned in Chapter 2 could also be used in stage sequence studies. For example, if X and Y are true Piagetian stages, then the cognitive contents of Stage X should be characterized by a more stable equilibrium level than those of Stage Y. Similarly, the cognitive contents of stages X and Y should be characterized by different underlying structures. Although these distinctions sound fine in principle, developmental psychologists do not know how to go about directly measuring "equilibrium level" and "underlying structures." Hence, stage sequence studies have focused on the more researchable invariant sequence prediction to the relative exclusion of other criteria discussed in Chapter 2.

Now, let us see how sequence studies work in the abstract. Actually, as psychological studies go, they are rather simple to do. Because studies of this sort are always concerned with invariant sequence predictions, the problem is how to test such predictions. Suppose that we again have two stages (or substages) X and Y. The first thing we need to know is what some of the cognitive contents of each stage are. These can easily be obtained from Piaget's writings as, for example, Uzgiris and Hunt (1974) did in constructing their sensorimotor intelligence test. After we have obtained some illustrative X contents and some illustrative Y contents, we construct two tests. The first one measures the X contents and the second one measures the Y contents. The next step is to select a large sample of children and to administer both tests to each child in the sample. We must be careful to select our children from the appropriate age ranges for X and Y. The age ranges, like the contents, are easily obtained from Piaget's own writings. After the tests have been administered, we score the children's responses to determine which subjects passed which tests. We are interested in the following prediction: If X is an earlier stage than Y, *then children should always pass the X test before they pass the Y test and they should never pass the Y test before the X test.*

If this prediction is correct, when the test data have been scored we should find that there are only three types of children: (*a*) those who fail both tests, (*b*) those who pass the X test and fail the Y test, and (*c*) those who pass both tests. The subjects in category (*a*) have not yet attained either Stage X or Stage Y; the subjects in category (*b*) have attained Stage X but not Stage Y; the subjects in category (*c*) have attained Stage Y after first passing through Stage X. We should not find any children who pass test Y and fail test X. If we did, it would mean that it is possible to attain Stage Y without first passing through Stage X. This would violate our assumption that the two stages form an invariant sequence. For certain statistical reasons having to do with measurement error and sampling error, we will usually find a *few* subjects who pass Y and fail X in any sample. But we should find that a vastly greater proportion of the subjects pass X and fail Y than fail X and pass Y. If this finding is observed, then we conclude that children invariably acquire the contents measured by the X test before they acquire the contents measured by the Y test.

As a specific illustration of the preceding remarks, consider a study by Gratch and Landers published in 1971. Gratch and Landers studied sensorimotor substages IV and V. The cognitive content was object permanence. According to Piaget (1954), the object permanence behavior of Substage IV and Substage V infants runs as follows: During Substage IV, infants will search for a hidden object at the *first* place where it is hidden but they will not search in new places; during Substage V, infants will search for hidden objects at new places provided that subsequent hidings are visible. In line with Piaget's descriptions, Gratch and Landers devised the following tests. They presented infants with a plastic tray that had two wells in it. The Substage IV test consisted of placing a toy in *one* of the wells and covering it with a cloth. They repeated this procedure several times with each infant they studied. Infants who searched for the toy under the cloth on all or nearly all the trials, were said to have passed the Substage IV test. Otherwise, they were said to have failed the test. The Substage V test consisted of hiding the toy first in one well and then in the other well. Infants who searched in the *second* hiding place on all or nearly all the trials, were said to have passed the Substage V test. Otherwise, they were said to have failed the test.

When Gratch and Landers examined their results, they found a pattern of responses inconsistent with the hypothetical pattern described above. Some infants failed both tests. These would be Substage III infants for Piaget. Some infants passed only the first test. These would be Substage IV infants for Piaget. Some infants passed both tests. These would be Substage V infants for Piaget. But a sizable group of infants passed only the second test. There is no way to classify these subjects with Piaget's model. These findings fail to confirm the hypothesis that Substage IV always precedes Substage V.

The method we have just examined is for the simplest possible case where only two stages are being studied. However, it is easy to see that the procedure would be the same if one wished to study a larger number of stages. To generalize the procedure, all that is required is that one have a test for some of the cognitive contents of each stage that one wishes to study.

Findings of stage sequence studies. Apart from the Gratch and Landers (1972) study and one other to be mentioned below, the trend of sensorimotor stage sequence research can be summarized in a word: supportive. It is generally found that infants acquire the cognitive contents that Piaget says belong to earlier substages before they acquire those that he says belong to later substages.

Taking macro studies first, the test construction projects mentioned in the preceding section (Corman and Escalona 1969; Uzgiris and Hunt 1974) were also stage sequence studies. The Uzgiris-Hunt project has been reviewed. It only remains to observe that when Uzgiris and Hunt examined the performance of infants on their tests, they discovered that sensorimotor contents tend to develop in the same order predicted by Piaget's substages. The sensorimotor intelligence test that Corman and Escalona devised is less comprehensive than Uzgiris and Hunt's. Although the Corman-Escalona test, like the Uzgiris-Hunt test, contains items that span the entire sensorimotor stage, the items deal with only two of the six contents discussed earlier, namely, object permanence and space. Corman and Escalona culled the items on their test from Piaget's infancy books and, therefore, the test may be presumed to be valid. Each item that they finally included on their test had to meet three criteria: (*a*) The behaviors assessed by the item could be readily measured in a small office by an examiner who was unfamiliar with the infants; (*b*) the behaviors assessed by the item were characteristic of *only one* sensorimotor substage; (*c*) the behaviors assessed by the item were easy to observe and to score. After preparing their test, Corman and Escalona administered it to 295 infants ranging in age from 1 month to 26 1/2 months. Thus, the sample of subjects covered the entire age range for sensorimotor intelligence. The sample was divided into two groups. An initial group of 247 infants was seen once. Each of them received one administration of the test. From the performance of this group, Corman and Escalona were able to determine that their test, like Uzgiris and Hunt's, was reliable. The remaining 48 infants in the sample were seen more than once. Each of these latter infants received one administration of the test every two months during the first two years of life.

Corman and Escalona found more or less the same thing as Uzgiris and Hunt. With both the 247 infants in the first group and the 48 infants in the second group, cognitive contents in the object permanence and space areas tended to be acquired in a fixed and invariant order. Moreover, the invariant order in which object permanence and space contents were acquired was the same as the order predicted by Piaget's substages. There were a few minor deviations from Piaget's predictions. But, on the whole, the measured contents were acquired in exactly the same order as Piaget says they should be.

Two other macro studies have been conducted at the University of Illinois by Leslie B. Cohen and Kennedy T. Hill (Miller, Cohen, and Hill 1970; Kramer, Hill, and Cohen 1975). The scope of these investigations was considerably narrower than the Uzgiris-Hunt and Corman-Escalona research. In particular, only Substages III–VI were studied and only object permanence content was tested. In both studies, the tests consisted of items borrowed from the object permanence sections of Uzgiris and Hunt's test. Hence, the tests may be presumed to be valid and reliable. An important feature of both studies is that the various items on the tests were administered in a *random order*. In other words, for any given subject, the order in which the various items were administered was determined by chance. This procedure differs from the one used by Piaget (1954), Uzgiris and Hunt (1974), and Corman and Escalona (1969). In each of the latter cases, items that measure contents associated with *earlier* substages were always administered *before* items measuring contents associated with later substages. Cohen and Hill argued that this procedure may *build in* an order of item difficulty that has nothing whatsoever to do with whether or not infants acquire sensorimotor contents in a fixed order. Infants, after all, have rather low attention spans and they tire very easily. Although most infants will be alert during the first few items, they may be drowsy or inattentive by the time we get to later items. This makes it seem as though the earlier items are easier and, therefore, as though the contents measured by the earlier tests develop before the contents measured by the later tests.

In tneir first study (Miller, Cohen, and Hill 1970), eighty-four infants between the ages of 6 and 18 months were tested. All eighty-four infants were seen once and received a single administration of the test. The results differed in two important respects from those of Piaget (1954), Uzgiris and Hunt (1974), and Corman and Escalona (1969). First, they found that Substage VI object permanence behavior (searching for an object after a series of invisible hidings) developed *before* Substage V object permanence behavior (searching for an object after a series of visible hidings). This, of course, is exactly the opposite of what Piaget predicts. Second and more important, when the data from all of the items were compared, it was found that the items could not be arranged in a single fixed order of difficulty. Items assessing contents associated with earlier substages were not any easier than the items assessing contents associated with later substages. As we saw above, if contents are acquired in an invariant sequence during the sensorimotor stage, then we should be able to arrange a set of items that assess these contents in a fixed order of difficulty.

Both results of Miller, Cohen, and Hill are blatantly inconsistent with what Piaget says we should find. These two results might pose a serious problem for Piaget's theory if it were not for a later investigation conducted by the same authors. As prudent scientists should, Cohen and Hill decided to see whether they could replicate their surprising results. It turns out that they could not. In their new study (Kramer, Hill, and Cohen 1975), a test of Substage III–Substate VI object permanence (the items again were borrowed from Uzgiris and Hunt) was administered to thirty-six infants. Each infant received the test on three separate occasions spaced over a six-month interval. At the time of the first administration, the infants ranged in age from 5 months to 32 months. At the time of the second administration, the infants ranged in age from 11 months to 38 months. When the data were examined, the earlier findings were not replicated. This time they found more or less what Uzgiris and Hunt and Corman and Escalona found.

Searching for objects following a series of invisible hidings (Substage VI) developed *later than* searching for objects following a series of visible hidings (Substage V). Also, the items on the test could be arranged in a fixed order of difficulty: Substage III items were easier than Substage IV items; Substage IV items were easier than Substage V items; Substage V items were easier than Substage VI items.

Briefly, the picture provided by micro stage sequence studies does not differ from that provided by macro stage sequence studies. I noted earlier that Gratch and his associates at the University of Houston have conducted several micro studies of Substage IV and Substage V using object permanence content. Among other things, Gratch has found that searching for objects in the *first* place they are hidden (Substage IV) is a behavior that develops earlier than searching for objects in the *last* place they are hidden (Substage V). This finding has been observed both in cross-sectional studies, in which each infant is tested only once, and in longitudinal studies, in which each infant is tested several times. Gratch and his associates also have observed that object permanence behaviors that Piaget associates with Substage III invariably precede object permanence behaviors that he associates with Substage IV.

To summarize, stage sequence studies, both macro and micro, have tended to find that infants acquire sensorimotor contents in the same order as the one predicted by Piaget's substages. The evidence is very extensive with object permanence content. With the exception of Miller, Cohen, and Hill's (1970) data, which are apparently unreplicable, no major disconfirmatory evidence has appeared on the horizon. However, I would caution the reader against making too much of this fact and, in particular, against interpreting the supportive data as though they confirm Piaget's stage model of sensorimotor intelligence. All that the available stage sequence research tells us is that infants tend to acquire certain behaviors in a certain order and, further, that the order is roughly the same one that Piaget observed in his own children. But stage sequence research does not tell us anything about whether Piaget's sensorimotor stages actually exist because we simply do not know how to recognize a Piagetian stage when we see one. All we can do is measure the behaviors that Piaget associates with them.

object permanence studies

No other aspect of Piaget's theory of sensorimotor intelligence has generated as much interest outside Geneva as his description (Piaget 1954) of the development of object permanence. As I write, over three dozen separate investigations of object permanence have been published by researchers in Great Britain and the United States. Most of the studies have used human infants as subjects, but some have assessed object permanence in monkeys and cats. Everything points to the publication of many more studies of object permanence, with infrahumans as well as humans, in the near future. What has caused all the excitement?

As might be expected, most of the research has been generated by the fact that investigators outside Geneva are uncertain about whether they ought to believe Piaget's account of object permanence. In particular, they are uncertain about whether *competence hypotheses* or *performance hypotheses* are the best way to explain infants' responses to hidden objects. Before we look at the general difference between competence and performance explanations, however, it will be helpful for us to recall the specific object permanence behaviors that Piaget says are characteristic of his six sensorimotor substages:

1. Substage I (0–1 month). Out of sight is out of mind. When an object disappears from view, the infant makes no attempt to search for it visually or to retrieve it manually.

2. Substage II (1–4 months). Same as Substage I.

3. Substage III (4–8 months). Infants show the first evidence of object permanence. When an object is completely hidden under a cover (e.g., a blanket), infants will not search for it visually or manually. They will search manually for a hidden object only if they were already moving in the direction of the cover at the time the object was hidden. They will search visually for an object if the object is only partially hidden by the cover.

4. Substage IV (8–12 months). The infant searches manually for hidden objects. When an object is placed under a cover, the infant will lift the cover and retrieve the object. However, if the object is hidden under several covers successively, with each successive hiding fully visible to the infant, then the infant will search under the *first* cover rather than the last cover.

5. Substage V (12–18 months). When an object is hidden under several covers, with each successive hiding fully visible to the infant, the infant correctly searches under the last cover. However, if some of the hidings are carried out in such a way that the infant cannot see them (e.g., by moving the object from one cover to another inside an opaque container), then the infant does not search for the object under the last cover.

6. Substage VI (18–24 months). Infants solve the invisible hiding problem. They correctly search under the last cover even if some of the steps in the series of hidings were invisible to them.

Competence theories vs. performance theories. Let us return now to the question of competence explanations vs. performance explanations. This is a question that will crop up again in later chapters, so it is advisable to discuss it in some detail here. Generally speaking, the question has to do with how one explains the fact that younger subjects fail a certain concept test while older subjects pass it. Piaget's account of object permanence development during infancy is what psychologists call a *competence theory*. A competence theory explains the fact that younger subjects fail tests, such as the ones used to assess object permanence, in terms of *the absence of some underlying concept or concepts*. Thus, when infants fail to search for a hidden object, Piaget says it is because their underlying assumptions (concepts) about the existence of objects are different from those of adults and children. Explicitly, Piaget says infants believe that an object's existence is contingent upon their own behavior—i.e., out of sight is out of mind. Adults and children, on the other hand, believe that objects continue to exist when they are not in direct perceptual contact with them. It is this conceptual difference between infants and older subjects that, according to Piaget, explains these differences in search behavior. The concept difference, in turn, is supposed to result from *differences in cognitive structure.*

Performance hypotheses, on the other hand, do not explain concept test failures in this way. Instead, they explain them in terms of *test difficulty variables.* There are many factors that can spuriously inflate test difficulty and cause subjects to fail even though they have the relevant concept. To take an extreme example, suppose we administered an arithmetic test to a group of English-speaking sixth graders and suppose the test was in Russian. Undoubtedly the subjects would fail the test, even though they understand the concepts of addition, subtraction, multiplication, and division, because they cannot read Russian. To take a more pertinent example, suppose we administer a Substage IV object permanence test to a group of 6-month-old infants (Substage III) and a group of 9-month-old infants (Substage IV). Let us say that the test consists of hiding an object under a single cover. We may expect that the infants in the first group will fail the test and the infants in the second group will pass it. How do we explain this difference? A performance explanation, unlike Piaget's competence theory, would not say that the difference is the result of a difference in underlying concepts. Instead, a performance explanation would assume that *both groups possess more or less the same concept,* but the younger group has not yet acquired certain supporting skills that are required to pass the test. What might some of these supporting skills be? In the case of a Substage IV object permanence test, the most obvious ones are *fine motor coordination* and *memory.*

Concerning fine motor coordination, our Substage IV test obviously makes some rather sophisticated motoric demands on infants. Among other things, it requires that infants be able to coordinate vision with arm movements (they must move their arms after they *see* the object being hidden), to grasp things (the cover), and to coordinate grasping movements with arm movements (they must withdraw the cover after they have grasped it). The motoric demands are, for an infant, not inconsequential. After all, most infants, to say the least, do not begin life with very good motor coordination. Hence, it could be that the fact that 6-month-olds fail Substage IV tests has nothing to do with the absence of a concept. It might just be that 9-month-olds have developed the supporting motor skills but 6-month-olds have not. Prima facie, this explanation is every bit as reasonable as Piaget's.

Concerning memory, this factor poses another problem for Piagetian infant tests. This is especially true for Substage V and Substage VI object permanence tests. In both cases, the infant is shown a series of hidings; in one instance all hidings are visible and in the other instance some hidings are invisible, and the infant is expected to search in the last hiding place. Piaget explains the fact that older infants pass such tests and younger infants do not by appealing to differences in underlying concepts. But it could also be that memory is the culprit with younger infants. Memory capacity is known to develop slowly throughout infancy and childhood. Therefore, it could be that the memory capacity of younger infants has not yet developed to the point where they can remember several different hiding places. If this were true, then the fact that older infants pass substage V and VI tests might simply be attributable to their larger memory capacity.

Any hypothesis that explains the fact that younger infants fail object permanence tests in terms of nonconceptual factors such as motor coordination and memory is a performance hypothesis. Further, *any hypothesis* that explains the fact that younger subjects fail *any test* by appealing to nonconceptual factors is a performance hypothesis. (In Chapter 5, for example, we shall see that performance hypotheses have frequently been advanced to explain why preschoolers fail tests for the cognitive contents of Piaget's concrete-operational stage.) A performance hypothesis says that younger subjects who fail a concept test actually possess the concept and, hence, their failures are "false negatives." Psychologists refer to such false negative failures as *measurement errors.*

Most of the research on object pemanence conducted by investigators outside Geneva has been designed to explore one or more performance hypotheses. Investigators have formulated specific performance hypotheses about object permanence tests—concerned with such variables as motor coordination and memory—and have then tested them on groups of infants. The general aim of these studies has been to discover whether specific test difficulty variables, on the one hand, or differences in underlying concepts, on the other, is the best way to explain object permanence test failures. The studies tend to fall into four categories: (*a*) those dealing with infants between the ages of 1 and 2 months (Substages I and II); (*b*) those dealing with infants between the ages of 3 and 9 months (Substage III); (*c*) those dealing with infants between the ages of 5 and 12 months (transition from Substage III to Substage IV); and (*d*) those dealing with infants between the ages of 9 and 24 months (substages IV, V, and VI). Virtually all of the studies in the first two groups have been conducted by T. G. R. Bower and his associates at the University of Edinburgh. The studies in the last two groups have been conducted primarily by P. L. Harris of the University of Lancaster and by Gratch and his associates at the University of Houston. To conclude this chapter, we briefly review the key findings of each group of studies.

Substages I and II. Contrary to Piaget, T. G. R. Bower (1974) has committed himself to the view that object permanence appears very early in infancy. Much of his research has been designed to show that infants acquire object permanence before they are 6 months old.

Bower (1967) reported three experiments designed to explore possible performance explanations of why Substage I and Substage II infants fail to search for hidden objects. In the first of these experiments, Bower trained 7- and 8-month-old infants to suck for a reward. During the training trials, a sphere was visible to the infant. By the usual laws of learning, pairing the sphere with a reward should cause the sphere to acquire rewarding properties. The sphere becomes, in the language of learning psychology, a "secondary reinforcer," and the infant will suck in the presence of the sphere even without the original reward. After training, Bower assessed the effects of four different methods of making the sphere disappear on suckling behavior: first, a screen was slowly lowered in front of the sphere; second, the sphere was made to fade gradually; third, the sphere was suddenly deflated; fourth, a screen was suddenly dropped in front of the sphere. Bower compared suckling behavior in each of these disappearance conditions with suckling behavior in a control condition in which the sphere was always visible. He found that infants in the first disappearance condition, but not in the remaining three, sucked the same amount as infants in the control condition. This suggests that the infants in the first condition believed that the sphere continued to exist behind the screen. But it could also be that suckling in the last three conditions was suppressed because something in these methods of disappearance startled the infants.

Bower conducted a second experiment in an attempt to rule out the latter possibility. This time he measured heart rate, which is known to change in certain ways when infants are startled, as well as suckling. Bower found that the four disappearance conditions did not have different effects on heart rate. In his third experiment, Bower studied the effects of repeated disappearance and reappearance of the sphere on suckling. Whenever the sphere disappeared, the infants' suckling rate dropped. Whenever the sphere reappeared, suckling rate increased to its predisappearance level *if the interval between disappearance and reappearance was not longer than five seconds.* This is an important finding because it suggests that memory may be an significant task difficulty factor on object permanence tests. If an object reappears within five seconds, then Substage I and II infants "remember" it as the same object they saw before. If an object does not reappear within this interval, they fail to "remember" it as the same object they saw before.

Bower's three experiments suggest that the object permanence skills of very young infants may be considerably more sophisticated than Piaget supposes. Also, the third experiment indicates that one of the test difficulty variables mentioned above, memory, may be responsible for the failure of very young infants to search for hidden objects. An important recommendation would seem to follow from this experiment: An object permanence test, to be considered valid, should allow the infant to begin searching within five seconds of disappearance.

Although Bower's experiments provide provocative data, they are by no means conclusive. Importantly, since Bower is the only investigator who has examined performance explanations for Substages I and II, it remains for other investigators to determine whether or not his findings are replicable.

Substage III. Bower has also conducted several experiments concerned with Substage III object permanence (Bower 1971; Bower, Broughton, and Moore 1971; Bower and Patterson 1973). The general aim of these studies was to show that, Piaget's claims to the contrary notwithstanding, 3- to 9-month-olds will search for a hidden object—thereby suggesting that they have the object permanence concept.

In his initial investigations (Bower 1971; Bower, Broughton, and Moore 1971), Bower seemed to have presented conclusive proof that very young infants search visually for hidden objects. Bower devised a simple but ingenious procedure for testing visual search in very young infants which is illustrated in Figure 3-1. The infant is seated in a small chair in front of a table. On the table, a toy railroad track is laid out and there is a train on the track. The train moves slowly across the infant's line of sight. Sometimes it moves from left to right [Fig. 3-1 (a) and (b)] and sometimes it moves from right to left [Fig. 3-1 (c) and (d)]. There is a tunnel somewhere on the track. What does the infant do when the train enters the tunnel? Suppose the infant immediately looks to the opposite end of the tunnel from the one the train entered. This would seem to indicate, first, that the infant expects the train to reappear momentarily and, second, that the infant must therefore believe that the train continues to exist after it has disappeared into the tunnel. Bower found that infants do, in fact, immediately look to the opposite end of the tunnel when they are about 3 months of age but not before. He concluded (Bower 1971) that, although object permanence probably is not present at birth, Piaget is incorrect in maintaining that the concept is not acquired until the second year of life.

The results of later research have made Bower's conclusions doubtful. Although it might be that 3-month-old infants look toward the opposite end of the tunnel from the one the train enters because they believe that the train will soon reappear there, it could also be that this behavior is simply *perseverative eye movement.* Infants track the movement of the train with their eyes and, hence, their eyes are already moving in the same direction as the train. Perhaps, after the train has entered the tunnel, their eyes continue moving in the same direction until they come to rest at a point further along the track near the opposite end of the tunnel. This would

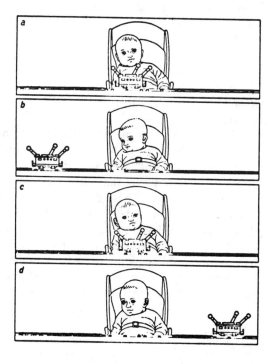

Figure 3-1. Illustration of the procedure used by
Bower (1971) to study object search behavior in
very young infants. The object shown in the pictures moves slowly through the infant's visual
field and tracking eye movements are measured.
(From T. G. R. Bower, The Object World of the Infant, *Scientific American*, 1971, *225*, 36. Copyright
©(1971) by Scientific American, Inc. All rights
reserved.

make it appear as though infants anticipate the reemergence of the train
from the tunnel when, in reality, they merely have difficulty stopping their
eyes once they are in motion. A simple method of examining the latter possibility suggests itself: Perform the same experiment as before, but stop the
train just before it enters the tunnel and determine whether the subject's
eyes continue to move. Bower and Patterson (1973) conducted such an experiment. Using 3- and 4-month-old subjects, they stopped the toy train just
before it entered the tunnel. Even though the train was still in full view, the
infants' eyes continued to move in the same direction as the train had been
moving until they came to rest at a point further along the track. Bower and
Patterson then removed the tunnel from the track, repeated the experiment,
and found the same thing. That is, when the train was stopped at a certain

point P_1, the infants' eyes continued to move in the same direction until they came to rest at a point P_2 further along the track. Next, Bower and Patterson trained their subjects to observe a train moving slowly along a track. On each training trial, the train stopped briefly at a point P_1 and at a point P_2 further along the track. After several of these trials, a test trial was administered. On the test trial, the train stopped for a much longer period at P_1 than it had on the training trials. The infants looked to point P_2 while the train was still stopped at P_1.

Insofar as performance and competence explanations are concerned, no definitive conclusions follow from Bower's research on Substage III. Concerning the performance view of why young infants fail to search visually for hidden objects, it now seems that Bower's early data on visual search were incorrectly interpreted. These data do not unequivocally support the conclusion that 3-month-olds have object permanence. But neither do they support Piaget's contrasting competence view. About the only thing that can be said with reasonable certainty is that the use of eye tracking movements as a measure of object permanence is objectionable. The fact that perseverative eye movements occur in very young infants makes it difficult, if not impossible, to use "anticipatory" eye movements as grounds for inferring that they are searching for a hidden object.

Substages III and IV. According to Piaget, the transition from Substage III to Substage IV is marked by the appearance of visually guided manual search for hidden objects. Prior to this time, infants will search manually for an object hidden under a cover only if their arms were already moving in the direction of the object at the time it was covered. Possible performance explanations of the transition from Substage III to Substage IV have been examined by Bower (Bower, Broughton, and Moore 1970; Bower and Wishart 1972). In addition, Gratch (1972; Gratch and Landers 1971) and Harris (1971) have attempted to provide an account of the development of manual search that is more detailed than Piaget's.

Earlier, I mentioned that manual search tests make some rather sophisticated motoric demands. At a minimum, infants must use vision to guide their reaching, must be able to grasp things, and must use grasping to guide their reaching. Hence, if we find that, say, 5-month-olds fail such tests while 9-month-olds pass them, this fact might not reflect differences in underlying concepts. It could very well be that 9-month-olds have developed the necessary motor skills but 5-month-olds have not. Bower and Wishart (1972) devised a simple procedure for evaluating this possibility. Their subjects were 5-month-olds who were administered two types of tests. First, they were given a standard Substage IV test in which an object was hidden by covering it with an opaque cloth. Second, they were given a modified Substage IV test in which an object was hidden by covering it with a *trans-*

parent cloth. In the latter test, the object remains fully visible after it is covered. If the "motor skill" interpretation of why 5-month-olds fail Substage IV tests is correct, we would expect that they will fail both tests with equal frequency. But if 5-month-olds possess the necessary motor skills but lack the appropriate concept (Piaget's competence interpretation), we would expect that many more of them will pass the second test than the first test. The latter is what Bower and Wishart found. This result does not provide direct support from Piaget's position. There are, after all, other test difficulty variables associated with Substage IV tests. However, the result does indicate that the difference between the performance of Substage III and Substage IV infants on manual search tests is not wholly attributable to differences in motor skill. This conclusion, while not directly supportive of Piaget's position, at least is not inconsistent with it.

Bower (1974) recently has proposed another performance explanation of why infants fail Substage IV tests. He argues that we must differentiate between two types of object disappearance: (*a*) the object is placed in a certain position and a cover is placed *over* it; and (*b*) the object is placed in a certain position and a screen is placed *in front* of it. Bower further argues that type (*a*) disappearance, which is almost always used in Substage IV tests (e.g., Corman and Escalona 1969; Uzgiris and Hunt 1974), tends to confuse the infant because the object and the cover occupy *the same spatial locus*. In contrast, the object and the cover do not occupy the same spatial locus in type (*b*) disappearance. According to Bower, type (*b*) disappearance therefore is a more valid Substage IV test than type (*a*) disappearance. Although I am oversimplifying things a bit, Bower's argument about the two types of disappearance says essentially this: When an object is out of sight, it not only *may* be out of mind (as Piaget maintains); it also is difficult to locate. The latter is a test difficulty variable. Hence, if we wish to determine whether out of sight is really out of mind, we should not make the object overly difficult to locate.

If Bower's argument is correct, then we would expect that, say, 5- or 6-month-olds would pass type (*b*) tests more frequently than they pass type (*a*) tests. On the other hand, if Piaget's competence explanation is correct, we would expect that infants will pass the two tests with equal frequency. These contrasting predictions were examined in a study conducted at the University of Edinburgh (Brown 1973). Brown administered both types of tests to a sample of infants. The type (*b*) tests were passed with much greater frequency than the type (*a*) tests. In the absence of alternative interpretations, this result suggests, first, that confusion of spatial location may be an important difficulty variable on Substage IV tests and, second, that this variable may be responsible for many failures on Substage IV tests.

Turning to the research of other investigators, Harris (1975) recently has summarized the available literature on the transition from Substage III to Substage IV. He concludes that his own studies, Gratch's studies, and others suggest that manual search for hidden objects develops in four stages that span Piaget's Substages III and IV. During the first stage (4 to 5 months), the infant will move an object that has been placed in her hand into her line of sight. During the second stage (6 to 7 months), the infant will withdraw an object that *is already in her hand* from under a cover. During the third stage (8 to 11 months), the infant will search manually for an object that is removed from her hand and then covered with a cloth. During the fourth stage (12 months), the infant will search manually for an object that she has seen covered but has not grasped. To review all of the separate studies that Harris uses to support this model would be far beyond the scope of the present chapter. Readers interested in these studies are directed to Harris' paper. However, I should note that if Harris' interpretation of the studies happens to be correct, it would mean that Piaget's account of the transition from Substage III to Substage IV is incomplete and, perhaps, at least two more substages need to be added between III and IV.

Substages IV, V, and VI. According to Piaget, the transition from Substage IV to Substage V is marked by the ability to search manually in the last place an object is hidden after a series of visible hidings. The transition from Substage V to Substage VI, on the other hand, supposedly is marked by the ability to search manually in the last place an object is hidden after a series of invisible hidings. Studies of the former transition have been conducted by Gratch and his associates and by Harris (1973, 1974). A study of the latter transition has been conducted by Webb, Massar, and Nodolny (1972).

For our purposes, the most interesting outcome of the studies of Gratch and his associates is that they have found very little support for Piaget's claim that manual search in the *first* place an object is hidden (Substage IV) is always developmentally prior to manual search in the *last* place an object is hidden (Substage V). Consider again the elementary procedure for assessing these two cognitive contents that was described earlier in the section on stage sequence studies. An object is hidden in either of two wells of a plastic dish. Sometimes the object is hidden in one well before the infant is allowed to search (Substage IV test). On other occasions, the object is hidden in one well and then is hidden in the second well before the infant is allowed to search (Substage V test). According to Piaget, infants should pass the first test with much greater frequency than the second test. However, in a study by Gratch and Landers (1971), infants passed the two tests with equal frequency. In the Gratch and Landers procedure, there was a three-second delay between the time the object was hidden and the time the infant was allowed to begin searching for it. This interval is well within the five-second maximum suggested by Bower's studies with younger infants. Other studies by Landers (1971), Evans and Gratch (1972), and Bower and

Patterson (1972) have also failed to find clear support for Piaget's claim that manual search at the first hiding place is developmentally prior to manual search at the last hiding place.

Harris (1973, 1974) has studied the effects of a test difficulty variable, memory, on Substage V object permanence. He has proposed that a short-term memory factor, *proactive inhibition,* may be responsible for failures on Substage V tests. Generally speaking, proactive inhibition refers to the fact that memory for an earlier event sometimes interferes with memory for a later event. Applied to Substage V tests, this performance hypothesis suggests that seeing an object hidden in several places may place a sufficiently severe strain on short-term memory that infants' ability to remember the last hiding place is impaired. Harris examined this hypothesis in two experiments. In the first experiment, he administered Substage V tests to 10-month-olds using a delayed response procedure. Harris reasoned that if proactive interference occurs on such tests, it should be possible to increase their difficulty by lenghtening the interval between successive hidings. This is precisely what he found. Subsequently, Harris' results were replicated in an experiment by Gratch et al. (1974).

Harris also examined the proactive inhibition hypothesis in a second and more complicated experiment. In this experiment, an object was successively hidden at two locations. At each location there was a screen that could be lowered to hide the object. Harris reasoned that *the order in which the screens were lowered* after the object had been placed at the *second* location should affect the difficulty of the test. He reasoned, more explicitly, that if the screen at the second location was lowered *before* the screen at the first location, infants would be more likely to pass the test than if the screens were lowered in the reverse order. Presumably, leaving the first screen up while the second screen is lowered in front of the object should help infants remember that the object is no longer at the first location. But if the screens are lowered in the reverse order, infants are denied the memory hint. In line with his hypothesis, Harris found that 10-month-olds pass Substage V tests with much greater frequency when the screen covering the second hiding place is lowered before the screen covering the first hiding place.

Harris's work on Substage V tests, like Bower's work on younger infants, strongly suggests that memory is an important difficulty variable on such tests. If Harris's argument about proactive inhibition is correct, then Substage V tests, to be considered valid, should make the delay between successive hidings as short as possible. Also, they should incorporate memory hints to remind the infant that the object is no longer at its earlier hiding place.

By comparison with the research on the transition from Substage IV to Substage V, relatively little work has been done on the transition from Substage V to Substage VI. It is true that several investigators have found support for Piaget's belief that searching in the last hiding place following a series of visible hidings (Substage V) is always developmentally prior to searching in the last hiding place following a series of invisible hidings (Substage VI). However, there has been very little research designed to explore possible performance explanations of why infants fail Substage VI tests. Harris (1975) has attempted to extend his memory interpretation of Substage V failures to Substage VI on the basis of an experiment by Webb et al. (1972). Webb et al. used a delayed response paradigm with 14- to 16-month-olds that was similar to the one Harris used in his first experiment with 10-month-olds. They hid objects in three successive locations and varied the time interval between successive hidings. The delays between successive hidings varied from a low of five seconds to a high of fifteen seconds. As was the case in Harris's experiment, Webb et al. found that the number of infants who failed to search in the last hiding place increased dramatically as the delay between successive hidings increased.

Some conclusions. We have seen that several studies designed to examine possible performance explanations of why infants fail object permanence tests have been published. Despite the fact that the number of relevant studies is fairly large, it would be imprudent and probably incorrect to conclude that these studies have resolved the complicated issue of performance vs. competence explanations of object permanence test failures. We saw that one prominent investigator, T. G. R. Bower, subscribes to the view that object permanence, though perhaps absent at birth, is acquired before the infant is 6 months old. Bower's interpretation notwithstanding, there is no single set of findings in all the wealth of object permanence research that shows Piaget's belief that the concept is not acquired until the second year of life to be untenable.

Although Piaget's account of object permanence has not been conclusively disproven, some important shortcomings and inconsistencies have been discovered. The question of test difficulty variables, which is rarely considered in Piaget's discussions of object permanence, has become a central issue. Bower's and Harris' research, for example, seems to establish beyond reasonable doubt that memory is a critical factor in object permanence tests. Clearly, some failures on object permanence tests are caused by the demands they make on infants' limited memory capacities. At a minimum, Bower's and Harris's research leads to the recommendation that traditional tests of object permanence should be revised to make less severe demands on memory. Bower's studies of Substage III infants show that, in addition to memory, the spatial locations of a hidden object and its cover may be important test difficulty variables. Among other things, these studies indicate that tests in which the object is hidden by placing a screen in front of it may be more sensitive than the Piagetian tests in which the object is covered with a cloth.

Thus, although the basic question of whether performance hypotheses or competence hypotheses are the best way of explaining object permanence test failures has not yet been resolved, we have learned a good deal from recent experiments. In particular, we have learned that test difficulty variables account for some failures on traditional Piagetian tests. Whether *all* failures result from test difficulty variables such as motor skill, memory, and so on is a question which must await future research.

Synopsis

Piaget's sensorimotor stage is a time of transition from cognitive contents that are entirely overt to cognitive contents that are internalized or "mental" The crucial ability to represent events mentally is acquired during this stage. Like Freud and William James, Piaget believes that infants are unable to distinguish between themselves and their environment.

Piaget emphasizes six types of sensorimotor cognitive content— imitation, circular reactions, object permanence, time, causality, and space. The ability to imitate seems to be an especially good index of mental representation. During the sensorimotor stage, imitation is said to progress from reflexive immediate responses to flexible responses that can be delayed for long periods of time. Imitation is an important source of reproductive assimilation. Circular reactions are behavior sequences that tend to be repeated because they produce internal stimuli that generate the sequences. Circular reactions promote accomodation through scheme consolidation. Primary circular reactions appear during Substage II, secondary circular reactions appear during Substage III, and tertiary circular reactions appear during Substage V. The newborn does not have any definite sense of time. During the sensorimotor stage, time progress from a wholly subjective phenomenon to an objective concept of duration.

The object concept is the most intriguing sensorimotor content. Piaget claims that newborns do not understand that objects exist independently of their actions on them. Instead, they think that objects cease to exist when they are not perceptually present. The complete concept of object permanence, which is Piaget's primary index of mental representation ability, is said to appear around 18 to 24 months. Causal concepts during the sensorimotor stage are very different from the casual concepts of adults and older children. Infants have difficulty distinguishing between psychological casuality (dynamism) and physical casuality (phenomenalism). Spatial concepts undergo a long process of development that is not complete until adulthood. During the sensorimotor stage, the chief advance is that space, like time, becomes less subjective and more objective. By the end of the second year of life, infants can relate objects to each other via an internal system of spatial coordinates.

Piaget slices the sensorimotor stage up into six substages. Substage I, Use of Reflexes, runs from birth to roughly 1 month. Substage II, First Acquired Adaptions and the Primary Circular Reaction, runs from 1 month to roughly 4 months. Substage III, Secondary Circular Reactions and Procedures Destined to Make Interesting Sights Last, runs from 4 months to roughly 8 months. Substage IV, Coordination of Secondary Schemes and Their Application to New Situations, runs from 8 months to roughly 12 months. Substage V, Tertiary Circular Reactions and the Discovery of New Means Through Active Experimentation, runs from 12 months to roughly 18 months. Substage VI, Invention of New Means Through Mental Combinations, runs from 18 months to roughly 24 months. Full-fledged mental representation appears during Substage VI.

Replication research. A substantial amount of replication research has been conducted on the sensorimotor stage in recent years. These studies may be grouped into three broad categories, namely, test construction research, stage sequence research, and object permanence research. Test construction research seeks to determine whether valid and reliable tests of sensorimotor contents can be devised. Stage sequence research is concerned with whether or not infants pass through the six sensorimotor substages in an invariant order. Object permanence studies are concerned with the various factors that contribute to infants' performance on object permanence tests.

The Uzgiris-Hunt and Escolona projects are large-scale test construction ingestigations. Of these, the Uzgiris-Hunt project is more comprehensive from the standpoint of both the range of behaviors studied and the detail in which the findings have been reported. The Uzgiris-Hunt project spanned approximately a decade, and it dealt with behaviors from five of the six sensorimotor content areas. Their tests seem to be valid, since all the items were culled from Piaget's original research. Interexaminer agreement data and test-retest correlations suggests that their tests are also quite reliable.

Stage sequence studies are of two types—micro studies and macro studies. Micro studies focus on behaviors from one content area and two or three stages. Macro studies focus on behaviors from more than one content area and more than three stages. Both types of studies are concerned with the prediction that subjects should invariably pass tests for behaviors from earlier stages before they pass tests for behaviors from later stages. Micro and macro studies have both produced findings that are consistent with Piaget's hypotheses. With the exception of a single experiment reported by Miller, Cohen, and Hill (1970), investigators have routinely observed that behaviors from the six sensorimotor substages appear in the same order that Piaget predicts.

Object permanence studies have been broadly concerned with the question of whether competence hypotheses or performance hypotheses are the most appropriate method of explaining infants' poor performance on object concept tests. Some investigators, notably T. G. R. Bower of the University of Edinburgh, have committed themselves to the view that object permanence appears early in the first year of life. Experiments inspired by this possibility have examined the effects of several test difficulty variables on object concept test performance. To date, the most thoroughly studied variables have been fine motor coordination, memory, and spatial confusion. The results have been mixed. Concerning fine motor coordination, experiments with transparent and opaque covers indicate that lack of fine motor coordination cannot explain infants' failure to search manually for a hidden object. However, memory limitations and spatial confusion may be able to explain such failures. Memory appears to play a definite role in object search. The available data indicate that the delay between object hiding and search should not exceed five seconds. Longer intervals may be beyond the infant's memory capacities. Experiments on spatial confusion suggest that object concept tests are more difficult when the hidden object and the occluding object occupy the same spatial coordinates than when they occupy different coordinates. On the whole, object permanence research has not yet provided a clear answer to the question of whether competence or performance hypotheses are better explanations of object concept test failures. The fact that some test difficulty variables have been shown to exert clear effects tends to favor performance explanations over competence explanations. However, the fact that no one has yet been able to produce unmistakable evidence of object permanence in infants below 6 months of age tends to favor competence explanations over performance explanations.

Supplementary Readings

The primary Piaget references for the sensorimotor stage were cited at the beginning of this chapter. More up-to-date information may be found in the following five readings.

1. BOWER, *Development in Infancy* (1974). Bower's little book is probably the most readable introduction to infant perceptual and cognitive capacities currently available.
2. COHEN and SALAPATEK, *Infant Perception* (1976). This two-volume set provides up-to-date scholarly reviews of the major research topics in the study of infant perceptual and cognitive capacities. The second volume contains two chapters on object permanence, one by Bower and the other by Gratch.
3. HARRIS, "Development of Search and Object Permanence During Infancy" (1975). At the present time, Harris' paper seems to be the most comprehensive

review of the object permanence literature available. The chapters by Bower and Gratch in Reading 2 tend to emphasize work conducted in their own laboratories to the relative exclusion of experiments by other investigators.

4. UZGIRIS and HUNT, *Toward Ordinal Scales of Psychological Development* (1974). This volume contains the full particulars of the Uzgiris-Hunt test construction project. Stage sequence findings also are reported.

5. B. L. WHITE, "The Initial Coordination of Sensorimotor Schemes in Human Infants—Piaget's Ideas and the Role of Experience" (1969). White's paper offers an advanced, research-oriented analysis of the concept of sensorimotor scheme.

chapter 4

Piaget on Early Childhood: The Preoperational Stage

There is widespread agreement among developmental psychologists that the second of Piaget's four stages of cognitive development is the one about which we know the least. In fact, we know so little about it that some scholars refused to regard it as a separate stage. Flavell (1963), for example, views the preoperational stage as a preparatory phase for the concrete-operational stage. The matter is further complicated by the fact that the pre-operational stage is treated somewhat equivocally in Piaget's own writings. In some of his summary works (e.g., Piaget 1967*a*; Piaget and Inhelder 1969), preoperational cognitive contents are discussed in a manner that would suggest they comprise a distinct stage of cognitive development. But in other summary works (e.g., Piaget 1973), Piaget seems to regard them as comprising the preparatory phase of the concrete-operational stage. For our purposes, fortunately, the difficult question of whether preoperations should or should not be viewed as a distinct stage need not concern us. My own reading of Piaget leads me to conclude that preoperations satisfy all necessary criteria for stages. For example, it is frequently stated that pre-operational and concrete-operational cognitive structures are qualitatively different. Hence, in this chapter, I shall treat preoperations as a separate stage. However, the reader is free to adopt the contrasting viewpoint.

A curious and interesting fact about the preoperational stage is that, by comparison with other stages, most of its cognitive contents are *negative.* That is, for the most part this stage is defined in terms of the *absence* of certain abilities. The nominal age range for the stage is from 2 to 7 years.

Piaget has conducted an enormous amount of research with children in this age range. In fact, by far the greatest amount of his research has dealt with children in the preschool and early elementary school years. But this research is concerned almost exclusively with discovering how children acquire *concrete-operational* contents. Such research tells us very little of a positive nature about the preoperational stage. It tends to leave one with the impression that preoperational children are those who possess all the cognitive contents discussed in Chapter 3 and none of the cognitive contents to be discussed in Chapter 5. Since the definition of preoperations that tends to emerge from Piaget's research is negative, this reinforces the belief of many investigators that the preoperational period is best interpreted as the preparatory phase of concrete operations.

Of Piaget's various research books, the two that provide the most *positive* information about preoperational contents are *The Language and Thought of the Child* (1926a) and *The Child's Conception of Physical Causality* (1930). Some additional evidence appears in two books dealing primarily with the sensorimotor stage, *Play, Dreams, and Imitation in Childhood* (1951) and *The Construction of Reality in the Child* (1954). Finally, *On the Development of Memory and Identity* (1968) presents a new preoperational content, identity, not discussed in earlier works.

In this chapter, we consider both the positive and negative sides of the preoperational stage. We begin with a discussion of the central thing that preoperational children do not have: *mental operations.* Next, the principal positive cognitive contents are reviewed. Last, the replication research on these contents is summarized.

The Negative Side of the Preoperational Stage: Mental Operations

general definition

As the term "preoperational" suggests, this is the stage just before children acquire something called "operations." In this section, we examine the concept of operation and consider the role it plays in Piaget's theory of intelligence.

The mental operation is where cognitive development is *going* in Piaget's view. The acquisition of mental operations is the supreme end-product of cognitive development. All the changes that occur during the sensorimotor and preoperational stages serve to prepare the child for the advent of operations. Operations are the great "something" that older children and adults have but infants and younger children do not. This concept of mental operation is the one indisputably unique feature of the Piagetian approach to intelligence.

The fact that mental operations are where cognitive development presumably is going is an important thing to bear in mind. Theories of intelligence can be classified with reference to the capacities they believe to be the essence of intelligence. In North American learning approaches to intelligence, the development of language is usually regarded as the essence of intelligence. In Gestalt psychology, the development of certain perceptual skills (e.g., closure) is the essence of intelligence. But for Piaget the development of the so-called mental operation is the supreme characteristic of intelligence. The acquisition of operations is the single most important event which occurs during post-infancy cognitive development.

To begin with, an operation is *mental* in the sense of being "internalized" and "in the mind." Regardless of whether a particular operation is concerned with abstract mathematical concepts or the most mundane of everyday objects, the operation is carried out *representationally* or, as it were, "inside the head." Thus, overt behaviors do not qualify as true Piagetian operations unless they are also represented internally. To illustrate, if a child physically combines a set of two objects with another set of three objects to yield a set of five objects, this is not an operation. But if the child adds 2 to 3 and obtains 5 without the aid of concrete props (as in doing mental arithmetic), this *may* be an operation if it satisfies the additional criteria that I shall mention presently. In this sense, Piaget's operations appear synonymous with what we call thought. However, we shall see that not all things that we might call thought qualify as operations, because they do not possess the additional characteristics that follow.

Operations develop from *action* or, what amounts to the same thing, *overt behavior.* Operations are internalized and mentally represented actions. According to Piaget, the internalization process goes something like this: (*a*) The child first develops the ability to perform a particular overt behavior (e.g., counting); (*b*) through repeated practice the behavior sequence is refined and generalized until it becomes a stable action scheme; (*c*) finally, the general properties shared by all the individual behaviors that make up the action scheme are internalized as mental representations. Returning to a distinction discussed in Chapter 2, step (*c*) is when an action scheme becomes a *cognitive* scheme. Piaget maintains that all true mental operations are internalized in this manner.

Piaget's stipulation that an operation must originate in action excludes three important mental phenomena from the definition of operation, namely, perception, memory, and imagery. In everyday parlance and in most psychological theories, perception, memory, and imagery are all viewed as representational phenomena. However, as they are usually defined, these three processes have very little to do with action schemes. Perception traditionally is defined as veridical representation of facts evident to sensation; memory traditionally is defined as a process of making, storing, and retrieving mental memoranda about past events; imagery traditionally is defined as a process whereby static sensations, usually visual or auditory, are stored mentally. In each of these processes, there is an emphasis on passively recording events without intervening interpretation. By comparison, the emphasis in Piagetian operations is on actively transforming and interpreting reality.

I should add here that Piaget's emphasis on activity as a cornerstone of intelligence is an absolutely fundamental characteristic of his approach. Over the years, Piaget has strongly criticized other theories of intelligence for being too concerned with processes that he regards as passive.

Another characteristic of Piagetian operations is that they are *organized.* This seems a trivial point at first, but becomes important because of the abstract mathematical systems Piaget has proposed to describe the mental organization of operations (Piaget 1942, 1949). When Piaget says that operations are organized, he means not just that they are tightly integrated, but that they obey certain abstract rules. Of these rules, the two most important ones are Piaget's *cognitive reversibility rules.* Piaget calls the first of these reversibility rules *inversion* or *negation.* The inversion reversibility rule says that an operation can always be inverted—i.e., an operation that is carried out mentally in one direction can always be carried out mentally in the opposite direction. Inversion reversibility is analogous to subtraction in arithmetic and, indeed, arithmetic provides an elementary example of this rule in action. Suppose, to use an earlier illustration, a child mentally adds 2 to 3 and obtains 5. According to Piaget, this may be regarded as a true mental operation only if the child can also carry out its inverse—i.e., can subtract 3 from 5 and obtain 2 or subtract 2 from 5 and obtain 3. This capacity to carry out the inverse of any mental operation, which Piaget calls inversion reversibility, is the first product of the tight organization that characterizes operations. The second is what Piaget calls *reciprocity reversibility* or *compensation.* According to this second reversibility rule, there exists, for every mental operation, a reciprocal operation. Given any mental operation, its reciprocal is an entirely different mental operation which *nullifies* or *compensates the effects of the given operation.* Again, the basic analogy is with arithmetic. But whereas the analogy for inversion reversibility is subtraction, the analogy for reciprocity reversibility is division: 1/2 is the reciprocal of 2; 1/3 is the reciprocal of 3; 1/4 is the reciprocal of 4; and so on. The key fact about reciprocity reversibility is that, unlike inversion, an operation is not reversed simply by carrying out the same operation in the opposite direction. Rather, the operation is reversed by carrying out a quite different operation whose effect is the opposite of the given operation. Thus, the effect of multiplying 2 by 3 to yield 6 may be reversed by dividing 6 by 3 to yield 2 or by dividing 6 by 2 to yield 3. To summarize, mental operations are *negated* via inversion reversibility and they are *compensated* via reciprocity reversibility. Later, in Chapter 5, we shall examine some cognitive contents that Piaget uses to defend his view that mental operations obey these two reversibility rules.

The fourth and final characteristic of operations is supposed to result from the fact that they are governed by systems of rules: Operations assemble themselves into organized and integrated systems which Piaget calls *structures d'ensemble* or "structures of the whole." This is, without doubt, the most difficult and poorly understood of the four attributes of mental operations. In fact, structures of the whole are so poorly understood that different investigators have managed to deduce contradictory empirical predictions from the concept. (For example, compare the predictions discussed in Bingham-Newman and Hooper 1975 to those discussed in Brainerd 1975a.) For these reasons, it should be noted that the remarks on structures of the whole that follow are hardly definitive. There is currently too much disagreement about the meaning of this idea for anyone to claim to possess the correct definition.

To begin with, I should assure the reader that although structures of the whole is a difficult concept, it is an absolutely indispensible feature of mental operations. According to Piaget, mental operations never occur in isolation from each other. An isolated mental act is the very antithesis of the concept of operation. Operations are always assembled into systems called structures of the whole. Within these systems, there is a large class of *potential* operations associated with every *actual* operation. Since there is no such thing as an isolated operation, any true operation must be part of a system of related operations. The distinction between operations that actually occur at a given time and those that might occur is fundamental to structures of the whole. To my mind, the distinction has always resembled the physicist's distinction between kinetic and potential energy. Kinetic energy, like actual operations, refers to the things that an object is really doing at some given moment. Potential energy, like potential operations, refers to the things that an object *might* have done or might do at some future time.

The structures of the whole principle says that the operations that characterize any given stage of development are not merely "associated" or "correlated" with each other. Instead, they are "organically" interrelated. At this point, it is becoming apparent that the structures of the whole principle is another example of the biological orientation of Piaget's theory. Piaget certainly seems to have a biological metaphor in mind when he says that operations group themselves into systems. The mouth, stomach, and intestines are organically connected to form the digestive system; sensory neurons, effector neurons, and adjustor neurons are organically connected to form reflex arcs in the nervous system; the bones are organically connected to form the skeletal system; and so on. Thus, it can be argued that structures of the whole are the intellectual counterparts of the familiar systems of human biology.

To summarize our definition, an operation is a mentally represented *action* (not a percept, not a memory trace, not an image) that obeys certain logical *rules of organization* (inversion and compensation) and combines with other operations to form tightly *integrated systems* called structures of the whole. With this definition in hand, we turn now to the salient differences between intelligence without operations (preoperational stage) and intelligence with them (concrete-operational stage).

nonoperational vs. operational intelligence

Although the cognitive processes of the preschooler are far more sophisticated than those of the infant, they are not operations. Piaget contends that mental representation of actions is present, but logical rules of organization and structures of the whole are not. Piaget does not believe that the two reversibility rules are evident during the preoperational stage. He says that the rules governing true operations are *logical* because they never generate contradictions. But preoperations are called *infralogical* because they produce contradictory conclusions. Finally, the mental processes of the preoperational stage are not gathered together to form structures of the whole. Piaget believes that structures of the whole are absent during the preoperational stage because the rules governing preoperations are not completely logical. The absence of structures of the whole leads to what is supposed to be a hallmark of preoperational mental processes: They are isolated from each other.

Three general characteristics of preoperational thinking are believed to follow from the fact that preoperations do not meet the criteria for true operations. First, and this is perhaps the feature that Piaget discusses most often, preoperational thinking is rigid and inflexible, presumably because it is not grounded in action. Second, preoperational thinking focuses on individual events one at a time and fails to seek the common denominators among events. This means that preoperational children are strongly influenced by the illusory effects of momentary experience, and they have a difficult time negating such influences. According to Piaget, this second characteristic results from the fact that preoperational thoughts do not form structures of the whole. Third, preoperational thinking is inadequate for solving reasoning problems that require that the child transform some given piece of information into some new piece of information. This lack of transformational (or deductive) ability is usually attributed to the absence of the reversibility rules.

These three aspects of preoperations are admittedly somewhat vague when discussed in the abstract. However, all of them are easily illustrated by the performance of preoperational children on Piaget's (1952*a*) so-called class inclusion problem. Suppose we show preoperational children a picture of five horses and two cows. First, we ascertain that they understand that horses and cows are animals by requiring that they successively count all the horses, count all the cows, and count all the animals. After all three sets have been counted, we pose the question, "Are there more horses or more animals in this picture?" Surprisingly, they answer "more horses," Further questioning (e.g., Inhelder and Piaget 1964, Chap. 3) reveals several interesting facts. Concerning the rigidity of preoperational thought, we discover that these children will not change their answer even if they are asked to recount the sets. Concerning the influence of momentary experience, we discover that the children are only interested in the fact that the horses are visibly more numerous than the cows and that it never occurs to them to consider the superordinate set. Concerning the nontransformational aspect of preoperational thought, we discover that these children are incapable of combining the two subordinate sets to obtain the superordinate set and are also incapable of decomposing the superordinate set to obtain the two subordinate sets. Now, suppose we administer the same problem to a concrete-operational child. According to Piaget, the concrete-operational child will answer "more animals." [1]

The terms *figurative* and *operative* normally are used to refer to the above differences between thinking with operations and thinking without them. The figurative intelligence of the preoperational stage consists of mental representations that are fairly uncritical "pictures" of events in the child's environment. These figurative representations, which Piaget describes as *imitations* (Furth 1968), lie somewhere between the direct sensory experience that is the stuff of sensorimotor intelligence and the interpretative operations of later stages. Figurative representations also incline toward a predominance of accomodation over assimilation.

The Positive Side:
Illustrative Cognitive Contents

The years that comprise the nominal age range for the preoperational stage witness many alterations in children's lives. More changes take place during this time than during any comparable portion of the life span. The most obvious changes are in the child's social environment. During the preschool years, the social sphere broadens to include playmates and neighbors. Upon entrance into elementary school, the social environment undergoes another

---

[1] Although further discussion will be deferred, I should at least note here that it is by no means certain that concrete-operational children can solve class inclusion problems. The usual age range that Piaget gives for this stage is 7 to 11. However, recent experiments (Brainerd and Kaszor 1974) indicate that most children do not consistently solve class inclusion problems until adolescence. Further, recent investigations by F. H. Hooper's research group at the University of Wisconsin have shown that the ability to solve such problems develops slowly during adolescence and that a majority of male college students cannot solve them.

transformation. Thus, while the social relationships of infants are confined to members of the immediate family, those of the early childhood years are characterized by a steadily decreasing frequency of interaction with immediate family members. At the same time, social interactions with outside groups increase. Another major change is that children receive their first systematic instruction in how to use language to denote both the objects in their everyday environments and their internal states (My stomach is upset. That smells nice. I certainly am hungry.) A third important change is that parents and other adults expect far more in the way of behavioral maturity from young children than they do from infants. Dressing, toilet training, and other self-maintenance skills are now mandatory. To encourage acquisition of such skills, adults reinforce young children for showing independence (Bijou 1975). Rewards are provided for a wide variety of achievements—ranging from such mundane things as feeding oneself to such sophisticated things as reading and writing—that utimately lead to self-reliance and reduced dependence on adults.

In view of the enormity of the environmental changes during early childhood, it is commonly supposed that they determine the basic course of psychological development after infancy. Consequently, most theories of child development—even ones as different as learning theory and Freudian theory—place almost exclusive emphasis on environmental variables when discussing the early childhood years. Among the major theories of development, Piaget's is the only exception to this rule. Piaget is concerned chiefly with what is going on in the minds of preoperational children—not with what is going on in their environments. No explicit consideration is given to factors such as the training of self-maintenance skills, changes in the social world, and adult encouragement of self-reliance. This is because Piaget, unlike other theorists, does not believe that development after infancy is wholly dependent on environmental changes. Instead, he maintains that the basic structure of development is fixed and cannot be altered by environmental influences. Piaget believes that such influences are capable of accelerating or retarding the *rate* of development—e.g., intelligence will develop more slowly in children who acquire language slowly, intelligence will develop more slowly in children who are not taught to read and write, etc. But the successive steps that comprise the course of intellectual development, regardless of *when* they may occur, always occur in the same order. This assumption is a consequence of Piaget's biological perspective.

Below, we examine four cognitive contents that are characteristic of the preoperational stage: (*a*) egocentrism, (*b*) causality concepts, (*c*) language, and (*d*) identity. Although others could have been discussed, these particular preoperational contents were selected because some replication data are available on each. Before discussing these contents, some general remarks about assimilation and accomodation during the preoperational stage are in order. In the discussion of adaption in Chapter 2, I noted that one of the central tasks of cognitive development in Piagetian theory is to establish a stable equilibrium between assimilation and accomodation. Before the final stage of cognitive development is attained, Piaget believes, assimilation and accomodation are in disequilibrium. Hence, the cognitive contents of earlier stages tend to be either overly assimilative or overly ac-comodative. In Chapter 3, for example, we saw some examples of over-assimilation during the sensorimotor stage. The sensorimotor conception of the world violates even the most primitive laws of reality: Objects surrender their existence as soon as the infant is no longer in perceptual contact with them; there is no sensation of time as an objective dimension that is in-dependent of the infant's behavior; space is not understood as an objective dimension that is independent of the infant's behavior. The imbalance between assimilation and accomodation continues during the preopera-tional stage, with an important difference. While the salient cognitive con-tents of the sensorimotor stage are predominantly overly assimilative, overly assimilative and overly accomodative contents are present in roughly equal proportions during the preoperational stage (Piaget 1967a). Piaget intro-duces a special term, *intuitive,* to denote overly accomodative contents. The first two contents discussed below, egocentrism and animism, are examples of overassimilation. The third content, identity, illustrates overaccomoda-tion. The fourth content, language, has some overassimilation features and some overaccomodation features.

egocentrism

The concept of egocentrism was introduced in Piaget's first book on children's language (Piaget 1926a) and it has played an important role both in his theory and in other theories about how preschoolers think ever since. Although one of North America's leading Piaget scholars, David Elkind (1967b), has proposed that vestiges of egocentrism may be found as late as adolescence, egocentrism remains chiefly illustrative of the preoperational stage. It is also the best known of the cognitive contents we shall be con-sidering.

In psychology, words beginning with "ego" usually connote selfish-ness (e.g., egoism, egotist). For example, they normally have this connota-tion in Freudian theory. But Piaget's notion of egocentrism does not, as is sometimes supposed, have anything to do with selfishness. In its broadest sense, egocentrism is a *dimension* concerned with the extent to which chil-dren view themselves as the center of reality. Any behavior that suggests children are preoccupied with themselves and/or unconcerned with things going on around them may be termed egocentric. At the level of emotional expression, for example, behaviors that indicate that the child has difficulty relating to others' feelings may be termed egocentric. More generally, any behavior that suggests children have difficulty telling the difference between what "I" think, feel, and believe and what "you" think, feel, and believe is, for Piaget, a sign of egocentrism. According to Piagetian theory, preoperational children are simply unaware that there are points of view other than their own. Preoperational children think that everyone experiences the world in the same way they do. Piaget's explanation of preoperational egocentrism is the same as his explanation of the absence of object permanence during the sensorimotor stage, namely, a lack of differentiation between the subject and the object. Thus, egocentrism is to the preoperational stage what object permanence is to the sensorimotor stage. As cognitive development proceeds, the subject and object become more thoroughly differentiated from each other. Piaget (e.g., 1962) calls this differentiation process *the law of decentration.* During the sensorimotor stage, the law of decentration produces a growing awareness that objects exist independently of our actions upon them. During the preoperational stage, the law of decentration produces a growing awareness that the people around us experience the world in ways that differ from our own experience.

It is interesting to note, in passing, that the concept of egocentrism can be applied to scientific theories as well as to cognitive development. For example, consider theories of cosmology. In particular, consider the Copernican and Ptolemaic models of the solar system. The Ptolemaic model is the more "egocentric" of the two because it accepts the assumption that our particular planet must be the center of the universe as a self-evident truth. Similarly, Newtonian cosmology is more "egocentric" than Einsteinian cosmology because it assumes that the laws of the universe are the same for all observers. Finally, in psychology, there are some theories (e.g., humanistic psychology) that posit that human behavior is unique in that it is governed by special laws that do not hold for animals. There are other theories (e.g., behaviorism) that hold that there is nothing special about the laws governing human behavior. The former theories obviously provide a more "egocentric" view of human behavior than the latter. It is also interesting to note that, historically, "egocentric" scientific theories tend to precede nonegocentric theories. Perhaps Piaget's law of decentration is both a phylogenetic principle and an ontogenetic principle.

Although egocentrism is only one of four preoperational cognitive contents, it is, for Piaget, perhaps the most pervasive characteristic of this stage. He believes that egocentrism, in some form, is to be found in most spheres of preoperational intelligence: "However dependent he may be on surrounding intellectual influences, the young child assimilates them in his own way. He reduces them to his point of view and therefore distorts them without realizing it, simply because he cannot yet distinguish his point of view from that of others through failure to coordinate or 'group' points of view. Thus, both on the social and on the physical plane, he is egocentric through ignorance of his own subjectivity" (Piaget 1950, p. 160).

How does one measure preoperational egocentrism? Since its chief attribute is the assumption on the part of children that everyone's point of view is the same as their own, a valid measure would seem to be one that taps the differentiation of the "I" and "you" points of view. Many such tests could no doubt be devised. However, a very simple and yet compelling one was introduced in *The Child's Conception of Space* (Piaget and Inhelder 1956). This particular test, which is usually called the mountain problem, is designed to determine whether children believe that others *see* things in the surrounding environment in the same way that they do. For this reason, it is called a *perspective-taking task*. Suppose we have a small table on which a simple geographical configuration of some sort is laid out. In the original problem devised by Piaget and Inhelder, the configuration consisted of three mountains of different heights. The child is asked to stand on one side of the table and to view the display from this particular location. After the child has observed the display from this position, a small doll is introduced. The child is told that she is going to play a game in which the doll will be placed at various locations within the display and her task will be to decide what the display looks like from the doll's location. To begin with, the doll is placed at the same location as the child. A series of photographs previously taken from various locations around the display are shown to the child. She is asked to select the photograph that shows what the doll sees. Of course, she selects the photograph that shows what the display looks like from her own position. To determine whether the child understands that there are points of view other than her own, the doll is moved to a new location that is different than the child's. The child is shown the same series of photographs and is again asked to select the one that shows what the doll sees. Next, the doll is moved to several other locations within the display. Each time it is moved, the child is shown the photographs and is asked to select the one that shows what the doll sees. For variety, the child may occasionally be asked to make a drawing of what the doll sees.

When children at the concrete-operational and formal-operational stages are administered this problem, they readily solve it. Wherever the doll is moved, they select the photograph showing what the display looks like from the doll's location. Preoperational children perform in a quite different manner. First, they do not select the correct picture when the doll is located at a position other than their own. Second, the picture they do select is usually the one that shows what the display looks like from their own position. Piaget interprets this second fact as unmistakable proof that preoperational children do not understand there are points of view other than their own. Recalling the distinction between performance and competence hypotheses discussed in Chapter 3, Piaget's interpretation is obviously a competence hypothesis (i.e., failing a test equals absence of a concept). Near the end of the preoperational stage, some improvements in mountain problem performance are observed. Children still do not routinely select the correct photograph. However, their incorrect responses are no longer systematic. Importantly, they do not automatically select the photograph showing what the display looks like from their own position. Although they still do not select the correct photograph, they usually select one that shows a view of the display different from their own. Piaget interprets this as evidence that some awareness of the existence of other points of view is beginning to dawn on the children. This is also a competence interpretation.

concepts of causality

By adult standards, preoperational children have some rather surprising ideas about cause-effect relations. We saw in Chapter 1 that during his tenure as director of research at the Rousseau Institute Piaget conducted a series of investigations concerned with children's causal philosophies. The findings were reported in three of Piaget's early books (1926*b*, 1929, 1930). It is to these investigations that we now turn. We shall consider three general features of preoperational children's causality concepts: *finalism, artificialism,* and *animism.*

Finalism. Finalism is concerned with the manner in which preoperational children answer the interrogatives "why," "what," "where," and "how"—but especially the interrogative "why." Piaget notes that the average adult attributes two meanings to "why." The first meaning concerns the goals or purposes that underlie one's behavior (e.g., "Why did you do that?"). The second meaning concerns the causes of various events (e.g., "Why does the sun shine?"). The former meaning refers to *effects* (where things are going) and the latter meaning refers to *causes* (where things come from). Thus, for the adult, the interrogative "why" is concerned with both causes and effects.

In contrast, Piaget maintains that preoperational children cannot distinguish between the cause and effect meanings of "why." When answering "why" questions, they seem to respond *simultaneously* about causes and effects. The result is some extremely confusing replies. While the adult always responds to "why" questions by reporting either causes or effects, the preoperational child wants to talk about the two interchangeably. Is it any wonder, Piaget asks, that when preoperational children ask "why," adults never seem to be able to give a satisfactory answer? There is a second important feature of preoperational children's replies to interrogatives. Unlike adults, they do not appear to accept the view that some events simply are accidental or chance occurrences. The preoperational child appears to believe that every event, no matter how inconsequential it may be, must have a specifiable cause. Hence, preoperational children will pose lengthy series of questions concerned with events about which adults find it meaningless to ask questions.

It is the second aspect of the replies of preoperational children to inter-rogatives that best illustrates the concept of finalism. When Piaget says that preoperational thinking is "finalistic," he means that it searches for a simple and direct cause for even the most trivial and accidental occur-rences. For Piaget, this fact illustrates the overly assimilative nature of pre-operational concepts of causality. Finalism fails to take account of an important law of reality, a law that underlies modern statistical theory, namely, *some events happen entirely by chance.*

Artificialism. Artificialism is closely related to finalism. It refers to the preoperational child's belief that everything that exists has been speci-fically created either by human beings or by a god who builds things the way people do. The notion of "the way people build things" is critical because people build things in a very special manner—i.e., according to some pre-viously devised plan that we may loosely term a blueprint. The notion of "the way people build things" may be contrasted with scientific laws gov-erning the existence of physical objects (e.g., the laws of entropy and thermodynamics) and the laws governing the evolution of biological organ-isms (e.g., the laws of inheritance and natural selection). In the latter case, there is no assumption of human or divine plans underlying the relevant laws. The laws of science are impersonal, mechanical, and obey the prin-ciples of probability rather than human or divine wishes.

The preoperational concept of artificialism dictates that all reality is manufactured according to the designs of some grand set of blueprints. As was the case for finalism, artificialism implies that no event can occur spon-taneously. Every object or event has a place in the grand blueprint. Piaget gives the following illustration of behaviors that he interprets as evidence of artificialism: "Mountains grow because stones have been manufactured and then planted; lakes have been hollowed out; and for a long time the child believes that cities are built before the lakes adjacent to them" (1967*a*, p. 28). Piaget believes that these examples show that the preoperational child's concept of causality fails to differentiate physical causes from psy-chological ones. In fact, this is the basic meaning of artificialism. To further illustrate this lack of differentiation, note that in each of the preceding examples some *humanlike* action is always an antecedent to the physical event. Stones do not arise spontaneously from geological processes, they are somehow "manufactured" and then "planted" in the ground; lakes do not arise spontaneously because gravitation causes water to collect in low regions, lakes are places that have been explicitly "hollowed out" for the purpose of holding water; cities are not built in certain places because the physical surroundings are pleasing, pleasing physical surroundings arise be-cause men have built cities.

Obviously, preoperational artificialism is implied to a certain extent by finalism. If children are searching for a cause for everything and will not admit chance events, then a certain amount of artificiality in their causal concepts will be an inevitable result. After all, one very simple method of resolving the problem of finding a direct cause for a perplexing event is to assume that all things have a place in some grand blueprint. In the adult world, this sort of artificialism has historically been the stock in trade of priests and mystics.

Animism. Of the three aspects of preoperational causality being considered, animism is far and away the most important historically. While the claim that preoperations are finalistic and artificialistic has provoked virtually no research by workers outside Geneva, the hypothesis that preoperational intelligence is animistic has precipitated an extensive series of investigations which began in the late 1930s and continue to the present. Some of these studies will be mentioned later when we consider replication research. Because the replication literature on animism is substantial, our discussion of animism must be somewhat more detailed than the discussions of finalism and artificialism.

By "animism," Piaget means more or less the same thing that the dictionary means—i.e., preoperational children attribute life to things that are not actually alive. Or, more precisely, they attribute life to things that adults do not believe are alive. Unfortunately, this rather elementary definition raises one horrendous problem. Adults have a habit of disagreeing about what things are and are not alive. Up until the time of the Renaissance, for example, even the most civilized Europeans believed that stones, castles, and ships were alive. Such things were believed to possess a life-giving spirit, called a dryad. The ancient Greeks even thought numbers were alive. From this fact, it is obvious that our definition of life must come from today's adults rather than those of previous generations. But this does not entirely solve the problem. The attribution of life to inanimate objects is still widespread today both in primitive cultures and in developing nations. Even in industrialized nations, the attribution of life to inanimate objects is not uncommon within some educational strata. Thus, to avoid endless confusion, it appears that we shall have to restrict the adult conception of life to well-educated contemporary adults. Presumably, these adults have some acquaintance with the biological definition of living matter.

Piaget (1929) proposed that the development of the child's conception of life consists of four substages. The first two substages occur during the preoperational stage and the last two occur during the concrete-operational stage. For the sake of convenience, we shall discuss all four substages here. During Substage I, the only criterion for life is the effect that an object has on people. As long as the object can do something (anything) that affects people, the object is said to be alive and to possess a will of its own. Examples of common objects that Substage I children believe are alive include bicycles, motor cars, lamps, and stoves. The following excerpt illustrates Substage I animism: "Vel (8:6): 'Is the sun alive? Yes. Why? It gives light. It is alive when it is giving light, but it isn't alive when it is not giving light. Is a gun alive? Yes, it shoots.' Vel even goes so far as to say that poison is alive—'because it can kill us'" (Piaget 1929, p. 196). Note that Vel emphasizes the effects that things have on us as his criterion for life. This emphasis is most apparent in his explanation of why poison is alive.

During Substage II, children restrict their definition of life to objects that are not immobile. To be viewed as living, an object must be capable of moving. It does not have to move by itself. What is important is that movement be one of its normal functions. Of the common inanimate objects cited in the preceding paragraph, bicycles, motor cars, and the sun are considered by the Substage II child to be alive because they all move. (Note that bicycles do not move by themselves.) But, because they do not move, lamps, stoves, guns, and poisons are not considered to be alive. The following excerpt illustrates Substage II animism: "Zimm (8:1): 'Is a stone alive? Yes. Why? It moves. How does it move? By rolling. Is the table alive? No, it can't move.'" (Piaget 1929, p. 199). Piaget also notes that Substage II children begin to attribute consciousness and other mental abilities to objects which they consider to be alive.

During Substage III, children further restrict their definition of life to objects that *move spontaneously* and do not require that human beings do something to get them moving. Thus, bicycles, motor cars, and stones are no longer considered to be living because, in each case, they only move when human beings do something to them. On the other hand, the sun is still considered to be living because it moves without any apparent human intervention. The following excerpt illustrates Substage III animism: "Sart (12:6): 'Is a fly alive? Yes. Why? Because if it wasn't alive it couldn't fly. Is a bicycle alive? No. Why not? Because it is we who make it go. Are streams alive? Yes, because the water is flowing all the time'" (Piaget 1929, p. 202).

During Substage IV, of course, children further restrict their definition of life to objects that adults consider living. More specifically, life is attributed only to plants and animals. In view of what was said at the outset about adult definitions of life, an obvious question arises about the universality of Substage IV behavior. All adults of a few generations ago and even a majority of adults in the present generation do not restrict the definition of life to plants and animals. Therefore, it seems likely that the only children who attain Substage IV are the offspring of "educated adults" of industrial nations. It should be noted that the children Piaget studied were of this sort. They were pupils in an elementary school run by the Rousseau Institute, and most of them were the offspring of university professors, physicians, lawyers, etc. This probably explains why Piaget was able to find clear evidence of Substage IV behavior. If his children had been selected from agrarian or semiliterate populations, it seems extremely unlikely that any Substage IV behavior would have been noted.

language

It will be recalled that Piaget has a rather special definition of language. Most psychologists interpret all vocalizations, even the babbling of infants, as examples of language. According to this view, language development begins when infants emit their first sound. Piaget's definition of language is considerably more restrictive. Importantly, he requires that the capacity for *mental representation* be present before vocalizations may be interpreted as evidence of language. Since, as we saw in Chapter 3, mental representation is not acquired until sensorimotor Substage VI, it is obvious that Piaget does not count language among the cognitive contents of the sensorimotor stage. For him, language is a preoperational acquisition.

As we saw in Chapter 1, Piaget's first book, *The Language and Thought of the Child* (1926a), was concerned with language. Most of the findings reported in this book were based on 1500 statements made by two Genevan schoolchildren who were roughly 6 1/2 years old. Although Piaget's key findings are based primarily on these two children, he also obtained statements from a larger sample of Genevan children between the ages of 2 and 11 years. The most important feature of Piaget's account of preoperational language is his conclusion that it serves two distinct functions, namely, an *egocentric* or private function and a *socialized* or public function. Piaget defines egocentric language as language that is used for purposes of self-stimulation. Egocentric language consists basically of talking to oneself. Negatively defined, egocentric language is language whose aim is not to communicate with others. When they are speaking egocentrically, children either do not speak to anyone in particular or, if they speak to some specific person, they do not seem to care whether that person listens. Recalling the general definition of egocentrism discussed above, egocentric language is not concerned with the listener's point of view and, consequently, egocentric statements are never phrased to take the informational limitations of listeners into account. Piaget views three types of linguistic behavior as signs of egocentrism: (*a*) *monologue*—i.e., talking aloud to oneself for extended periods of time, usually without a listener being present; (*b*) *repetition*—i.e., rehearsing aloud the same statement over and over, either with or without a listener being present; (*c*) *collective monologue*—i.e., holding a conversation with another person but without taking that person's half of the conversation into account. From the standpoint of our earlier definition of egocentrism, linguistic behaviors of the first two types are unmistakably egocentric because they do not even require the presence of another person. Type (*c*) behavior is more difficult. If a child engages in a conversation with another person, how can we tell whether the conversation is a collective monologue or is truly communicative? Piaget suggests a simple test, namely, after the conversation is over ask the child what the other person talked about. If the child is incapable of reporting what the other person said or if she reports that the other person said the same things she did, then the conversation was a dual monologue.

The crucial feature of all egocentric language is that it is not truly communicative, at least not in an interpersonal sense. When they speak egocentrically, preoperational children are not actually trying to communicate with others nor are they trying to solicit communication from others. They are merely talking to themselves. By comparison, socialized language is truly communicative. When speaking socially, preoperational children speak directly to one or more listeners and attempt to communicate with them. They adjust their statements to accomodate listeners' informational limitations, and they explain statements that listeners do not understand. They also listen to what others say, and adjust subsequent statements of their own to reflect the points of view expressed by listeners. Piaget regards statements that attempt to persuade listeners or to provide them with some useful item of information as clear signs of socialized language.

In his original studies, Piaget found that most children's spontaneous verbalizations could be classified as either egocentric or socialized. He reported considerable evidence of egocentric language during the preoperational stage. For the two intensively studied children, he judged roughly 40% of their utterances as clearly egocentric and roughly 45% of their utterances as clearly socialized. It will be recalled that these children's ages fell within the second half of the nominal age range for the preoperational stage (2 to 7 years old). Piaget found much higher percentages of egocentric language in some of the children in his larger sample. Virtually all of the statements of the youngest children were judged to be egocentric, while virtually all of the statements of the oldest children were judged to be socialized. Piaget interpreted these findings as evidence of a gradual shift from egocentric to socialized language during the preoperational stage. When language is first acquired at the onset of this stage, it is entirely egocentric. At this initial level, language is just one of several forms of behavior being used for self-stimulative purposes. Eventually, however, the child discovers that language may also be used to communicate with others. During the middle years of the preoperational stage, egocentric and socialized language exist along side each other. Sometimes children speak for self-stimulative reasons, while at other times they speak for communicative reasons. Near the end of the preoperational stage, egocentric language is suppressed and socialized language comes to dominate. By the beginning of the concrete-operational stage, egocentric language has disappeared almost completely.

Piaget maintains that the shift from egocentric language to socialized language is a symptom of the general waning of egocentrism discussed earlier. This, of course, is a competence hypothesis. Piaget also believes that the evolution of socialized language is dependent upon social interactions with peers and adults. In other words, the gradual acquisition of socialized language and the suppression of egocentric language is supposed to be a function of the social interactions that occur during the preschool years. Later in this chapter, we shall see that this particular explanation is made doubtful by recent research on egocentric and socialized language.

identity

A seemingly universal characteristic of theories of intelligence is that a great deal is made of what I shall call *cognitive invariants.* A cognitive invariant is a concept or idea that helps add stability to the endless flux of reality. Much psychological research in fields such as perception, language, and memory is concerned with cognitive invariants. The field of perception provides some well-known examples. Perceptual psychologists devote considerable research to a class of behaviors that they call perceptual constancies. The general phenomenon is simply stated. There are certain properties of objects that we perceive as constant even though the information about these properties reaching our sense receptors varies greatly from moment to moment. The properties of shape and size are among the simplest examples of perceptual constancy. Concerning the former, the objective shape of the desk at which I am writing is rectangular. But it only *looks* rectangular when I am suspended in midair directly over its center, which I never am. I am usually located either at one side of the desk or at one end. From either of these positions, the desk looks like a trapezoid rather than a rectangle. And yet, if I were asked about the shape of my desk, I should say that it is rectangular even though I invariably see it as trapezoidal. This is an illustration of *shape constancy.* Similarly, an object located six inches from my nose looks much larger than an object several feet away because its projection takes up more space on my retina. As an object moves away from me, its perceived size decreases. From this fact, I can either infer that the object itself is growing smaller, a conclusion favored by the projection on my retina, or I can infer that the object's size remains constant. The latter inference is an example of *size constancy.*

Like other approaches to intelligence, Piaget's theory is concerned with cognitive invariants. During each of his four stages, one or more of the key cognitive contents turns out to be a cognitive invariant. We have already encountered a very important cognitive invariant in the preceding chapter— the sensorimotor object concept. When babies are not in direct perceptual contact with an object, they have no objective grounds for supposing that the object continues to exist. And yet, we saw that they develop a belief in the permanent existence of objects no later than the second year of life and perhaps much earlier. In Chapter 5, we shall encounter another interesting cognitive invariant, namely, the concrete-operational conservation concept. The conservation concept, which is concerned with the maintenance of *quantitative* relationships (e.g., number, length, weight) between objects, is by far the most important cognitive content in Piaget's theory. In this particular chapter, however, our illustrative cognitive invariant is the preoperational concept of identity.

I noted above that perceptual constancies are concerned with the invariance of certain perceived properties of objects. In contrast, Piagetian cognitive invariants are concerned with the invariance of certain *abstract* or *inferred* properties of objects. Psychologists usually call these properties concepts rather than percepts. The conceptual properties of objects fall into two broad categories: (*a*) *qualitative* or *absolute* properties and (*b*) *quantitative* or *relative* properties. Qualitative properties are concerned with differences in kind, whereas quantitative properties are concerned with differences in amount. By virtue of a given qualitative property, an object belongs to a certain class or type of objects. Common examples of such properties include racial type, sexual gender, and species. By virtue of a given quantitative property, an object occupies a position on a certain *dimension* or *continuum*. Common examples of quantitative properties include length, mass, and any other property that involves measurement operations.

The preoperational concept of identity is concerned with the invariance of the "all-or-none" and "yes-or-no" features of objects that we are calling qualitative properties. The identity concept may be precisely defined as follows. Any object consists of a long and perhaps infinite list of properties P_1, P_2, P_3, ... Some of these properties are qualitative and others are quantitative. The identity concept comes into play when we *alter* one or more of these properties. It consists of the inference that unaltered *qualitative* properties remain invariant when other properties are altered. Given some object with the properties P_1, P_2, P_3, ... , suppose we alter some subset P_i, P_j, ... , P_n of these properties. The identity concept refers to the preoperational child's understanding that the other qualtitative properties on the list that were not in the altered set of properties *remain unchanged*. But this definition is rather abstract. Let us consider two simple illustrations of the preoperational identity concept.

First, suppose we show a preoperational child a drawing of a nude female form. The child, when asked to state the sexual gender of the drawing, of course says, "It's a girl." Next, we alter the drawing in some way that is irrelevant to gender. For example, we color the drawing blue or we erase the hair on its head or we draw a beard on its chin. When the alteration is complete, the child is again asked to state the gender of the drawing. If the child asserts that the drawing is still female, Piaget would interpret this as evidence of the presence of the preoperational identity concept. Second, suppose the same child is shown a small dog. The child is asked to state the name of the animal, and the response is "It's a dog." Next, suppose we cover the dog's head with a mask that has the facial features of a cat painted on it. After the mask is in place, the child is again asked to state the name of the animal. If the response is "It's a dog," Piaget would conclude that the identity concept is present. But if the response is "It's a cat," he would conclude that identity concept is absent.

According to Piaget (e.g., 1968), the concept of identity, like animism and egocentrism, evolves gradually during the preoperational stage. At the onset of the stage, children fail most tests of the sort just described. During the middle of the stage, various intermediate reactions are observed. In particular, children will assert that some qualitative properties remain invariant but others do not. Finally, near the end of the preoperational stage, children appear to understand that all qualitative properties remain invariant when other irrelevant properties are altered. But these same children do not yet understand that *quantitative* properties of objects remain invariant when other irrelevant properties are altered. To illustrate, suppose we have a piece of string that is stretched out to its full length. We show the string to a late-preoperational child (say, a five-year-old). After the child has examined the string, we bend it into a circle. To test for the identity concept, we ask the child, "Is this string the same string as before?" Children of this age level normally respond affirmatively. But suppose we also ask the child, "Is this string the same *length* as before?" Surprisingly, children of this age level say no. It is not until the latter half of the concrete-operational stage that they seem to grasp the invariance of quantitative properties.

Replication Studies

We turn now to research on preoperational cognitive contents conducted by investigators outside Geneva. There is some research available on all of the cognitive contents discussed in the preceding section. This research is reviewed in the same order as the cognitive contents were considered above. We shall see that much of it has been concerned with the same issues that prompted some of sensorimotor replication studies discussed in Chapter 3.

egocentrism

Piaget's claim that preoperational children are profoundly egocentric has precipitated considerable replication research in the past few years (e.g., Borke 1971, 1972, 1975, 1977; Chandler and Greenspan 1972; Flavell et al. 1968; Rubin and Maioni 1975). The focus of much of this research has been the same issue that led to some of the object permanence studies reviewed in Chapter 3, namely, performance hypotheses vs. competence hypotheses. According to Piaget's competence interpretation, children fail egocentrism tests such as the mountain problem because they do not yet understand that other people have points of view that differ from their own. Since children below that age of 5 consistently fail such tests, Piaget concludes that they are profoundly egocentric. However, this conclusion does not necessarily follow. It could also be that Piaget's egocentrism tests, like his infant object concept tests, are too difficult for preschool children. In other words, it could be that preschool children are aware that other people have their own unique points of view. But they are simply not as skillful at *communicating* this knowledge as older children and, consequently, they tend to fail complicated perspective-taking tests like the mountain problem. To examine this possibility, we need to devise simpler tests that still measure children's understanding that other people have their own unique points of view.

Borke's findings. Much of the recent research on preoperational egocentrism has been conducted by Helene Borke (1971, 1972, 1973, 1975, 1977). This work is to preoperational egocentrism what T. G. R. Bower's work is to sensorimotor object permanence. The guiding theme of Borke's research is a discrepancy between Piaget's hypothesis that preoperational children are profoundly egocentric and some of the views of the American sociologist George H. Mead (1934) and the American psychiatrist Harry Stack Sullivan (1940). According to Sullivan, infants as young as 6 months are aware that others have emotional experiences that are different than their own. Although Sullivan also believed that the capacity to perceive the feelings of others improves gradually during the infant and preschool years, he maintained that the basic awareness of the existence of other emotional points of view is present as early as 6 months. Mead (1934) argued that the development of the self-concept requires that children be aware of the existence of other points of view from a very early age. For example, Mead believed that children as young as 2 1/2 years can take the role of another child in a game or put themselves in another child's place in a game. Mead reported some anecdotal observations that supported his conclusions.

In her first study, Borke (1971) devised an entirely new procedure for measuring children's awareness of others' points of view. Her subjects were 200 children between the ages of 3 and 8. Each child was tested as follows. First, the child was shown line drawings of four faces depicting the emotional expressions "happy," "sad," "afraid," and "angry." The child was asked to identify the emotional expression on each face. Children who did not know the correct name for the expression on a given face were told the name by the experimenter. Next, the child was read a series of short stories. In each story, there was a central character. Certain things happened to the central character that would make most children feel happy, sad, afraid, or angry (e.g., he ate a favorite food, he lost a favorite toy, he lost his way in the woods at night, he was forced to go to bed when he did not want to). After each story had been read, the child was shown the series of facial drawings and was asked to pick the one that showed what the central character was feeling. Borke's data supported Mead's and Sullivan's views rather than Piaget's. With three of the four types of stories (happy, sad, angry), the youngest children in the sample (3- to 3 1/2-year-olds) selected the correct emotional expression with a frequency much higher than would be expected by chance alone. On the happy stories, 60% of the 3-year-old children responded perfectly on all of the tests. These same children did not perform quite as well on the sad and angry stories, but their performance was still far above chance expectations. On the afraid stories, the 3-year-old children did not perform above chance. However, the next-youngest group of children (3 1/2- to 4-year-olds) and all older children performed far above chance on afraid stories. Borke concluded that these findings "support the hypothesis that the task used to measure interpersonal perception [egocentrism], especially with very young children, significantly influences the child's ability to communicate his awareness of other people's feelings. ... The present results challenge Piaget's position that the child between the ages of 2 and 7 years is primarily egocentric and unable to take another person's point of view. Instead, it is suggested by the data that children as young as 3 years of age are aware that other people have feelings and that these feelings vary according to the situation in which the individual finds himself" (1971, pp. 268–69).

The preceding study was subsequently repeated by Chandler and Greenspan (1972), and their findings agreed with Borke's. In a later study, Borke (1975) investigated Piaget's mountain problem. She observed that previous research on the mountain problem by Flavell et al. (1968) had shown that the number of children who solve the problem varies dramatically as a function of the display laid out on the table. Borke devised a new version of the mountain problem which she administered to 3- and 4-year-olds. In the new problem, children were shown four different displays. One of the displays was used to familiarize the child with the requirements of the task, and the other three displays were used to test for egocentrism. The familiarization problem is shown schematically in Figure 4-1. The display consisted of a large toy fire engine located in the center of a small table. The child was seated at one side of the table. A turntable with a small replica of the fire engine was located on the child's left. The child's attention was drawn to the fire engine on the table. She was told that an imaginary child, Grover, was going to look at the fire engine from different locations around the table. Each time Grover looked at the engine from a different location the child was asked to rotate the turntable on her left so that she saw what Grover saw. After the familiarization problem had been completed, the child was successively shown three more displays. Two of them consisted of toy people, animals, and buildings. One of them consisted of three toy mountains like those used in Piaget's original mountain problem. The testing procedure for each of these three displays was the same as the familiari-

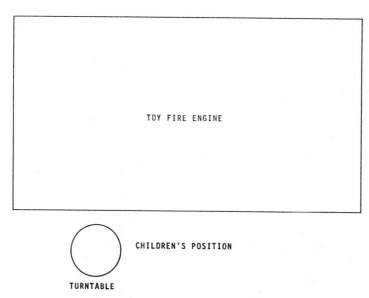

Figure 4-1   Diagram of the familiarization problem used in Borke's (1975) egocentrism experiment. The subject is told that a second, imaginary child is viewing the fire engine from various positions around the table. There is a small replica of the fire engine on the table on the turntable at the subject's left. The subjects's task is to turn the turntable to show what the imaginary child sees from each position around the table.

zation problem—i.e., a miniature version of the display was located on a small turntable on the child's left and the child's task was to rotate the turntable to show what the other child saw. On displays that consisted of toy people, animals, and buildings, Borke found that her subject's responses were very accurate. On one of these displays, 80% of 3-year-old children's responses were correct and, on the other, 79% of 3-year-old children's responses were correct. On the other hand, the frequency of correct responses dropped to 42% with the mountain display. Borke concluded that Piaget's original findings may have resulted from the particular display that he used. Borke also concluded that the high frequencies of correct responses on her new displays "raise considerable doubt about Piaget's conclusion that young children are primarily egocentric and incapable of taking the viewpoint of another person. When presented with tasks that are age appropriate even very young subjects demonstrate perceptual role-taking ability" (1975, p. 243).

Rubin and Maioni's findings. Rubin and Maioni (1975), like Borke, investigated a modified version of Piaget's mountain problem. Also like Borke, they observed a higher frequency of correct responses with their new test than Piaget did with his. Rubin and Maioni's test employed three different displays. First, the child was shown a large box that had pictures of a sailboat, a house, a drum, and a flower, respectively, attached to four of its six sides. The box was placed in the center of a small table. The child sat at one side of the table, and was given a small box with the same four pictures on it. The child was then asked to show what an imaginery person would see from various locations around the table by pointing to the appropriate picture on her own box. Second, a red and white ball was placed in the center of the table. The child was asked to describe what the ball would look like from various locations around the table. Third, a papier-maché village was placed on the table. The child was given a set of materials similar to those on the table and was asked to use these materials to construct models of what the papier-maché village looked like from various locations around the table. Rubin and Maioni administered this test to 3- and 4-year-old children who were pupils of a preschool at the University of Waterloo. Although their test was rather more complicated than Borke's, Rubin and Maioni observed that roughly half of their subjects' responses were correct. This particular value was far above chance expectations.

Summary. In his original studies, Piaget reported, first, that very young children (3-year-olds) almost never solve perspective-taking tests such as the mountain problem and, second, that the frequency of correct responses on perspective-taking tests increases gradually during the preschool and early elementary school years. As usual, Piaget assigned competence interpretations to these findings. Explicitly, he inferred that children are unaware of the existence of other viewpoints at the beginning of the preoperational stage and this awareness emerges very gradually during early childhood through social interaction with peers and adults. However, according to recent research findings, these conclusions do not now seem to be correct. Investigators such as Borke, Chandler and Greenspan, and Rubin and Maioni have found high frequencies of correct responses on perspective-taking tests using 3-year-old subjects. In the absence of alternative explanations, these data suggest that children are very much aware of the existence of other viewpoints even at the beginning of the preoperational stage. The aforementioned investigators have confirmed Piaget's finding that performance on perspective-taking tasks improves between the ages of 3 and 8. However, given that even 3-year-olds probably are aware of the existence of other viewpoints, a new interpretation of this age trend seems to be called for. The most reasonable one appears to be that it reflects an increasing ability to *communicate* one's awareness of the existence of other viewpoints rather than the gradual acquisition of this awareness. This, of course, is a performance hypothesis.

Piaget's early studies of children's casual concepts stimulated considerable research by investigators outside Geneva. Nearly all of the research has been concerned with childhood animism. In fact, only Laurendeau and Pinard (1962) have undertaken a systematic replication of all of Piaget's findings on children's causal concepts. For this reason, we shall examine only animism research in this section.

Although some research on childhood animism was published during the past decade (e.g., King 1961; Looft and Charles 1969), most of the available studies were published during the 1930s, 1940s, and 1950s. Although interest in animism all but disappeared during the late 1950s, animism research was an especially lively topic during the 1930s and 1940s. Much of this research was prompted by an early study published by Johnson and Josey (1931–32). In his original research, Piaget (1929) claimed that young children were profoundly animistic, but he failed to provide any supporting quantitative data. In particular, he failed to report the exact percentages of animistic responses given by children of different age levels. The lack of quantitative information led Johnson and Josey to undertake their replication. They questioned a sample of 6-year-olds about their conceptions of life using Piaget's clinical method. However, they found no evidence of animism in their subjects.

Dennis and Russell's studies. The names which loom largest in the animism research of the 1930s and 1940s were Wayne Dennis and Roger Wolcott Russell. Beginning with an early paper by Dennis (1938), Dennis and Russell made extensive contributions which spanned three decades. Among other things, Dennis and Russell sought to discover whether certain objectionable features of Piaget's questioning procedures could have produced the high levels of animism that he observed in young children. For example, many of the questions Piaget asked appeared to be *leading* ones that may have suggested animistic replies to children. Dennis and Russell developed a standardized questioning procedure. Their main improvements over Piaget's clinical procedure were, first, exactly the same questions were posed to each subject, second, the concrete objects that the questions referred to were the same for each subject, and third, there was an objective scoring procedure for assigning each reply to one of Piaget's four stages of animism. The complete standardized procedure was first reported in 1939 (Russell and Dennis 1939). The procedure was then used in several follow-up studies.

Dennis and Russell's animism test may be summarized as follows. For each question on the test, the subject first is shown a concrete object of some sort (e.g., a wristwatch). The subject is then asked whether the object is living or dead. If the subject says that the object is dead because it is not moving, the experimenter moves the object and asks whether it was alive when it was moving. If the subject says that the object was alive when it was moving, the experimenter also asks whether objects must move spontaneously to be considered alive. During the course of their many studies, Dennis and Russell administered this test to several hundred American school children and adults (e.g., Russell 1940, 1942). Two findings emerged from these studies which are consistent with Piaget's views. First, unlike Johnson and Josey (1931–32), Dennis and Russell reported that the attribution of life to inanimate objects was common among the children they tested. Second, the criteria these children used to declare things alive or dead tended to change with age in the manner reported by Piaget. At first, anything that is useful was said to be alive; second, anything that moved was said to be alive; third, anything that moves spontaneously was said to be alive; finally, only plants and animals were said to be alive. On these points, Dennis and Russell's investigations agree with Piaget's.

Two other findings from the Dennis-Russell studies failed to support Piaget's model of animism. The first and most important of these concerns the persistance of animism into adolescence and beyond. It will be recalled that Piaget believes that most children attain Substage IV by the end of the concrete-operational stage (roughly age 11 or 12). However, Dennis and Russell found that although animism decreased as their subjects got older, even their oldest subjects continued to attribute life to many inanimate objects. The clearest evidence of the persistence of animism beyond childhood came from a study using older adults (Dennis and Mallinger 1949). In this study, the animism test was administered to a group of 70-year-old subjects. The great majority of these subjects (75%) said that at least some of the inanimate objects on the test were alive. A second finding from the Dennis-Russell studies that tends to contradict Piaget's model of animism concerns *stage mixture*. In Piaget's model, children are supposed to pass through the four substages in an invariant order, and they are supposed to use a different set of criteria for life during each substage. However, Dennis and Russell found that children typically use criteria from more than one stage rather than from a single stage. For example, a given child may say that a wristwatch is alive because it helps us tell time (Substage I) and she may also say that the sun is alive because it is capable of spontaneous movement (Substage III).

Other animism studies. Several other investigators have verified Dennis and Russell's finding that animism persists into adolescence and beyond. In a review of animism research, Looft and Bartz (1969) concluded that between 50% and 75% of adult subjects may be expected to attribute life to inanimate objects. In view of what I said earlier about cultural and historical differences in the concept of life, this finding is not too surprising. The existence of these cultural and historical differences also suggests a reasonable explanation of adult animism which would allow us to save Piaget's model: Adults who attribute life to inanimate objects are simply ignorant of the appropriate scientific criteria for living matter. If they knew these criteria, then they presumably would not give animistic responses. Unfortunately, this very simple explanation is not confirmed by the available data. One way to test the explanation is to measure animism in university students. These subjects are highly educated and may be assumed to be aware of the biological definition of life. Several animism studies with college students have been published (e.g., Bell 1954; Crannell 1954; Crowell and Dole 1957; Lowrie 1954; Simmons and Goss 1957; Voeks 1954). In all of these studies, large proportions of the subjects attributed life to inanimate objects. In fact, the exact percentages of university students who attributed life to inanimate objects were not much smaller than the corresponding percentages for less-educated adults. A second way to test the explanation is to train subjects on the appropriate criteria for life and *then* measure animism. Lowrie (1954) conducted an experiment of this sort. He gave university students a series of lectures that carefully delineated the distinction between living and nonliving matter. During the course of these lectures, the subjects were informed of several unique properties of living matter (e.g., it grows, it reproduces). After the lectures had been completed, an animism test was administered. The students still attributed life to many inanimate objects.

Interpretation. In brief, investigators outside Geneva have confirmed Piaget's original finding that young children attribute life to inanimate objects and that the frequency of these animistic responses decreases with increasing age. They have also confirmed Piaget's finding that the stated reasons for declaring objects living or dead change as children grow older. However, investigators outside Geneva have found that children typically state reasons from more than one animism substage and that animism persists into adolescence and adulthood. From the standpoint of Piaget's model of animism, both findings are problematical. The fact that a given child invokes criteria for life belonging to different substages appears inconsistent with Piaget's hypothesis that children pass through the substages in an immutable order. The fact that animism persists in adults, even in highly educated ones, appears inconsistent with Piaget's hypothesis that Substage IV is attained by the beginning of adolescence. Satisfactory explanations of these two facts, which would allow us to retain Piaget's model, have not yet been given. Concerning the persistence of animism into adulthood, several writers have attempted to reconcile Piaget's model with adult animism by arguing that the animism of adults has a different meaning than the animism of children (e.g., Laurendeau and Pinard 1962, Chap. 3; Looft and Bartz 1969, pp. 13–14). According to this argument, the underlying causes of animism are different in adults and children. At present, however, this explanation is strictly ad hoc. We do not know enough about the underlying causes of animism in either adults or children to say that the causes are different. Hence, no one has been able to put this explanation to the test as yet. For my part, I prefer to believe that if Piaget's model is correct, then adult animism must be primarily a reflection of ignorance of the biological criteria for life. This leads me to expect that further training experiments such as Lowrie's (1954) might eventually show that adult animism can be reduced to negligible levels by, first, carefully training them on biological criteria for life and, second, carefully training them on how to apply these criteria to the objects used on animism tests.

language

Piaget's (1926*a*) claim that the language of very young children is almost entirely egocentric has stimulated a considerable amount of replication research and four decades of theoretical controversy. The first replication studies began to appear during the 1930s and others are still being conducted today. Excellent scholarly reviews of research on egocentric and socialized language have been written by several authors. Dorothea McCarthy (1954) published a review of research conducted during the 1930s and 1940s. Reviews of research conducted during the 1950s and 1960s have been published by Flavell et al. (1968), by Kohlberg, Yeager, and Hjertholm (1968), and by Looft (1972). Insofar as Piagetian theory is concerned, the key finding from this research is that it shows more or less the same thing as the research on perspective-taking tasks examined earlier. Therefore, the present discussion of this research will be brief. We begin with a brief overview of the salient issues and the results of early studies. We conclude with a summary of the procedures and findings of a recent illustrative experiment by Garvey and Hogan (1973).

Early studies. It will be recalled that Piaget believes that language is profoundly egocentric at the beginning of the preoperational stage. Very young children are supposed to use language primarily for self-stimulative purposes. Their utterances are directed toward themselves and are not intended to communicate with other people. Piaget reported that as much as 70% of young children's utterances are egocentric. These views prompted Dorothea McCarthy to undertake the earliest replication study. McCarthy's subjects were 140 children between the ages of 1 1/2 and 4 1/2. A total of 20 children were included from each six-month age interval. McCarthy obtained fifty spontaneous utterances from each of her subjects. She then used the criteria discussed by Piaget (e.g., monologue, repetition, collective monologue) to classify her subject's utterances as egocentric or socialized. She found no support for Piaget's claim that young children's language is highly egocentric. Depending on the subject's age, the proportion of utterances classified as egocentric varied between roughly 1 1/2% and roughly 6 1/2%. The average proportion of utterances classified as egocentric was 3 1/2% for the entire sample of 140 children. For all intents and purposes, therefore, these utterances were entirely socialized and communicative. Since the ages of all of McCarthy's subjects fell within the first half of the nominal age range for the preoperational stage, her results are obviously inconsistent with Piaget's account of preoperational language.

Later studies by other investigators (e.g., Smith 1935; Weir 1962) have found much larger percentages of egocentric utterances than McCarthy observed. In line with Piaget's original research, these studies have found that the frequency of egocentric utterances decreases with increasing age (e.g., Glucksberg and Krauss 1967). A number of situational and demographic variables have been shown to affect the observed proportion of egocentric utterances. For example, lower-class children make more extensive use of egocentric language than middle-class children (e.g., Cowan 1967). The frequency of egocentric utterances also has been observed to decrease as children become more familiar with their listeners and as they become more familiar with the social situation in which language is measured (e.g., Cazden 1970). There now appears to be a consensus among language researchers that (*a*) a substantial proportion of young children's utterances are truly egocentric and (*b*) the frequency of egocentric utterances decreases during the preschool and early elementary school years (Looft 1972).

From our standpoint, the crucial fact which has emerged from all the research on egocentric and socialized language is this: Although different percentages of egocentric language have been reported by different investigators and although these percentages vary as a function of demographic and situational factors, *the observed proportion of egocentric utterances never reaches 50% in even the very youngest subjects.* Contrary to Piaget's original studies, egocentric language apparently never predominates in children's speech. This is an extremely important finding because it suggests that, from the beginning of the preoperational stage, the primary aim of children's language is to communicate with other people. As one Piaget expert, Hans G. Furth, has put it "No normal child at any period of development uses language primarily for purposes of self-communication" (1969, p. 118). Although this conclusion is inconsistent with Piaget's belief that preoperational intelligence is egocentric, the reader should note that it *is not* consistent with our earlier discussion of preoperational children's performance on perspective-taking tasks such as the mountain problem. We saw that research on such tasks has shown that even 3-year-olds are well aware of the existence of other people's points of view.

Garvey and Hogan's study. To make the preceding remarks more concrete, let us conclude our brief examination of research on egocentric language by reviewing a recent experiment reported by Garvey and Hogan (1973). The subjects were eighteen 3- and 4-year-old children. The children were studied in pairs. Each pair of children was placed in a room containing several toys that they could play with (e.g., telephones, stuffed animals, wooden blocks). The children were left alone in the playroom for fifteen minutes, and their activity was video taped. After all the children had been video taped, the tapes were reviewed and the children's verbalizations were transcribed for scoring. Each child's verbalizations were divided into *utterance units*. An utterance unit was defined as any sample of speech interrupted either by pauses of greater than one second by the speaker or by speech from the listener. Each of these units was then classified as egocentric or socialized. To be classified as socialized, a unit had to be judged to be specifically adapted to the speech or nonverbal behavior of the listener. Generally speaking, a unit was considered an example of socialized language if it served to elicit some specific behavior from the listener or to convey some piece of information to the listener. Garvey and Hogan reported that their subjects talked quite freely during their fifteen-minute sessions. On the average, the utterance rate was one utterance unit every 4.6 seconds. In line with my earlier remarks, Garvey and Hogan observed that socialized language predominated in their subjects. The mean proportion of utterances judged to be socialized was 59% for the entire sample. These utterances also were observed to increase with age. The mean proportion of socialized utterances ranged from 21% to 64% for 3-year-olds and from 48% to 77% for 4-year-olds. Thus, even the youngest subjects spent considerable time engaged in communicative conversation. Garvey and Hogan concluded "that the children were mutually engaged the majority of the time and that most of their utterances were mutually responsive, that is, adapted to the speech or nonverbal behavior of their partner. Social speech, as defined here, appeared in abundance, and all dyads were able to sustain mutually responsive speech beyond simple exchanges. Furthermore, both younger and older dyads used a conventionalized series of verbal moves to create a state of mutual involvement (1973, p. 567)."

identity

Since Piaget's discussions of identity are very recent, there has not yet been time for a substantial replication literature to accumulate. However, two reasonably comprehensive studies of this cognitive content are available (DeVries 1969; Brainerd 1977a). The nominal aim of both studies was to determine whether Piaget's claim that the identity concept belongs to the preoperational stage could be verified. In this section, these two studies are reviewed in some detail. In Chapter 5 we shall consider some further studies concerned with the part played by identity in the concrete-operational conservation concept.

DeVries' study. It will be recalled that the identity concept is concerned with children's understanding of qualitative invariance. Specifically, it is concerned with children's understanding that qualitative attributes of objects (color, sex, shape, etc.) remain constant when other irrelevant attributes are altered. According to Piaget, this understanding evolves during the preoperational stage. De Vries (1969) was the first investigator to examine this claim. She studied the development of *generic identity* in sixty-four children between the ages of 3 and 6. Generic identity refers to children's understanding that an animal's *species* does not change when some of the features of its appearance are altered. De Vries reasoned that if identity belongs to the preoperational stage, as Piaget maintains, then children's grasp of generic identity should gradually improve between the ages of 3 and 6.

De Vries constructed an ingenious test for generic identity. The test made use of a live animal—a trained black cat named Maynard. The test also made use of two realistic masks made of rubber and monkey fur which could be fitted over the cat's head. One of the masks was designed to resemble the head of a dog. The other was designed to resemble the head of a rabbit. To measure the generic identity concept, De Vries divided her sixty-four subjects into three testing conditions. Condition 1 involved a cat-to-dog transformation. To begin with, each child in this condition was shown the black cat and was asked to state the animal's name. Next, the experimenter fitted the dog mask on the cat's head. After the masking was complete, the experimenter placed the animal in front of the child and said, "Look, now it has a face like a dog. What is this animal now?" Further questions were posed to determine whether the child thought that the animal was a dog or a cat. (Can it bark? Would it rather eat dog food or cat food? Would it rather play with a dog or a cat?) Finally, the mask was removed and the child was again questioned about the animal's generic identity. Condition 2 involved a cat-to-rabbit transformation. The procedure for Condition 2 was the same as for Condition 1, except that the rabbit mask rather than the dog mask was placed over the cat's head. Condition 3 involved a dog-to-cat transformation. The procedure for Condition 3 was the reverse of the procedure for Condition 1. The child was first shown the cat with the dog mask already in place. After the child had identified the animal as a dog, the mask was removed and the child was questioned about the animal's generic identity. The dog mask was then replaced on the cat's head and the generic identity questions repeated.

On the whole, De Vries' results were consistent with Piaget's hypothesis that the identity concept is acquired during the preoperational stage. De

Vries found that children's performance on her test gradually improved between the ages of 3 and 6. The youngest children in her sample usually concluded that masking transformations altered the animal's generic identity, whereas the oldest children usually were not deceived. Detailed analysis of the children's responses revealed six specific levels in the development of generic identity. At the first and most primitive level, there is no evidence identity—i.e., the animal's generic identity is said to change whenever a mask is fitted or removed. At the second level children *predict* constancy of generic identity before masking transformations, but they revert to nonconstancy following transformations. Children functioning at both of these first two levels believe that the posttransformational animal is *entirely different* than the pretransformational animal. At the third level, children assert that the animal's physical substance remains the same after masking transformations. However, they still believe the animal's generic identity has changed. At the fourth level, only the animal's name is believed to change after masking transformations. At the fifth level, children usually assert that generic identity remains constant when a mask is fitted or removed. However, they still admit the remote possibility that generic identity might change under certain magical circumstances. Finally, at the sixth level, children believe that an animal's generic identity must always remain constant.

There is an important shortcoming in De Vries' research, namely, she did not include any additional tests to determine her subjects' stage of cognitive development. Since the nominal age range given by Piaget for the preoperational stage is 2 to 7 years old, it was simply assumed that the subjects were preoperational. However, this assumption is problematical. The age ranges for Piaget's stages are only rough guidelines. Within the specified age range for any given stage, a substantial percentage of children will presumably be functioning at earlier or later stages. Within the age range for preoperations, for example, many 2-year-olds will still be functioning at the sensorimotor level while many 5- and 6-year-olds will already have made the transition to the concrete-operational stage. The latter fact poses interpretational difficulties for De Vries' research. It is possible that those particular subjects in her sample who achieved the highest level on the generic identity test *had already made the transition to concrete operations.* If so, then identity is a concrete-operational cognitive content rather than a preoperational one. To explore this possibility, it is necessary to compare children's performance on identity tests with their performance on tests for selected concrete-operational cognitive contents.

Brainerd's study. I now summarize a recent experiment conducted in my own laboratories (Brainerd 1977*a*) that also dealt with whether identity belongs to the preoperational stage or the concrete-operational stage. Children's performance on identity tests was compared with their performance on tests for three cognitive contents from the concrete-operational stage: (*a*) quantitative invariance, (*b*) inversion reversibility, and (*c*) compensation reversibility. Concerning (*a*), it will be recalled from our earlier discussion of identity that Piaget contends that children understand that an object's *qualitative* properties remain invariant during the preoperational stage, but they do not understand that an object's *quantitative* properties remain invariant until the concrete-operational stage. Hence, if we administer an identity (qualitative invariance) test and a quantitative invariance test to a group of children, we should find that our subjects pass the former test before they pass the latter test. Concerning (*b*) and (*c*), it will be recalled from our earlier discussion of mental operations that concrete-operational reasoning is supposed to be rule-governed. Specifically, children are supposed to grasp two rules, inversion reversibility and compensation reversibility, during the concrete-operational stage that they do not understand during the preoperational stage. Therefore, if tests of identity, inversion, and compensation are administered to a group of children, we should find that the first test invariably is passed before the latter two tests.

To evaluate these predictions, tests of identity, quantitative invariance, inversion, and compensation were administered to 188 5- and 6-year-old children. This particular age level was selected because although it falls within the latter half of the nominal range for preoperations, many children will already have made the transition to concrete operations. Hence, the 5- to 6-year-old range should contain an optimal mixture of preoperational and concrete-operational children. The four tests made use of the same stimulus materials. In fact, the four tests were virtually identical except for the questions that were posed. The tests were precisely equated in this manner to eliminate the possibility that the observed order in which children passed them could be attributed to trivial differences in stimulus materials. The materials for each test consisted of two glasses. One glass was a *standard* or *referent* glass while the other was a *nonstandard* or *variable* glass. The referent glass was 25 centimeters high and 9 centimeters in diameter. The variable glass was the same height as the referent glass, but it was of a considerably different diameter (6 centimeters on some tests and 12 centimeters on others). On each of the four tests, the experimenter placed the referent and variable glasses in front of the subject and filled the referent glass half full of water. On the identity test, the experimenter poured the contents of the referent glass into the variable glass and asked the subject whether the water in the variable glass was the "same water" as the referent glass had contained. The quantitative invariance test was the same as the identity test except that the experimenter asked the subject whether the water in the variable glass was the "same amount of water" as the referent glass had contained. The inversion test was the same as the identity and quantitative invariance tests except that the subject was asked to predict what the height of the water would be if the contents of the variable glass were poured back into the referent glass. Finally, the compensation test was the reverse of the inversion test. The water in the referent glass was never poured into the variable glass. Instead, the subject was asked to predict what the height of the water would be if the contents of the referent glass were poured into the variable glass.

There were three major findings. First, it did not appear that children understood the identity concept before age 5 or 6. Less than half of the youngest subjects in the sample passed the identity test. This particular result is consistent with De Vries' finding that only her oldest children attained the highest level of performance on the generic identity test. Second, Piaget's prediction that children understand identity before quantitative invariance was confirmed. Only 75 of the 105 subjects who passed the identity test also passed the quantitative invariance test, but 83 of the 91 subjects who passed the quantitative invariance test also passed the identity test. Third, Piaget's prediction that children understand identity before either inversion or compensation was disconfirmed. Concerning inversion, the children clearly understood this reversibility rule *before* they understood identity. Only 106 of the 163 subjects who passed the inversion test also passed the identity test, but 113 of the 122 subjects who passed the identity test also passed the inversion test. In other words, if a subject passed the inversion test, it was 93% certain that he would also pass the identity test. But if a subject passed the identity test, it was only 65% certain that he would also pass the inversion test. While the subjects understood inversion before identity, they seemed to grasp identity and compensation at about the same time: Of the 105 subjects who passed the identity test, 77 also passed the compensation test; of the 104 subjects who passed the compensation test, 77 also passed the identity test.

Implications of findings. To conclude our discussion of identity research, let us briefly consider the implications of the findings for Piaget's views on identity. As with children's life concepts but in contrast to their use of socialized language and their perspective-taking skills, it appears that the average preschooler is unaware that objects' qualitative properties remain invariant across irrelevant alterations. De Vries' findings and my own both suggest that children are unaware of this fact until roughly age 5 or 6. In addition, my findings show that children grasp identity before quantitative invariance. All of these results are consistent with Piaget's hypothesis that identity belongs to the preoperational stage. However, they do not prove the hypothesis. It still could be that the identity concept, like the life concept, develops more slowly than Piaget believes. This conjecture is supported by the fact children do not seem to understand identity until after they understand inversion and about the same time as they understand compensation. Since the inversion and compensation rules are concrete-operational cognitive contents, the hypothesis that identity is a preoperational concept may not be correct. The best guess that can be made on the basis of available evidence is that identity, like inversion and compensation, is an *early concrete-operational acquisition* rather than a late preoperational acquisition.

Synopsis

The preoperational stages runs from roughly age 2 to age 7. Piaget scholars disagree about whether this age range does, in fact, qualify as a separate stage of cognitive development. This disagreement is due in large measure to the fact that preoperations are frequently defined as the absence of concrete operations.

The concept of "operation" is probably the most unique feature of Piaget's view of intelligence. The acquisition of operations is the central goal of cognitive development. Operations have four defining characteristics. First, they are symbolic representations—i.e., they are "mental" events. Second, they originate in motor activity. Third, they obey certain logical rules, especially the reversibility rules of inversion and compensation. Fourth, they always gather together in tightly integrated systems called structures of the whole. The connections between operations in such systems resemble the connections between the parts of bodily systems. Therefore, in sum, an operation is an internally represented action that obeys specified logical rules and is part of some larger system of operations. When intelligence is governed by operations, Piaget says that it is *logical*. By this he means that operations do not generate internal contradictions. When intelligence is not governed by operations, Piaget says that it is *infralogical* because contradictions occur regularly.

Preoperational intelligence is usually described as rigid, inflexible, incapable of deduction, and as being unconcerned with relations among different events. Piaget uses the word *figurative* to denote these aspects of preoperations.

Enormous environmental changes occur during the early childhood years. Piaget is less concerned with these changes than are other theorists. He tends to be more interested in what is going on inside the child than in what is going on around him. He believes that the basic structure of development is fixed and cannot be altered by environmental influences. It is claimed that such influences can affect the rate of development but not its form.

The four major cognitive contents of the preoperational stage are egocentrism, causality concepts, language, and identity. These are the contents on which the most data are available. Egocentrism has played an important role in Piaget's theory since the 1920s. According to the law of decentration, egocentrism decreases as development proceeds. Evidence of egocentric thinking during the preoperational stage comes primarily from perspective-taking tests such as the mountain problem. Piaget reports that preoperational children have difficulty on such tests because they cannot take the point of view of another person. Three stages are proposed. First, very young children do not even understand that there are viewpoints other than their own. Second, somewhat older children understand that other viewpoints exist, but they cannot say precisely what they are. Third, still older children can readily identify others' viewpoints.

Preoperational causal concepts contain some surprising ideas about how the world is put together. They are characterized by finalism, artificialism, and animism. Finalism refers to an inability to separate causes from effects. It also refers to the fact that preoperational children do not acknowledge the existence of chance events. Artificialism is the belief that everything, including geological details of the physical environment, is constructed according to blueprints. The third aspect of causal concepts, animism, is historically the most important. Piaget's ideas about animism have provoked considerable research by investigators outside Geneva. By "animism," Piaget means the attribution of life to inanimate objects. Four substages are posited. During Substage I, anything that affects people is considered alive. During Substage II, life is restricted to objects capable of movement. During Substage III, life is further restricted to objects capable of spontaneous movement. During Substage IV, the biological definition of life is adopted.

Concerning language, Piaget maintains that language requires mental representation and, hence, is absent during the sensorimotor stage. The babbling of infants does not count as language. Language first appears during the preoperational stage. It serves two functions, namely, an egocentric (or "self-stimulating") function and a socialized (or "communicative") function. Three types of verbal behavior are interpreted as signs of egocentric language: monologue, collective monologue, and repetition. Language is said to be primarily egocentric at the outset of the preoperational stage. However, socialized language comes to predominate as the child approaches the concrete-operational stage. The crucial point about egocentric language is that it is not intended to communicate with others. The shift from egocentric to socialized language during the preoperational stage is viewed as a symptom of the general waning of egocentrism that occurs during this time of life.

Identity is a cognitive invariant. Cognitive invariants are concepts that lend stability to our ever-changing environments. Simple perceptual constancies dealing with size and shape are classic examples. The preoperational identity concept is an extension of the sensorimotor concept of object permanence. It maintains the invariance of *qualitative* properties (gender, species, etc.) of objects in the face of irrelevant transformations. The concept of identity is said to develop gradually. At the outset of the preoperational stage, it is absent. During the middle of the stage, the child maintains the invariance of some qualitative properties of objects but not others. By the end of the stage, children understand that all qualitative properties remain invariant when other irrelevant properties are altered.

Replication research. The claim that preoperational children, at least in the beginning, do not understand that there are points of view other than their own has been the focus of considerable experimentation in recent years. This research makes use of perspective-taking tasks that resemble Piaget's mountain problem. Some investigators, in particular Helene Borke, have argued that children's poor performance on the mountain probably is caused by performance factors rather than egocentrism. According to this argument, preoperational children are aware of the existence of other viewpoints but they are not very skillful when it comes to communicating this awareness. The recent evidence, though by no means conclusive, seems to favor this performance interpretation over Piaget's competence hypothesis. In a series of experiments, Borke has found consistent evidence of perspective-taking ability in children as young as age 3. The key feature of Borke's perspective-taking tasks, as compared to the mountain problem, is that they make it easier for children to communicate their awareness of the existence of other viewpoints. Some of Borke's findings have been replicated in other laboratories. Rubin and Maioni (1975), using different tasks than Borke, also found evidence of perspective-taking ability in 3-year-olds.

The first replication studies on animism were published in the early 1930s. An initial study by Johnson and Josey (1931–32) created some controversy because it failed to find evidence of animism in children. However, a series of follow-up studies by Russell and Dennis produced more positive findings. Russell and Dennis replaced Piaget's clinical interview with a standardized questionnaire concerned with everyday objects. When this questionnaire was administered to children, animistic responses were common. Moreover, children tended to rely on the same criteria for life that Piaget had originally reported. Although these findings supported Piaget's views, others did not. Russell and Dennis obtained no evidence of distinct animism substages. Typically, a given subject would rely on criteria from two or more substages. Russell and Dennis were also unable to confirm the existence of Substage IV. The great majority of older subjects, even adults, routinely attributed life to inanimate objects. This finding has been replicated by so many other investigators that there now seems little doubt that animism persists into adulthood. A high incidence of animistic responses is even observed in college students who are familiar with the biological criteria for life. Some writers have attempted to reconcile these data with Piagetian theory but, so far, available explanations are all ad hoc.

Piaget's views on language, like his views on animism, have been the subject of replication experiments since the early 1930s. The early replication work was dominated by Dorothea McCarthy's research. McCarthy classified the spontaneous utterances of preschool children as "egocentric" and "socialized" according to the same criteria used by Piaget. At all age levels, she found that the percentage of egocentric utterances averaged less than 10%. Other investigators failed to confirm this low estimate. Most subsequent studies have found much higher percentages of egocentric speech. They have also shown that the proportion of egocentric utterances decreases with age. These findings tend to support Piaget's views, but others do not. Importantly, although the observed percentage of egocentric language is usually higher than McCarthy's values, investigators have repeatedly observed that this percentage never exceeds 50% in even the youngest subjects. The fact that egocentric utterances never predominate in children's language has prompted some investigators to conclude that language never serves a primarily self-stimulating function and, instead, communication is always paramount. Therefore, while Piaget's claim that preoperational children use egocentric language has been verified, his hypothesis that language originates as a purely self-stimulative ability is open to serious doubt.

The volume of replication research on identity is small in comparison with that on egocentrism, animism, and language. The most detailed findings appear in a monograph by DeVries (1969). DeVries studied the development of generic identity in 3- to 6-year-olds. The results supported Piaget's hypothesis that identity develops during the preoperational stage. There was no evidence of identity in the youngest subjects. Somewhat older children predicted identity prior to a physical transformation, but they immediately reverted to nonidentity when the transformation was performed. The oldest subjects maintained identity both before and after physical transformations. The results of another investigation of identity (Brainerd 1977*a*) were less supportive of Piaget's claims. Tests of identity and the concrete-operational reversibility rules were administered to 5- and 6-year-olds. In line with Piaget's hypothesis that identity develops during the preoperational stage, it did not appear that children could pass the identity test before age 5 or 6. But contrary to the same hypothesis, the subjects understood the inversion rule before they understood identity and they understood the compensation rule at the same time as they understood identity.

Supplementary Readings

The recommended readings which follow are research-oriented books and papers dealing with individual preoperational contents.

1. BINGHAM-NEWMAN, and HOOPER, "Classification and Seriation Instruction and Logical Task Performance in the Preschool," (1974); BRAINERD, "Structures-of-the-whole and Elementary Education" (1975a); BINGHAM-NEWMAN and HOOPER, "The Search for the Woozle Circa 1975: Commentary on Brainerd's Observation," (1975); and BRAINERD, "Rejoinder to Bingham-Newman and Hooper," (1975b). These papers are an integrated discussion and analysis of the research implications of the structures-of-the-whole property of mental operations. Of particular interest is the fact that the authors were able to deduce conflicting empirical predictions from structures of the whole.

2. BORKE, "Piaget's View of Social Interaction and the Theoretical Construct of Empathy" (1977). Borke analyzes Piaget's claims about egocentrism and discusses the implications of her own series of experiments in this chapter.

3. DEVRIES, "Constancy of Generic Identity in the Years Three to Six" (1969). DeVries' monograph offers the most comprehensive analysis of the identity concept of any source currently available.

4. FLAVELL et al., *The Development of Role-taking and Communication Skills* (1968). This book is widely regarded as a classic in the study of egocentric behavior in children. In addition to new findings on perspective-taking tasks, it also presents a review of previous egocentrism research.

5. LAURENDEAU and PINARD, *Causal Thinking in the Child* (1962). The Laurendeau-Pinard project is the only known attempt to replicate all aspects of Piaget's causality research. The early chapters provide an overview of Piaget's hypotheses and a review of previous research.

6. LOOFT, "Egocentrism and Social Interaction Across the Life Span" (1972). This paper is a scholarly review of egocentrism research concerned with both language and perspective-taking tasks. It is somewhat more up-to-date than the review in Reading 4.

7. LOOFT and BARTZ, "Animism Revived" (1969). Looft and Bartz' paper appears to be the only comprehensive review of animism research from the 1930s to the present. Since very little animism research has been published since this paper was written, it is still very timely.

chapter 5

Piaget on Middle Childhood: The Concrete-Operational Stage

While, as we have noted, developmental psychologists agree that the preoperational stage is the Piagetian epoch on which the least information is available, exactly the reverse is true of the concrete-operational stage. Here there is a real information glut. To begin with, the vast majority of Piaget's own works are concerned in one way or another with this stage. A representative sample of these works might include *The Child's Conception of Movement and Speed* (Piaget 1971*a*), *The Child's Conception of Number* (Piaget 1952*a*), *The Child's Conception of Geometry* (Piaget, Inhelder, and Szeminska 1960), *The Child's Conception of Space* (Piaget and Inhelder 1956), *The Child's Conception of Time* (Piaget 1971*b*), *The Early Growth of Logic in the Child* (Inhelder and Piaget 1964), *Memory and Intelligence* (Piaget and Inhelder 1973), *Mental Imagery in the Child* (Piaget and Inhelder 1972), and *On the Development of Memory and Identity* (Piaget 1968). And this is only a sample!

Furthermore, most of the research on Piaget's theory conducted by investigators outside Geneva deals with cognitive contents belonging to the concrete-operational stage. And there is an enormous amount of it. At present, journals that publish research on the psychological development of children receive more papers on the concrete-operational stage than on any other subject. In fact, the editors of one of these journals, *Child Development,* have reported that papers concerned with just one concrete-operational cognitive content, the conservation concept, far out number papers submitted on any other topic!

For these reasons, the available information on the concrete-operational stage long ago exceeded the capacity of any one person to comprehend it. I seriously doubt that it is possible for anyone to digest all the information available in the English language alone. The present chapter is, therefore, extremely selective. Only a very small proportion of the total range of concrete-operational contents is examined.

Although it has been necessary to be selective, my grounds for including some things and excluding others were not entirely arbitrary. First, cognitive contents that appear in Piaget's own works on the concrete-operational stage may, for the sake of argument, be divided into two categories: (*a*) "classic" contents and (*b*) "nonclassic" contents. The contents in category (*a*) were introduced long ago in the books that Piaget wrote around the time of World War II. These contents are the ones that are always discussed in Piaget's summary works (e.g., Piaget 1950, 1967*a*; Piaget and Inhelder 1969). Consequently, they appear to be the ones he considers most important and the ones on which the theory must stand or fall. Category (*a*) includes elementary concepts of arithmetic (e.g., number), logic (e.g., relations and classes), and the physical sciences (e.g., conservation laws and space). Since category (*a*) contents have been available for so long, there had been sufficient time for adequate replication literatures to accumulate. This is crucial because, as we have seen on previous occasions, the anomolies of Piaget's methods of doing research make it essential that the replicability of his findings be established. Category (*b*) contents appear in the more recent series of works mentioned at the end of Chapter 1. In these works, it will be recalled, Piaget is attempting to bridge the gap between his own views on intelligence and more traditional approaches. The contents discussed in these works include such familiar variables as imagery, learning, memory, and perception. Since category (*b*) contents have been around for a relatively short period, there has not yet been time for much replication research to accumulate. Therefore, we do not yet know which of Piaget's findings can and cannot be replicated. Also, these contents are not discussed in Piaget's summary works.

In this chapter, category (*b*) contents have been largely excluded. Some of them are growing tips of research, and a few interesting findings have been reported. But, at present, there is not enough replication research available to justify including them in this book. There is one important exception to this rule: learning. Although a comprehensive statement of Piaget's views on learning was published only recently (Inhelder, Sinclair, and Bovet 1974), there is an extensive literature on how children learn concrete-operational contents which dates back to the late 1950s.

Within category (*a*), not all of the "classic" contents are discussed below. Only those for which solid replication literatures are available are included. Contents that have not piqued the interest of researchers outside

Geneva are not discussed. Thus, for example, there is no consideration of time, movement, and speed. Although these particular contents have been around for many years (Piaget 1946*a*, 1946*b*), they have generated only occasional follow-up studies (e.g., Weinreb and Brainerd 1975).

The Transition
to Operational Intelligence

Piaget says that children enter his concrete-operational stage around age 7 or 8, on the average. He maintains that entry into this stage should be viewed as the most "decisive turning point" in the entire course of cognitive development (Piaget and Inhelder 1969). Intellectually, children who have attained the concrete-operational level bear a much more marked resemblance to adults than they do during the sensorimotor and preoperational stages. Several features of adult intelligence that most of us take for granted become evident for the first time.

In Chapter 4, we noted that in Piaget's theory the great goal toward which cognitive development proceeds is a state of intelligence that is called *operational*. We also examined what Piaget means when he uses this word. We saw that operational intelligence consists of internalized (or "mental") actions that are reversible in two senses (inversion/reciprocity) and are gathered together in integrated systems called structures of the whole. These internalized, reversible, and tightly organized systems of action are what Piaget calls operations. And getting operations is what cognitive development is all about. The reason the concrete-operational stage is the "decisive turning point" in cognitive development is that it is the first stage during which intelligence is officially operational. Piaget supports this claim with data showing that, by about age 7 or 8, children acquire a variety of cognitive contents that, he says, require reversible and structured reasoning. In the present section we examine two basic categories of concrete-operational intelligence—logico-arithmetic operations and spatial operations. Later, we shall consider some illustrative contents drawn from these categories. First, however, we examine the phases or levels of transition involved in the development of truly operational intelligence.

Piaget speaks of three distinct levels of transition in the emergence of operational intelligence. The first level is the sensorimotor stage discussed in Chapter 3. We saw that, during this first transition phase, intelligence is firmly rooted in overt action. But internalized actions, one of the key attributes of operations, have not yet appeared. Consequently, the infant fails problems, such as those concerned with object permanence, that require internal representation of overt actions. In the discussion of replication research, we saw that there are reasonable alternative hypotheses for such failures that can be grouped under the heading "performance explanations."

The second level of transition to truly operational intelligence is the preoperational stage. Preoperational intelligence has some but not all the defining features of operational intelligence. Unlike the sensorimotor child, the preoperational child can solve problems that require internal representation of overt action. But the other key attributes of operational intelligence are lacking. In particular, the preoperational child fails problems that require reversible and/or structured reasoning—e.g., the mountain problem. We again saw that there are equally reasonable performance explanations of these failures.

The concrete-operational stage is the third transition phase. It is considered a transition phase rather than a final phase because the development of operational intelligence is still not complete. Although it is true that concrete-operational intelligence evinces all the defining attributes discussed in Chapter 4, it suffers from one important flaw. These attributes can only be brought to bear when children are dealing with concrete and tangible information—hence, the name "concrete" operations. The mental operations of this stage work only when they are being applied to information that the child has directly perceived. They do not work when they are being applied to information that is abstract and purely hypothetical. Piaget's favorite illustration of this distinction between bringing operations to bear on concrete information and on hypothetical information involves a cognitive content that we shall come to presently, transitive inference. Generally speaking, transitive inference refers to a person's understanding that when a certain type of relation obtains between two objects *A* and *B* and between two objects *B* and *C*, then it must also obtain between objects *A* and *C*. Length relationships provide a classic illustration. If some object *A* is longer than some other object *B* and if *B* is longer than some third object *C*, it follows that *A* is longer than *C*. Suppose we give a concrete-operational child three sticks (*A, B,* and *C*) that differ by very small amounts (say, 1/4 centimeter). The child is allowed to determine the relative length of *A* and *B* and to determine the relative length of *B* and *C*. He is then asked to deduce the relative length of *A* and *C*. Piaget reports (e.g., Piaget, Inhelder, and Szeminska 1960) that children begin to solve this problem around age 7 or 8. But suppose we present an entirely hypothetical version of this problem. For example, we ask the child, "John is taller than Jim and Jim is taller than James, but who is tallest?" According to Piaget, the same children who solve the first problem will fail the second until the age of 11 or 12. Because concrete-operational children can use operations in some situations but not in others, Piaget concludes that the concrete-operational stage is a transition phase in the development of operations.

Piaget claims (e.g., Piaget 1967*a*; Piaget and Inhelder 1969) that concrete mental operations can be grouped into two broad categories based on the kinds of information available in our environments: *logico-arithmetic operations* and *spatial operations*. Given the names "logico-arithmetic" and "spatial," one might suppose that the former are concerned with concepts borrowed from arithmetic and logic and the latter are concerned with concepts borrowed from geometry. While it is true that most of the contents in the first category belong to logic or arithmetic and most of the contents in the second category belong to geometry, this is not the crux of the distinction. The environment confronts us with two basic types of information, namely, *discontinuous* information and *continuous* information. Examples of continuous and discontinuous information are considered below. For now, the important fact to bear in mind is that logico-arithmetic operations are contents that involve discontinuous information and spatial operations are contents that involve continuous information.

Logico-arithmetic Operations

From the standpoint of Piaget's own writings and the existing replication literature, logico-arithmetic operations are a much richer source of cognitive contents than spatial operations. The three best-known categories of concrete-operational contents—*relations, classes,* and *numbers*—fall under the logico-arithmetic heading. Contents from these three categories are far and away the most strongly emphasized ones in Piaget's theoretical treatises on the concrete-operational stage (e.g., Piaget 1942, 1949, 1953, 1970*b*) and in his summary works. The largest proportion of replication research also focuses on these contents.

The distinction between information that is discontinuous and information that is continuous is fundamental to Piaget's account of the concrete-operational stage. The things in our environments provide some information that is continuous and some that is discontinuous (or "discrete"). For example, consider a circle. On the one hand, we can view the circle as a single discrete object and consider how it relates to other objects. For example, how does it relate to other circles? What is its diameter relative to other circles? What is its area relative to other circles? Answers to questions such as these are what Piaget calls discrete or discontinuous information. When operations deal with such information, they are called logico-arithmetic. On the other hand, we might ignore the relations between our given circle and other objects and consider the circle as a unified whole. Now, we are interested in how certain features of our circle relate to other features of the same circle. For example, what is the relationship between the area of the circle and its radius? Or what is the relationship between the circumference of the circle and its radius? When operations deal with this second type of information, they are called spatial. In this illustration, the reader will note that answers to the first two questions are given by arithmetic and answers to the second two questions are given by geometry (i.e., πr^2 and $2\pi r$).

The category of operations that concerns us in this section is the one in which operations are brought to bear when objects are considered as discrete entities. As the continuous-discrete distinction suggests, logico-arithmetic operations are concerned with *relations between objects*. These relations fall into two general categories, namely, difference relations and equivalence relations. That is, two objects may be the same with respect to some property or they may be different. When they are the same with respect to some property, we say that a *symmetrical* relationship exists between them. But when they differ with respect to some property, we say that an *asymmetrical* relationship exists between them. Returning to our preceding example, the diameters of two circles are said to be symmetrical if they are equivalent and asymmetrical if they are not equivalent. Similarly, we say that the height relationship between two people is symmetrical if they are the same height and asymmetrical if one person is taller. Logico-arithmetic operations deal with both symmetrical and asymmetrical relationships between objects. As we shall see below, some of the specific cognitive contents that fall under the logico-arithmetic heading are exclusively concerned with asymmetrical relations (e.g., seriation), others are exclusively concerned with symmetrical relations (e.g., classification), and still others are concerned with both types of relations (e.g., conservation).

We now consider some cognitive contents that, according to Piaget, illustrate children's use of logico-arithmetic operations. Although others could be mentioned, the four most important logico-arithmetic contents are *conservation concepts, relational concepts, classification concepts,* and *number concepts.*

conservation

The theory says that the best single indicator that children have passed from the preoperational stage to the concrete-operational stage is the presence of conservation concepts. For example, two of Piaget's chief collaborators, Inhelder and Sinclair, have observed that conservation concepts should be viewed as "the main symptoms of a budding system of operational structures" (1969, p. 3). Conservation concepts are concerned with both symmetrical and asymmetrical *quantitative* relationships between objects.

Let us first define conservation in the abstract and then proceed to some specific examples. Generally speaking, conservation refers to children's understanding that quantitative relationships between two objects remain invariant (are "conserved") in the face of irrelevant perceptual deformations of one of the objects. An "irrelevant perceptual deformation" is any transformation that does not involve either addition or subtraction. In the standard conservation test, the child is first shown two objects that are known to be equivalent with respect to some quantitative relationship between them. The two objects are also perceptually identical in the beginning. The experimenter proceeds to deform one of the objects in such a way that the perceptual identity is destroyed but the quantitative relationship is not affected. After the deformation has been completed, the experimenter questions the child to determine whether the child knows that the objects are still quantitatively equivalent. Children who say the objects are still quantitatively equivalent are said to *conserve* that relationship. Children who say the objects are not quantitatively equivalent, are said to fail to conserve that relationship.

Examples of conservation. We now consider some examples of conservation. A child and an experimenter are seated across from each other at a table. On the table, there are three glasses (*X, Y,* and *Z*) and a large pitcher of colored water. Two of the glasses (*X* and *Y*) are identical, but the third glass (*Z*) is *taller* and *thinner* than the other two. First, the experimenter fills glasses *X* and *Y* with equal amounts of water from the pitcher. Since the two glasses are the same size, the *height* of the water in the glasses will be identical. Next, the child is asked whether or not *X* and *Y* contain the same amount of water and, of course, answers that they do. After the child has agreed that *X* and *Y* contain the same amount of water, the experimenter pours the contents of *Y* into *Z*. Now, the child must determine the quantitative relationship between the water in *X* and the water in *Z*. Although the two quantities are still equal, note that they are no longer perceptually identical. In particular, note that since *Z* is thinner than *X*, the height of the water in *Z* will be greater than the height of the water in *X*. The experimenter asks the child whether or not *X* and *Z* contain the same amount of water. Children who say that they do are said to conserve the relationship of quantity. Children who say that one of the glasses contains more water than the other are said not to conserve quantity.

As our second example, we consider the length conservation problem. The only equipment that is used in this test are two pieces of string. To begin with, the experimenter places two pieces of string (*A* and *B*) on the table in front of the child. The two pieces of string are the same length. The experimenter makes this fact apparent to the child by placing the strings side by side so that their end points correspond:

String *A* ＿＿＿＿＿＿＿
String *B* ＿＿＿＿＿＿＿

After the child has agreed that *A* and *B* are in fact the same length, the experimenter performs a perceptual deformation of some sort—by bending string *B* into a circle, for example, or a "*V*," or a zig-zag. Although the two strings are still the same length, they are no longer perceptually identical.

The experimenter asks the child whether A and B are still the same length. Children who respond affirmatively are said to conserve the relationship of length. Those who respond negatively are said not to conserve length.

I noted earlier that conservation concepts are concerned with both symmetrical and asymmetrical relationships. However, the examples which we have just considered are entirely symmetrical—i.e., the two objects were always quantitatively equivalent. It is easy to see how these examples could be converted to conservation of asymmetrical relations. In the quantity example, suppose we began with X containing slightly more water than Y. After the child has agreed that X contains more water, the experimenter pours the contents of Y into Z. As before, the height of the water in Z is greater than the height of the water in X. However, Z contains less water than X. Similarly, the length conservation problem could be converted to conservation of an asymmetrical relationship merely by beginning with two strings of unequal length.

Findings on how children perform on the sort of tests just described are reported in virtually all of Piaget's main works on the concrete-operational stage (e.g., Piaget 1952a; Piaget and Inhelder 1941, 1956; Piaget, Inhelder, and Szeminska 1960). These works contain a wide variety of rich and occasionally contradictory speculations about conservation. However, we shall focus on two themes that run through most of these discussions: (*a*) developmental stages in children's understanding of conservation, and (*b*) specific antecedent concepts or "rules" that children must grasp before they can conserve a given quantitative relationship.

Conservation development. Piaget maintains that children's capacity to conserve any given quantitative relationship always goes through three global stages. Moreover, it is assumed that children always pass through the stages in the same invariant order. During Stage I, children do not conserve at all. Whenever a perceptual deformation is performed, Stage I children conclude that the quantitative relationship between the two objects has been altered. In the two illustrations given above, for example, Stage I children would say that glass Z contains more water than glass X and that string A is longer than string B. During Stage II, children give responses that Piaget calls "intermediate reactions." In other words, sometimes they conserve and sometimes they do not. There are two general types of intermediate reactions. First, Stage II children will sometimes give a conserving response when the perceptual deformation is rather small, but they will revert to nonconservation as soon as the size of the deformation is increased. For example, in the water illustration discussed above suppose that the diameters of the first two glasses were $X = 6$ centimeters and $Y = 6$ centimeters. Suppose that we have *two* deformation glasses with diameters $Z_1 = 5$ centimeters and $Z_2 = 2$ centimeters. We first pour the contents of Y into Z_1 and ask the child whether X and Z_1 have the same amount of water. The one-centimeter difference in the diameters of X and Z_1 is sufficient to produce a clear difference in heights of the two quantities of water. However, Stage II children may say that the two quantities are equal because the height difference is small. However, suppose that the water in Z_1 is poured into Z_2 and we ask children whether X and Z_2 have the same amount of water. The three-centimeter difference in their diameters produces an enormous difference in the heights of the quantities of water in X and Z_2. Consequently, Stage II children may change their minds and say that X contains more water than Z_2. The second type of intermediate response is concerned with conservation prediction. According to Piaget, Stage II children will usually *predict* that the quantitative relationship between objects will be conserved if they are questioned just prior to the deformation. But they relinquish their prediction and revert to nonconservation as soon as a large deformation is performed. Finally, during Stage III, children invariably say that quantitative relationships between objects are not affected by irrelevant perceptual deformations. Stage III children both predict conservation before deformation *and* do not change their minds once the deformation has been performed. They conserve regardless of whether the actual deformations are small or large.

Piaget's three stages of conservation development are related to his stages of cognitive development. Stage I corresponds to the preoperational stage discussed in Chapter 4. Thus, most preschoolers and kindergarteners would be expected to be functioning at Stage I of conservation. Stage III corresponds to Piaget's concrete-operational stage. Thus, most children in the later elementary school grades would be expected to be functioning at Stage III of conservation. Stage II is perhaps the most interesting of the three. It supposedly corresponds to the transition phase between the preoperational and concrete-operational stages. This transition phase is said to be a relatively short and highly unstable period during which the cognitive structures of the preoperational stage and the cognitive structures of the concrete-operational stage coexist side by side. This latter assumption presumably explains why Stage II children sometimes give preoperational responses (nonconservation) and sometimes give concrete-operational responses (conservation). Since the nominal age for attainment of the concrete-operational stage is 7 or 8, we would expect to find most Stage II children somewhere in the 6-year-old range.

A final interesting feature of Piaget's stages of conservation development is the principle of *horizontal décalage*. According to this principle, children progress through the three stages at different rates for different quantitative relationships. That is, children will conserve some quantitative relationships long before they conserve others. For example, consider number conservation, which was discussed in Chapter 4, and consider quantity and length conservation, which were both used as illustrations above. Piaget claims that children reach Stage III for number before they reach

Stage III for length and, in turn, that they reach Stage III for length before they reach Stage III for quantity. A good deal of research has been devoted to verifying the existence of these conservation *décalages*.

Reversibility rules and conservation. One could reasonably ask what it is that makes conservation possible in some children but not in others. More simply, what is it that Stage II and Stage III children have that Stage I children do not? At first glance, this appears to be a rather easy question to answer: Stage II and Stage III children have cognitive structures composed of things called "operations." Although this is an easy answer to give, it is not a very satisfactory one. The problem is that operations and cognitive structures are exceedingly difficult things to measure. In fact, they cannot be measured at all. As we saw in Chapter 2, they can only be *inferred* from behavior. This leaves us in a dilemma. If we do not measure something besides conservation behavior, then the preceding "answer" is merely a circular statement rather like saying, "Sleeping pills make you drowsy because they have a soporific power." Circular explanations are exceedingly poor form in science.

Hence, if we wish to explain why some children conserve and others do not, we require something else that we can measure in addition to conservation. From Piaget's standpoint, this other thing is children's ability to apply the two reversibility rules discussed in Chapter 4 to conservation tests. To explicate the meaning of this statement, let us first reformulate conservation tests in abstract terms. It is easy to see from what has already been said that every conservation test makes use of two objects. We might call the first object the *standard* and denote it with the letter S. Object S is called the standard because it never changes during the test; it always remains the way it was when the test began. We might call the other object the *variable* and denote it with the letter V. Object V is called the variable because, unlike S, it changes during the test. When V is in its initial state, V_1, S and V are both quantitatively equivalent and perceptually identical. But when V is in its second state, V_2, S and V are still quantitatively equivalent but they are no longer perceptually identical.

Now, let us recall the two reversibility rules discussed in Chapter 4—inversion (or negation) and compensation (or reciprocity). Children who have acquired concrete-operational cognitive structures, by definition, possess these reversibility rules and their reasoning is influenced by them. It follows that children who possess the reversibility rules know certain things about the two states of V that preoperational children could not know. For example, they know that the deformation performed by the experimenter ($V_1 \rightarrow V_2$) can also be carried out in the opposite direction ($V_1 \leftarrow V_2$). Further, they know that if the deformation were carried out in the opposite direction, then V would look exactly like it did when the test began. This is quite obviously an example of our previous definition of the inversion reversibility rule. Children mentally invert some operation. Concrete-operational children also know some other things about the two states of V. Explicitly, they know that the experimenter's deformation produces more than one change in V and, what is more, these various changes tend to compensate one another. That is, if the experimenter's deformation produces a certain change in a certain feature of V (height, length, width, etc.), it also produces an equal and opposite change in some other feature of V. This appears to be a case of the compensation rule in action. Instead of simply inverting the deformation, the child nullifies it.

According to Piaget, children must be able to apply both reversibility rules in the manner just described before they can conserve. Thus, the presumed difference between Stage II and III children, on the one hand, and Stage I children, on the other, is that the latter do not know the above-mentioned things about the two states of V. Piaget's evidence for this claim comes from the explanations that children give on conservation tests. To illustrate, consider the liquid quantity problem described earlier. After the contents of Y have been poured into Z, the child is asked whether X and Z contain the same amount of water. Suppose the child responds affirmatively. We might then ask, "How do you know that?" When questions of this sort are posed, Piaget reports that children tend to offer two basic rationales. First, they may say something like, "The glasses contain the same amount because if the water in this glass (Z) were poured back into this glass (Y), it would be just the same as before." Answers of this sort look suspiciously like the inversion rule in operation. Second, children say something like, "The glasses contain the same amount because even though the water in this glass (Z) is taller than the water in this glass (X), it is also skinnier." This, of course, suggests that children are compensating the change in one dimension (height) with an equal and opposite change in another dimension (width).

Now, suppose we have a child who does not give conserving responses but says, rather, that there is more water in glass Z than in glass X. Suppose that we also ask this child, "How do you know that?" Piaget reports that such children do not tend to provide the two rationales just considered. Instead, they give explanations that emphasize changes in one perceptual dimension. Piaget views this evidence as grounds for the conclusion that nonconservers do not possess the reversibility rules. This is obviously a competence interpretation.

We have just seen that Piaget uses children's explanations of their conservation test answers as a basis for inferring the presence or absence of reversibility rules. However, it is relatively easy to devise tests of these rules that are entirely independent of the conservation test itself. We saw that the rules are actually concerned with the relation between V_1 and V_2 rather than the relation between S and V. Therefore, we could devise a test of inversion and compensation that makes use of only a single variable object. For example, suppose we have only glasses Y and Z from the quantity conservation test. First, we pour some water into Y. We then ask the child to predict the height of the water before it is poured into Z. Children who say that pouring the water into the much narrower glass will force it to a greater height are apparently aware of the compensatory relationship between height and width. Next, we pour the water from Y into Z. We now ask the child to predict the height of the water if it were poured back into Y. Children who say that pouring the water back into Y will cause it to look like it did originally apparently grasp the inversion rule. By taking independent measures of rule knowledge in this manner, we can test Piaget's hypotheses about why Stage II and III children conserve and Stage I children do not by merely relating children's performance on rule tests to their performance on conservation tests.

Identity rules and conservation. Finally, one may ask whether there are still other rules about the two states of V that could help children pass conservation tests. Two prominent investigators, Jerome Bruner (1964; Bruner, Olver, and Greenfield 1966) of Oxford University and David Elkind (1967a; Elkind and Schoenfeld 1972), believe that there are. Bruner and Elkind propose that knowledge of the *identity rule* is a necessary prerequisite for conservation. Bruner even claims that the identity rule must be understood before children can grasp either of the two reversibility rules.

To see why the identity rule is presumed to be important in conservation, let us recast the conservation test as a conditional law of the following form. If $A = B$, then $B = C$ where A is S, B is V_1, and C is V_2. What does one need to know to decide whether or not this statement is true? To begin with, it is apparent that statements of this form are not true in general. For example, when $A = 5$ pennies, $B = 5$ pennies, and $C = 2$ pennies, the statement is clearly false. But precisely when are statements of this form true? Obviously, they are true when and only when it happens that $B = C$. Naturally, this is the case in a conservation test because $B = V_1$, $C = V_2$, and $V_1 = V_2$. It is children's grasp of the latter fact which is called the identity rule.

In conservation tests, the identity rule always comes in two varieties, namely, *qualitative* identity and *quantitative* identity. The first type of identity, which resembles the preoperational identity concepts examined in Chapter 4, is emphasized by Bruner and the second type of identity is emphasized by Elkind. Bruner's qualitative identity rule refers to children's understanding that, despite the experimenter's deformation, V_2 is still the "same object" as V_1. Elkind's quantitative identity rule refers to children's understanding that, despite the experimenter's deformation, V_2 is still the "same amount" as V_1. The distinction between qualitative and quantitative identity can be made more concrete by reconsidering the test for inversion and compensation rules outlined above. First, we pour some water into glass Y and then we transfer the water into glass Z. Suppose we now ask the child two questions. Is the water in this glass (*Z*) the same water that was in this glass (*Y*)? Is there the same amount of water in this glass (*Z*) as there was before in this glass (*Y*)? If the child answers the first question affirmatively, this is an example of qualitative identity. If the child answers the second question affirmatively, this is an example of quantitative identity.

Summary. Piaget describes the development of conservation concepts in terms of three global stages. During Stage I, which corresponds to the preoperational stage, there is no evidence of conservation. During Stage II, which corresponds to the transition phase between preoperations and concrete operations, conservation occurs in some situations but not in others. During Stage III, which corresponds to the concrete-operational stage, children conserve in all situations. Piaget believes that children pass through these stages more rapidly for some quantitative relationships than for others, and he believes that children must possess reversibility rules before they can conserve. Bruner and Elkind believe that children must also possess identity rules before they can conserve.

relations

The cognitive contents in this category are chiefly concerned with asymmetrical relations. They are concerned, more especially, with the concrete-operational child's ability to use the asymmetrical relations that exist between the members of a set of objects to *order* these objects in some manner.

Before we examine some specific relational cognitive contents, we must first distinguish between relations that are merely asymmetrical and relations that are both asymmetrical and transitive. As we saw earlier, asymmetrical relations are difference relations—i.e., given two objects *A* and *B*, any property that serves to differentiate them is an asymmetrical relation. Asymmetrical relations are quite obviously *unidirectional.* If they hold in one direction, they cannot possibly hold in the other. For example, if *A* is taller or longer or heavier or wider than *B,* it cannot possibly be the case that *B* is taller or longer or heavier or wider than *A.* In addition to being unidirectional, some special asymmetrical relations also happen to be transitive. In general, we say that some asymmetrical relation **R** is transitive if and only if the following statement is always true. Given three objects *A*, *B*, and *C*, when **R** holds between *A* and *B* and between *B* and *C* it must also hold between *A* and *C*. Asymmetrical quantitative relations of the sort we have been considering up to this point are invariably transitive. Thus, if *A* is taller or longer or heavier or wider than *B* and if *B* is taller or longer or heavier or wider than *C,* then it is clear that *A* must also be taller or longer or heavier or wider than *C*. More simply, if any asymmetrical relation **R** is transitive, then $A \mathbf{R} C$ follows logically from $A \mathbf{R} B$ and $B \mathbf{R} C$.

Although quantitative relations are always transitive, there are many other asymmetrical relations which are not transitive. A familiar case in point is the relation "is the father of." This relation is asymmetrical because it is unidirectional. If *A* is the father of *B*, it cannot possibly be true that *B* is the father of *A*. But the relation is not transitive. If we know that *A* is the father of *B* and we also know that *B* is the father of *C*, it does not follow that *A* is the father of *C*. Actually, it follows that *A* is the grandfather of *C*.

This distinction between transitive and nontransitive asymmetrical relations must be borne in mind because relational cognitive contents are concerned with the asymmetrical-transitive relations. Relations of this sort are important because they may be used to order a set of objects from first to last. For example, suppose we have a set of five coins—a penny, a nickel, a dime, a quarter, and a half-dollar. We could order these coins from first to last by using the asymmetrical-transitive relation "is worth more than." If we did, the penny would come first, the nickel would come second, and so on. We could also order the coins according to the asymmetrical-transitive relation "is larger than." This ordering would be very different than the ordering by worth. Now, the dime would come first, the penny second, and the nickel third.

Relational cognitive contents. As the preceding example should suggest, Piaget's relational contents are concerned with using asymmetrical-transitive relations for purposes of ordering sets of objects. There are three key cognitive contents in the relational category: (*a*) seriation (e.g., Inhelder and Piaget 1964); (*b*) multiple seriation (e.g., Inhelder and Piaget 1964); (*c*) transitive inference (e.g., Piaget, Inhelder, and Szeminska 1960). Each of these three contents, as well as the tests used to measure them, is designed to tap a different aspect of the general ability to order objects according to asymmetrical-transitive relations.

Seriation resembles the coin-ordering illustration considered earlier. The child is presented with a moderately large collection of objects (usually about five to ten) that differ from each other on some quantitative dimension such as length or weight. The differences between the objects are fairly small so that their overall ordering cannot be determined simply by looking at them. For example, the child is given a set of five dowling sticks whose lengths differ by only 1/2 centimeter—e.g., the first stick is 10 centimeters, the second stick is 10 1/2 centimeters, etc. The child's task is to order the five sticks from shortest to longest. This problem is quickly solved by instituting a planned series of pairwise comparisons of the sticks. By comparing them two at a time, the child can find the shortest, the next shortest, and so on. A very similar test of seriation ability would involve giving the child a set of rubber balls which all look alike (i.e., they are all the same size, the same color, the same texture, etc.). Although the balls all look the same, they do not *weigh* the same. The child is asked to arrange the balls from lightest to heaviest, and is provided with a pan balance for weighing them. Using the balance to execute a series of pairwise comparisons, the child can solve the problem by finding the lightest ball, the next lightest ball, and so on.

Multiple seriation is simply a more complicated version of seriation. Rather than having to order a collection of objects according to a single asymmetrical-transitive relation, the child is asked to order them simultaneously according to two such relations. For reasons that will become apparent momentarily, the test for multiple seriation ability is usually called the matrix problem. Suppose we present the child with four cylindrical cans whose heights and widths differ as follows. The first can is 7 centimeters tall and 3 centimeters wide, the second can is 9 centimeters tall and 3 centimeters wide, the third can is 7 centimeters tall and 5 centimeters wide, and the fourth can is 9 centimeters tall and 5 centimeters wide. The child's task is to order the cans according to both height and width simultaneously. To solve this problem, one constructs a 2×2 table or matrix. The first can occupies the top left cell of the matrix, the second can occupies the top right cell of the matrix, the third can occupies the bottom left cell of the matrix, and the fourth can occupies the bottom right cell of the matrix. This yields a *doubly seriated* collection. Height increases as we go from left to right: The cans in the left column of the matrix are both 7 centimeters tall, but the cans in the right column are both 9 centimeters tall. Width increases as we go from top to bottom: The cans in the upper row of the matrix are both 3 centimeters wide, but the cans in the bottom row are both 5 centimeters wide. A very similar test of multiple seriation would involve presenting the child with four rubber balls which differ in diameter (say, 3 or 5 centimeters) and in weight (say, 50 or 100 grams). Again, the task is to order the balls according to both relations simultaneously. The problem can be solved by constructing a 2×2 matrix in which diameter increases from left to right and weight increases from top to bottom, or by constructing a 2×2 matrix in which weight increases from left to right and diameter increases from top to bottom.

Transitive inference is the third and most difficult type of ordering skill. With the seriation and multiple seriation problems just examined, children are allowed to make pairwise physical comparisons of all the objects in the set as a means of ordering them. In transitive inference tests, on the other hand, children cannot compare all the objects. Instead, they must do part of the ordering "in their heads." An illustrative transitive inference problem involving weight relationships is shown at the left of Figure 5–1. The child is given three balls (*A*, *B*, and *C*) that look identical, but actually are of different weights (e.g., *A* = 50 grams, *B* = 100 grams, and *C*

Figure 5-1 Illustrations of tasks frequently employed to test children's grasp of transitivity of weight (left illustration) and transitivity of length (right illustration). (From Charles J. Brainerd, the Origins of Number Concepts. Copyright ©(1973c) by *Scientific American, Inc.* All rights reserved.)

= 150 grams). First, the child is asked to compare A to B and determine which is heavier. Second, the child is asked to comare C to B and determine which is heavier. But the child is not allowed to compare A and C. After A and C have each been compared to B, the child is asked to deduce the relative weight of A and C. Children who reason that A must be heavier than C because B is lighter than A but heavier than C are said to be capable of transitive inference. A second test of transitive inference is shown at the right of Figure 5-1. The child is given three dowling sticks (X, Y, and Z) whose lengths differ by very small amounts (e.g., $X = 11$ centimeters, $Y = 10\ 1/2$ centimeters, and $Z = 10$ centimeters). After X and Z have both been compared to Y, the child is questioned about the relative length of X and Z. Children who conclude that X must be longer than Z because Y is both shorter than X and longer than Z are said to be capable of transitive inference.

  Relational development. Piaget (e.g., Beth and Piaget 1966) claims that relational development, like conservation development, is characterized by three invariant stages. During Stage I, which corresponds to the preoperational stage, children fail all of the tests outlined above. On seriation tests, Stage I children may be able to determine a few of the pairwise differences, but they cannot construct the overall ordering. The same is true of their performance on multiple seriation tests. On transitivity tests, Stage I children cannot deduce the relationship between A and C simply by knowing the relationships between A and B and B and C. Typically, they say that $A = C$ because they look alike. During Stage II, which corresponds to the transition phase between preoperations and concrete operations, children pass some relational tests and fail others. They pass seriation tests. If given enough time to make all the pairwise comparisons, the Stage II child will usually be able to order five to ten objects according to a single asymmetrical-transitive relation. However, there is only partial success on the multiple seriation problem. Stage II children can seriate the objects separately according to either of the two relations, but they cannot seriate the objects *simultaneously* according to *both* relations. In the height × width tests mentioned earlier, for example, Stage II children can construct two sets of objects which differ in either height or width, but they cannot construct the 2×2 matrix. On transitivity tests, Stage II children perform more or less like Stage I children.

  During Stage III, which corresponds to the concrete-operational stage, children pass all ordering tests of the sort we have considered. On seriation tests, there is quantitative improvement. Stage III children order the objects much more rapidly than Stage II children. Piaget says that this is because Stage II children order the objects exclusively by trial and error, while Stage III children order the objects mentally. On multiple seriation tests, Stage III children construct 2×2 matrices. Given enough time, Stage III children can also construct higher-order multiple seriation matrices (2×3, 3×3, 3×4, etc.). Finally, Stage III children also pass transitive inference tests. If three objects A, B, and C can be ordered according to some asymmetrical-transitive relation, Stage III children can deduce the relationship between A and C by knowing the relationships between A and B and B and C. They can also make transitive inferences about much larger sets of objects. For example, suppose there are five objects, A, B, C, D, and E that can be ordered according to some asymmetrical-transitive relation. If Stage III children know the pairwise relationships between A and B, B and C, C and D, and D and E, they can deduce all the remaining pairwise relationships.

  Piaget's description of relational development leads to some fairly obvious predictions that will be examined more thoroughly when we come to the replication research. First, it is clear that most children should pass seriation tests before they pass either transitive inference or multiple seriation tests. Recall that seriation is a Stage II content, while multiple seriation and transitive inference are both Stage III contents. Consequently, if we administered tests of all three to a large sample of children, we would expect to find many children who pass the seriation test and fail the other two tests. But we would not expect to find any children who pass the other two tests and fail the seriation test. A second obvious prediction is that most children should not pass multiple seriation and transitive inference tests until they reach the first or second grade. Recall that multiple seriation and transitive inference are both Stage III contents and Stage III corresponds to the concrete-operational stage. Since the nominal age for the onset of concrete operations is 7 to 8 years, there certainly should be no evidence of either in children as young as, say, 3 or 4 years old.

classes

The cognitive contents in this category are concerned with a very special symmetrical relation, namely, the relation of *belonging* or *membership.* The relation is special because we use it to group things into classes, and classes are very important and useful things. It would be difficult to imagine what thinking, reasoning, and language would be like if it were not for classes. Without classes, we could not slice the world up into manageable collections of objects. Instead, we would have to deal with every object in isolation.

The relation of membership is both symmetrical and transitive. Concerning symmetry, if A belongs to B then B belongs to A. Concerning transitivity, if A belongs to B and B belongs to C, then A belongs to C. Although membership is both symmetrical and transitive, this should not be taken to mean that symmetrical relations are *generally* transitive. Some are and some are not. As was the case for asymmetrical relations, it is easy to see that symmetrical quantitative relations must always be transitive. If A is the same height or length or weight or width as B and B is the same height or length or weight or width as C, then A must be the same height or length or weight or width as C. Some symmetrical nonquantitative relations are also transitive. For example, if A is the brother of B and B is the brother of C, then A and C are brothers. But other symmetrical nonquantitative relations are not transitive. A case in point is the relation of marriage. The relation is symmetrical because if A is married to B, then B is married to A. But it is not transitive. If A is married to B and B is married to C, then it does not follow that A and C are married. Our best guess would be that B is probably a bigamist.

Cognitive content of class concepts. The cognitive contents falling under the present heading are all supposedly concerned with the same general ability: the ability to categorize objects. As was the case for relations, there are three basic contents: (*a*) classification (e.g., Inhelder and Piaget 1964); (*b*) multiple classification (e.g., Inhelder and Piaget 1964); (*c*) class inclusion (e.g., Piaget 1952*a*). As was also the case for relations, these contents and the tests which measure them are presumed to reflect slightly different aspects of the general ability to categorize things.

Classification is the classes counterpart of seriation. That is, whereas seriation refers to one-dimensional ordering, classification refers to one-dimensional categorization. The child is confronted with a moderately large collection of objects (usually ten or more) that belong to two or more *mutually exclusive* classes and is asked to sort the objects into categories. For example, the child is shown an array consisting of six toy animals (e.g., a dog, a cow, a bird, a sheep, a cat, and a pig) and six toy pieces of furniture (e.g., a lamp, a chair, a bed, a sofa, a footstool, and a table). The child's task is to sort these twelve objects into two mutually exclusive categories. After the child has had an opportunity to look the collection over, the experimenter says, "Put the things together which go together." More difficult versions of this basic test involve confronting the child with arrays whose members belong to more than two mutually exclusive classes. In each case, the child's task is to sort the objects into however many mutually exclusive classes there are.

Multiple classification is to classification as multiple seriation is to seriation—i.e., it is simply a more complicated version of the classification task. Rather than classify objects along a single dimension of mutually exclusive categories, the child must now classify objects simultaneously along two dimensions of mutually inclusive categories. The test for this content, like the test for multiple seriation, is known as a matrix problem. Suppose the child is given the following four objects: a red plastic circle, a green plastic circle, a red plastic triangle, and a green plastic triangle. This set of objects varies in terms of two overlapping categorical dimensions—color (red or green) and shape (circle or triangle). The dimensions overlap because each belongs to one of the two categories that comprise each dimension. As before with multiple seriation, the child's task is to categorize the four objects along both dimensions *simultaneously*. The solution is the same as for multiple seriation tests, namely, construct a 2×2 matrix. The red circle occupies the top left cell of the matrix, the green circle occupies the top right cell of the matrix, the red triangle occupies the bottom left cell of the matrix, and the green triangle occupies the bottom right cell of the matrix. This yields a double classification table in which color changes as we go from left to right and shape changes as we go from top to bottom. By using other categorical dimensions (e.g., animal species, plant species), it is easy to see that many different matrix tests of multiple classification ability could be devised. In all of them, the child's task is to classify objects along two categorical dimensions simultaneously.

Although classification and multiple classification bear a marked resemblance to seriation and multiple seriation, respectively, the resemblance between the third class content, class inclusion, and the third relational content, transitive inference, is slight. About the only similarity is that class inclusion, like transitive inference, is supposed to require that children must do something "in their heads." Class inclusion refers to children's understanding that a class must always be smaller than any more inclusive class in which it is contained. There are many illustrations of this principle in everyday life: There are fewer robins than there are birds; there are fewer spaniels than there are dogs; there are fewer women than there are people; there are fewer tulips than there are flowers; there are fewer nouns than there are words. In each of these cases, the second class mentioned is a class that contains all of the members of the first class plus other things. The second class is called a superordinate class and the first class is called a subordinate class. It is obvious that a superordinate class must always be larger than any of its subordinate classes. This fact—or, more precisely, children's knowledge of this fact—is what Piaget means by class inclusion.

Many different class inclusion tests have been employed by Piaget and his coworkers over the years. But all of them share some common attributes. First, children are presented with a collection of objects. Each object belongs to one of two mutually exclusive classes, which we may denote A and A'. In addition, the class A is larger than class A'—i.e., more of the objects belong to A than belong to A'. In addition, the members of A and A' all belong to some superordinate class B. After looking the collection over, children are asked questions of the following form. Are there more As than Bs? Are there fewer Bs than As? Are there the same number of Bs and As? That is, they are questioned about the relative size of the superordinate class and the larger of the two subordinate classes. Piaget introduced the first version of this test, which was called "additive composition of classes" at the time, more than three decades ago (Piaget and Szeminska 1941). Children were shown a box containing a large number of wooden beads (class B). Most of the beads were brown (class A), but two of them were white (class A'). The children were asked whether the box contained more wooden beads or more brown beads. They were also asked whether the wooden beads or the brown beads would make a longer necklace. Finally, they were asked whether there would be any beads left in the box if all the wooden beads were removed and if all the brown beads were removed. Later versions of the class inclusion test (Inhelder and Piaget 1964) make use of common objects such as flowers and animals. For example, the child is shown a picture of sixteen flowers (B). Some of them are yellow (A) and some of them are blue (A'). The child is asked questions of the following form. Are there more yellow flowers or more flowers? Will a bouquet made up of all the yellow flowers be larger or smaller than a bouquet made up of all the flowers?

Development of class concepts. In view of our earlier discussions of conservation and relations, it is not surprising that Piaget believes that classification development is characterized by three invariant stages. During Stage I, which corresponds to the preoperational stage, children fail all of the tests we have just considered. On class inclusion tests, Stage I children are unaware that class *A* is contained in class *B* and, consequently, they always say that *A* is larger than *B*. On classification tests, Stage I children engage in a very interesting form of behavior known as the construction of *graphic collections.* When the experimenter says, "Put the things together which go together," Stage I children take this to mean that they are supposed to *group the objects into spatial configurations.* For example, they may group the objects into simple geometric shapes. In the first illustrative classification test mentioned above, a typical Stage I strategy would be to arrange all twelve toys in a large circle or a large square. As might be expected, Stage I children also construct graphic collections on multiple classification tests. During Stage II, which corresponds to the transition phase between preoperations and concrete operations, children pass some of the aforementioned tests and fail others. On classification tests, Stage II children succeed in sorting collections of objects into two or more mutually exclusive categories. As was true for multiple seriation, Stage II children achieve partial success on multiple classification tests. Explicitly, they can sort objects into categories along one dimension or they can sort objects into categories along two or more dimensions *successively.* But they cannot sort objects into categories along two dimensions simultaneously. In the color × shape test outlined earlier, Stage II children could sort the objects by color and immediately resort them by shape. But they could not simultaneously sort them according to both color and shape by constructing a 2 × 2 matrix. On class inclusion tests, Stage II performance is somewhat better than Stage I performance. Unlike Stage I children, Stage II children do not automatically say that class *A* is larger than class *B.* They are aware that *A* is subordinate to *B* and, occasionally, they discover that *B* is larger than *A* by trial and error. For the most part, however, they continue to maintain that *A* is larger than *B.*

During Stage III, which corresponds to the concrete-operational stage, children pass all of the aforementioned tests. On classification tests, there is quantitative improvement. Stage III children sort objects into mutually exclusive classes at a much more rapid pace and they rarely make errors. According to Piaget, this is because Stage III children classify the objects mentally before they sort them whereas Stage II children do not. On multiple classification tests, Stage III children construct 2 × 2 matrices. Stage III children can also construct matrices involving two dimensions with more than two categories. Stage III children also pass class inclusion tests. Stage

III children are aware that *A* is included in *B* and they realize that this fact logically implies that *B* must always be larger than *A* no matter how large *A* is. Stage III children do not *discover* the fact that *B* is greater than *A* when they are confronted with some given array. They already know the general principle and apply it rapidly in any given test.

The preceding description of classificatory development generates some elementary predictions that are easily tested. For example, preschool children, who fall within the first half of the nominal age range for pre-operations, should be completely incapable of classificatory behavior. On classification tests, preschoolers should overwhelmingly tend to construct graphic collections rather than sort the objects into mutually exclusive categories. They should do the same thing on multiple classification tests, and they should fail class inclusion tests across the board. A second prediction is that children should always pass classification tests before they pass either multiple classification or class inclusion tests. Recall that classification is a Stage II content, whereas multiple classification and class inclusion are Stage III contents. If it is true that these stages are invariant, then a given child should always be able to sort objects along one dimension before he can either sort them along two dimensions or understand that subordinate classes are smaller than superordinate classes. Since multiple classification tests are simply more difficult versions of classification tests, the first of these two relationships is bound to be confirmed and, consequently, it is not really worth studying. However, the second relationship is worth studying because class inclusion and classification tests are quite different. A third and final prediction is that most children should pass all of these tests by the time they reach first or second grade. Multiple classification and class inclusion are both Stage III contents and Stage III presumably corresponds to concrete operations. Since the nominal age for the onset of concrete operations is 7 to 8, we would expect children to fail these tests infrequently after they have reached this age.

number

When Piaget speaks of number, he does not mean precisely what you or I would mean. When we think of number, most of us think of the elements of the basic number systems (e.g., natural numbers, integers, rational numbers, real numbers). We also think of performing the standard operations of arithmetic and algebra with these elements (e.g., adding, multiplying, squaring, factoring). But when Piaget (e.g., 1952a, 1970c; Beth and Piaget 1966) discusses number, he is almost always concerned with a very special type of conservation, namely, *number* conservation.

Number conservation has already been examined in Chapter 4. Recall that, in general, number conservation focuses on the conditions under which children believe that two sets of objects either do or do not contain the same number of elements. Although there are other possibilities, the traditional test

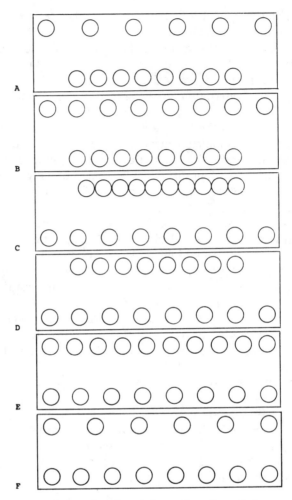

Figure 5-2   A series of six configurations that may be used to illustrate Piaget's hypotheses about how children's number judgments are affected by length and density cues.

for number conservation begins with two parallel rows of objects (say, two rows of coins). Initially, the rows are exactly the same length and they contain the same (or different) number of elements. After the child has examined the rows, the experimenter shortens (or lengthens) one of them. The experimenter then questions the child about the relative numerousness of the rows to determine whether or not the child conserves the initial numerical relationship between them.

Stages in number development. Since number is a special type of conservation, it is obvious that Piaget's description of number development will consist of three invariant stages. These are the same three stages examined earlier in the section on conservation, but they have some special features not discussed previously. These features may be conveniently summarized by referring to the six configurations appearing in Figure 5-2. During Stage I, children's numerical judgments are completely dominated by the relative lengths of the two parallel rows. If, for example, we begin with two rows containing eight elements and then shorten one of them [Fig. 5-2 (B) and (D)], the Stage I child says that the longer row now has more elements. If the experimenter constructs two rows that contain different numbers of elements but are exactly the same length [Fig. 5-2 (E) and (F)], the Stage I child says that the rows contain the same number of elements. Finally, if the experimenter constructs one row and then asks the child to construct a parallel row with the same number of elements as the given row, the Stage I child simply constructs a row which is the same length as the given row. Forgetting number conservation tests for the moment, what would happen if we present Stage I children with the six configurations in Figure 5-2 and ask them to judge the relative numerousness of the two rows in each configuration? If the numerical judgments of Stage I children are completely dominated by the relative lengths of the rows, they should judge the upper rows in configurations (A) and (B) to be more numerous than the lower rows, they should judge the lower rows in configurations (C) and (D) to be more numerous than the upper rows, and they should judge the rows in configurations (E) and (F) to be equally numerous.

There are two cues that provide information about the relative numerous of parallel rows such as those shown in Figure 5-2. Taken together, the relative length and relative density of any pair of rows determines their relative numerousness: If two rows are the same length but one row is denser, then the denser row is more numerous; if one row is shorter and denser and the length-density differences exactly balance each other, then the two rows are equally numerous; if one row is longer and denser, then that row is more numerous. As we have just seen, Stage I children only pay attention to the relative length of the rows. Stage II children, on the other hand, consider both relative length and relative density. On the number conservation test, Stage II children, like Stage I children, frequently say that the longer row is more numerous. But, unlike Stage I children, Stage II children occasionally say that the shorter row is more numerous because its elements are closer together. Stage II children's dependence on both length and density cues is further illustrated by their performance when shown configurations like those in Figure 5-2. On configurations (A), (B), (C), and (D), Stage II children perform like Stage I children most of the time and say that the longer row is more numerous. On configurations (E) and (F), however, Stage II children do not say that the rows are equally numerous. Instead, they say that the denser row contains more elements. Although Stage II performance is a clear improvement over Stage I, Stage II children still lack the ability to *coordinate* length and density information. They usually make correct judgments whenever a test can be passed by depending on length or density alone [Fig. 5-2 (E) and (F)]. However, they usually make incorrect judgments whenever a test can only be passed by equating length and density information.

During Stage III, children coordinate length and density information when making numerical judgments. On number conservation tests, for example, Stage III children conclude that the initial numerical relationship between the rows (whatever it may be) is conserved when one of the rows is lengthened or shortened. When a row's length increases, Stage III children understand that its density decreases by a comparable amount. When a row's length decreases, Stage III children understand that its density increases by a comparable amount. These two forms of knowledge look like special cases of the compensation rule. Since they can now coordinate length and density information, Stage III children make correct numerical judgments with those configurations in Figure 5-2 in which length and density are inversely related to each other [(A), (B), (C), and (D)].

Number development and other logico-arithmetic operations. An important feature of Piaget's description of number development is his belief that it is very closely connected to development in the relational and classificatory spheres. To be accurate, Piaget claims that the concrete-operational number concept *develops from* the coordination of the relational and classificatory contents considered earlier. Or in Piaget's words:

> When we study the development of the notion of number in children's thinking, we find that it is not based on classifying operations alone but that it is a synthesis of two different structures. We find that along with the classifying structures ... number is also based on ordering structures, that is, a synthesis of the two different types of structures. It is certainly true that classification is involved in the notion of number. Class inclusion is involved in the sense that two is included in three, three is included in four, etc. But we also need order relationships, for this reason: if we consider the elements of classes to be equivalent (and this of course is the basis of the notion of number), then by this very fact it is impossible to distinguish one element from another—it is impossible to tell the elements apart. ... Given all these elements, then, whose distinctive qualities are we ignoring, how are we going to distinguish them? The only possible way is to introduce some order. The elements are arranged one after another in space, for instance, or they are considered one after another in time, or they are counted one after another. This relationship of order is the only way in which elements, which are otherwise being considered as identical, can be distinguished from one another. ... *number is a synthesis of class inclusion and relationships of order.* [Piaget 1970c, p. 38, my italics]

Piaget's view that number development is closely connected with relational and classificatory development leads to several predictions on which a large amount of replication research has been conducted. For convenience, these predictions may be divided into two groups. The first group is broadly concerned with developmental and correlational predictions about the relational, classificatory, and numerical tests we have considered up to this point. Insofar as number development in particular is concerned, we would expect that children's performance on number conservation tests and on configurations of the sort shown in Figure 5–2 would conform to the three stages just examined. That is, we would first expect children to pass only tests in which the length cue is correct, then to pass tests in which either the length or density cue is correct, and finally to pass tests in which length and density information must be equated. When relational, classificatory, and numerical development are taken together, we would expect that development in each area should be parallel to development in the remaining two areas. That is, children functioning at some given stage in one sphere should be functioning at the same stage in other spheres. This means that children should evince the respective cognitive contents for corresponding relational, classificatory, and numerical stages at about the same time. When children are constructing graphic collections (classificatory Stage I), they should be failing ordering problems across the board and they should be basing their numerical judgments entirely on relative length. When children are sorting objects into mutually exclusive categories (classificatory Stage II), they should be passing seriation tests and basing their numerical judgments alternatively on length and density. Finally, when children are passing both multiple classification and class inclusion tests (classificatory Stage III), they should be passing multiple seriation and transitive inference tests and they should be basing their numerical judgments on coordinated length and density information. A final set of predictions within the first group is correlational in nature. Although children's performance on classificatory and relational tests should correlate strongly with their performance on numerical tests of the sort discussed above, if Piaget's account of number development is to have any generality at all, their performance on classificatory and relational tests should also correlate strongly with more traditional tests of numerical competence. In particular, these tests should correlate with basic arithmetic skills such as counting, adding, subtracting, etc.

Ordinal, cardinal, and natural numbers. The second group of predictions that follow from Piaget's account of number development are not directly concerned with any of the cognitive contents considered up to this point. Rather, they are concerned with children's understanding of the most basic of all the elementary number systems—the system 1, 2, 3, 4, ... of so-called "natural numbers." These are the numbers used in ordinary arithmetic computation. What makes the natural numbers so important is that all of the other types of numbers with which most of us are familiar—integers, rationals, irrationals, etc.—are built up in a stepwise manner from the natural numbers. Therefore, whenever one speaks of number concepts one is, in the final analysis, speaking of the natural numbers. Likewise, when Piaget speaks of the number concepts of the concrete-operational stage, he means the natural numbers. Consequently, his main justification for employing number conservation tests to measure concrete-operational numerical skills is that he believes these tests assess children's understanding of the natural numbers (e.g., Piaget 1952*a*; Beth and Piaget 1966).

Now, the natural numbers 1, 2, 3, ... have a very interesting property that they share with no other number system: Each of them has two quite different meanings. One meaning is relational and the other meaning is classificatory. When 1, 2, 3, ... have their relational meanings, they are called *ordinal numbers.* Ordinal numbers are concerned with collections of objects that have been ordered according to some asymmetrical-transitive relation. The sets of objects used in the seriation and transitive inference tests described in the earlier section on relations are cases in point. Whenever a set of objects has been ordered according to some asymmetrical-transitive relation, it is obvious that there is a "first" object, a "second" object, a "third" object, and so on until we reach the last object. Whenever 1, 2, 3, ... are being used as ordinal numbers, the number 1 refers to the first object in an ordered set, the number 2 refers to the second object in an ordered set, and so on. On the other hand, when natural numbers have classificatory meanings, they are called *cardinal numbers.* Cardinal numbers are concerned with *how many* elements different classes contain. When 1, 2, 3, ... are being used as cardinal numbers, the number 1 refers to all classes containing a single thing (e.g., the set of all current presidents of the United States), the number 2 refers to all classes containing a pair of things (e.g., the set of equinoxes), the number 3 refers to all classes containing a trio of things (e.g., the set of outfielders on any baseball team), and so on. We can see from these definitions that the number tests discussed earlier in this section are not so much natural number tests as they are cardinal number tests. We can also see from these definitions that although natural numbers can have both ordinal and cardinal meanings, all higher-order number systems can have only ordinal meanings. Integers, rationals, irrationals, etc., can easily be given ordinal meanings by thinking of them as ordered sets of points falling along a straight line. But it is impossible to think of them as classes containing certain numbers of elements.

In line with what was said earlier about the close connections between development in the relational, classificatory, and numerical domains, Piaget also contends that children's concepts of ordinal, cardinal, and natural number are closely related. In particular, he believes that children's natural number concepts are constructed from their ordinal and cardinal number concepts:

> There is then no doubt as to the explanation of the coordination between ordinal and cardinal numbers during the third stage. A cardinal number is a class whose elements are conceived as "units" that are equivalent, and yet distinct in that they can be seriated, and therefore ordered. Conversely, each ordinal number is a series whose terms, though following one another according to the relations of order that determine their respective positions, are also units that are equivalent and can therefore be grouped in a class. Finite [i.e., natural]

numbers are therefore necessarily at the same time cardinal and ordinal, since it is of the nature of number to be both a system of classes and of asymmetrical relations blended into one operational whole. [1952*a*, p. 157]

This statement generates some interesting predictions about how children acquire number concepts. Suppose we measure children's understanding of ordinal, cardinal, and natural number concepts by administering separate tests of their ability to use 1, 2, 3, ... to denote the members of ordered sets of objects (ordinal number), of their ability to use 1, 2, 3, ... to denote how many elements different sets contain (cardinal number), and of their ability to use 1, 2, 3, ... in ordinary arithmetic computation (natural number). It follows from Piaget's view of number development that each of these abilities should emerge more or less in unison with the others. Recall that development in each of these areas is supposed to run parallel to development in the other two areas. Thus, Piaget's approach entails that children's ordinal, cardinal, and natural number concepts develop in tight synchrony. The opposite of this view is that children's ordinal, cardinal, and natural number concepts emerge *sequentially*. For example, it could be that there are three invariant stages in number development: During Stage I, children acquire one of the three forms of number; during Stage II, children acquire another of the three forms of number; during Stage III, children acquire still another of the three forms of number. Later, we shall see that a good deal of research has been devoted to determining whether number development is synchronous, as Piaget predicts, or whether it is sequential.

Spatial Operations

We turn now to the second of the two basic types of concrete operations—spatial operations. As noted earlier on, spatial operations are brought to bear whenever concrete-operational children consider objects as unified wholes—i.e., spatial operations are concerned with relations within objects rather than between them. We shall consider some specific contents that are believed to exemplify this definition below. For now, however, it will suffice to think of spatial operations as the realm of elementary geometric concepts. While all of the contents discussed in the preceding section would be found in arithmetic and logic textbooks, the contents mentioned below are the sort of thing one might encounter in a high school geometry text.

geometric relations

Before we can discuss Piaget's views on spatial development, a few preliminary remarks are required about mathematics in general and geometry in particular. Mathematics is considered to consist of two branches—the mathematics of numbers and mathematics of space. The mathematics of numbers consists of three divisions—arithmetic, algebra, and analysis (the calculus and its extensions). The second branch of mathematics, geometry, also consists of three divisions. Most of us remember one of the three divisions, Euclidean geometry, from high school. However, there are two more known as topology and projective geometry. It is critical to delineate the distinctions between these divisions of geometry because Piaget's account of spatial development depends on them.

Euclidean geometry, projective geometry, and topology are all concerned with *spatial relations* and with the *scales of measurement* that can be derived from these relations. They differ in terms of the specific types of relations and scales of measurement on which they focus. Euclidean geometry deals with the sorts of spatial relations that are most familiar to us, namely, relations of *distance* which can be measured by instruments such as rulers, compasses, protractors, etc. Euclidean relations are concerned, therefore, with how much distance there is between different objects. Distance relations can always be represented by numbers. They also give rise to two important types of measurement scales: *interval* scales and *ratio* scales. Whenever one has a set of measurements for which the underlying scale is either interval or ratio, one can assign numbers to the individual measurements and, what is more, one can proceed to carry out all the usual operations of arithmetic and algebra on these numbers. Interval and ratio scales are called Euclidean metrics. Euclidean metrics are of very great importance in the physical and biological sciences. In these sciences, virtually all of the measurements taken in the course of research are assumed to involve either interval or ratio scales. Although Euclidean metrics are also important in social sciences like psychology, they are not as important as in other sciences.

Projective geometry and topology are not concerned with distance at all. They are concerned with much simpler types of spatial relations. Projective geometry deals with *relations of order*—i.e., it focuses on relations that permit us to order things in space relative to each other but not on relations that permit us to determine how far apart these objects are. Projective relations are best exemplified by the straight line. Suppose we have three distinct points *A, B,* and *C* that all fall along the same horizontal line. It is obvious that we can order these points relative to each other. The first point (say, *A*) is the one that is to the left of both of the other points; the second point (say, *B*) is the one that is to the right of the first point and to the left of the other point; the third point (say, *C*) is the one that is to the right of both the first and second points. Relations of this sort give rise to *ordinal* scales of measurement. Ordinal scales of measurement have two important properties. First, when one has a set of measurements for which the underlying scale of measurement is ordinal (e.g., points along a line), one can assign numbers to these points. But, second, one cannot do arithmetic and algebra with these numbers. In the preceding illustration, suppose we assign point A the number 1 because it is first, point B the number 2 because it is second, and point C the number 3 because it is third. To see that we cannot do arithmetic with such numbers, let us assume that A, B, and C are points along a one-foot ruler. Explicitly, let us assume that A is the one-inch mark, B is the three-inch mark, and C is the nine-inch mark. If we assign numbers to these points as before, it is clear that none of the following simple arithmetic statements is true: $1 + 2 = 3$; $2 \times 1 = 2$; $3 - 2 = 1$; $2 - 1 = 1$; $3 \times 1 = 3$; $3 - 1 = 2$. Measurement scales which have these properties are not very important in the physical or biological sciences. However, they are widely used in the social sciences.

Topology is not concerned with either distance relations or ordering relations. Instead, it deals with relations which are purely qualitative or categorical in nature. Examples of spatial relations that are qualitative include open-closed, connected-disconnected, and near-far (also called proximity). Topological relations give rise to *nominal scales* of measurement. Since topological relations are qualitative rather than quantitative, one cannot assign numbers to a set of measurements for which the underlying scale of measurement is nominal. Consequently, one cannot do arithmetic with such measurements. Nominal scales of measurement may be illustrated by any group of mutually exclusive categories. Most familiar systems of political classification (e.g., democratic-republican, liberal-conservative) and psychiatric classification (neurotic, schizophrenic, manic-depressive, etc.) are nominal scales. Since nominal measurements cannot be quantified, they have very few applications in science. However, nominal scales are very common in the arts, history and philosophy.

spatial development

We turn now to Piaget's views on spatial development. Piaget has proposed an account of spatial development which makes use of the Euclidean-projective-topological distinctions just examined. This account first appeared in two important books published in 1948: *La représentation de l'espace chez l'enfant* and *La géométrie spontanée de l'enfant*. The former work, which traces the development of various topological, projective, and Euclidean concepts, was translated in 1956 (Piaget and Inhelder 1956). The latter work, which is exclusively concerned with children's grasp of Euclidean concepts such as the measurement of distance, was translated in 1960.

Piaget describes spatial development as consisting of two invariant stages. During Stage I, which corresponds to the preoperational stage, children understand topological concepts but not projective or Euclidean ones.

As we shall see when we come to some illustrations below, when Piaget says that Stage I children grasp topological concepts he means that they understand spatial ideas which may be said to characterize objects considered one at a time. When he says that Stage I children do not grasp projective or Euclidean concepts, he means that they do not understand spatial ideas which involve locating objects in space relative to each other. During Stage II, which corresponds to the concrete-operational stage, children do understand projective and Euclidean ideas and, consequently, are capable of locating objects in space relative to each other. Since topology belongs to Stage I while projective and Euclidean geometry belong to Stage II, it is apparent that Piaget predicts a developmental lag between the former and the latter. That is, a given child will always acquire topological concepts before beginning to make any progress with either projective or Euclidean concepts. But, interestingly, Piaget does not predict any such lag between projective and Euclidean concepts. He maintains that children work out their notions of projective and Euclidean space in parallel rather than in sequence.

Before taking up illustrative contents, perhaps Piaget should speak for himself on the matter of spatial development. He has summarized his views as follows:

> Historically, scientific geometry began with Euclidean metric geometry; then came projective geometry, and finally topology. Theoretically, however, topology constitutes a general foundation from which both projective space and the general metrics from which Euclidean metrics proceeds can be derived in a parallel manner. What is remarkable is that the line of development from the preoperatory intuitions through the spatial operations in the child is much closer to the theoretical order than to the historical genealogy. The topological structures of ordinal partition (proximities, separations, envelopment, openness and closedness, coordination of proximities in linear, bidimensional, or tridimensional order, etc.) precede the others in a rather clear-cut manner. These basic structures then given rise simultaneously and in parallel fashion to the projective structures (rectilinearity, coordination of viewpoints, etc.) and the metrical structures (displacements, measurement, coordinates or systems of reference) as an extension of measurement to two or three dimensions. [Piaget and Inhelder 1969, p. 107]

I would add two observations to these remarks. First, it is not as remarkable as Piaget would have us suppose that children acquire topological concepts first. The truth of the matter is that topological concepts are much, much simpler than either projective or Euclidean ones. Thus, the fact that children grasp topological concepts first is not any more surprising than, say, the fact that children learn arithmetical concepts before they learn algebraic concepts. Second, it is very remarkable that Piaget does not expect a developmental lag between projective and Euclidean geometry. Projective geometry is simpler and more basic than Euclidean geometry (e.g., Russell

1897). Whereas the former is based entirely on the notion of spatial order, the latter involves both order and the notion of distance. Therefore, common sense suggests that children should grasp projective ideas before Euclidean ones for the same reason they learn to add before they learn to multiply—i.e., Euclidean geometry consists of projective geometry "plus some other things." However that may be, Piaget maintains, for reasons that have never been carefully spelled out, that projective and Euclidean concepts develop in parallel.

contents of spatial operations

To conclude our discussion of spatial operations, we now consider some examples of topological, projective, and Euclidean contents. The best single source of topological concepts is Part 1 of *The Child's Conception of Space* (Piaget and Inhelder 1956). The topological contents tested by Piaget and Inhelder included proximity (nearbyness), separation, succession, enclosure, and continuation. One of the most intriguing of these tests involved the recognition of shapes by the sense of touch. Preoperational children (2- to 7-year-olds) were presented with a series of everyday objects (e.g., a pencil, a comb, a key) and series of flat geometric cutouts (e.g., a circle, a cross). The objects were always presented behind a screen. The children were allowed to examine the objects with their hands but not to see them. These objects differed in terms of the aforementioned topological properties. After children had examined a particular object behind the screen, they were asked to pick out that object from a collection of drawings. Children were also questioned about the topological properties of the objects they had felt, and they were sometimes asked to make drawings of the objects. In general, Piaget and Inhelder found that preoperational children could discriminate these objects on the basis of their topological properties.

Part 2 of *The Child's Conception of Space* contains many examples of projective contents. An interesting case in point is what Piaget and Inhelder call "rotation and development of surfaces" or, more simply, projective imagery. The basic task is to visualize what three-dimensional objects look like when they are "opened up" or to visualize what two-dimensional objects look like when they are "closed up." In the language of projective geometry, the task is to convert three-dimensional objects into their two-dimensional projections, and conversely. Piaget and Inhelder's method of measuring projective imagery may be illustrated by referring to Figures 5-3 and 5-4. Suppose a child is presented with four simple three-dimensional objects—a cigar box, a plastic cube, an unopened soup can, and a toy pyramid. After examining each object, the child is asked to visualize what the object would look like if it were opened up. The correct answers for the preceding four objects appear in Figure 5-3. To measure the accuracy of the

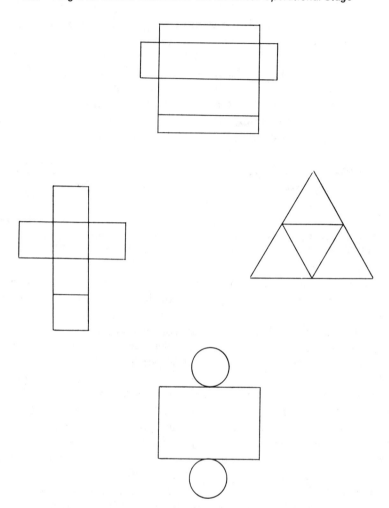

Figure 5-3   Examples of the two-dimensional projections of four common objects. The objects are a box, a cube, a pyramid, and a soup pan.

child's projective imagery, she might be shown a collection of several different two-dimensional drawings for each solid object and asked to choose the correct drawing. For example, she might be shown the collection in Figure 5-4 and asked which drawing is what the cigar box looks like when it is opened up. The child might also be asked to draw her own pictures of what each object looks like when it is opened up. Piaget and Inhelder report that concrete-operational children pass such tests but preoperational children do not.

I noted earlier that *The Child's Conception of Geometry* (Piaget, Inhelder, and Szeminska 1960) is exclusively concerned with the development of Euclidean concepts. The conservation paradigm provides two of the best-

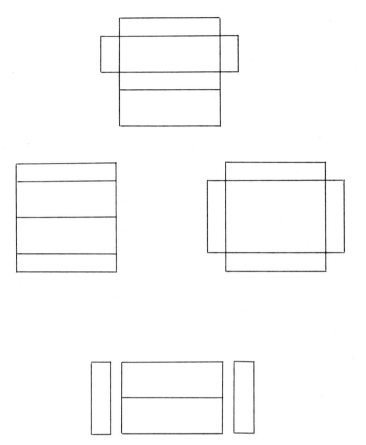

Figure 5-4   A recognition array for the two-dimensional projection of a box. Each item in the array is what a box might look like when it is "opened up." Only one of the items is correct.

known illustrations: distance conservation and area conservation. In the distance conservation test, the child's attention is first drawn to the distance between two objects A and C. A third object, B, is then inserted between A and C. Finally, the child is questioned to determine whether she conserves the original distance (i.e., $AC = ABC$) and whether she understands that the two intervals created by inserting C are equal to the original interval (i.e., $AB + BC = AC$). An illustrative distance conservation test might begin by placing two toy trees one foot apart on a table. A third tree would then be inserted between the first two. Area conservation tests are very similar. We might begin with two one-foot square pieces of green cardboard and a toy cow. The child is asked to pretend that each square is a field of grass for the cow to eat. Next, the experimenter proceeds to reduce the area of each square by placing toy buildings on it. Each time a toy building is placed on one square, an identical toy building is placed on the other square. The difference is that the buildings on one square are grouped tightly together in one corner of the square while the buildings on the other square are widely dispersed. The child is questioned to determine whether she believes that the cow has the same amount of grass to eat in each field. Piaget, Inhelder, and Szeminska report that concrete-operational children pass tests like these, but preoperational children fail them. On distance conservation tests, pre-operational children do not conserve the original interval; they believe that the sum of the two new intervals is less than the original interval. On area conservation tests, preoperational children believe that the amount of area reduction is greater when the buildings are widely distributed than when they are packed closely together.

A final Euclidean content, which I personally find very interesting, is the concept of horizontality (Piaget and Inhelder 1956). Suppose we have a large cylindrical container of water that is *closed at both ends*. Suppose the container is sitting upright on a table. Now, it is obvious that the level of the water in the container must be parallel to the surface of the table. But what happens to the water level if we rotate the container in various ways? For example, what happens to the water level if we tilt the container slightly to the right, tilt the container slightly to the left, lay the container on its side, or turn the container upside down? Of course, the water level remains parallel to the surface of the table no matter how we tilt the container. According to Piaget and Inhelder, preoperational children do not understand this. They think that when the container is tilted the water level must tilt in the same direction. In contrast, Piaget and Inhelder report that concrete-operational children understand that the water level always remains parallel to the surface of the table.

Learning

In Chapter 2, we saw that perhaps the single most distinctive feature of Piaget's theory of intelligence is its biological flavor. We saw, more particularly, that Piaget assumes that biological laws also govern intellectual development, that he treats cognitive growth as though it were a special case of growth in general, that he believes that understanding biological development is the route to understanding intellectual development, and that he views the study of intellectual development as a branch of embryology. This reliance on biological meta-phors is the principal difference between Piaget's theory and those approaches to children's intelligence that have traditionally been popular in North America. These latter approaches are characterized by their emphasis on learning as a source of intellectual development (e.g., Ferguson 1954; Stevenson 1970), and by their reliance on metaphors borrowed from the simple conditioning para-digms of animal psychology (respondent conditioning and instrumental condi-tioning). By comparison, learning does not play a central role in Piaget's theory. In fact, it plays essentially no role at all. To illustrate this point, the reader should note that there has been no mention of the influence of learning on the acquisition of any of the cognitive contents considered in this or the preceding two chapters.

In past attempts to assess the strengths and weaknesses of Piaget's theory, the absence of any explicit analysis of learning has always been counted among the theory's most important weaknesses. Unless we are all very much mistaken, children learn a great deal and, more important, they learn some of the concepts associated with Piaget's stages. So, we may reasonably ask, what role does learning play in the development of these concepts? For many years, Piaget loftily dismissed inquiries of this sort on the ground that they were strictly "American questions." More recently, however, Piaget's attitudes toward learning appear to be thawing. In a series of papers and two important books published since 1966, Piaget and some of his collaborators have attempted to spell out the basic principles of the Genevan approach to learning (Inhelder 1972; Inhelder et al. 1966; Inhelder and Sinclair 1969; Inhelder, Sinclair, and Bovet 1974; Piaget 1967b, 1970b, 1970d; Sinclair 1973). These principles are summarized in the remainder of this section. At the end of the present chapter, we consider research designed to test their validity.

The thrust of Piaget's approach to learning is twofold. First, he acknowledges that learning has an effect on cognitive contents of the sort we have been discussing. Although this may appear to be a thoroughly unsurprising statement to readers not previously steeped in Piaget's theory, it is nevertheless an historically important admission. At one time, it was widely believed by most students of Piaget's writings that his theory predicts negligible learning effects (e.g., Flavell 1963). Second, having admitted the possibility that learning influences cognitive contents, Piaget's biological perspective takes over and he begins to recant. The remainder of his ideas about learning are negative. Essentially, they consist of a list of constraints on children's ability to learn things such as conservation, transitive inference, classification, etc. These constraints may be grouped into two categories: (*a*) limitations on how much a child can learn about cognitive contents and (*b*) limitations on the specific learning procedures that may be used to train cognitive contents.

readiness to learn

Piaget's approach to learning is a readiness approach. In developmental psychology, readiness approaches emphasize that children cannot learn something until maturation gives them certain prerequisites. Toilet training is probably the best example of a true readiness phenomenon. We assume that children cannot be toilet trained until neural maturation reaches the point where they can control their bowel and bladder sphincters. Substitute "cognitive structures" for "bowel and bladder sphincters" and one is well on the way to understanding Piaget's approach to learning. According to this view, the ongoing process of cognitive development determines when and how learning can occur: "learning is no more than a sector of cognitive development which is facilitated by experience" (1970*b*, p. 714). This leads to the hypothesis that children's ability to learn any cognitive content is always "subject to the general constraints of the current developmental stage" (1970*b*, p. 713). Thus, when we try to teach children concepts such as conservation or transitive inference or classification, Piaget believes that their ability to learn these concepts will "vary very significantly as a function of the initial cognitive levels of the children" (1970*b*, p. 715). In line with these statements, Piaget also believes that "teaching children concepts that they have not already acquired in their spontaneous development...is completely useless" (1970*d*, p. 30).

We have previously seen that, for Piaget, cognitive development is a stagelike process in which children pass through an invariant series of qualitatively distinct phases. Each stage is ostensibly characterized by its own unique set of cognitive structures. When children learn any of the contents of a given stage, Piaget says that they actually are *learning how to apply previously acquired cognitive structures to new content.* If the structures appropriate to a given stage have been acquired, then children can be taught the contents associated with that stage. But if they have not yet acquired these structures, then they cannot be trained. Again, the analogy with toilet training should be obvious.

What these statements appear to add up to is this. Children's ability to learn any cognitive content is always related to their stage of cognitive development. Children who are below the stage at which a given content normally develops cannot possibly be taught contents from the next stage of cognitive development. Thus, no amount of training will cause truly preoperational children to conserve or to produce transitive inferences. Also, the more a child already knows about a given content the easier it should be to train the content. Recall from Chapter 2 that the presence of cognitive structures is inferred from the presence of cognitive contents. Consequently, the more evidence there is of a given content, the more likely it is that children possess the relevant structures. The more likely it is that children possess the relevant structures, the easier they are to train.

learning procedures

It is necessary to draw a distinction between two basic types of learning procedures: *tutorial* procedures and *self-discovery* procedures. Both procedures seek to do the same thing, namely, to teach children something they do not already know. But each goes about it in a different way. The distinction between tutorial and self-discovery training may be illustrated by considering how we might set about training children who fail conservation tests. Suppose, for example, that we have children who fail the liquid quantity test and we wish to train them to pass the test. If we decided to train them tutorially, we might institute a correction procedure. Whenever they say that glasses X and Z do not contain the same amount of water, we tell them that they are wrong and carefully explain why they are wrong (e.g., "we did not add or subtract any water when we poured it"). Whenever they say that glasses X and Z contain the same amount of water, we tell them that they are right and explain why they are right. This careful specification of correct and incorrect responses is the essence of tutorial instruction. It is rather like doing one's mathematics homework and having it graded by the instructor. But we might also take a quite different approach in which we rigorously avoid telling the children that their responses are right or wrong. For example, we might give them a series of training trials in which their task is to pour liquid back and forth between glasses of various shapes and sizes. If they pay attention to what they are doing and think about it, they may discover rules such as inversion and compensation for themselves. That is, children may discover how to conserve without the necessity of our having to tell them which responses are correct and which are incorrect.

Of the two methods just described, self-discovery training is supposed to be more effective than tutorial training. This no doubt will surprise most readers. Since there obviously is no guarantee with self-discovery training that children will, in fact, discover the error of their ways, it might seem reasonable to suppose that tutorial training would work better. Piaget believes that the reverse is true. If training is to be effective, Piaget contends that it must reflect the laws of spontaneous cognitive development. Although tutorial procedures are used in the classroom, they are not so common outside it. The spontaneous cognitive development which occurs in everyday life results primarily from an active self-discovery process or, in the words of one of Piaget's coworkers, *"active discovery* is what happens in development" (Sinclair 1973, p. 58). Since the most effective training is assumed to be training that reflects spontaneous development and since spontaneous development is an active discovery process, it follows that the best training methods are those in which "the subject himself is the mainspring of his development, in that it is his own activity on the environment or his own active reactions that make progress" (Sinclair 1973, p. 58).

To summarize the Genevan approach to learning, Piaget admits that learning can influence the cognitive contents associated with his stages. However, he also contends that learning will only occur if two conditions are met. First, children must already possess the cognitive structures of a given stage before they can be taught contents from that stage. Since cognitive structures cannot be directly measured, what this condition actually says is that the only children who can be taught a given content are those who already have a slight (but not complete) understanding of it (e.g., Stage II conservers). Second, our training methods should always reflect Piagetian laws of spontaneous cognitive growth. Specifically, our methods should be self-discovery procedures.

Replication Studies

We turn now to findings from research conducted by investigators outside Geneva. We consider research on each of the major categories of cognitive contents discussed up to this point in the same order in which the categories were originally examined.

logico-arithmetic operations:
1. conservation

Since developmental psychologists seem to be doing more research on children's conservation concepts than on just about any other topic, we shall only be considering the tip of an enormous iceberg in this section. In particular, the discussion will be restricted to illustrative findings on three earlier topics: (*a*) stages of conservation development; (*b*) horizontal *décalages* in the development of different forms of conservation; (*c*) the role of reversibility and identity rules in the development of conservation.

Stages of conservation development. There is credible evidence that children acquire the contents associated with Piaget's three stages of conservation development in an invariant sequence. As a case in point, we consider an investigation conducted by my wife and me (Brainerd and Brainerd 1972). It focused on two different types of conservation—number and liquid quantity. For each type of conservation, separate tests of Stage I, Stage II, and Stage III content were devised. These tests were then administered to kindergarteners, first graders, and second graders. If it is true that children pass through the three stages of conservation in an invariant sequence, we would expect that children should pass tests for these stages in the same order—i.e., we should find only four types of children: those who fail all three tests; those who pass only Stage I tests; those who pass only Stage I and Stage II tests; those who pass all three types of tests. Moreover, we would expect to observe this same pattern for both number conservation and liquid quantity conservation. This was exactly what we found. For number conservation, 10% of the subjects passed only the Stage I test, 3% of the subjects passed both the Stage I and Stage II tests but not the Stage III test, and 87% of the subjects passed all three tests. None of the subjects deviated from the predicted order. For liquid quantity conservation, 10% of the subjects failed all three tests, 18% passed only the Stage I test, 42%

passed the Stage I and Stage II tests but not the Stage III test, and 20% passed all three tests. Once again, none of the subjects deviated from the predicted order.

Horizontal décalages in conservation development. There also is credible evidence that children acquire conservation concepts at different times in different areas. What is notable about the claim that there are *horizontal décalages* in conservation concepts is not merely Piaget's idea that children acquire different conservation concepts at different times (it hardly seems likely that a child would acquire all of the many different varieties of conservation at exactly the same time), but his belief that all children learn to conserve different quantitative relationships in the same invariant order. For example, we saw that Piaget predicts that children always conserve number before they conserve quantity. Thus, if we administer tests for number and quantity conservation to a group of children, we expect to find only three types of children—i.e., those who fail both sorts of tests, those who pass only number tests, and those who pass both number and quantity tests. We do not expect to find children who pass quantity tests and fail number tests. This predicted pattern has been observed by several investigators (e.g., Brainerd and Brainerd 1972; Gruen and Vore 1972). Another *horizontal décalage*, usually considered to be the most important one of all, is quantity conservation → weight conservation → volume conservation. According to this sequence, children conserve quantity relations before they conserve weight relations and they conserve weight relations before they conserve volume relations (Piaget and Inhelder 1941). This sequence has been investigated many times (e.g., Chittenden 1964; Kooistra 1965; Sigel and Mermelstein 1966; Uzgiris 1964). Uzgiris (1964) conducted what is usually regarded as the classic study of the sequence. She administered four tests of quantity conservation, four tests of weight conservation, and four tests of volume conservation to children in grades one through six. If these three forms of conservation are acquired in the predicted order, we expect to find only four types of children—i.e., those who fail all the tests, those who pass only quantity tests, those who pass only quantity and weight tests, and those who pass all the tests. This is what Uzgiris found. In all, 93% of the children she tested fell into one of these four categories.

Reversibility and identity rules in conservation development. There has also been a substantial amount of research on the role of reversibility and identity rules in the development of conservation. For the sake of argument, let us assume that Piaget's, Bruner's, and Elkind's hypotheses are all correct. In other words, suppose that inversion, compensation, qualitative identity, and quantitative identity are all necessary preconditions for conservation. What predictions about the relationship between children's rule knowledge and their conservation knowledge are generated by this assumption? For one thing, it is obvious that children should pass rule tests and conservation tests in an invariant order. If we administer tests for any one of these rules and tests for conservation to a group of children, we certainly would not expect to find children who pass the latter while failing the former. Second, suppose we have a group of children who fail conservation tests and that we wish to teach them to conserve. If knowledge of the rules is necessary for conservation, it follows that teaching children one or more of the rules should improve their conservation skills. Third, suppose that we have another group of children who fail conservation tests whom we wish to teach to conserve. Suppose that we administer rule tests to these children just before we begin to train them. What should we find? If rule knowledge is *really* necessary for conservation, it should prove very difficult to train children who fail the rule tests. On the other hand, children who pass the rule tests should be much easier to train.

We now consider what research has had to say about the relationship between rule knowledge and conservation:

1. The order in which children pass rule tests and conservation tests has been a much-investigated topic in recent years and the basic finding is simply stated. It appears that children grasp each of the four rules before they conserve. The developmental relationship between qualitative identity and conservation has been studied by Bruner (1966) and by Hamel (1971; Hamel, van der Veer, and Westerhof 1972). According to Bruner and Hamel, their subjects understood that the variable stimulus is the "same object" as before deformation at a much younger age than they understood conservation. The developmental relationship between quantitative identity and conservation has been the subject of more than a dozen studies. F. H. Hooper and I have summarized the findings of these studies (Brainerd and Hooper 1975). We concluded that, on the whole, there was evidence that children understand that the variable stimulus is still the "same amount" before they understand conservation. However, the lag between quantitative identity and conservation is much shorter than the corresponding lag between qualitative identity and conservation. The developmental relationship between compensation and conservation has been studied by Larsen and Flavell (1970), Gelman and Weinberg (1972), Curcio et al. (1972), Blanchard (1975), and Brainerd (1976b, 1977a). Early studies (Larsen and Flavell 1970; Gelman and Weinberg 1972) reported no consistent relationship. However, more recent studies (Curcio et al. 1972; Blanchard 1975; Brainerd 1976b, 1977a) show that children grasp compensation before they conserve. Finally, the developmental relationship between inversion and conservation has been studied by Murray and Johnson (1969) and in a series of investigations conducted in my laboratories (Blanchard 1975; Brainerd 1977a). A consistent finding has been that children understand that inverting the deformation of the variable stimulus recreates the original state of affairs long before they can conserve the quantitative relationship

between the standard and variable stimuli. For most quantitative relations, the lag between inversion and compensation appears to be as much as 1 1/2 to 2 years. The last study (Brainerd 1977*a*) provided evidence about a possible invariant sequence in the development of the rules themselves. The children in this study understood inversion first, compensation and qualitative identity second, and quantitative identity third.

2. All four rules have been employed in experiments designed to improve the conservation performance of children who initially fail conservation tests. Hamel (1971; Hamel and Riksen 1973) and Siegler and Liebert (1972) have studied the effects of qualitative and quantitative identity instruction. They report that conservation test performance of nonconservers improves dramatically after they are given identity rule training. The effects of compensation training on children's conservation abilities have been studied by Goldschmid (1968) and by Halford and Fullerton (1971). In both cases, children who initially failed conservation tests tended to pass these tests after they had been trained on the compensation rule. Finally, several experiments have dealt with the effects of inversion rule training on conservation. There have been more than two dozen such experiments, and they have been examined in several reviews of the conservation learning literature (e.g., Beilin 1971*b*; Brainerd 1973*b*; Brainerd and Allen 1971*a*; Glaser and Resnick 1972). Like identity and compensation, inversion rule instruction produces clear improvements in the conservation test performance of children who failed these tests before they were trained. In fact, there was a time not too many years ago when inversion rule instruction was just about the only form of training which was known beyond reasonable doubt to produce conservation learning. This situation has changed dramatically in recent years, and many different forms of training are now known to be effective.

3. Both of the preceding forms of research suffer from an important weakness. Neither proves that any of the rules is an absolutely essential prerequisite for conservation. If one finds that children always understand some rules before they conserve or that training some rule improves subjects' conservation test performance, both findings are *consistent* with the hypothesis that the rule is a necessary prerequisite for conservation but neither actually proves the hypothesis. The third type of research on the relationship between rules and conservation is designed to provide more direct evidence on this question. Children who fail conservation tests are also given tests for some rule. They are divided into two groups—nonconservers who grasp the rule and nonconservers who do not. The two groups then receive identical conservation training procedures. If children must know the rule before they can conserve, we would expect the children who fail the rule test to be very difficult to train. We would also expect that the children who pass the rule test will be much easier to train. Experiments of this sort have

begun to be conducted only in the past few years. However, all four of the rules have been studied in more than one experiment. Curcio et al. (1972) reported that nonconservers who understood the compensation rule could be taught to conserve but nonconservers who did not understand the compensation rule could not. But this finding could not be replicated in three other experiments (Blanchard 1975; Brainerd 1976*b*, 1977*a*). In each of these latter experiments, there was no relation between nonconservers' compensation knowledge and their susceptibility to conservation training. In two of these latter experiments (Blanchard 1975; Brainerd 1977*a*), the relations between conservation learning and knowledge of inversion, qualitative identity, and quantitative identity also were examined. A strong relationship was observed between nonconservers' knowledge of inversion and their susceptibility to conservation training. No such relationship was observed for the other three rules. On the whole, therefore, the available evidence suggests that children probably have to understand inversion before they can conserve. The data on the other three rules are simply inconclusive at present.

logico-arithmetic operations:
2. relations

Although some replication research on relations has been devoted to testing the invariant sequences in relational contents predicted by Piaget's three stages (e.g., Murray and Youniss 1968; Youniss and Murray 1970), the great bulk of the research has focused on transitive inference. It has focused, in particular, on just how old children must be before they can make transitive inferences. This is the research that will concern us in the present section.

It will be recalled that transitive inference is supposed to be a Stage III content. It follows that most children should not possess this ability until age 7 or 8. We would certainly not expect to find that the great majority of kindergarteners and preschoolers are capable of making transitive inferences. But this is precisely what recent research has shown.

Several years ago, Martin Braine (1959, 1962) criticized the tests that Piaget uses to measure transitive inference (e.g., Piaget, Inhelder, and Szeminska 1960). His criticism will sound familiar because it is the sort of objection that Bower lodged against Piaget's object permanence tests (Chapter 3) and Borke lodged against Piaget's egocentrism tests (Chapter 4). Braine claimed that Piaget's transitivity tests are much more difficult than they should be because they measure many things other than transitive inference. It is easy to see that Braine's criticism is sound. Piaget's transitivity tests measure at least three factors that do not necessarily have anything to do with the ability to make transitive inferences: (*a*) the ability to resist visual illusions; (*b*) language ability; (*c*) memory ability. Concerning factor (*a*), Piaget incorporates visual illusions into his transitivity tests. In Figure 5-1, for example, after the child has compared sticks *A* and *C* to stick *B*, Piaget would attach outward-pointing arrowheads to the shorter stick (*C*) and attach inward-pointing arrowheads to the longer stick (*A*). This procedure, which is known as the Müller-Lyer illusion, makes *A* *look* shorter than *C* even though it actually is longer. Or suppose, in the weight transitivity test, that we make the lighter of the two outside balls (*C*) twice as large as the heavier of the two balls (*A*). This is called the size-weight illusion. In both cases, children who are perfectly capable of making transitive inferences might fail the test because they could not resist the visual illusion. Concerning factor (*b*), Piaget always requires that children who pass his transitivity tests be able to explain each of their inferences logically. It is quite possible that many children who are otherwise capable of making transitive inferences would not be verbally sophisticated enough to provide a logical justification of their inferences. Concerning factor (*c*), if subjects are to conclude that $A > C$, it is clear that they are going to have to *remember* the fact that $A > B$ and the fact that $B > C$. But what happens if they forget either or both facts? Clearly, they will fail no matter how good they are at making transitive inferences.

What happens when factors (*a*), (*b*), and (*c*) are eliminated? Several studies have shown that children will pass transitivity tests many years earlier than Piaget has reported. If one or two of these three factors is eliminated, the average age at which the majority of children make transitive inferences drops to about 5. In a series of studies conducted in my laboratories (Brainerd 1973*a*, 1974*a*; Brainerd and Vanden Heuvel 1974) and in F. H. Hooper's laboratories (e.g., Toniolo and Hooper 1975), factors (*a*) and (*b*) were eliminated by not incorporating visual illusions and by not requiring children to give logical explanations of their inferences. The majority of kindergarteners passed these tests. Similarly, Roodin and Gruen (1970) eliminated factors (*b*) and (*c*) by not requiring children to give logical explanations of their inferences and by providing memory hints. Regarding the latter, Roodin and Gruen reminded their subjects of the relationships between *A* and *B* and *B* and *C* just before they were asked about the relationship between *A* and *C*. When kindergarten children were given this memory hint, 75% of them passed the test. But when the memory hint was omitted, only about one-quarter of them passed the test.

When all three factors are eliminated, the available research indicates that preschoolers make transitive inferences. Experiments of this sort have been conducted by Siegel (1971*a*, 1971*b*) and by Bryant (1974; Bryant and Trabasso 1971). Siegel uses a discrimination learning procedure to eliminate the three factors. She trains children to acquire some simple discrimination that they simply cannot learn unless they can make transitive inferences. Then, if they learn the discrimination, we can conclude that they are capable of transitive inference. One such discrimination, is "middle-size" or "between-size." Given three objects *A, B,* and *C,* the child is taught that *B* is "between" *A* and *C.* To learn this discrimination, the child must be able to understand that *B* is *simultaneously* smaller than *A* and larger than *C.* This is a transitive inference. Bryant uses a lengthy stimulus pretraining procedure to eliminate the three factors. His subjects are given a series of five stimuli *A, B, C, D,* and *E.* They are then carefully trained to remember *A* > *B, B* > *C, C* > *D,* and *D* > *E.* When *and only when* all of these relationships have been very thoroughly learned, children's transitive inference abilities are assessed by questioning them about the relationship between stimulus *B* and stimulus *D.* When either Siegel's or Bryant's procedures are used, the majority of 3- and 4-year-olds are found to be able to make transitive inferences.

These findings on transitive inference pose serious problems for Piaget's account of relational development. Transitivity, after all, is supposed to be a Stage III content. But replication research makes it look as though transitivity is not a concrete-operational ability at all. On the whole, our best guess on the basis of the available evidence is that transitivity is a preoperational content.

logico-arithmetic operations:
3. classes

In this section, we shall consider two questions. First, what has replication research on children's classificatory concepts had to say about the validity of Piaget's three-stage model of development in this area? Second, what has replication research had to say about the age at which children understand the class inclusion concepts? We examine these two questions separately below.

Classificatory development studies. Although Piaget's three-stage model of classificatory development was first published in 1959 (Inhelder and Piaget 1959), it was not widely known until after a translation appeared in 1964. As a result, the bulk of the replication research has been conducted fairly recently. We shall be interested in what this research has shown about (*a*) the existence of graphic collections and (*b*) the order in which children acquire Stage I, Stage II, and Stage III contents.

Concerning (*a*), there have been a number of investigations in which preschool and elementary school children have been administered classification (object sorting) tests (e.g., Allen 1970; Annett 1959; Hooper et al. 1974; Kofsky 1966; Lovell, Mitchell, and Everett 1962; Ricciuti 1965; Ricciuti and Johnson 1965). It will be recalled that, according to Inhelder and Piaget (1964), Stage I children do not sort objects into mutually exclusive categories. Instead, they group them into simple geometric configurations that Inhelder and Piaget term "graphic collections." The findings of the available replication research suggest a pattern which is remarkably like the one noted for egocentric language in Chapter 3. It will be recalled that although preschoolers use egocentric language and although this usage decreases with age, egocentric utterances never predominate in children's language. More or less the same thing is true of children's construction of graphic collections. Several investigators (e.g., Annett 1959; Lovell, Mitchell, and Everett 1962) have found that very young children do indeed construct graphic collections when they are given a set of objects to sort. Moreover, the frequency of these graphic sortings is known to decrease with age. For example, they are almost never observed with elementary schoolers. But although graphic sorting exists and decreases with age, it never predominates in even the youngest children. In children as young as two or three, it is more common for objects to be sorted into mutually exclusive categories than into graphic collections. This point is well-illustrated in a recent study conducted by Hooper et al. (1974). They administered a reasonably complicated object sorting test involving more than two mutually exclusive categories to forty preschoolers. The subjects sorted the objects correctly 54% of the time on the average. In short, the replication research on children's classification test performance raises some important doubts about Piaget's three-stage model of classificatory development. On the one hand, there appears to be no doubt that children do make graphic sortings and that the frequency of such sortings decreases as children get older. On the other hand, it appears to be equally certain that even preoperational children prefer to sort objects into mutually exclusive categories. Since this is Stage II behavior, it may be that Stage I simply does not exist.

Concerning (*b*), Piaget's description of classificatory development leads to some predictions about the order in which children pass tests for various classificatory contents. The predictions resemble those discussed earlier for conservation. Since classification is a Stage II content while multiple classification and class inclusion are both Stage III contents, it follows that children should pass classification tests before they pass either multiple classification or class inclusion tests. Conversely, since multiple classification and class inclusion tests are both Stage III contents and since (as we saw in Chapter 2) invariant sequences are Piaget's way of distinguishing different stages, we would not expect that children would pass tests for one of these contents before they pass tests for the other. A study by Kofsky (1966) is usually considered the classic investigation of the order in which children acquire classificatory contents. Although Kofsky's study is very comprehensive, an even more thorough study has recently been conducted by Hooper et al. (1974). I shall discuss this second study, but the findings mentioned are consistent with those reported by Kofsky.

Hooper et al. administered tests of classification, multiple classification, and class inclusion to 280 children between the ages of 4 and 13. In line with Piaget's model, children passed the classification test before they passed either the multiple classification test or the class inclusion tests. For example, roughly 90% of the preschool and kindergarten children in the sample, taken as a group, passed the classification test but only about half of these same subjects passed the multiple classification test. A more interesting finding is that there also was an invariant sequence between classification and class inclusion. Only 7.5% of the preschool and kindergarten children passed the class inclusion test. Therefore, Hooper et al. confirmed Piaget's prediction that children always understand classification before they understand either multiple classification or class inclusion. However, they did not confirm the prediction that children understand multiple classification and class inclusion at about the same time. Instead, they found a very large invariant sequence in which the children always understood multiple classification before class inclusion. To illustrate this latter finding, suppose we say, merely for the sake of argument, that we shall regard the age at which 50% of the children pass a test for a given content as the age at which most children acquire that content. If we do this, the acquisition age for multiple classification is 6 years. Roughly 55% of Hooper et al.'s kindergarteners (average age: 6 years, 3 months) passed the multiple classification test, but only 7.5% of them passed the class inclusion test. The acquisition age for class inclusion appears to be 10 years. Roughly 52% of Hooper et al.'s fourth graders (average age: 10 years, 3 months) passed the class inclusion test. Thus, there seemed to be a lag of *four years,* on the average, between the development of multiple classification and the development of class inclusion. Even by the time children reached age 12, their performance on the class inclusion test was far from perfect. Fully 35% of Hooper et al.'s sixth graders (average age: 12 years, 2 months) failed the class inclusion test. By comparison, these same subjects performed perfectly on the multiple classification test. It therefore seems that children invariably understand how to classify objects simultaneously according to two dimensions by constructing a matrix long before they understand the principle of class inclusion.

On the whole, we may say that the replication research on children's classificatory concepts does *not* tend to confirm the broad outlines of Piaget's three-stage model of development in this area. Since even very young children have been shown to be capable of sorting objects into mutually exclusive categories, there is no evidence that Stage I even exists. Moreover, the fact that very young children pass object sorting tests suggests that it would be more proper to regard classification as a preoperational content than as a concrete-operational content. Concerning Stage III, there is an invariant sequence between multiple classification and class inclusion. Since there may be a gap of as much as four years between these two contents, it would seem improper to regard them as belonging to the same stage of classificatory development.

Class inclusion studies. As was the case in the preceding section on relations, the preponderance of research on classificatory development is concerned with only one of Piaget's contents, class inclusion. We have just seen that children seem to pass class inclusion tests much later than the nominal 7- to 8-year-old norm for the onset of concrete operations. We shall now examine research designed to investigate this phenomenon in greater detail.

In Chapters 3 and 4, we saw that performance explanations may be used to challenge Piagetian theory. Whenever Piaget interprets failures on a certain concept test as evidence that children do not possess the underlying competence that the test ostensibly measures, one can always lodge the argument that the underlying competence actually is present but the test is too difficult. Although this argument normally is used to challenge Piaget's views, it can also be used to save them on occasion. In the case of class inclusion, for example, one might be able to save his model of classificatory development if performance explanations of class inclusion failures could be found. According to such explanations, children actually understand the class inclusion principle at about the same time they understand multiple classification but they fail class inclusion tests because of extraneous test difficulty factors. Performance explanations of this sort have now been explored in several papers (e.g., Ahr and Youniss 1970; Brainerd and Kaszor 1974; Jennings 1970; Klahr and Wallace 1972; Kohnstamm 1967; Winer 1974; Winer and Kronberg 1974; Wohlwill 1968).

Recall that when children fail class inclusion tests they seem to respond in terms of the relative size of the two subordinate classes (*A* and *A* ') rather than in terms of the relative size of the superordinate class and the larger subordinate class (*B* and *A*). To date, investigators have proposed two different performance explanations of this error: the *perceptual set* hypothesis and the *misinterpretation* hypothesis. Both explanations look very plausible at first glance. The perceptual set hypothesis focuses on the stimulus materials and the misinterpretation hypothesis focuses on the type of question posed. Both hypotheses were originally advanced by Wohlwill (1968). Concerning the perceptual set hypothesis, recall that there is a marked discrepancy in the relative sizes of *A* and *A* ' in class inclusion tests. In Piaget's (1952*a*) first test, children were shown forty brown beads (*A*) and two white beads (*A* '). According to our first performance explanation, this enormous discrepancy generates a "perceptual set" which causes children to focus on the *A/A* ' relation (because it is so salient) rather than the A/B relation. According to the misinterpretation hypothesis, class inclusion questions are downright tricky. In fact, questions such as "Are there more *A*s or more *B*s?" are so deceptive that children misinterpret them. Explicitly, when the experimenter says, "Are there more *A*s or more *B*s?" children think they have been asked, "Are there more *A*s or more *A* 's?" Thus, our second performance hypothesis explains class inclusion test failures on the ground that children think they have been asked one question when, in reality, they have been asked another.

The perceptual set and misinterpretation hypotheses lead to some simple predictions that should be easy to verify if these hypotheses are true. The perceptual set hypothesis leads to two predictions. First, class inclusion tests should be much easier if they are presented in a completely verbal manner. For example, suppose we show one group of children eight toy horses and two toy cows and ask them, "Are there more horses or more animals?" But suppose we test another group of subjects without the toys by simply saying, "If a farmer has eight horses and two cows, does he have more horses or more animals?" If the perceptual set hypothesis is correct, then the children in the second group should say "more animals" much more frequently than the children in the first group. Second, if the marked numerical discrepancy between A and A' causes a perceptual set, we should be able to eliminate the set by making A and A' equal. We show one group of children five horses and five cows. We ask both groups, "Are there more horses or more animals?" We again expect that the children in the second group should say "more animals" more often than the children in the first group. Turning to the misinterpretation hypothesis, this performance explanation leads one to predict that children will not be very good at recalling the experimenter's class inclusion questions. Suppose we again show a group of children eight horses and two cows and ask them, "Are there more horses or more animals?" Immediately after they have answered, the experimenter says, "Now, what was the question I just asked you?" If the misinterpretation hypothesis is correct, we would expect that children who answer "more horses" will not recall the question very accurately. We would expect them to say that they had been asked, "Are there more horses or more cows?"

All three of these predictions have been examined in more than one experiment. The data have failed to confirm any of them. Concerning the first prediction, Wohlwill (1968) reported some preliminary evidence that seemed to show that verbal class inclusion tests are much easier than Piaget's original ones. However, subsequent experiments (Brainerd and Kaszor 1974; Jennings 1970; Winer 1974) have not borne out Wohlwill's findings. In these latter experiments, verbal and concrete class inclusion tests turned out to be equally difficult. Further, Winer (1974) was able to show that Wohlwill's original findings were artifacts of an extraneous variable that has nothing to do with whether or not class inclusion tests are presented verbally. Concerning the second prediction, Youniss (1971; Ahr and Youniss 1970) conducted three experiments that seemed to show that class inclusion tests were much easier to pass when $A = A'$ than when $A > A'$. But Youniss' findings, like Wohlwill's, proved to be artifactual. Brainerd and Kaszor (1974) reported data showing that the Youniss tests incorporated an extraneous variable that had nothing to do with whether or not the two subordinate classes were the same size. Brainerd and Kaszor eliminated the extraneous variable and found that class inclusion tests were somewhat easier when $A > A'$ then when $A = A'$! Finally, Brainerd and Kaszor tested the third prediction in two experiments. In both experiments, elementary school children were asked several class inclusion questions. After they answered each question, they were also asked to recall the question. There was absolutely no evidence that children misinterpret class inclusion questions. That is, they almost never said that a question about the A/B relation had been concerned with the A/A' relation. Moreover, by the time the children had reached about 7 years of age, they *recalled* virtually every question correctly but they rarely *answered* any question correctly.

To summarize, attempts to save Piaget's model of classificatory development by invoking performance explanations of class inclusion test failures have not met with conspicuous success so far. At present, our best evidence is that most children do not understand the class inclusion principle until early adolescence or very late childhood. If this conclusion is correct, then it would be more proper to regard class inclusion as belonging to the formal-operational stage than to the concrete-operational stage. However, this conclusion may not stand the test of time. Tomorrow, some investigator may isolate an extraneous difficulty factor that no one has yet thought of, conduct a clever experiment, and convince all of us that children understand the class inclusion principle at about the time Piaget says that they do.

logico-arithmetic operations:
4. number

Since numbers are so important in our everyday lives, it will probably surprise no one that there has been an unbroken string of research on children's numerical ideas since the turn of the century (e.g., Brownell 1928, 1941; Douglass 1925; McLellan and Dewey 1896). However, we shall be concerned here with only research pertaining to Piaget's account of number development. In particular, we shall be concerned, first, with research designed to test the validity of the three-stage model of number development and, second, with research designed to evaluate Piaget's claim of parallel rather than sequential development in the relational, classificatory, and numerical spheres. We shall see that although Piaget's three-stage model is sometimes criticized for being incomplete (e.g., Mehler and Bever 1967; Pufall and Shaw 1972; Pufall, Shaw, and Syrdal-Lasky 1973), the available data are about as consistent with this model as one could possibly wish. We shall also see that the reverse is true for Piaget's claim that relational, classificatory, and numerical development are parallel. As many readers will no doubt have guessed from the replication research on relations and classes, the data suggest sequential development in these areas.

Tests of the three-stage model. In view of the importance of number conservation in Piaget's theory of number development, it hardly seems surprising that a great many investigations of children's performance on number conservation tests have been published (e.g., Achenbach and Weisz 1975; Bearison 1969; Calhoun 1971; Rothenberg and Courtney 1968; Winer 1968). What is surprising is that although there has been an enormous amount of research on number conservation, virtually none of it has sought to test Piaget's three-stage model. Although there has been a good deal of research on this model, most of it makes use of tests other than number conservation. These other tests may be illustrated by referring to Figure 5-5.

As we saw earlier, Piaget's stages of number development are concerned with children's dependence on length and density information when they are asked to judge the relative numerousness of parallel rows of objects like those in Figure 5-5. During Stage I, children only pay attention to the relative length of the two rows. If the rows are the same length, they are said to be equally numerous; otherwise, the longer row is said to be more numerous than the shorter row. During Stage II, children pay attention to both the relative length of the two rows and their relative density, but they do not combine length and density information. During Stage III, children combine length and density information. Now, consider the sixteen stimuli in Figure 5-5. Note that three different factors are varied in these stimuli—i.e., cardinal number (equal or unequal), relative length (equal or unequal), and relative density (equal or unequal). Suppose we administer the stimuli in Figure 5-5 to preschool and elementary school children, and we ask them to make cardinal number judgments about each stimulus. If we consider each stimulus as a separate test, we should be able to use children's performance on these tests to evaluate Piaget's three-stage model. It is clear that if this model is correct, then children should tend to pass the sixteen tests in an invariant sequence. First, they should pass only tests 1, 4, 11, 12, 13, 14, 15, and 16. On these eight tests, the correct answer can be derived by simply responding to the relative length of the rows. Second, the children should pass the preceding tests plus tests 7, 8, 9, and 10. In these latter four cases, the correct answer can be derived by simply responding to the relative density of the rows. Third, the children should pass the preceding tests plus tests 2, 3, 5, and 6. In the latter four cases, the correct answer can be derived only by combining relative length information with relative density information.

Several investigations that make use of the procedure just described have been conducted in the past few years (e.g., Baron, Lawson, and Siegel 1975; Brainerd 1973c, 1973d, 1977d; Gelman 1972; Lawson, Baron, and Siegel 1974; Pufall and Shaw 1972; Siegel 1974; Smither, Smiley and Rees 1974). One finding that these studies seem to have established beyond reasonable doubt is that children base their judgments on relative length at a very young age, whereas they do not base their judgments on relative

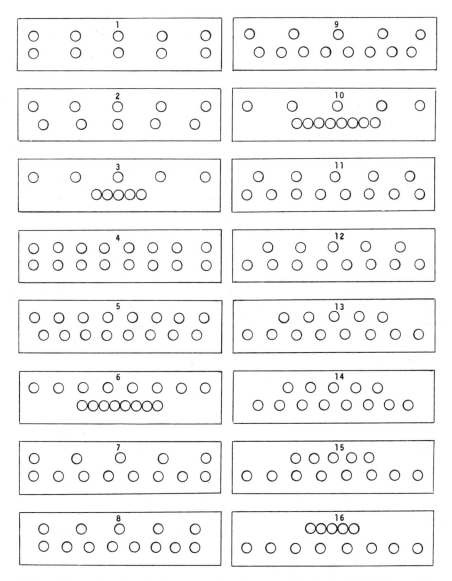

Figure 5-5 A series of sixteen configurations used by Brainerd (1977*d*) to study the effects of length and density cues on the number judgments of preschool and elementary school children.

density until much later. This is quite obviously consistent with Piaget's model. These investigations also provide support for the three-step invariant sequence just discussed. To illustrate this support, we briefly examine a study in which sixteen tests like those in Figure 5-5 were administered to preschool and elementary school children (Brainerd 1977*d*). The percentage of children who passed tests 1, 4, 11, 12, 13, 14, 15, and 16 were 95%, 93%, 92%, 99%, 96%, 99%, 98%, and 100%, respectively. Thus, these eight tests, all of which could presumably be passed by Stage I children, proved to be extremely easy even for preschoolers. The percentage of children passing tests 7, 8, 9, and 10 were 72%, 83%, 71%, and 61%, respectively. Thus, these four tests, all of which could presumably be passed by Stage II children, were clearly more difficult than the first eight tests. Moreover, virtually all of the children who failed one or more of these tests were preschoolers. This latter result is consistent with Piaget's view that most preschoolers are functioning at Stage I. Finally, the percentages of children passing tests 2, 3, 5, and 6 were 27%, 27%, 13%, and 15%, respectively. Thus, these last four tests, which could only be passed by Stage III children, were far and away the most difficult. The only children who passed them were elementary schoolers. This finding is consistent with Piaget's view that the transition to Stage III occurs at about 7 or 8 years of age.

Forgetting everything else for the moment, the chief empirical claim of Piaget's three-stage account of number development is that children employ length and density information as a basis for cardinal number judgments in the following manner. First (Stage I), they rely entirely on length; second (Stage II), they rely on both length and density but do not combine the two forms of information; third (Stage III), they combine length and density information. The research on children's judgments about parallel rows of objects, and there is a good deal of research available, provides consistent support for this claim.

Tests of the parallel development hypothesis. I noted at the beginning of this section that replication research has not borne out Piaget's hypothesis of parallel development in the relational, classificatory, and numerical areas. As some readers will have already guessed, the replication research suggests sequential development. Explicitly, it suggests that relational development precedes both numerical and classificatory development and numerical development precedes classificatory development. We examine two sources of evidence for this suggestion: (*a*) studies in which children's acquisition of *Piagetian* cognitive contents have been studied and (*b*) studies which have focused on children's understanding of ordinal and cardinal number.

Before considering the evidence in category (a), we recall that Piaget's account of development in each of the three spheres consists of three stages. In each case, development is presumed to be complete when children possess Stage III contents. As we saw in the earlier quotations from Piaget's writings on number, the key Stage III contents from these areas are transitive inference (relations), number conservation (number), and class inclusion (classes). If there is parallel development in these areas, one would expect that children should not tend to pass tests for these three contents in an invariant sequence. But this is not what the replication research has shown. There have now been several investigations in which preschool and elementary school children were administered transitivity, conservation, and class inclusion tests (Achenbach and Weisz 1975; Brainerd 1973*a*, 1974*a*; Brainerd and Fraser 1975; Brainerd and Vanden Heuvel 1974; Peterson et al. 1975; Tonolio and Hooper 1975; Winer and Kronberg 1974). The general finding in all these studies is that children who are administered such tests fall into only four groups. The youngest children (early preschool) fail all the tests; slightly older children (late preschool) pass only transitivity tests; still older children (early elementary school) pass only transitivity and conservation tests; the oldest children (late elementary school) pass all three types of tests. Also, when children who fail all three types of tests are trained on each of the three contents, transitive inference is easier to train than either conservation or class inclusion and conservation is easier to train than class inclusion. We now consider studies by Brainerd and Fraser (1975) and Winer and Kronberg (1974) which illustrate this invariant sequence.

Brainerd and Fraser (1975) investigated the first half of the transitivity → conservation → class inclusion sequence. They administered tests of transitivity of length, transitivity of weight, and number conservation to kindergarteners and first graders. The children tended to fall into three groups. Exactly 16% failed all the tests; 38% passed only the transitivity tests; 37% passed both the transitivity and conservation tests. Only 9% of the children failed to conform to this ordering. Winer and Kronberg (1974) investigated the second half of the transitivity → conservation → class inclusion sequence. They administered number conservation and class inclusion tests to children between the ages of 5 and 12. Again, the children tended to fall into three groups. Roughly 31% failed all the tests; roughly 47% passed only the conservation tests; roughly 19% passed all the tests. Only 3% of the children failed to conform to this ordering.

Thus, there is ample evidence that children acquire Stage III relational, classificatory, and numerical contents sequentially. On the whole, the currently available data indicate that a majority of children can make transitive inferences by age 4 or 5, can conserve number by age 6 or 7, and can understand the class inclusion principle by age 9 or 10.

As for the evidence in category (b), recent investigations of children's ordinal and cardinal number concepts (and the relationship between these concepts and arithmetic) are consistent with the sequential pattern of development just discussed. It will be recalled that if Piaget's hypothesis of parallel development is correct, we would expect that children should understand ordinal and cardinal number at about the same time. That is, they should be able to use numbers to refer to sets of objects ordered according to asymmetrical-transitive relations (ordinal number) at about the same time as they are able to use numbers to refer to how many elements different sets contain (cardinal number). Moreover, children's understanding of ordinal and cardinal number should be closely connected with their ability to do simple arithmetic computations (natural number).

Research on children's ordinal and cardinal number concepts, like research on Piagetian contents, has failed to bear out these predictions. Research of this sort has been a very popular topic in recent years. Many empirical reports and reviews of the literature have appeared (e.g., Brainerd 1973c, 1973d, 1974b, 1976c, 1977b; Gonchar 1975; Lesh 1976; Siegel 1974). The general trend in this research parallels the transitivity → conservation → class inclusion sequence. First, children understand ordinal number. Second, they can do basic arithmetic computations. Third, they understand cardinal number. In view of the findings on Piagetian relational, classificatory, and numerical contents that we have already examined, this three-step sequence does not seem very surprising. Research has also shown that when children who do not possess either ordinal or cardinal number are trained on these concepts, it is much easier to teach them ordinal number than it is to teach them cardinal number (Brainerd 1974b). It is also known that knowledge of ordinal number is more closely connected with arithmetic computation ability than knowledge of cardinal number. If children who are not yet very good at arithmetic (e.g., kindergarteners) are given special training on either ordinal number or cardinal number, it turns out that the arithmetic computation skills of children given ordinal number training improves more than the arithmetic computation skills of children given cardinal number training (Brainerd 1973c).

In conclusion, there certainly do not appear to be any grounds for supposing Piaget's hypothesis of parallel development of relational, classificatory, and numerical contents to be true. Regardless of whether one considers research on Piagetian logico-arithmetic contents or research on children's ordinal and cardinal number concepts, development in the three areas appears to be sequential.

spatial operations

There is much less to report in the way of replication research on spatial operations than there was on logico-arithmetic operations. For some reason, Piaget's two books on spatial development (Piaget and Inhelder 1956; Piaget, Inhelder, and Szeminska 1960) have not stimulated as much follow-up research as his books on conservation, number, etc. Moreover, it is symptomatic of the replication research that is available that it consists primarily of one-shot studies. Typically, investigators tend to conduct one or at most two studies on spatial development and then move on to other matters. In contrast, topics such as conservation and number have prompted cumulative research efforts over several years by individual investigators.

I believe only two findings from the replication literature on spatial development merit discussion. First, it is generally acknowledged that the age at which children pass tests for Euclidean contents such as distance, area, and horizontality is much later than Piaget's books on spatial operations would lead one to expect. It will be recalled that Euclidean contents are supposed to belong to the concrete-operational stage. But the replication research suggests that most of them probably are not acquired until early adolescence. Area conservation is a case in point. It appears that a majority of children do not pass area conservation tests until early adolescence (e.g., Beilin 1964, 1966; Goldschmid and Bentler 1968). A similar pattern has been observed for horizontality (e.g., Beilin, Kagan, and Rabinowitz 1966; Smedslund 1963; Thomas, Jamison, and Hummel 1973). Such tests are very difficult for concrete-operational children to pass, and it is also quite difficult to train horizontality in such children. Of the various horizontality studies, an experiment by Thomas, Jamison, and Hummel (1973) provides by far the most dramatic findings. Thomas, Jamison, and Hummel found that even *college students* do not perform perfectly on horizontality tests. In fact, they found that a substantial minority of college men and a majority of college women actually fail such tests. Moreover, when they tried to train college students who did not understand horizontality, the students did not learn very well. Generally speaking, the available normative data on horizontality indicate that the youngest age at which we may expect that a majority of children will pass horizontality tests is 12 years. If this finding holds up, it would be more proper to regard horizontality as a formal-operational content.

The second finding which merits discussion pertains to Piaget's hypothesis that topological contents invariably develop before either projective or Euclidean ones. I noted earlier that this hypothesis actually is not terribly interesting because topological ideas are so very much simpler than projective or Euclidean ones. Nevertheless, a fair amount of replication research has been conducted on this hypothesis (e.g., Dodwell 1963; Lovell 1959; Lovell, Healey, and Rowland 1962; Laurendeau and Pinard 1970). Predictably, it turns out that young children pass topological tests while failing Euclidean and projective ones. A more interesting question would be whether they also pass projective tests while failing Euclidean ones. Unfortunately, there is virtually no information available on this question.

learning

As we saw earlier, Piaget long dismissed the effects of learning on his concrete-operational contents as an "American question." This rather cavalier attitude toward what is quite clearly a very important psychological process prompted many investigators outside Geneva to conduct learning experiments on concrete-operational contents. This research began with two experiments by Smedslund (1959) and Wohlwill (1959) concerned with conservation. It has continued at an unabated pace ever since. Virtually all of the subsequent research has focused on the learning of conservation concepts, befitting their status as "the main symptoms of a budding system of operational structures" (Inhelder and Sinclair 1969, p. 3). The number of experiments has now grown quite large and, as a result, several scholarly reviews of them have been written in recent years (Beilin 1971*b*; Brainerd 1973*b*, 1977*c*, 1977*e*; Brainerd and Allen 1971*a*; Glaser and Resnick 1972; Strauss 1972). Readers who wish to acquaint themselves with Neo-Piagetian learning research are directed to such scholarly reviews. In the present section, we shall only be concerned with some special selected findings from learning experiments.

We have noted that Piaget's theory of learning makes three basic claims: (*a*) Learning can influence children's acquisition of concrete-operational contents; (*b*) children's ability to learn any concrete-operational content is limited by their stage of cognitive development; (*c*) learning procedures based on active self-discovery do work and tutorial learning procedures do not because active self-discovery is the process that governs cognitive development in everyday life. We have seen that hypothesis (*a*) is trivial because it would be difficult to find anyone who would not say that learning could have at least some influence on concrete-operational contents. Hence, we consider only what learning research has shown about hypotheses (*b*) and (*c*). We shall see that, so far, there do not appear to be any grounds for supposing either hypothesis to be correct.

Tests of stage constraints on learning. Beginning with an important and pioneering experiment by Beilin (1965), hypothesis (*b*) has been examined in more than a dozen conservation learning experiments. (For a detailed review of these experiments, see Brainerd 1977*e*.) All of them follow a three-step procedure. First, children are administered a series of conservation tests in order that they may be assigned to Piaget's three stages of conservation development. Children who fail all of the tests are assigned to Stage I. Children who pass a few of the tests but fail all of the others are assigned to Stage II. Children who pass all or virtually all of the tests are assigned to Stage III. Since Stage III children already possess a thorough grasp of conservation, they do not continue any further in the experiment. Children assigned to Stage I and Stage II proceed to the second phase of the experiment. During the second phase, the Stage I and Stage II children are given a training procedure of some sort that is supposed to help them learn to conserve. After the training has been completed, the children proceed to the third phase. During the third phase, the series of conservation tests administered at the outset is administered over again. To determine how much individual children learned, their performance during the first phase is compared to their performance during the third phase.

In the type of experiment just described, Stage I children are assumed to be in the transition phase between preoperations and concrete operations. Consequently, according to hypothesis (*b*) above, Stage II children should learn a good deal more from the training procedure than Stage I children. In fact, strictly speaking, Stage I children should not learn at all if they are really at the preoperational level. However, we would be quite satisfied if we simply found that Stage I children learn much less than Stage II children. This hypothesis has now been examined in more than a dozen experiments and it has never been confirmed. No matter what specific training procedure has been used, it has always been found that the amount of improvement in Stage I subjects' conservation test scores is equal to the amount of improvement in Stage II subjects' scores.

There is a second way to approach the prediction that learning is constrained by children's stage of cognitive development. It involves teaching concrete-operational contents to preschoolers. Preoperational children should not be able to learn contents such as conservation because they do not yet possess the cognitive structures of the concrete-operational stage. Since the preschool years comprise the first half of the nominal age range for the preoperational stage, it follows that it should be essentially impossible to teach preschoolers contents such as conservation. Research has failed to confirm this expectation. Several conservation learning experiments have been conducted with 3- and 4-year-old children (e.g., Brainerd 1974*a*, Bucher and Schneider 1973; Emrick 1968; Rosenthal and Zimmerman 1972; Denny, Zeytinoglu, and Selzer 1977). In these experiments, the investigators were able to teach their subjects conservation concepts. Taken as a group, the experiments leave little doubt that it is possible to teach preschool children to conserve quantitative relationships between stimuli.

Generally speaking, the available research fails to support the hypothesis that children's learning is related to Piaget's stages of cognitive development. Experimenters have failed to show that children learn better when they know a little bit about a certain content than when they know nothing at all. Also, it appears possible to teach concrete-operational contents to children whose ages place them in the first half of the preoperational stage.

Self-discovery vs. tutorial procedures. Learning research has also failed to support the hypothesis that active self-discovery procedures are better methods of teaching children concrete-operational contents than tutorial procedures. The reverse is true. The available data suggest, first, that tutorial methods work quite well as training strategies and, second, that where comparison is possible tutorial procedures seem to work better than active self-discovery procedures.

Concerning the first of the preceding suggestions, research has shown that at least four tutorial methods are excellent procedures for teaching contents such as conservation: *rule instruction, observational learning, conformity training,* and *feedback.* The first method was pioneered by

Beilin (1965) and has been used in many subsequent experiments (e.g., Hamel and Riksen 1973; Siegler and Liebert 1972). Rule instruction consists of providing children who fail conservation tests with a verbal rule that should help them understand why quantitative relationships between objects are conserved across irrelevant deformations (e.g., "I did not add or subtract anything"). The second method is inspired by the theories of Albert Bandura (e.g., 1969; Bandura and Walters 1963) of Stanford University. Zimmerman and Rosenthal (e.g., 1974) are chiefly responsible for applying the method to concrete-operational contents. The procedure consists of having children who fail tests for some content watch a *model* who performs perfectly on such tests. The model may be either live or filmed. Conformity training has been used by Murray (1972) and by Silverman and Geiringer (1973). The procedure involves using children who already possess a certain content to teach children who do not possess the content. For example, a child who fails conservation tests is paired with a child who passes them. The experimenter administers a series of conservation tests to the two children simultaneously. Each time a question is posed, the experimenter asks the two children to debate their respective answers and arrive at a consensual response. Finally, feedback training is primarily associated with a series of experiments conducted in my laboratories (e.g., Brainerd 1972*a*, 1972*b*, 1974*a*, 1976*b*, 1977*a*). The procedure is extremely simple. A series of tests for some content is administered to children who fail such tests. Each time a wrong response is given, the experimenter says, "No, that is the wrong answer. The right answer is. ..." Each time a correct response is given, the experimenter says, "Yes, that is the right answer," and gives the child a reward (token, candy, etc.).

Contrary to Piaget's emphasis on self-discovery learning, the preceding methods, which all de-emphasize self-discovery, are known to work very well. Each of them has proved capable of teaching children who fail conservation tests across the board (Stage I) to progress to perfect or nearly perfect performance on conservation tests.

Concerning the second of the preceding suggestions, research also indicates that tutorial training is generally superior to self-discovery training. There are two main sources of evidence bearing on this point. The first comes from a few experiments in which tutorial and self-discovery training have been compared (e.g., Botvin and Murray 1975), and the former proved more effective. The second source comes from learning experiments conducted in Geneva by Piaget's coworkers (Inhelder, Sinclair, and Bovet 1974). As might be expected, these experiments have made exclusive use of self-discovery training. The findings indicate that self-discovery training suffers from an important weakness. It does not appear to work for children who do not already possess some understanding of conservation (Stage I). In all of these experiments, only children who passed some conservation tests (Stage II) derived benefit from self-discovery training. Thus, the conclusion that seems to follow from Genevan learning research is that self-discovery training is only effective for Stage II children. This may be contrasted with results from tutorial experiments conducted outside Geneva. Tutorial methods such as the four mentioned above have been shown to work as well for children who fail conservation tests across the board as for children who have a partial understanding of conservation. Moreover, as we saw earlier, tutorial procedures have even proved effective at teaching preschoolers to conserve.

Synopsis

The concrete-operational stage is by far the most important one in Piaget's theory. The great bulk of Piaget's writing and research is concerned, in one way or another, with this stage. Concrete-operational contents have also provoked more research by investigators outside Geneva than the contents of any other stage.

Theoretically, the concrete-operational stage is the last of the three levels of transition to mature operational intelligence. During the first level of transition, the sensorimotor stage, intelligence is confined to overt action and mental representation is absent. During the second level, the preoperational stage, mental representation is present but true operations have not yet appeared. During the third and last level, true operations are present but they are limited to concrete information. At the level of mature operational intelligence, the formal-operational stage, mental operations are freed from their previous reliance on concrete information and can now deal with abstract ("hypothetical") information as well.

There are two principal types of concrete operations: logico-arithmetic operations and spatial operations. Logico-arithmetic operations process discrete data, and spatial operations process continuous data. Logico-arithmetic operations are the richer of these two sources of cognitive contents. The four key contents in this category are conservation, relations, classification, and number.

Logico-arithmetic operations. Conservation is the single most important content in Piagetian theory. It is regarded as an unequivocal behavioral indicator of the presence of mental operations. Conservation refers to children's understanding that quantitative relationships between pairs of perceptually identical objects remain invariant when the perceptual identity is destroyed. These relationships may be either symmetrical or asymmetrical. Conservation tests have been devised for several everyday quantitative relations (number, length, weight, volume, area, etc.) Three global stages of conservation development have been posited. During Stage I, which corresponds to the preoperational period, children fail conservation tests across the board. During Stage II, which corresponds to the transition phase between preoperations and concrete operations, various intermediate reactions are observed. In particular, children usually predict conservation before a deformation is performed, and they sometimes conserve after small deformations. During Stage III, which corresponds to the concrete-operational period, children pass conservation tests across the board. Children are said to pass through the three stages at different rates for different concepts. For example, Stage III is presumably attained earlier for number than for length and earlier for length than for quantity. In order to conserve, Piaget believes, children must grasp the reversibility rules that govern mental operations. Other theorists, notably Jerome Bruner and David Elkind, have proposed that knowledge of identity rules is a necessary prerequisite for conservation.

Relational cognitive contents are concerned with relations of order (asymmetrical-transitive relations). The three most important contents in this category are seriation, multiple seriation, and transitive inference. Seriation refers to children's ability to order a collection of objects according to a single asymmetrical-transitive relation. Multiple seriation refers to children's ability to order a collection of objects simultaneously according to two asymmetrical-transitive relations by constructing a matrix. Given the premises $A > B$ and $B > C$ (or $A < B$ and $B < C$), a transitive inference occurs when the child deduces that $A > C$ (or $A < C$). Relational development, like conservation development, involves three stages. During Stage I, which corresponds to the preoperational period, children fail seriation, multiple seriation, and transitive inference tests across the board. During Stage II, which corresponds to the transition phase between preoperations and concrete operations, children pass seriation tests but they continue to fail multiple seriation and transitive inference tests. During Stage III, which corresponds to the concrete-operational phase, children pass all three types of tests.

Classificatory cognitive contents are concerned with a special symmetrical relation, the relation of membership or belonging. It is by virtue of this relation that things are grouped together to form classes. The three basic classificatory cognitive contents are classification, multiple classification, and class inclusion. Classification refers to children's ability to sort a large collection of objects exhaustively into two or more categories. Classification is one-dimensional in the sense that each object belongs to one and only one class. Multiple classification is the counterpart of multiple seriation. It refers to children's ability to categorize a collection of objects simultaneously according to two properties by constructing a matrix. Finally, class inclusion is concerned with children's understanding of the fact that any superordinate class is numerically greater than any subclass contained in it (there are more dogs than spaniels, more birds than robins, etc.). Classificatory development also consists of three stages. During Stage I, which corresponds to the preoperational period, children fail classification, multiple classification, and class inclusion tests across the board. The most interesting feature of this stage is that children form graphic collections on classification tests. During Stage II, which corresponds to the transition phase between pre-operations and concrete operations, children pass classification tests while continuing to fail multiple classification and class inclusion tests. During Stage III, which corresponds to the concrete-operational period, children pass tests for all three types of classificatory content.

Usually when we speak of "number" we are referring to the elementary number systems (integers and fractions) and, perhaps, to arithmetic as well. But when Piaget discusses number, he is normally speaking of number conservation. Number conservation refers to children's understanding that the numerical relationship between two perceptually identical collections remains invariant when the perceptual identity is destroyed. As is the case for conservation, relations, and classification, three developmental stages are posited. During Stage I, children base their numerical judgments exclusively on relative length. They ignore both density information and numerical information. During Stage II, children base their numerical judgments alternately on relative length and relative density. They continue to ignore numerical information. During Stage III, children base their numerical judgments exclusively on relative number. Piaget believes that this reliance on number arises from coordinating length and density information rather than simply ignoring it. Another important aspect of Piaget's account of number development is his hypothesis that development in the numerical sphere closely parallels development in the relational and classificatory spheres. In fact, he speaks of the mature number concept as a "synthesis" of relational and classificatory achievements (especially transitive inference and class inclusion). This leads one to predict an absence of invariant sequences between relational and classificatory stages, on the one hand, and the three number stages, on the other. It also leads one to predict that children should grasp ordinal and cardinal number at about the same time.

Spatial operations. Spatial operations comprise the second category of concrete-operational cognitive contents. These operations are brought to bear on continuous information. Piaget's spatial contents are primarily geometrical in nature. His views about development in the spatial area hinge on a distinction between three basic types of geometric concepts: topological concepts, projective concepts, and Euclidean concepts.

All three types of concepts are concerned with spatial relations and with the underlying scales of measurement that can be derived from such relations. Euclidean concepts deal with familiar relations of distance that can be measured with the instruments of high school geometry. Distance relations can be represented by numbers, and they give rise to so-called interval and ratio scales. These scales, which are also called Euclidean metrics, are very important in the biological and physical sciences. One can do arithmetic with the numbers from such scales. Projective concepts deal with relations of order. Such relations permit us to localize objects in space relative to each other, but they do not tell us how far apart objects are. Projective relations give rise to ordinal scales. Although such scales can be represented by numbers, we cannot do arithmetic with the numbers. Finally, topological concepts are concerned with spatial relations of a purely quantitative (categorical) nature. Such relations neither permit us to localize objects relative to each other nor tell us how far apart objects are. Proximity, open-closed, and connected-disconnected are topological relations. Such relations give rise to nominal scales. Nominal scales cannot be represented by numbers. Although such scales are of little importance in science, they are very common in the arts, humanities, and philosophy.

Piaget describes spatial development in terms of two invariant stages. During Stage I, children grasp topological relations but not Euclidean or projective ones. Consequently, they cannot order objects in space nor determine how far apart they are. During Stage II, projective and Euclidean concepts both appear. The topological contents for which Piaget has devised tests include proximity, separation, succession, enclosure, and continuation. Consistent with his two-stage theory, he reports that such relations are understood by preoperational children. Piaget has also devised tests for several projective and Euclidean contents. The former include rotation of surfaces and development of surfaces. The latter include conservation of area and horizontality. Consistent with his two-stage theory, Piaget reports that preoperational children fail projective and Euclidean tests, but concrete-operational children pass them.

Learning. Whereas learning plays a central role in most other theories of cognitive development, it is rarely mentioned by Piaget. This has caused many investigators to wonder about the influence of learning procedures on contents from Piaget's stages—particularly contents from the concrete-operational stage. Piaget long dismissed such inquiries as "the American question." Recently, however, a Genevan theory of learning has been published. It makes three claims, one trivial and the other two important. First, it is proposed that learning procedures will, in fact, produce improvements in concrete-operational contents. Second, it is proposed that the amount of improvement is strictly dependent on the child's stage of cognitive development. In the case of conservation, for example, attempts to train Stage I children to conserve are viewed as "completely useless." Third, it is proposed that the amount of improvement also depends on the type of training method used. The training methods that the theory regards as correct are those which incorporate some provision for active self-discovery of the content being trained.

Replication research. Logico-arithmetic contents have received substantially more attention than spatial contents in the replication literature. The replication research on conservation has examined stages of conservation development, horizontal *décalages,* and the role of reversibility and identity rules in conservation acquisition. Concerning stages of conservation development, the available evidence indicates that children show the various reactions Piaget associates with these stages in the same order predicted by the stages. The concepts for which this finding has been reported include number conservation and liquid quantity conservation. Concerning horizontal *décalages,* there is also a good deal of evidence showing that children acquire different conservation concepts in an invariant order. Specific conservation concepts for which *décalages* have been observed include number conservation vs. length conservation, number conservation vs. quantity conservation, and quantity conservation vs. weight conservation vs. volume conservation.

Concerning the role of rules in conservation acquisition, there have been both invariant sequence studies and training experiments. The invariant sequence studies, on the whole, show that children understand rules before they understand conservation. Explicitly, they appear to grasp inversion, compensation, qualitative identity, and quantitative identity before they conserve. The picture provided by training experiments is more mixed. There have been two general types of experiments. First, some investigators have trained rules as a means of inducing conservation. All four rules have been used as training procedures in more than one experiment. Each of them has been found to produce improvements in conservation. Second, other investigators have measured children's prior knowledge of the rules, and have used this information to predict how easily children learn conservation in a training experiment. If a given rule is actually a necessary prerequisite for conservation, then we would expect that children would be more likely to learn conservation in a training experiment if they already grasped the rule. In experiments of this sort, inversion is the only rule that has been observed to predict learning.

Most of the replication research on relations has been concerned with transitive inference. Several investigators, in particular Martin Braine, have argued that Piaget's transitive inference tests measure many things other than the mere ability to make a transitive inference. This criticism is fundamentally the same as Bower's objections to Piaget's object permanence tests and Borke's objections to Piaget's perspective-taking tests. Transitivity tests appear to measure at least three extraneous abilities, namely, the ability to resist visual illusions, language comprehension, and memory ability. It is possible that many children who fail transitive inference tests do so because they lack one of the extraneous skills rather than because they cannot make transitive inferences. A large number of studies suggests that this supposition is correct. Several investigators have devised transitivity tests in which two extraneous skills are eliminated. As a rule, the mean age of transitive inference drops to 5 years. Transitive inference tests in which all three extraneous skills are eliminated have been employed in a series of experiments by P. E. Bryant. The mean age of transitive inference drops below 5 years in these experiments. These data pose serious difficulties for Piaget's theory of relational development. They suggest that relational contents may be preoperational rather than concrete-operational.

Replication research on classificatory contents has tended not to support Piaget's three-stage model of development in this area. There have been a number of studies in which preschool and elementary school children were administered classification tests. Although the existence of graphic collections has been confirmed, it appears that they never predominate. Even very young children prefer to sort objects into mutually exclusive classes rather construct graphic collections. Piaget's three-stage model leads to some definite predictions about the order in which children acquire classificatory contents. Multiple classification and class inclusion should appear at about the same time because they are both Stage III contents. However, the research suggests that children invariably pass multiple classification tests before class inclusion tests. It also suggests that class inclusion is a surprisingly difficult concept that is not acquired until the several years after the nominal acquisition age reported by Piaget. Some experimenters have reported that a large percentage of high school and college students, though by no means a majority, fail class inclusion tests. Experiments have been conducted that were designed to examine the possibility that the inordinate difficulty of class inclusion tests is caused by performance variables. Two performance hypotheses, the perceptual set hypothesis and the misinterpretation hypothesis, have been studied. The perceptual set hypothesis says that numerical disparities between the two subclasses increase the difficulty of class inclusion tests. Experiments in which equal subclasses are used and experiments in which class inclusion tests are presented verbally have failed to confirm this hypothesis. The misinterpretation hypothesis says that class inclusion questions are tricky and, consequently, children misunderstand them. However, an experiment by Brainerd and Kaszor (1974) showed, first, that children rarely misunderstand class inclusion questions and, second, that such errors do not predict performance on class inclusion tests. At present, therefore, the difficulty of the class inclusion concept remains unexplained.

The available findings on Piaget's account of number development are consistent with his three-stage model and inconsistent with his hypothesis of parallel development among classificatory, relational, and numerical contents. Concerning the three-stage model, children's use of length, density, and number information as a basis for making numerical judgments has been examined in several studies. The data seem to indicate that children use length information before they use either density or number and that they use density before number. This is what Piaget's model predicts. Concerning the parallel development hypothesis, classificatory, relational, and numerical contents appear to be acquired sequentially. Relevant data come from two sources: studies in which tests for Piagetian contents have been administered and studies concerned with ordinal and cardinal number. Studies of the former sort show that children grasp transitive inference (Stage III relations) before number conservation (Stage III number) and that they grasp number conservation before class inclusion (Stage III classification). Similarly, studies of ordinal and cardinal number show that children normally understand ordinal number (Stage III relations) before they understand cardinal number (Stage III classification).

Piaget's work on spatial development has not stimulated as much follow-up research as his work on logico-arithmetic operations. However, there is enough research to conclude that certain aspects of Piaget's two-stage model of spatial development have received support. In particular, it seems that children grasp topological relations before projective or Euclidean relations. In view of the enormous differences in the complexity of such relations, this is probably a trivial finding. On the negative side, it is generally conceded that Euclidean relations are understood at much later ages that Piaget's model would lead one to expect. Area conservation and horizontality are cases in point. Neither appears to be present before adolescence. The concept of horizontality may never be acquired by most subjects. Experiments by Thomas, Jamison, and Hummel (1973) revealed that a majority of college students fail horizontality tests and that the failure rate remains high after training on the concept.

Piaget's views about the effects of learning on his conrete-operational contents do not appear to be correct. The hypothesis that learning affects performance on tests for such contents is trivial, and it has been confirmed in any number of experiments. The two nontrivial hypotheses, that stage constrains learning and learning procedures based on active self-discovery work best, have not received support. The hypothesis that stage constrains learning causes one to predict that children who know a little about some content should learn more than children who know nothing. This prediction has been tested in several conservation learning experiments. On the whole, children who failed conservation pretests across the board (Stage I) derived as much benefit from training as children who passed some tests while failing others (Stage II). The hypothesis that effective training procedures should incorporate provisions for active self-discovery of the target content has also not been confirmed. The available evidence indicates that methods that do not provide for self-discovery (tutorial procedures) work quite well and that they probably work better than self-discovery procedures. Four tutorial procedures have produced large learning effects in children with no prior knowledge of conservation (Stage I): rule instruction, observational learning, conformity training, and simple feedback. Contrary to Piaget's emphasis on self-discovery learning, these particular methods actually de-emphasize self-discovery.

Supplementary Readings

1. BRAINE, "The Ontogeny of Certain Logical Operations: Piaget's Formulation Examined by Nonverbal Methods" (1959). Braine's monograph, based on his doctoral dissertation, is widely regarded as the classic reference on the influence of performance variables on Piagetian tests. The introductory section contains a series of closely reasoned arguments about how such variables affect transitive inference.

2. BRAINERD, "NeoPiagetian Training Experiments Revisited: Is There Any Support for the Cognitive-developmental Stage Hypothesis?" (1973b); "Cognitive Development and Concept Learning: An Interpretative Review" (1977e); and "Learning Research and Piagetian Theory" (1977c). At the time of this writing these three papers were the most recent reviews of learning research on concrete-operational contents. The first two papers review the data from the standpoint of Piaget's hypothesis that stage constrains learning. The last paper discusses Piaget's views on self-discovery learning.

3. BRAINERD, *The Origins of the Number Concept* (1977b). This book is concerned with recent work on the development of children's number concepts. Piaget's theory is examined and relevant findings are summarized.

4. BRUNER, OLVER, and GREENFIELD, *Studies in Cognitive Growth* (1966). In this classic work, Bruner and his coworkers argue that the acquisition of concrete-operational contents results from processes different than those posited by Piaget. The roles of language and culture are stressed in place of operations and cognitive structures.

5. FLAVELL, "Concept Development" (1970). Flavell's unusually comprehensive chapter provides a broad introduction to research on the development of concepts. By far the greater portion of the chapter deals with the acquisition of concrete-operational contents.

6. GELMAN, "The Nature and Development of Early Number Concepts" (1972). Gelman's chapter, like Flavell's, is unusually comprehensive. It covers most of the research on number development conducted during this century and examines the implications of the findings for Piaget's views on number development.

7. KOHNSTAMM, *Piaget's Analysis of Class-inclusion—Right or Wrong?* (1967). Kohnstamm's monograph is a detailed analysis of Piaget's model of classificatory development with special reference to class inclusion concepts.

8. LAURENDEAU and PINARD, *The Development of the Concept of Space in the Child* (1970). I noted earlier on that the replication literature on spatial contents consists primarily of one-shot experiments. Laurendeau and Pinard's book is the most important single exception to this rule. It is clearly the best source of evidence on the replicability of the findings reported in Piaget's space books.

9. ZIMILES, "The Development of Conservation and Differentiation of Number" (1966). This may be the most comprehensive investigation of conservation development ever reported. Piaget's views on conservation are discussed in some detail, and normative findings based on a sample of several hundred children are presented.

chapter 6

Piaget on Adolescence:
The Formal-Operational Stage

We turn now to Piaget's fourth and last epoch of cognitive development, the stage of formal operations. The nominal age range for the onset of this stage is what we usually call adolescence—i.e., from puberty (roughly 11 years old) to the middle of high school (roughly 15 years old). We saw in Chapter 4 that Piaget's account of the preschool years differs in important respects from what most theorists have to say about this period. The same thing is true of his views on adolescence. The common denominator in most psychological theories of adolescence is their emphasis on the emotional and social upheavals that occur during this time of life. To use a popular phrase, adolescence is routinely portrayed as a period of "trouble and turmoil." The views of Erik Erikson (e.g., 1963, 1968) about adolescent "life crises" and "identity crises" afford classic illustrations of this school of thought.

The one conclusion that seems to follow inescapably from the trouble-and-turmoil position is that adolescence is just not a very pleasant phase to go through. Adolescents are pictured as being in a state of constant and unrelieved conflict. They are said to be incapable of coming to grips with their newly acquired sexuality. They are also said to be emotionally unstable and subject to bouts of depression. Statistics show that they are prone to delinquency and other varieties of antisocial behavior. They seem to be torn between the desire to remain children and the need to assume the responsibilities of adulthood. In short, the traditional view of adolescence is somewhat gloomy. In fact, one wonders upon reading Erikson, Freud, and others how most of us managed to make it through with a whole skin. One is also tempted to ask why, if adolescence is so bad, most of us have such warm and blissful memories of it.

Piaget is not, to say the least, especially concerned with the socio-emotional problems of adolescence. In sharp contrast to the trouble-and-turmoil view, he regards adolescence as perhaps the most exhilarating and productive time of life. It is the time when one plans one's future and fixes the goals for one's life; it is a time of altruism and accute awareness of injustice; it is a time of great hopes and a time when simple answers to burning questions are just not good enough. It is perhaps arguable whether this is a valid description of the behavior of most adolescents. But, as we saw in Chapter 1, it is probably a valid description of Piaget's own adolescence.

Piaget finds the thinking and reasoning of adolescents to be similarly praiseworthy. He believes that between the ages of 11 and 15 intelligence reaches its peak. The thinking and reasoning of this period is clearly superior to that of childhood. What is more, Piaget has even suggested that it may be superior to that of adulthood. For example, he once proposed (Tanner and Inhelder 1960) that the reasoning capabilities of untrained adolescents may be superior to those of college-trained young adults. This surprising claim was based on a series of investigations conducted in Great Britain. These investigations indicated that young adults at the University of Bristol did worse on the abstract reasoning tests we shall be discussing in this chapter than adolescents Piaget has tested in Geneva. Interestingly, these tests call for the use of reasoning skills on which the college subjects had been specifically trained as part of their university educations. The message seems to be that it is all downhill after adolescence.

The standard reference for the formal-operational stage is *The Growth of Logical Thinking from Childhood to Adolescence* (Inhelder and Piaget 1958). This book focuses on two themes. The first, which consumes by far the greater share of the book, is a report of several experiments conducted during the early 1950s by Piaget's chief collaborator, Barbel Inhelder. As we shall see below, Inhelder's experiments were supposed to get at "scientific" and "propositional" reasoning in adolescents. The second theme is a theoretical account of the formal-operational stage that was written primarily by Piaget. This account is offered as an explanation of the findings of Inhelder's experiments. In addition to the Inhelder-Piaget book, discussions of the formal-operational stage may be found in most of Piaget's summary works (e.g., Piaget 1967 *a*; Piaget and Inhelder 1969).

The analysis of the formal-operational stage that follows takes the same general form as our discussions of earlier stages. First, we consider some broad features of formal-operational thought that serve to distinguish it from the intelligence of earlier stages (especially the concrete-operational stage). In particular, we consider the fact that the reasoning of this stage is said to be *hypothetico-deductive, scientific*, and *reflective-abstractive*. In conjunction with these general properties, we also examine what factors are ostensibly responsible for the transition from concrete to formal operations. Second, we review some illustrative cognitive contents. These contents, like those associated with the concrete-operational stage, may be divided into two groups—*propositional* or *combinatorial operations* and *formal-operational schemes*. Third and finally, we take up the available replication research. Three general varieties of replication investigations are examined: *(a)* studies of propositional operations; *(b)* studies of formal-operational schemes; *(c)* learning experiments. For the most part, the empirical questions posed in these studies are the same as those which have arisen in earlier chapters.

General Features
of Formal-Operational Thought

The nominal age range given by Piaget for the first glimmers of formal-operational intelligence is 11 to 12 years. Piaget posits a lengthy transition or "preparation" phase for this state. While one may expect some evidence of formal thinking by age 11 or 12, Piaget believes that formal operations are not solidly established until around age 15. Naturally, this leads one to expect that between the ages of 11 and 15 subjects will tend to behave as though they were formal-operational in some situations and as though they were still concrete-operational in other situations. But after age 15, when formal operations are in full control, their behavior should become more consistent.

During the four or five years required for formal operations to become completely established, three new features of intelligence emerge. These features are, in their approximate order of importance, hypothetico-deductive reasoning, scientific reasoning, and reflective abstraction. Below, we examine these abilities in turn with an eye toward the question of how each serves to distinguish formal operations from concrete operations. After each of them has been discussed, we turn to the question of what underlying changes are supposed to be responsible for their emergence. That is, we take up the matter of how the transition from concrete to formal operations is supposed to occur.

hypothetico-deductive reasoning

This first characteristic of formal operations, which Piaget sometimes also calls "transcendentalism," harks back to some issues raised in the preceding chapter. We noted in Chapter 5 that the "concrete" in concrete-operational means that reasoning operates on hard tangible facts rather than on hypotheses. We saw that one of Piaget's favorite illustrations of this point involves transitive inference. When concrete-operational children are administered a test in which the initial premises ($A < B$ and $B < C$) are asymmetrical-transitive relations that they have *directly perceived*, then they make the appropriate transitive inference ($A < C$). But they do not automatically make such inferences when the premises are hypothetical. For example, they do not automatically conclude "Chicago is west of New York" after being told "Chicago is west of Detroit" and "Detroit is west of New York." But formal-operational children do—or at least so Piaget claims.

In its broadest sense (which happens to be the sense Piaget uses), hypothetico-deductive reasoning refers to *any* type of reasoning that goes beyond the confines of our everyday experience to things of which we have no experience. In particular, hypothetico-deductive reasoning extends beyond the boundaries of both perception and memory. Such reasoning always involves deducing conclusions from premises which are *hypotheses* rather than from facts that the subject has actually verified. For convenience, the premises on which hypothetico-deductive reasoning is based may be said to be of two general sorts: (*a*) testimony and (*b*) pure conjecture. Type (*a*) premises include statements that happen to be true but that, for some reason, the subject cannot verify at the moment. They include statements such as "The Babylonians discovered arithmetic before the Greeks," "Plato was a student of Socrates," and "The cotton gin was invented before the automobile." In each case, the subject could verify these statements only if there was a history book handy. Type (*b*) premises refer to hypotheses that may be true but cannot be directly verified ("The Vikings discovered America before Columbus"), statements that are fictitious ("Apollo was the son of Zeus"), and even statements that contradict verifiable facts ("Napoleon was taller than DeGaulle"). This leads to the interesting prediction that, given invalid premises, formal-operational children will deduce the appropriate conclusions even if they know these conclusions are factually incorrect. Thus, formal-operational children will deduce "Los Angeles is east of Philadelphia" given the premises "Los Angeles is east of St. Louis" and "St. Louis is east of Philadelphia" even though they know that Los Angeles is west of Philadelphia. A concrete-operational child would never do this. The capacity to deduce conclusions that are presumably at variance with the facts is significant because it plays a central role in mathematics.

From the above features of hypothetico-deductive reasoning, Piaget draws the following important conclusion: The mental operations of the formal-operational stage, unlike those of the concrete-operational stage, *may be executed from start to finish at a purely symbolic level.* This is where the "formal" in formal-operational comes from. It will be recalled from Chapter 5 that concrete-operational children always need some informational input from the external environment to get their mental operations going. At the formal-operational level, concrete props and points of reference are no longer required. Intelligence seems to have severed many of its ties with the real world. To Piaget, this suggests that intelligence has moved away from "things" toward "ideas." This makes it possible to think about things that are quite abstract and may even have no solid basis in the real world (e.g., What is probable? What is possible?). In this sense, formal-operational intelligence *transcends* reality.

It goes without saying that language plays a central role in hypothetico-deductive reasoning. In fact, Piaget believes that such reasoning would be impossible if it were not for the capacity to pose questions verbally. This ability to formulate conjectures (What is truth? How much is $8 + 9$?) provides a mechanism for informational inputs which are entirely self-generated. This new-found question-formulating ability is supposed to rest on a new form of mental representation. Since advances in mental representation have played a central role in our discussions of earlier stages, it is hardly surprising to find that there are new representational powers at the formal-operational level. As might be expected from what has already been said, the mental representations of adolescence are, for the first time, no longer restricted to extrapolations from external reality. That is, they are no longer confined to generalizations from sensory and perceptual experience. Instead, formal representations form a *language-based system* that, upon examination, bears little resemblance to concrete experience. To make this point about formal representations slightly clearer, one might contrast them with another form of mental representation, namely, imagery. Images bear a definite prima facie resemblance to the concrete experiences that they represent. In other words, images possess a *quasi-sensory* aspect. Images, especially visual images, are usually described as being "pictures" of the things they represent. In contrast, formal-operational representations bear no obvious resemblance to things in the real world. They are abstract symbols of some sort. Since formal-operational representations are so abstract and so unrelated to anything in our everyday experience, it is, almost by definition, very difficult to say what they are actually like. But it is fairly easy to say what they are not like.

Mathematics is the supreme example of hypothetico-deductive reasoning. As anyone who has studied some mathematics beyond arithmetic knows, mathematical reasoning can be exceedingly abstract and hypothetical. These qualities were aptly described in the following definition of mathematics that Bertrand Russell proposed around the turn of the century.

> Mathematics consists entirely of assertions to the effect that, if such and such a proposition is true of *anything*, then such and such another proposition is true of that thing. It is essential not to discuss whether the first proposition is really true. ... We then take any hypothesis that seems amusing, and deduce

its consequences. *If* our hypothesis is about *anything*, and not about some one or more particular things, then our deductions constitute mathematics. Thus mathematics may be defined as the subject in which we never know what we are talking about, nor whether what we are saying is true. People who have been puzzled by the beginnings of mathematics will, I hope, find comfort in this definition, and will probably agree that it is accurate. [Quoted from Newman 1956, pp. 1576–77]

Deduction. Up to this point, we have been concerned primarily with the hypothetical half of hypothetico-deductive reasoning. But what about deduction? Adult human reasoning is sometimes said to consist of two general types of inference, namely, from general to specific and from specific to general. The former is called deductive reasoning. The latter, which will be taken up in the next section, is called inductive or "scientific" reasoning. Deductive reasoning is also commonly described as a process of reasoning from *premises to conclusions.* Sherlock Holmes novels provide a popular illustration of such reasoning: At breakfast, Holmes observes that the right side of Watson's face is more cleanly shaven than the left side, and he deduces that there must be a window on the right side of Watson's shaving glass and that this window must face east. More academic illustrations of deductive reasoning are provided by mathematics, where premises are called axioms (or postulates) and conclusions are called theorems. High school geometry is a familiar case in point.

Most readers will no doubt remember that high school geometry consisted of proving a large body of theorems about plane geometric forms (triangles, circles, rectangles, etc.). Even though we may no longer be able to recall the exact steps in these proofs, the key theorems are still etched in most of our memories: The sum of the interior angles of a triangle is two right angles; the square of the hypotenuse of a right triangle equals the sum of the squares of the other two sides; the opposite angles of two intersecting lines are equal; and so on. How did we manage to prove these theorems? Our textbooks told us that we first had to accept five axioms originally set down by Euclid in the fourth century B.C.

1. A straight line may be drawn from any one point to any other point.
2. A terminated straight line may be extended to any length in a straight line.
3. A circle may be described from any point at any distance from that point.
4. All right angles are equal.
5. If a straight line meets two straight lines, so as to make the sum of the two interior angles less than two right angles, these two straight lines, if extended, will eventually intersect on that side on which the sum of the two interior angles is less than two right angles.

These five axioms appeared at the very beginning of our geometry textbooks. We were told to accept them on faith or we would not be able to get on with the business of proving theorems. Since one has to prove theorems to pass a geometry course, we naturally accepted them. Any lingering doubts could be dispelled by considering that textbook authors were experts who knew what they were talking about. Moreover, the axioms begin to seem self-evidently true after one has done a little geometry. But, just for the sake of argument, what if one of the axioms happens to be false? Then, obviously, the theorems proved via the axiom are also false.

It turns out that, despite what we all learned in high school, the axioms of Euclid are not all true. The fifth axiom, which is usually called the axiom of parallels, is not true. This fact was discovered in the nineteenth century by the Hungarian mathematician Lobachevski and the German mathematician Riemann. They showed that the axiom of parallels is only true when one is drawing straight lines on a *flat* two-dimensional surface—e.g., a table or a desk, a piece of paper lying on a table or a desk. (Note that the fifth axiom does not stipulate that the two straight lines must lie on a flat surface.) Whenever a two-dimensional surface has either positive curvature (convex surface) or negative curvature (concave surface), the fifth axiom is false. The outside of an inflated balloon is a common example of a convex two-dimensional surface, and the inside of a soup bowl is a common example of a concave two-dimensional surface. On either of these surfaces, the two straight lines mentioned in the fifth axiom may go on forever and never intersect. This makes some of the most cherished theorems of high school geometry false. For example, it is not true that the sum of the interior angles of a triangle is two right angles. This fact may come as a shock to some readers. However, it can easily be verified by drawing a triangle on the flat surface of a deflated balloon, then inflating the balloon and measuring the angles.

Our high school geometry example is important because it points out a grave flaw in deductive reasoning that escaped the attention of theologians and philosophers until the time of Galileo and Newton. When reasoning from general to specific, our conclusions are true only if our premises are secure. If our premises are not secure, then our conclusions are false and perhaps also silly (e.g., St. Louis is east of Philadelphia). If deductive reasoning is to be useful, then we must have some way of verifying the truth of our premises. This is the task of inductive reasoning.

scientific (inductive) reasoning

According to Piaget, the advent of the formal-operational stage heralds the emergence of inductive reasoning. We already have a general definition of inductive reasoning in hand. This sort of reasoning is commonly called "scientific" in honor of its chief practitioners. The quantitative laws of science illustrate what inductive reasoning can achieve. The fundamental equations of physics (e.g., Boyle's law, Newton's law, Ohm's law) are usually regarded as the supreme examples of such laws.

To understand what Piaget means when he says that formal-operational intelligence is scientific, we must be more precise about what science is really all about. Initially, scientists are interested in systematically investigating some fairly narrow set of questions (the tensile strengths of metals, the behavior of laser beams, the structure of the cell, etc.). But they are also interested in drawing *inductive generalizations* from their research. Systematic investigation means taking precise measurements and quantifying the results. It also means doing experiments.

To conduct an experiment, scientists formulate an easily (or not so easily) testable hypothesis about "what would happen" to the phenomena they study if certain things were done to them. For example, which metals bend under a fixed amount of stress or how much stress is necessary to bend a beam consisting of a certain metal? After the hypothesis is formulated, an experiment is conducted in which variables specified in the hypothesis are manipulated and the results are measured. The things that scientists manipulate in an experiment are usually called independent variables (or causes) and the things that are measured are usually called dependent variables (or effects).

After conducting several experiments, scientists have a catalogue of the changes produced in certain variables by changes in certain other variables. Now comes the second step in scientific inference: inspection of the mass of specific findings in the hope of ascertaining some general functional relationship between the things that were being manipulated and things that were being measured. If a functional relationship of some sort does emerge and if the same relationship is observed by other investigators in other laboratories, scientists conclude that a general rule governing the things they study has been isolated. All of the so-called "laws of nature" discussed in physics textbooks are functional relationships of this type. For example, the physicist Boyle found after studying several different gases that their volume could always be predicted if one knew their temperature and pressure. This observation led to Boyle's law, which states that the volume of *every* gas is a function of its temperature and pressure. The third and final step in scientific reasoning comes when several different rules are put together in a coherent framework. When laws of nature are combined in a coherent system, the result is called a scientific theory. Relativity theory, quantum theory, and Newtonian mechanics are examples of putting several physical laws together to form a theory. Evolutionary theory is an example of putting several biological laws together to form a theory. In the more advanced sciences, where experimentation is sophisticated and findings are subtle, the people who put rules together to form theories are generally not the same people who conduct the experiments that isolate the rules in the first place. In the case of extremely advanced sciences such as physics, the rule discoverers and the rule synthesizers belong to different generations.

Piaget argues that, in many situations, adolescent intelligence behaves according to this model of scientific inference. Several specific findings from the research reported in *The Growth of Logical Thinking* (Inhelder and Piaget 1958) are invoked to support this claim. First, when adolescent subjects are confronted with complicated problem-solving situations, they seem to formulate hypotheses. That is, instead of focusing on the facts that are immediately before them, they seem to generate hypotheses about what may be going on. In Piaget's language, their thinking focuses on the anticipation of possible facts and potential states of affairs. This anticipatory aspect of formal-operational thought is analogous to the first step in scientific reasoning: Rather than concentrate on the immediate facts, adolescents first formulate some hypotheses that will allow them to systematize the facts as they come along. Second, adolescents *experiment*. When confronted with a complicated problem-solving situation, adolescents "study" the situation carefully before attempting a solution. They may directly manipulate certain things in an attempt to discover how they effect other things. This behavior can be contrasted with that of concrete-operational children. Although concrete-operational children are able to solve simple problems in which all the relevant facts are given at the outset (e.g., conservation), they fail problems that require that some relevant facts be *discovered* through experimentation.

After adolescents have carefully studied a problem and have undertaken a few experiments, they may arrive at a solution. These solutions are analogous to the rules that are isolated in the second step of scientific reasoning. Finally, adolescents, like scientists, construct grand systems or theories. Owing to ignorance, adolescents' theories are rather naive and unsophisticated by comparison with scientific theories. They are typically concerned with religion, justice, morality, ethics, and other philosophical questions. Piaget has conjectured that the adolescent tendency to construct grandiose theories may be partially responsible for the trouble and turmoil of this era.

The pendulum problem. Since the above description of scientific reasoning during the formal-operational stage is very general, we conclude this section by considering one of the problem-solving situations that elicits this behavior. The situation we shall examine is the so-called *pendulum problem* (Inhelder and Piaget 1958, Chap. 4). The subject is shown an apparatus like the one in Figure 6-1. It consists of three strings of different lengths ($S_1 < S_2 < S_3$) and three pieces of metal of different weights ($W_1 < W_2 < W_3$). Each piece of string can be tied to the center of the stick in Figure 6-1. If one of the weights is tied to the other end of the string, the string may be swung freely back and forth. Sometimes the string swings more rapidly than at

STICK FROM WHICH WEIGHTED STRINGS ARE SUSPENDED

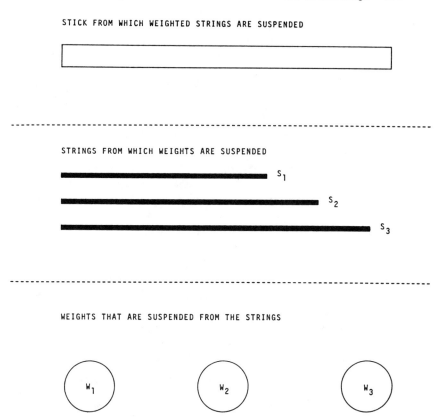

STRINGS FROM WHICH WEIGHTS ARE SUSPENDED

S_1

S_2

S_3

WEIGHTS THAT ARE SUSPENDED FROM THE STRINGS

W_1 W_2 W_3

Figure 6-1 A schematic example of Inhelder and Piaget's (1958, Chap. 4) pendulum problem. Imagine that one end of a string is attached to the stick somewhere near the middle of the stick. Imagine that one of the three weights is attached to the other end of the string and that the string is then permitted to swing freely from side to side. W_3 is heavier than W_2 and W_2 is heavier than W_1. There are a total of nine (3 strings × 3 weights) possible combinations of strings and weights. The subject's task is to determine why some string-weight combinations swing more rapidly than others.

other times. The experimenter demonstrates this fact to the subject. For example, string S_1 is attached to the stick with weight W_3 suspended from its other end. The string is then given a push and allowed to swing freely back and forth. Next, the same procedure is repeated with string S_3 and weight W_1. The experimenter calls the subject's attention to the fact that the string swings more rapidly in the former case than in the latter. The experimenter may then repeat this demonstration with other pairs of strings and weights.

After the demonstrations have been completed, the problem is posed: What, exactly, is it that makes the string swing more rapidly on some occasions than on others? The answer is that it is the length of the string—shorter strings always swing more rapidly than longer ones. It is not so much the solution that we are interested in as it is the method by which subjects arrive at the solution. Inhelder and Piaget report that concrete-operational children simply guessed. But their adolescent subjects did not guess. They proceeded to isolate the solution in a manner resembling the initial steps of the scientific reasoning model discussed earlier. First, like the scientist, they formulated hypotheses about what specific factors might possibly influence the speed of the string's oscillations. At the outset, most subjects thought that one or more of four variables might be influential: (*a*) the length of the string; (*b*) the weight of the piece of metal attached to the string; (*c*) how high the string is raised before it is released; (*d*) how strong a push the string is given when it is released. It was clear that adolescent subjects were formulating hypotheses about these variables because, in many cases, the hypotheses were stated aloud. For example, Inhelder and Piaget report the following protocol for a subject named JOT: "JOT (12;7) believes that '*you have to pull down* (lengthen) *the string.*' He suspends 20 grams and varies the length: '*It goes more slowly when you lower* (lengthen) *the string and faster when it's high up.*'—That's all?'—'*Maybe the weight does something*'" (Inhelder and Piaget 1958, p. 73).[1]

JOT had obviously formulated hypotheses about at least two of the factors mentioned above. Next, Inhelder and Piaget's adolescent subjects proceeded to test their hypotheses by experimenting with the apparatus. They compared the effects of using strings of different lengths and weights of different amounts. They compared the effects of releasing the string at different heights and of giving it different amounts of impetus. Although concrete-operational children also experimented with the apparatus on occasion, they seemed to conduct their experiments in an unsystematic and almost random manner—thereby suggesting that they had not formulated hypotheses. But the experiments of adolescents seemed to be very systematic. Each time an experiment was performed it usually eliminated one of the possible factors. Moreover, adolescent subjects typically continued their experiments until all of the factors except one had been eliminated. On the other hand, concrete-operational subjects, when they experimented at all, would perform one or two experiments and then guess. This formal-operational strategy of systematic and exhaustive experimentation is typified by a protocol reported for a subject named EGG: "EGG (15;9) at first believes that each of the four factors is influential. She studies different weights with the same string length (medium) and does not notice any appreciable change: '*That doesn't change the rhythm.*' Then she varies the length of the string with the same 200 gram weight and finds that '*when the string is small, the swing is faster.*' Finally, she varies the dropping point and the

[1] *The Growth of Logical Thinking: From Childhood to Adolescence,* by Barbel Inhelder and Jean Piaget, translated by Anne Parsons and Stanley Milgram, ©1958 by Basic Books, Inc., Publishers, New York; and Routledge & Kegan Paul, Ltd., London.

impetus (successively) with the same medium length string and the same 200 gram weight, concluding for each one of these two factors: '*Nothing has changed*'" (Inhelder and Piaget 1958, pp. 75–76).

Thus, EGG behaved more or less the way scientists do in their laboratories. First, she formulated hypotheses about everything that might possibly be influencing the speed of the pendulum's oscillations. Second, she conducted a series of tests designed to eliminate the irrelevant factors one at a time and isolate the relevant factors. Finally, she concluded that the rule governing the pendulum is that the speed of its oscillations is inversely related to its length.

reflective abstraction

The third characteristic of formal operations is considerably less important than the two we have already examined. This is so for two basic reasons. First, reflective abstraction is assumed to be a direct consequence of hypothetico-deductive and scientific reasoning. That is, both forms of reasoning are involved in reflective abstraction. Second, none of Inhelder and Piaget's (1958) studies of formal operations were designed to get directly at reflective abstraction. Hence, we have hard data on hypothetico-deductive and scientific reasoning, but not on reflective abstraction.

To see what reflective abstraction is all about, we must consider a further distinction that Piaget draws between the mental operations of the concrete-operational and formal-operational stages. Piaget says that the mental operations of the concrete-operational stage are *first-order* and the mental operations of the formal-operational stage are *second-order*. Generally speaking, the term "second-order" is supposed to mean that the mental operations of the formal-operational stage *are capable of operating* (or "reflecting") *on themselves*. By comparison, the mental operations of the concrete-operational stage are not supposed to be capable of operating on themselves—hence, the name "first-order."

Piaget's distinction between first-order and second-order operations actually is implicit in some things mentioned earlier. We have seen that, during the concrete-operational stage, children's mental operations are limited to dealing with concrete informational inputs from the real world. Concrete-operational thinking is assumed to operate exclusively on the hard data of sensation and perception. An important implication of this assumption, not previously discussed, is that concrete-operational children *can gain no new information from internal reflection*. They cannot meditate on their knowledge. Consequently, the sorts of inferences that can be generated by concrete-operational thinking are confined to generalizations or extrapolations from everyday experience. Primarily, they are confined to rules concerned with simple regularities that can be observed in the child's environment—e.g., objects fall when released from a height; men are larger than women; the sun rises in the east and sets in the west. In each of these cases, the function of concrete operations is to recognize the facts and draw the most obvious conclusions.

The principle of conservation, Piaget's chief index of concrete-operational intelligence, illustrates the limited generalizations that first-order operations are capable of. It will be recalled that the principle of conservation specifies that two equal quantities do not suddenly become unequal because the appearance of one of them has been altered. Now, the point to be emphasized with respect to conservation is that it is obviously a very simple rule that can be derived from observing what goes on in the environment. It is certainly not a complex intellectual construction. It is a simple physical regularity like objects falling when they are released from a height. By executing a few overt actions (counting, weighing, measuring, etc.), the child can easily verify that the conservation principle always holds. Thus, the principle of conservation is there in the real world and the child's major task is simply to assimilate this empirical fact.

By comparison, Piaget maintains that second-order operations are capable of arriving at generalizations and extrapolating rules that either cannot be or have not been directly observed in everyday experience. Many instances of such behavior can be gleaned from the preceding discussion of scientific inference. The clearest examples come from the hypothesis formation phase that precedes experimentation. During this phase, formal-operational subjects devise several *possible* rules about what *might* be going on even though they have not yet observed any events that would tend to confirm any of these rules. They must then conduct experiments to isolate the correct rules and eliminate the incorrect ones. In the pendulum, EGG apparently had constructed four rules: the shorter the string, the faster the swing; the heavier the weight, the faster the swing; the higher the release point, the faster the swing; the stronger the push, the faster the swing. But note that all of these rules were formulated *in advance of any hard facts about how the pendulum actually operates*. According to Piaget, rules have to be demonstrated to concrete-operational children before they can formulate them.

The process of formulating possible rules in advance of the facts is what Piaget calls reflective abstraction. The simple hypotheses governing experimentation are, therefore, reflective abstractions. By implication, so are all the laws of science. Although scientists do not like to be reminded of it, their laws are not merely statements of observed environmental regularities. They are *idealizations* of such regularities that are never exactly confirmed in practice. Anyone who has studied physics or chemistry knows that even these very precise laws are never exactly verified in any given experiment. The results always deviate somewhat from predictions. But this does not cause us to reject the laws that make the predictions. As long as the deviations are small, we attribute them to measurement error (or some other extraneous variable) and continue to believe the laws. We only give up the laws when the deviations from predictions become very large. Since scientific laws are never exactly confirmed in practice, they are not simply statements of environmental regularity. They are, in Piaget's words, reflective abstractions.

From what has just been said, it is apparent that reflective abstraction is, at bottom, another way of reiterating the key distinction between concrete and formal operations. If one were forced to reduce this distinction to a single statement, that statement might be: Concrete operations consist of thought thinking about the environment, but formal operations consist of thought thinking about itself.

the transition to formal operations

Before taking up formal-operational contents, it remains to consider what changes in underlying competence are presumed to be responsible for the general features of formal operations discussed up to this point. We have seen in earlier chapters that Piaget's method of explaining cognitive development centers on changes in mental operations. There are no operations during the sensorimotor stage; there are only unstructured and nonlogical operations during the preoperational stage; there are structured logical operations during the concrete-operational stage. It should come as no surpise, therefore, to find that further changes in mental operations are believed to be responsible for the transition from the concrete-operational stage to the formal-operational stage. Piaget has proposed two specific changes: (*a*) coordination of the two reversibility rules and (*b*) the ability to represent potential actions as well as real ones. We shall explore these two changes separately.

Coordination of the reversibilities. We recall that the most important of the various logical rules that operations obey are the two reversibilities—inversion and reciprocity. We saw in Chapter 5 that there is some behavioral evidence suggesting that concrete-operational thinking is guided by these rules. The best evidence comes from performance on conservation tests. Children will sometimes say that the quantitative relationship between the standard and transformed stimuli remains invariant after deformation because the deformation could always be carried out in the opposite direction. Piaget interprets this as evidence that the inversion rule is present. Children will also sometimes say that the quantitative relationship remains invariant because changes in one perceptual dimension caused by the deformation are compensated by equal and opposite changes in some other dimension (e.g., width compensates height in the quantity conservation test). Piaget interprets this as evidence that the reciprocity rule is present.

You may have noticed that the various illustrations of inversion and reciprocity we have examined do not contain a single example in which the two rules were used *together*. There were tests (e.g., of relations) that could be passed by using only the reciprocity rules, tests (e.g., of classes) that could be passed by using only the inversion rule, and tests (e.g., of conservation) that could be passed by using either rule. But there were no tests which could be passed only by using both rules. This was no coincidence. According to Piaget, concrete-operational children can use either reversibility rule by itself, but they cannot use them together.

The coordination of the two reversibility rules presumably is achieved by reciprocal assimilation. In Chapter 2, we said that the mental structures and the operations of which they consist are supposed to undergo two basic changes during cognitive development. First, they become more numerous. New structures are constructed to handle an ever widening array of information. These structures evolve from the internal differentiation and discrimination of existing structures. But as structures proliferate there is a danger that they may become isolated from each other. Hence, there is a need for tighter and tighter structural integration as cognitive development proceeds. Piaget calls the process by which this integration is achieved *reciprocal assimilation.* Since the coordination of the two reversibilities is an example of previously diverse structures becoming more tightly integrated, it follows that the governing mechanism must be reciprocal assimilation. More important, because the formal-operational stage is the final level of cognitive development, Piaget views the coordination of the two reversibilities as the culmination of all the reciprocal assimilations that have taken place since birth.

The INRC group. The coordination of reversibilities is said to lead to the emergence of an important new mental structure. For Piaget, this structure, the INRC group, is the sine qua non of adult intelligence. Given that this structure is absolutely central to Piaget's view of adult intelligence, it is clear that we should familiarize ourselves with its properties. This is somewhat difficult to do because Piaget has never spelled out the connections between the INRC group and formal-operational contents in the same detail as he has spelled out the connections between, say, the two reversibility rules and concrete-operational contents. Consequently, the remarks that follow will be rather general in comparison to earlier remarks about mental operations during the preoperational and concrete-operational stages. They say what an INRC group is, but no attempt will be made until later to point out formal-operational contents that are obvious examples of this structure.

Piaget borrowed the notion of "group" from a branch of mathematics called abstract algebra. As mathematical concepts go, groups are rather simple things. A group is merely any set *G* of elements plus some operation "o" that satisfies four properties: (*a*) closure (when elements of *G* are combined via "o" the result is always an element of *G*); (*b*) *associativity* (when three elements are combined the result of combining the first with the combination of the second and third is the same as the result of combining the third with the combination of the first and second); (*c*) *identity* (there is an element of *G* that leaves other elements unchanged when it is combined with them); (*d*) *inverse* (for every element of *G* there is some other element of *G* such that the identity element results when the two are combined). In abstract algebra, the standard examples of groups are elements that are numbers together with operations from arithmetic or algebra. For example, if *G* is the set of integers 0, ±1, ±2, ±3, ±4, ... and "o" is addition, it is very easy to see that all four properties are satisfied. But, and this is the important point, there is no reason that a group *must* consist of numbers and arithmetic or algebra operations. *Any* set of elements and *any* operation can be a group if properties (*a*) through (*d*) are satisfied. In particular, it is possible that a group may consist entirely of *operations*—i.e., the elements of *G* are certain operations and "o" is some other operation. This is what the *INRC* group is, a group of operations.

To see that groups may be comprised entirely of operations, let us consider a very simple illustration. Suppose you have two coins arranged side by side in front of you. Suppose that *H* means a coin shows heads and *T* means that a coin shows tails. If you happen to have two coins handy (any two will do), you may empirically verify everything that I am about to say regarding groups.

To begin with, it is apparent that there are exactly four conceivable arrangements of our two coins, namely *HH* (both coins show heads), *HT* (the coin on the left shows heads and the coin on the right shows tails), *TH* (the coin on the left shows tails and the coin on the right shows heads), and *TT* (both coins show tails). Suppose that we are permitted to perform any of the following operations on the coins: (operation *a*) turn the left coin over; (operation *b*) turn the right coin over; (operation *c*) turn both coins over; (operation *d*) do nothing, leave the coins as they are. Finally, suppose that there is another operation, "o", which is defined as carrying out any two operations from the set {*a, b, c, d,*} *in succession*. Thus, the formulae (*a* o *b*) and (*b* o *c*) mean "turn over the left coin then turn over the right coin" and "turn over the right coin then turn over both coins," respectively. A compound formula such as (*b* o *a*) o (*c* o *a*) simply means "turn over the right coin and the left coin then turn over both coins and the left coin." The result of carrying out operations from the set {*a, b, c, d,*} will always depend on the particular arrangement one begins with. For example, the result of doing (*a* o *b*) will be *TT* if we start with arrangement *HH*, but it will be *HH* if we begin with arrangement *TT*. However, this is not a crucial point. The really important thing is that, forgetting the specific arrangements that we begin with, *it can be shown that the set of operations {a, b, c, d}* *carried out in succession are a group.* To prove this statement, it is only necessary to show that each of the four properties mentioned above is present.

We begin with closure. To establish this property, one merely lists all possible pairwise combinations. There are 16 equations in all:

1. $(a \text{ o } a)$	$= d;$	9. $(b \text{ o } c)$	$= a;$
2. $(b \text{ o } b)$	$= d;$	10. $(c \text{ o } b)$	$= a;$
3. $(c \text{ o } c)$	$= d;$	11. $(a \text{ o } d)$	$= a;$
4. $(d \text{ o } d)$	$= d;$	12. $(d \text{ o } a)$	$= a;$
5. $(a \text{ o } b)$	$= c;$	13. $(b \text{ o } d)$	$= b;$
6. $(b \text{ o } a)$	$= c;$	14. $(d \text{ o } b)$	$= b;$
7. $(a \text{ o } c)$	$= b;$	15. $(c \text{ o } d)$	$= c;$
8. $(c \text{ o } a)$	$= b;$	16. $(d \text{ o } c)$	$= c.$

Each of these statements may be separately verified for any pair of coins beginning with any one of the head-tail arrangements. Since no matter what operations you carry out you always get one of the members of the set $\{a, b, c, d\}$, this set is closed and the first group-defining property is present.

Concerning associativity, given any three operations to be carried out in succession, the result of carrying out the third on the result of the first and second is the same as carrying out the second and third on the result of the first. In other words given three operations to be carried out in succession, it does not matter which two are executed first. To show that our four operations are associative, all the possibilities must be considered. Rather than list all of them, two illustrations are given that may be verified with any pair of coins.

Illustration 1. $(a \text{ o } b) \text{ o } c = (c \text{ o } c)$ by Eq. 5. $(c \text{ o } c) = d$ by Eq. 3. $a \text{ o } (b \text{ o } c)$ $= (a \text{ o } a)$ by Eq. 9. $(a \text{ o } a) = d$ by Eq. 1. Therefore, $(a \text{ o } b) \text{ o } c = a \text{ o } (b \text{ o } c)$.

Illustration 2. $(b \text{ o } d) \text{ o } c = (b \text{ o } c)$ by Eq. 13. $(b \text{ o } c) = a$ by Eq. 9. $b \text{ o } (d \text{ o } c)$ $= (b \text{ o } c)$ by Eq. 16. $(b \text{ o } c) = a$ by Eq. 9. Therefore, $(b \text{ o } d) \text{ o } c = b \text{ o } (d \text{ o } c)$.

By using the method outlined in these two illustrations, associativity is easily established for all combinations of three operations carried out in succession.

Turning to identity, this is the easiest of the four properties to demonstrate. Remember that the identity property means that there is some member of the set that leaves the other members unchanged when it is combined with them. The presence of an identity element is confirmed by examining Equations 11 through 16. Operation d ("stay as you were") leaves operations a, b, and c unchanged when it is combined with them.

Finally, the inversion property is also easy to establish. According to this property, for every operation in the set $\{a, b, c, d\}$ there is some other operation in the set such that the identity element results when the two operations are combined. The presence of this property is verified by examining Equations 1 through 4. Note that whenever a given operation is performed twice in succession, the result is operation d. Since we have just seen that d is the identity element, it follows that each operation has an inverse—itself.

Piaget's *INRC* group does not differ in principle from the two-coin game we have just reviewed. In fact, the set of four operations in this game *is an INRC group.* Or, in somewhat more academic language, the two-coin game is a concrete representation of an abstract structure that mathematicians happen to call an *INRC* group.[2] As Piaget defines it, an *INRC* group is *any* set of operations $\{I, N, R, C\}$ that has the four group properties and whose individual operations are defined as follows:

$$I = (N \circ R \circ C) = (N \circ C \circ R) = (R \circ N \circ C) = (R \circ C \circ N)$$
$$= (C \circ N \circ R) = (C \circ R \circ N);$$
$$N = (R \circ C) = (C \circ R);$$
$$R = (N \circ C) = (C \circ N);$$
$$C = (N \circ R) = (R \circ N).$$

The two-coin game clearly satisfies this definition. All we have to do is interpret the set $\{I, N, R, C\}$ as $I = d$, $N = a$, $R = b$, and $C = c$. More generally, any system that consists of two discrete variables that can take on either of two discrete values can be shown to be an *INRC* group. Although the proof is too complicated to undertake here, the crucial point to bear in mind is that any set of operations whose elements may be defined in terms of each other in the manner just considered is an example of what Piaget calls an *INRC* group. Later, when we come to formal-operational contents, we shall examine what Piaget views as the most important illustration of the *INRC* group—propositional operations.

representation
of potential actions

The principal shortcoming of concrete operations is that they can only deal with hard observable data. We saw in Chapter 2 that mental operations spring from the internal representation of action. When it comes to representing actions, concrete-operational children are limited to representing events that they are actually capable of performing. This does not mean that they must actually execute an operation before they can represent it inter-

[2] Actually, this is only Piaget's name for the structure. In abstract algebra, it is called the Klein-group and is denoted D_2. Readers who desire a more formal exposition of the Klein-group should see Budden (1972, Chap. 11).

nally. On the contrary, one of the major advantages of concrete operations over preoperations is that the former are capable of representing actions that children have not actually performed while the latter are not. Thus, on the quantity conservation test, concrete-operational children say that the standard and variable stimuli are still the same amount after deformation because "you could always pour the water back." They give this answer without benefit of actually carrying out the repouring.

Thus, in theory, the reason that concrete-operational children solve problems like conservation is that they can internally represent the various actions that they see the experimenter engaging in and, further, they can represent negations and compensations of these actions. But note that, although the actions being represented do not actually have to be performed, they are nevertheless the sorts of actions that can be easily observed. According to Piaget, the concrete-operational child is representing *real actions* rather than *potential actions*. The formal-operational child is said to be capable of representing both.

The distinction between representing real actions and potential actions will become clearer in the next section when we consider illustrative formal-operational contents. All of the actions that one must take account of in order to solve the types of problems discussed in Chapter 5 are perfectly concrete and observable. There is nothing hidden about them. Regardless of whether the child carries them out or the experimenter does, the various pourings and measurings that are necessary to establish the equivalence of the two stimuli on the quantity conservation test are directly observable events. None of them needs to be inferred or deduced. This situation contrasts sharply with the requirements of some of the formal-operational tests that we shall discuss in the next section. For example, we shall consider a more complicated version of the conservation problem, conservation of motion in a horizontal plane. In this problem, subjects are required to isolate factors that determine how far a ball will roll along a horizontal plane. To solve this problem, we shall see that, as in concrete-operational conservation tests, subjects must take account of all the actions they see the experimenter perform. But this problem differs from concrete-operational conservation tests in that subjects must also take account of the unseen influence of friction. Friction cannot be directly observed and its influence must be inferred by the subject before the problem can be solved.

Two Categories of Formal Operations

We now take up the main categories of formal operations and their associated cognitive contents. As was the case for concrete operations, Piaget divides formal operations into two broad classes, namely, *propositional* (or combinatorial) *operations* and *formal-operational schemes.* The distinction between these two classes is, unfortunately, not so clear-cut as the continuous-discrete distinction between the logical and spatial operations of the concrete-operational stage. In general, both categories of formal operations are regarded by Piaget as the immediate underlying genotypes that make the phenotypes of hypothetico-deductive reasoning, scientific reasoning, and reflective abstraction possible. Propositional operations appear to be most closely connected to hypothetico-deductive reasoning and reflective abstraction. Formal-operational schemes appear to be most closely connected to scientific reasoning. In fact, we shall see that some formal-operational schemes bear the names of familiar scientific principles.

Propositional operations and formal-operational schemes are both presumed to be direct consequences of the coordination of the two reversibilities that occurs during the transition between the concrete-operational and formal-operational stages. The two categories of formal operations are discussed separately below. In each case, the theoretical definition of the category is first reviewed and then several illustrative cognitive contents from Inhelder and Piaget's (1958) experiments are presented.

propositional (combinatorial) operations

Generally speaking, any given formal operation is always supposed to be more abstract and less closely connected to reality than any corresponding concrete operation. However, this does not preclude that formal operations may differ among themselves in their degree of abstractness. Piaget's two main categories of formal operations, for example, clearly differ in their relative proximity to the real world. The propositional operations that we shall be considering in the present section are exceedingly abstract. They are, as we shall see, analogous to a branch of symbolic logic. They are also an embodiment of the *INRC* group structure discussed earlier. Formal-operational schemes are more concrete. Generally speaking, they may be regarded as rules stating functional relationships that govern the behavior of objects in the environment. These rules are, of course, more complex than, say, the simple conservation laws that we encountered in Chapter 5.

Piaget has, subject to later qualifications, taken the most elementary branch of symbolic logic, propositional logic, and put it inside the adolescent's (and adult's) head as a system of mental operations. Therefore, it is necessary to understand what propositional logic is all about to understand what propositional operations are all about. This problem is taken up below. First, we consider the subject matter of propositional logic. Second, we examine the connection between propositional logic and Piaget's *INRC* group. Third, we review the thinking and reasoning skills that propositional operations are supposed to be responsible for.

Propositional logic. The brief overview I shall give of propositional logic is only intended to give readers who are unfamiliar with it a nodding acquaintance sufficient to get on with explicating formal operations. But it is not a substitute for the real thing. Readers who want to know about propositional logic, as distinct from formal operations, are directed to any good introductory logic textbook (e.g., Copi 1961; DeLong 1970; Ennis 1969; Quine 1951).

Broadly defined, propositional logic is the logic of all systems that satisfy three conditions: (*a*) There are two or more *factors* (or variables), (*b*) each factor can take on two discrete *values*, and (*c*) all combinations of these factors take on the same two values. It is crucial that the values be mutually exclusive and not overlap in any way. In principle, propositional logic deals with systems in which there are any number of variables and any number of mutually exclusive values. But the simplest possible example of propositional logic, the example that we shall use, consists of two variables and two values. By convention, the variables are called *propositional functions* and are denoted *P* and *Q*. The two values may be just about anything, but they are usually called true and false to emphasize their mutual exclusivity.

Suppose we let our first propositional function, *P*, be "*x* composed operas" and we let our second propositional function, *Q* be "*x* was president of the United States." When a specific person is substituted for the *x* in either statement, the statement becomes either true or false. For example, *P* is true if Mozart or Verdi or Wagner is substituted but is false if Aristotle or Plato or Socrates is substituted. Similarly, *Q* is true if Washington or Jackson or Lincoln is substituted but is false if Alexander or Caesar or Pericles is substituted. The substitution of a specific person for the *x* in either statement is called *interpretation*. When a propositional function is interpreted and becomes true or false, it is called a proposition. This is where the "propositional" in propositional logic comes from.

Through the process of interpretation *P* and *Q* each becomes true or false. Consequently, there are four possible results of interpreting both statements: (*a*) *P* = true and *Q* = true (e.g., Verdi composed operas and Jackson was president of the United States); (*b*) *P* = true and *Q* = false (e.g., Verdi composed operas and Caesar was president of the United States); (*c*) *P* = false and *Q* = true (e.g., Socrates composed operas and Jackson was president of the United States); (*d*) *P* = false and *Q* = false (e.g., Socrates composed operas and Caesar was president of the United States). Since there are exactly four possible outcomes, hereafter referred to as *a, b, c,* and *d*, of interpreting *P* and *Q*, we may think of *P* and *Q* as forming a new *compound propositional function* which we denote *P* + *Q*. The compound proposition *P* + *Q* takes on exactly four interpretations which correspond to the four possible outcomes for interpreting *P* and *Q*. Since all propositional functions in our system must be either true or false once they have been interpreted, $P + Q$ must be either true or false when it is assigned one of its four interpretations. Suppose we assign $P + Q$ each of its four interpretations one after the other. How many different patterns of true-false outcomes are there? The answer is that there are 4^2 or 16 possible outcomes. At one extreme, it might be that $P + Q$ turns out to be true for interpretations *a, b, c,* and *d.* At the other extreme, it might be that $P + Q$ turns out to be false for interpretations *a, b, c,* and *d.* In between, there are fourteen other outcomes where $P + Q$ is true for some interpretations and false for others. These sixteen possible outcomes, along with the names that are usually given to them in propositional logic, are shown in Table 6–1.

TABLE 6–1   The Sixteen Outcomes From Combining Two Binary Propositions

Outcome	Component propositions			
	$P = true$ $Q = true$	$P = true$ $Q = false$	$P = false$ $Q = true$	$P = false$ $Q = false$
1. Affirmation $(P*Q)$	true	true	true	true
2. Disjunction $(P \lor Q)$	true	true	true	false
3. Reverse Implication $(P \leftarrow Q)$	true	true	false	true
4. Implication $(P \rightarrow Q)$	true	false	true	true
5. Nonconjunction (P/Q)	false	true	true	true
6. Affirmation of P (P)	true	true	false	false
7. Affirmation of Q (Q)	false	false	true	true
8. Equivalence $(P \equiv Q)$	true	false	false	true
9. Denial of Q $\sim(Q)$	false	true	false	true
10. Denial of P $\sim(P)$	false	false	true	true
11. Nonequivalence $\sim(P \equiv Q)$	false	true	true	false
12. Conjunction $(P \cdot Q)$	true	false	false	false
13. Nonimplication $\sim(P \rightarrow Q)$	false	true	false	false
14. Nonreverse implication $\sim(P \leftarrow Q)$	false	false	true	false
15. Nondisjunction $\sim(P \lor Q)$	false	false	false	true
16. Negation $\sim(P*Q)$	false	false	false	false

It is easy to grasp the significance of Table 6–1 if one thinks of $P + Q$ as some special propositional function, R, which can take on a set of four different interpretations. Suppose $R = $ "x is an integer between 1 and 4 inclusive," and suppose we denote the set of possible interpretations that R may take on as $\{a, b, c, d\}$. Now, consider the two extremes where R is true for every interpretation (Row 1, Table 6–1) and where R is false for every interpretation (Row 16, Table 6–1). Concerning the former, suppose the set of possible interpretations is $\{a = 1, b = 2, c = 3, d = 4\}$. The pattern of true-false outcomes for R corresponds to Row 1. Concerning the latter, suppose the set of possible interpretations $\{a = 25, b = 26, c = 27, d = 28\}$. The pattern of true-false outcomes for R corresponds to Row 16. The other fourteen outcomes shown in Table 6–1 can be produced by assigning appropriate numbers to *a, b, c,* and *d*. But, importantly, no matter what *a, b, c,* and *d* happen to be, there are no possible outcomes other than those shown in Table 6–1.

Piaget endows the adolescent with the system of propositional logic depicted in Table 6–1. He renames the sixteen possible patterns of true-false outcomes of a compound propositional function "the system of 16 binary propositional operations." There is one important difference between the propositional endowment that Piaget gives to adolescents and the logicians' propositional logic. In the final analysis, the logician's system consists of symbols on pieces of paper (e.g., Table 6–1). But, as the name "16 binary propositional operations" should suggest, Piaget's system consists of *mental operations*. This means that it must have three characteristics that the logician's system is not required to have. First, it must be comprised of internalized actions. Second, these actions must obey certain logical rules—more particularly, they must be reversible in two senses. Third, these actions must be gathered together in a coherent structure of some sort. The structure that the sixteen propositional operations are said to form is the *INRC* group.

I think there can be very little doubt that adolescents are capable of propositional logic. Piaget's work aside, the fact that high school and junior high pupils learn symbolic logic nowadays in their mathematics classes provides strong supportive evidence. However, it does not follow, as Piaget seems to suppose, that much younger children are incapable of propositional logic. Consequently, we shall see when we come to the replication research that much of it has focused on propositional logic in concrete-operational children.

The INRC group and propositional operations. We examined Piaget's *INRC* group earlier. We saw that it is a special structure that has the usual four properties of a group. The two things that set it apart from all other groups are, first, its elements (denoted by the letters *I, N, R,* and *C*) are four operations and, second, each of these operations is defined in terms of at least two of the remaining three operations.

We now return briefly to the *INRC* group for purposes of spelling out the relationship between this structure and the sixteen propositional operations. I do this chiefly as a means of accomplishing something that I have been unable to do before, namely, illustrate the third ("structuring") principle of mental operations. When the concept of mental operations was defined in Chapter 4, I noted that it is by far the murkiest of the three characteristics of operations. With Piaget's first two stages, no one knows precisely what the structures are. In the case of Piaget's third stage, some structures have been proposed (e.g., Piaget 1942, 1949, 1972) but they are difficult to discuss because Piaget and his coworkers keep changing them—in fact, in one book alone (Piaget 1972), two different and contradictory versions of these structures are given! These internal inconsistencies have been meticulously documented in a doctoral dissertation by Sheppard (1973). Piaget's concrete-operational structures also are difficult to discuss because it is hard to see clear connections between them and the logico-arithmetic and spatial contents associated with the concrete-operational stage. The mist clears somewhat when we come to the formal-operational stage. The *INRC* group has remained unchanged since it was first introduced as a structural model. No doubt this is because it was borrowed intact from abstract algebra. Moreover, the connections between the *INRC* group and the sixteen propositional operations are easy to identify.

To establish the relationship between propositional operations and the *INRC* group, we might begin by noting some obvious points of agreement. First, propositional logic was previously defined as the logic of systems in which there are two variables that may take on either of two values. Systems of this sort are called *binary systems*. It is apparent that the two-coin game is a binary system: There are two variables (the coins), and they have either of two values (heads or tails). Similarly, there are four possible outcomes of interpreting two propositional functions (*t/t, t/f, f/t,* and *f/f*) and four possible outcomes in the two-coin game (*H/H, H/T, T/H,* and *T/T*). If we were to interpret "propositional function" as "coin," "true" as "head," and "false" as "tail," the two systems would be indistinguishable. These underlying similarities strongly suggest that propositional logic and the *INRC* group must, somehow, be related.

We saw above that the members of the set $\{I, N, R, C, \}$ are defined in terms of each other as follows: $I = NRC$, $N = RC$, $R = NC$, and $C = NR$. That is, carrying out the operation on the left is the same as carrying out the operations on the right. But what *are* these operations? What specific *mental* operations do these four letters denote? Since we know that operations obey reversibility rules, it should come as no surprise that these letters stand for *reversibility* operations. Suppose that we have some given operation; it may be almost anything (e.g., turning coins over in the two-coin game). The letter "*I*" signifies the given operation itself and, for this reason, it is called an *identity* operation. If it happens to be some form of behavior, such as turning coins, then *I* is its mental representation. The letter "*N*" signifies the *negation* of the given operation. It is also called the *inverse* operation of the group. In the two-coins game, we saw that each operation was its own inverse. If the given operation consists of turning over the coin on the left (operation *a*), then the inverse operation consists of turning the coin over a second time. The letter "*R*" signifies the reciprocal of the given operation and is called the *reciprocal* operation of the *INRC* group. If the given operation consists of turning over the coin on the left, then the reciprocal of this operation consists of turning over the coin on the right. Finally, the letter "*C*" signifies the inverse of the reciprocal operation and it is called the *correlative* operation. If the given operation is turning the left coin over and its reciprocal is turning the right coin over, then the correlative operation is turning both coins over. As should be apparent from these examples, the definitions of *N*, *R*, and *C* always depend on how we define *I*. Depending on the definition of *I*, *a single set of operations can generate many different INRC groups*. This point can be illustrated by returning to the two-coin game and defining *I*, in turn, as *a*, *b*, and *c*. The result is four distinct *INRC* groups:

1. $I = a^2$	2. $I = b^2$	3. $I = c^2$	4. $I = c^2$
$N = a$	$N = b$	$N = c$	$N = c$
$R = b$	$R = a$	$R = a$	$R = b$
$C = c$	$C = c$	$C = b$	$C = a$

In short, any set of operations satisfies Piaget's definition of an *INRC* group if, for the element *I* of the set, one of the remaining operations is its inverse, another is its reciprocal, and another is its correlative. Suppose you have a much larger set of operations such that the members of the set satisfy three properties. First, each operation is the inverse of one and only one other member of the set. Second, each operation is the reciprocal of one and only one other member of the set. Third, each operation is the correlative of one and only one other member of the set. Such sets will generate *n* different *INRC* groups, where *n* is the number of operations in the set.

The sixteen propositional operations are an example of a set which has these three characteristics. Consequently, we expect sixteen different *INRC* groups to result when we define *I*, in turn, as each of the sixteen operations appearing in Table 6-1. This is precisely what happens. The sixteen *INRC* groups generated by defining *I* as one of the propositional operations are shown in Table 6-2. These groups were originally worked out by William Bart, and Table 6-2 is based on a table constructed by Bart (1971, p. 543). Let us now examine Table 6-2. To begin with, it shows the inverse, reciprocal, and correlative of each of the propositional operations. It also shows that each propositional operation has one and only one inverse, reciprocal, and correlative elsewhere in the set. It is sometimes the case that a propositional operation is its own inverse, reciprocal, or correlative. But we have already encountered this phenomenon with the two-coin game, and we know that it does not pose any problems. To construct each of sixteen possible *INRC* groups, we merely examine each row in turn. When a given row has been selected for examination, the *name of that row* is the name of the *I* operation of the *INRC* group being constructed. The *N*, *R*, and *C* operations are then filled in by reading from left to right and locating the specific operations which serve as the *N*, *R*, and *C* operations for the given *I* operation. Put the four operations together and you have an *INRC* group.

TABLE 6-2

The Relationship Between Propositional Operations and the *INRC* Group

	1	2	3	4	5	6	7	8	9	10	11	12	13	14	15	16
1. Affirmation	I = R															N = C
2. Disjunction		I			N							C			R	
3. Reverse Implication			I	R									C	N		
4. Implication			R	I									N	C		
5. Nonconjunction		N			I							R			C	
6. Affirmation of P						I = C				N = R						
7. Affirmation of Q							I = C		N = R							
8. Equivalence								I = R			N = C					
9. Denial of Q							N = R		I = C							
10. Denial of P						N = R				I = C						
11. Nonequivalence								N = C			I = R					
12. Conjunction		C			R							I			N	
13. Nonimplication			C	N									I	R		
14. Nonreverse implication			N	C									R	I		
15. Nondisjunction		R			C							N			I	
16. Negation	N = C															I = R

To conclude our discussion of the relationship between the *INRC* group and propositional operations, let us consider one illustration of how some given propositional operation generates an *INRC* group. The example is one that Piaget himself has provided (Inhelder and Piaget 1958, p. 134). First, consider the operation of disjunction (Row 2, Table 6–1). Note that disjunction is a compound proposition of the form $P + Q$ that produces the outcome pattern true/true/true/false for the four possible values of P and Q. Going to Row 2 in Table 6–2, we look up the inverse, reciprocal, and correlative operations. We find the inverse, or *mirror image* operation in Column 15 (false/false/false/true). We find the reciprocal operation in Column 5 (false/true/true/true). Finally, we find the inverse of the reciprocal operation in Column 12 (true/false/false/false). We have now isolated that particular *INRC* group in which *I* is the disjunctive outcome pattern from Table 6–1, *N* is the nondisjunctive outcome pattern from Table 6–1, *R* is the nonconjunctive outcome pattern from Table 6–1, and *C* is the conjunctive outcome pattern from Table 6–1. The same mechanical procedure may be used to find the *N*, *R*, and *C* operations for any given *I*.

Combinatorial thinking. We come now to the much larger question of what, generally speaking, propositional operations are supposed to do for our thinking and reasoning. What is it that formal-operational subjects can do, by virtue of these propositional operations, that concrete-operational subjects cannot do? I have already said that these operations are supposed to be responsible both for hypothetico-deductive reasoning and for reflective abstraction. They are also supposed to allow subjects to think in a manner which Piaget calls *combinatorial.*

What Piaget usually seems to have in mind when he speaks of combinatorial thinking is the type of reasoning involved in solving permutation and combination problems. Most of us spent a good deal of time on such problems in high school algebra. Generally speaking, permutation and combination problems are concerned with the question of how many different ways a certain operation can be performed on a certain set of things. A *permutation* is a subset of a certain set of things that has a definite order— i.e., there is a first term, a second term, and so on. Given a set of *n* terms, the number of permutations of this set consisting of exactly *r* terms is $n(n - 1)(n - 2) \ldots (n - r + 1)$. That is, giving some set of *n* things, the number of ordered subsets of size *r* is given by the preceding rule. A *combination* is a subset of a certain set of things that has no definite order. Given a set of *n* things, the number of combinations consisting of *r* things equals the number of permutations consisting of *r* things divided by $r(r - 1)(r - 2) \ldots (r - (r - 1))$.

To solve permutation and combination problems, it is clear that one must at least be able to conceive or imagine all possible hypothetical arrangements of a set of objects. This ability, which is believed to be absent at the concrete-operational stage, is said by Piaget to be a direct consequence of propositional operations. We now examine some formal-operational cognitive contents that are presumed to rely on propositional operations.

Cognitive contents. In the present section, we discuss the cognitive contents found in Part 1 of Inhelder and Piaget's *Growth of Logical Thinking* (1958). Later, when we come to formal-operational schemes, we discuss the cognitive contents found in Part 2.

Inhelder and Piaget used six different tests to study the development of propositional operations: (*a*) angle of incidence versus angle of reflection problems, (*b*) density problems, (*c*) flexibility of rods problems, (*d*) oscillation of pendulums problems, (*e*) falling bodies problems, (*f*) magnetization problems. Each of these six types of problems will be briefly described before examining the main findings.

Type (*a*) problems are designed to get at a concept that most of us remember from high school physics or geometry: the angle of incidence equals the angle of reflection. The main apparatus for these problems is a billiard table. Pictures of various common objects (houses, flowers, trees) are placed at various locations on the surface of the billiard table. Subjects are requested to "hit" specific targets (e.g., "Hit the house") *by bouncing a billiard ball off one of the cushions of the table.* The stated objective of these problems is to assess subjects' knowledge that the angle of incidence on the cushion equals the angle of reflection. Type (*b*) problems are concerned with floating objects. The apparatus consists of a number of large vessels containing liquids of different densities and several solid objects which are successively placed in the various containers to determine whether or not they float. For example, a piece of metal is first placed in a container of water and then in a container of mercury. It sinks in the former case and floats in the latter case. The aim of such problems is to measure subjects' understanding of what Inhelder and Piaget call the "law of floating bodies." This law is the principle of specific gravity taught in high school physics. An object will float in a liquid if and only if the weight per unit volume of the liquid (*density*) is greater than the weight per unit volume of the object.

Type (*c*) problems are concerned with the factors that make rods bend. The apparatus consists of a square wooden frame that contains several parallel metal rods. The apparatus looks almost exactly like a child's abacus except that, first, there are no counting beads on the rods and, second, the rods protrude through one side of the wooden frame. The rods vary as to their thickness, their cross-sectional shape (circular or square), how much they protrude through the side of the frame, and the metal of which they are made. The subject is given several objects of various weights that may be attached to the ends of the rods that protrude through the frame. When the weights are attached, the rods bend by various amounts. The subject's task is to isolate all of the different factors that are varying and to group them into two categories, namely, relevant factors that determine how much a rod bends (e.g., the weight of the object suspended from it) and irrelevant factors that do not determine how much the rod bends (e.g., its cross-sectional shape). Type (*d*) problems were described earlier in the section on scientific reasoning.

Type (*e*) problems are concerned with balls rolling down an inclined plane. The main apparatus consists of a board that is inclined at an angle from the horizontal. At the bottom of the board there is a spring. The experimenter releases balls from the top of the inclined board. The balls roll down toward the spring. When they hit the spring, the spring gives them a "push." The subject's task is to isolate the factors that determine how far the ball will roll along the horizontal plane on which the apparatus is set up *after it hits the spring.* There are two main determinants. First, if the board is always tilted at the same angle, then the distance that the ball rolls is a function of how far up the board the experimenter releases it. The higher the release point the greater the distance the ball rolls. On the other hand, if the ball is always released at the same point, then it is the angle of incline that counts. A ball released from a given point will roll further if the board is inclined at a sixty-degree angle than it will if the board is inclined at a forty-five-degree angle.

Finally, type (*f*) problems make use of an apparatus that resembles a roulette wheel. Instead of a roulette wheel with the usual thirty-seven or thirty-eight sections, imagine one that is divided into only eight sections. Instead of the numbers that mark each section on a roulette wheel, the eight sections of this wheel are marked with four different geometric shapes (a circle, a diamond, a pentagram, and a square). Each figure appears twice, and the two instances of each figure are directly opposite one another on the wheel. In the center of the wheel there is a pointer that replaces the ball used in roulette. The pointer is made of metal and, like the ball used in roulette, it identifies the "winner" after each spin of the wheel. Before the wheel is spun, a small magnet is placed under one or more of the geometric forms on the surface of the wheel. The wheel is then spun and, because the pointer is made of metal, it always ends up pointing at one of the geometric forms under which a magnet is located. That is, only magnetized sections of the wheel ever "win." The objective of the problem is to assess subjects' understanding of the fact that, unlike a standard roulette wheel which (hopefully) always behaves in a random manner, the present wheel will behave in a predictable nonrandom manner whenever magnets are located under the geometric forms. According to Inhelder and Piaget, this particular problem is an especially good test of propositional operations because it elicits all sixteen of the operations depicted in Table 6-1 (cf. Inhelder and Piaget 1958, pp. 103, 104).

Piaget's analysis of how children's solutions of these six problems change with age leads him to propose three broad stages in the development of propositional operations. He further divides the third stage into two substages that correspond to the preparation and achievement phases of formal operations. Stage I corresponds to the second half of the preoperational phase. Three characteristic reactions are observed when Stage I children are confronted with the preceding problems. First, they almost always concentrate on *momentary states* of each system and ignore the *transformations* that are taking place. This is another way of saying that Stage I children tend to focus on *perceptually salient* features of a task. Second, although Stage I children pay little attention to the transformations taking place in a problem, when they do pay attention to them they fail to see that these transformations are reversible. Third, the reasoning of Stage I children appears unorganized and unstructured. All three of these features of Stage I children's behavior on propositional operations tests have been previously discussed as defining traits of preoperations.

Stage II corresponds to concrete operations. Although Stage II children still do not solve propositional operations problems, they perform much better than Stage I subjects do. In particular, Stage II subjects are more likely to focus on transformations and are less likely to be concerned with momentary perceptual configurations. They are also more likely to recognize that various transformations are reversible. These two characteristics of Stage II behavior are reminiscent of the differences between preoperational and concrete-operational children's behavior on conservation tests. These apparent improvements notwithstanding, Piaget contends that the development of propositional operations is still far from complete. In particular, he notes three important shortcomings of Stage II performance. First, the range of information that Stage II children are capable of assimilating and retaining is quite limited. As we have seen earlier, it appears that Stage II children only make use of information provided by concrete sensory experience. Hence, while Stage II children focus on the transformations taking place in the above problems, they usually focus on only *actual* transformations and ignore *potential* ones. Second, there appear to be definite limitations on the extent to which Stage II children can generalize a functional relationship they have discovered in one physical situation to a new but related situation. We have already encountered an example of this in our discussion of conservation in Chapter 5. When the conservation principle has been discovered for one quantitative relation (e.g., number or length), the concrete-operational child does not understand that the law also applies to other quantitative relations. Instead, the conservation principle must be reacquired for each such relation. We saw that Piaget calls these reacquisitions *horizontal décalages*. Third, Piaget argues that the performance of Stage II children suggests that thought is not yet characterized by an overall, systematic structure. The main evidence for this claim comes from situations in which Stage II children fail to see that one conclusion which they have arrived at implies one or more further conclusions.

During Stage III, the remaining difficulties are overcome. When solving propositional operations problems, Stage III subjects (between 11 and 15 years of age) assimilate and retain a broader range of information. In particular, they take account of potential as well as actual transformations. In type (*f*) problems, for example, Stage III subjects deduce that a certain variable (magnetization) is determining where the pointer comes to rest even though they cannot directly observe the operation of that variable. (The magnets are always hidden, and subjects never know ahead of time exactly where they are hidden. Hence, it is impossible for them to observe a direct correlation between where the pointer points and where the magnet is located.) Stage III children also evidence an expanded capacity to generalize a law to new situations. In type (*b*) problems, for example, when Stage III children observe that a certain piece of brass sinks in a certain container of water, they immediately deduce that all other pieces of brass, regardless of their size or shape, sink in water. Stage II children, on the other hand, either would not make this inference at all or would only do so after checking several pieces of brass of various shapes and sizes. Finally, Stage III thinking seems to be tightly interconnected. Whenever Stage III children reach a certain conclusion, usually through experimenting with the apparatus, they recognize that other conclusions also follow. An example of this sort of behavior occurs on type (*c*) problems. One of the irrelevant factors in these problems is the cross-sectional shape of the rods. From observing that only two shape variations (circular and square) do not affect flexibility, the Stage III subject concludes all other shape variations (triangular, rectangular, etc.) also are irrelevant.

formal-operational schemes

We turn now to the other category of formal operations, the so-called formal-operational schemes. Although these schemes are certainly cognitive structures in the sense in which we have been using this notion, they are considerably more complex and highly specialized than anything encountered in earlier chapters. On the one hand, formal-operational schemes are less abstract than propositional operations and the *INRC* group. But, on the other hand, they are also more highly specialized. For these reasons, they are more closely related to scientific reasoning than propositional operations are. Like propositional operations, however, they are believed to emerge between 11 and 15 years of age in most subjects. We begin by considering the similarities and differences between formal-operational schemes and propositional operations. We then consider illustrative cognitive contents.

Formal-operational schemes and propositional operations. Piaget says that formal-operational schemes are derived from propositional operations. They are thought to be actualizations of certain things that are inherent both in propositional operations and in the underlying *INRC* group. Specifically, they are thought to be methods whereby propositional operations are applied to certain reasoning situations that occur with great regularity in the environment. Formal-operational schemes are, therefore, broadly defined by Piaget as *latent potentialities* of propositional operations that are elicited by certain common but restricted situations in the environment.

As we noted earlier, the acquisition of propositional operations is supposed to bring with it a wide variety of new cognitive skills. Formal-operational schemes, taken as a group, are one of these new skills. Inhelder and Piaget (1958) summarize the connection between the system of propositional operations and formal-operational schemes as follows:

> The system itself implies a set of potential transformations which may become manifest or remain latent depending on particular conditions. ... operational schemata are defined as the concepts which the subject potentially can organize from the beginning of the formal level *when faced with certain kinds of data*, but which are not manifest outside these conditions. ... formal thinking makes its presence known not only by the constant utilization of the sixteen binary propositional operations. ... but also by the sporadic elaboration of some concepts or schemata which are inaccessible at the concrete level. ... These operational schemata consist of concepts or special operations (mathematical and not exclusively logical), the need for which may be felt by the subject when he tries to solve certain problems. When the need is felt, he manages to work them out spontaneously. ... [p. 308, my italics]

In other words, there are certain rules governing the behavior of certain systems in the environment. What is more, these rules can be worked out via the application of propositional operations. If the rules are especially important ones, as in the case of the basic laws of physics, the subject will discover them by applying propositional operations to relevant facts. This process generates formal-operational schemes.

The key difference between propositional operations and formal-operational schemes lies in their degree of specialization. Formal-operational schemes are adapted to the demands of certain forms of information from the environment, whereas as propositional operations are extremely general and equally applicable to all forms of information. While propositional operations supposedly pervade all areas of adolescent and adult thought, formal-operational schemes do not. In fact, they only come into play when certain specific reasoning situations call them forth. Consequently, formal-operational schemes are closely related to the formulation of scientific laws because they are adapted to extracting the functional relationships such laws are concerned with. We now consider examples of such functional relationships.

Cognitive contents. Piaget has reported findings bearing on four schemes: the proportionality scheme, the scheme of double reference, the scheme of mechanical equilibrium (or the *action-reaction principle*), and the probability scheme. Data on the first three are reported in Part 2 of the *The Growth of Logical Thinking*. Data on the fourth are reported in a separate work (Piaget and Inhelder 1951). These four schemes do not comprise an exhaustive list of all conceivable formal-operational schemes. They are merely the four that have been most strongly emphasized in Piaget's writings. Theoretically, the number of possible schemes is limited only by the number of recurrent functional relationships in the environment. One might, in principle, hypothesize a scheme for each elementary law of physics. We examine the four given schemes separately below.

1. The proportionality scheme, in its broadest sense, refers to subjects' understanding of the fact that the ratio of two quantities (X/Y) is equal to the ratio of two other quantities (X'/Y'). The simplest examples of this proportionality (or "equal ratios") scheme occur with fractions in arithmetic. In North America, children usually begin working with fractions in the sixth grade. Among other things, they soon learn that certain fractions are equal to certain other fractions—$1/2 = 3/6$, $1/3 = 9/27$, etc. As is obvious from these illustrations, none of the quantities on the left side have to be the same as the quantities on the right side for the fractions to be equal. The rule, which children learn when they are taught how to reduce fractions, is that the fraction on the right side is always an integer multiple of the fraction on the left side.

Inhelder and Piaget (1958) claim that children cannot solve problems involving ratios until they reach the formal-operational stage. This claim receives some a priori support from the fact that most experts in mathematics education believe that the study of fractions should not be introduced until sixth or seventh grade (e.g., cf. Payne 1976). However, Inhelder and Piaget's method of studying the proportionality scheme involved concrete problem-solving situations in which a balance scale was used.

The main apparatus for studying the proportionality scheme is depicted in Figure 6-2. To begin with, subjects are shown the balance and are told that their task is to determine how it works. Next, subjects are given two unequal weights (W_1 and W_2) which can be suspended at different lengths (L_1 and L_2) from the pivot point of the balance. Subjects are asked to determine through experimentation how to suspend the weights, one on either side of the pivot point, so that the arm is exactly balanced—i.e., so that the arm is parallel to the table on which the entire apparatus rests. Subjects are asked to perform the same task with many different pairs of weights. The rule governing the balance is that the effect of a given weight is always proportional to its distance from the pivot. In fractional terms, $W_1/W_2 = L_1/L_2$ where L_1 is the distance of W_1 from the pivot and L_2 is the

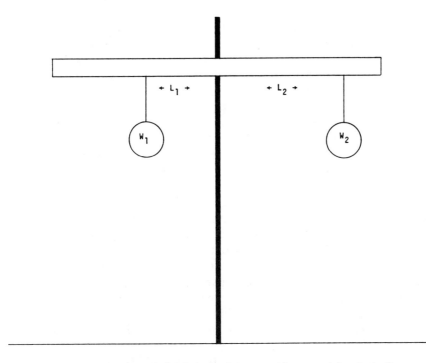

Figure 6-2 An illustration of the balance beam problem used to study the proportionality scheme. The beam will tilt to the left if W_1L_1 is greater than W_2L_2. The beam will tilt to the right if W_1L_1 is smaller than W_2L_2. The beam will remain where it is if W_1L_1 equals W_2L_2.

distance of W_2 from the pivot. What the experimenter is *really* interested in is whether subjects can discover this proportional relation for themselves after they have balanced the scale several times. We might say that they had discovered the rule if they concluded that (*a*) equal weights must be hung at equal distances from the pivot and (*b*) a lighter weight must be hung at a greater distance from the pivot than a heavier weight.

Inhelder and Piaget report that subjects do not discover this proportion until they reach the formal level. Before age 11 or 12, subjects can only solve each separate balancing task by trial and error. Although they eventually balance the arm by trial and error, preformal subjects give no evidence of having discovered the general principle $W_1/W_2 = L_1/L_2$. This conclusion follows from the fact that they continue to make the same errors on each successive task. Moreover, the number of these errors does not decrease very much with practice. Preformal subjects' basic difficulty on the proportionality test seems to be a tendency to focus on the weight ratio (W_1/W_2) while ignoring the length ratio (L_1/L_2) or to focus on the length ratio while ignoring the weight ratio. To illustrate, children younger than 11 or 12 will frequently discover that the effect of a small weight can be increased by increasing its distance from the pivot. But these same subjects fail to see that this fact must imply the corresponding relationship in which the effect of a large weight can be reduced by decreasing distance from the pivot. In contrast, subjects between the ages of 11 and 15 gave definite evidence of having discovered the proportion. When subjects in this age range were given several consecutive balancing tasks, they behaved like younger subjects for the first few trials. In other words, they solved each task by experimentation and committed many errors. Eventually, however, they discovered the rule and thereafter they made no errors.

2. Systems of double reference refer to subjects' understanding that an event that occurs in one system can either be canceled or enhanced by an event that occurs in some second system that is linked to it. In modern science, perhaps the most famous examples of systems of double reference come from Einstein's theory of relativity. According to Einstein, motion or speed is never absolute; it always depends on two different frames of reference. These are the speed of a particular object and the speed of any observer attempting to measure the speed of the object. Thus, if one attempts to measure the speed of a train, the value is larger if the observer is moving *toward* the train than if he is stationary or is moving away from the train.

Our example of systems of double reference is drawn from Piaget and Inhelder (1969) rather than from Inhelder and Piaget (1958). The apparatus consisted of a board which is placed on a table. A snail is then placed on the board. The snail can travel from left to right or from right to left relative to the board and table. The board can be moved from left to right and from right to left relative to the snail and table. Thus, when the snail moves in one direction, the board can be moved in the same direction or in the opposite direction. The board can also move while the snail remains immobile. The subject's task is to determine, under all of these conditions, just where the snail will end up relative to some *external* system of reference such as the table or the room in which the apparatus is set up. What we are interested in is whether the subject can combine the two systems of reference to make predictions. In particular, can the subject predict that the movement of the snail relative to an external system of reference (e.g., the table) will be enhanced when the board moves in the same direction and canceled when the board moves in the opposite direction?

Inhelder and Piaget found that preformal children do not make predictions based on both systems of reference. Subjects between the ages of 8 and 11, when questioned, showed that they clearly understand that *both* the snail and the board can move relative to each other and relative to the external reference system. But, curiously, they did not make use of this fact when making predictions. They seemed incapable of coordinating the behavior of the two systems of reference relative to the external system. Their predictions were always based on the movement of the snail alone or on the movement of the board alone. Piaget attributes this behavior to the lack of coordination of the two reversibility rules at the concrete-operational stage. He says that the coordination of the two reversibilities would allow the subject to understand that the snail's movement relative to the external referent can either be negated (by reversing the movement of the snail itself) or compensated (by moving the board). Inhelder and Piaget found that subjects between the ages of 11 and 15 could make predictions that took account of both the movement of the snail and the board relative to each other. Naturally, Piaget attributes this advance to the coordination of the two reversibilities and the concomitant acquisition of propositional operations and the *INRC* group.

3. The scheme of mechanical equilibrium refers to subjects' grasp of Newton's action-reaction principle: For every action there is an equal and opposite reaction. Piaget believes that a formal-operational scheme that embodies this principle is activated when the subject is confronted with a problem-solving situation in which some given event is visible but the cause which engenders it is not.

Not surprisingly, the method used by Inhelder and Piaget to study the scheme of mechanical equilibrium is rather like the techniques used to study the action-reaction law in high school physics. The apparatus consists of a scaled-down version of the hydraulic press used to raise and lower automobiles in service stations. Two large glass tubes *A* and *B* are connected at the bottom by a small rubber hose. Tube *A* is fitted at the top with a small piston. The piston can be loaded with objects of various weights, which cause it to press down on any liquid that is in tube *A*. The hydraulic system —consisting of the two tubes, the hose which connects them, and the piston—is filled with liquids of different densities (e.g., water, alcohol). By placing objects of different weights on the piston at the top of tube *A*, the subject can vary the amount of pressure exerted on the liquid in the system. Of course, the height of the liquid in tube *B* rises whenever a weight is placed on the piston at the top of tube *A*. The subject's task is to discover, by placing objects of different weights on the piston, what factors determine how high the liquid in tube *B* will rise. The answer is that there are two determining factors, namely, the amount of weight placed on the piston (the greater the weight the greater the rise) and the density of the liquid in the system (the denser the liquid the greater its resistance to a given amount of weight). In presenting this problem, Inhelder and Piaget's main objective was to discover the extent to which their subjects understood that the force exerted by the piston is transmitted through the system in such a way that an equilibrium is produced between the action of the piston and the reaction (resistance) of the liquid.

Inhelder and Piaget observed that the action-reaction principle, as measured by subjects' understanding of how a hydraulic press operates, does not appear until the formal level. Concrete-operational children performed in somewhat the same manner as they performed on the snail problem. They tended to focus on the weight factor and ignore the intrinsic resistance of the liquid. Piaget attributes this behavior, first, to lack of coordination of the two reversibilities at the conrete level and, second, to the failure to take account of both real and potential factors. By the age of 11 or 12, children begin to take account of both the weight on the piston and the resistance of the liquid. This leads many of them to formulate a general action-reaction principle governing the hydraulic system. The best single indicator of these advances, according to Inhelder and Piaget, is a change in subjects' conception of *how* the piston exerts force on the system. Formal-operational subjects believe that the piston exerts a force that is always proportional to the resistance of the liquid—i.e., the weight and density factors compensate each other. In contrast, concrete-operational subjects believe that the piston will descend just as far as a given weight will "push" it. This belief leads to the incorrect prediction that a given weight (say, 100 grams) will cause the liquid in tube *B* to rise just as high when the system contains a very dense liquid as when it contains a less dense liquid.

4. Piaget has written a separate book on the development of the probability scheme, *La Genèse de l'idée de hazard chez l'enfant*. Although there is some discussion of probability in Chapter 15 of *The Growth of Logical Thinking*, the empirical evidence appears in the former work. Although this book was originally published in 1951, it has never been translated. We first consider the general model of probability development presented in this book. We then consider two of the experiments used to study children's probability concepts.

Piaget says that the development of the probability scheme depends on the development of formal operations in general and the development of the proportionality scheme in particular. His guiding hypothesis is that subjects cannot understand what sorts of events are only probable ("chance occurrences") unless they also understand which events are absolutely necessary. According to this view, intelligence slices the world up into two broad categories: (*a*) things that absolutely must happen because they are governed by natural laws and (*b*) things that only *should* happen because they are not governed by any natural law. If you drop a rock from the top of a building, it must fall thanks to the law of gravity. But if you flip a coin 100 times, you should get in the neighborhood of 50 heads.

Dividing events into these two classes, which is the heart of the probability scheme, is said to presuppose formal operations. According to Piaget, the development of the probability scheme consists of three global stages that correspond to the preoperational, concrete-operational, and formal-operational levels. During Stage I, subjects fail to grasp the distinction between events governed by natural law (dropping a rock) and events governed by chance (flipping a coin). Interestingly, they tend to think that chance events may actually be governed by natural laws. This is reminiscent of our discussion of preoperational finalism in Chapter 4. During Stage II, subjects begin to distinguish chance events from lawful ones. Concrete-operational children realize that there are certain situations in which they cannot figure out a rule that allows them to make perfect predictions. But within the domain of purely chance occurrences, concrete-operational children have great difficulty distinguishing between events that are more and less likely to happen. For example, they might not understand that of all the possible results of flipping a coin 100 times, 50 heads and 50 tails is a much more likely result than 20 heads and 80 tails. It appears that concrete-operational children do not understand the frequency principles that govern systems of chance events. These principles are not discovered until the formal-operational stage. According to Piaget, this is because they always involve *statements of proportion*. The formulation of such statements calls for the application of the proportionality scheme which, as we have seen, is a formal-operational achievement.

One very simple experiment that Piaget and Inhelder used to study the probability scheme involved drawing different colored objects from a bag. A mixed set of blue, red, yellow, and green objects was placed in a bag. The bag was opaque so the children could not see the objects inside it. However, an identical set of objects was visible to the child. The subjects were asked to withdraw objects from the bag in pairs. Before withdrawing each pair, they were asked to predict the color of the objects. Although the task required guessing, there were two rules that could be used to maximize the number of "hits." First, by looking at the visible objects, the subject could see that some were more frequent than others. Second, by matching up each pair of withdrawn objects with the set of visible objects, the subject could also see how the initial frequency was changing. A subject who used both principles was said to grasp the probability concept. Piaget and Inhelder reported that preoperational children did not tend to make use of either rule. Concrete-operational children made use of the first rule but not the second. Their initial guesses were fairly accurate because they were based on the frequency of each color in the set of visible objects. But accuracy degenerated on later trials because they failed to see that color frequencies were changing as objects were withdrawn. Formal-operational children made use of both principles. They used the frequency of each color in the visible set to guide their initial judgments, and they altered the frequencies of the visible set as objects were withdrawn from the bag.

The roulette wheel apparatus mentioned earlier as a method of studying propositional operations was also used by Piaget and Inhelder to study the probability scheme. The specific aim of the experiment that made use of this apparatus was to assess the extent to which subjects could partition sets of events into the lawful and chance categories mentioned earlier. The metal pointer on the wheel was spun under two sets of conditions. First, it was spun without any magnetization. The subject was asked to predict which section of the wheel the pointer would arrive at after each spin. The object of this series of spins was to show the child that the wheel behaves in an entirely unpredictable manner when it is not magnetized. Second, the wheel was spun with some segments magnetized. During this second series of spins, a matchbox was placed on each section of the wheel. Some of the boxes contained a magnet and others did not. The object of this second series of spins was to show the subject that the behavior of the wheel was predictable when the matchboxes were present. Piaget and Inhelder reported the following results. Preoperational children failed to draw a clear distinction between unpredictable and predictable spins of the wheel. When the boxes were absent, they thought the pointer was more likely to stop at certain sections than others. When the boxes were present, they thought that the pointer would occasionally stop at unmagnetized sections. Concrete-operational children could distinguish between the two series of spins with tolerable accuracy. They understood that the behavior of the wheel was more predictable when the boxes were present than when they were absent. But they did not understand that the behavior of the wheel was *completely* random when the boxes were absent and completely predictable when they were present. For example, when the boxes were absent, some concrete operational children thought that the pointer would be less likely to stop at a certain section if it had stopped at that section on the *immediately preceding trial.* Formal-operational children understood that the behavior of the wheel was completely unpredictable when the boxes were absent and completely predictable when they were present.

Replication Studies

To conclude this chapter, we turn to research conducted by investigators outside Geneva that bears, in one way or another, on Piaget's account of the formal-operational stage. For convenience, the research is subdivided into three categories: (*a*) research on propositional operations; (*b*) research on formal-operational schemes; (*c*) learning experiments. These categories differ markedly in terms of the amount of research that has been published and the extent to which definitive conclusions can be drawn from the available data. Research on propositional operations is quite extensive, and it seems possible to draw a few conclusions that are beyond reasonable doubt. Categories (*b*) and (*c*) are quite another matter. Although there seem to be some definite themes underlying research on formal-operational schemes, the findings are far less extensive and, thus, empirical generalizations are correspondingly more hazardous. Finally, learning research on formal-operations is still in its infancy.

research on propositional operations

On the very first page of *The Growth of Logical Thinking*, it is proposed that subjects do not grasp propositional logic until they reach adolescence. This contention serves as the background for the experiments on angles of incidence vs. angles of reflection, floating objects, etc., that we considered earlier. Inhelder and Piaget's specific hypothesis runs like this: "If we are to explain the transition from the concrete thought of the child to the formal thought of the adolescent, we must first describe the development of propositional logic, *which the child at the concrete level* (stage II: from 7-8 to 11-12 years) *cannot yet handle*" (1958, p. 1, my italics).

These remarks bring us back to the performance-competence question which has cropped up in each of the preceding three chapters. Inhelder and Piaget say that concrete-operational children "cannot yet handle" propositional logic. But, as we have found before, the key findings used to support this claim are negative. A series of problem-solving tests are administered that, according to Inhelder and Piaget, require a grasp of propositional logic. Let us assume, purely for the sake of argument, that the six problems discussed earlier in this chapter cannot be solved without understanding propositional logic. Therefore, when subjects (almost always adolescents) solve one of these problems, it seems safe to conclude that they possess propositional logic. But when subjects (usually elementary schoolers) fail one of these problems, it is not equally safe to conclude that they lack propositional logic. Problems such as invisible magnetization, oscillation of pendulums, etc., require, in addition to propositional logic, a vast array of supporting skills. It may be that it is an absence of these other skills ("performance factors"), not propositional logic, that explains why elementary schoolers fail Inhelder and Piaget's problems. Consequently, it may be that purified tests that tap propositional logic but require fewer extraneous skills would show that elementary schoolers can handle propositional logic.

We now examine three sources of evidence bearing on the hypothesis that propositional logic is not understood until the formal-operational stage. First, we review conceptual criticisms of Piaget's use of propositional logic. Second, we review a rather extensive series of studies concerned with one particular propositional operation, the operation of implication. Third, we review studies concerned with propositional operations other than implication.

Conceptual criticisms. Earlier, I observed that Piaget has essentially taken propositional logic and placed it inside the adolescent's head as a system of mental operations. Actually, this statement is not quite accurate. I should have said that Piaget *tried* to put propositional logic inside the adolescent's head. But logicians say that what was actually put in there is not propositional logic.

Since *The Growth of Logical Thinking* first appeared in translation, it has been widely criticized by English-speaking logicians for faulty logic. Inhelder and Piaget's discussions of the abstract principles of propositional logic is never very rigorous and occasionally is downright sloppy. More important, however, the degree of correspondence between what Piaget calls "propositional logic" and the real item (i.e., what one finds in a logic textbook) is imperfect. It is one thing to give an informal presentation of a very formal subject. It is quite another to give a presentation that is not faithful to the original. This general criticism was first lodged by the logician Charles Parsons (1960) in a review of *The Growth of Logical Thinking*. But lately the criticism has been associated with the work of Robert H. Ennis of the University of Illinois. In a series of papers spanning more than a decade, Ennis has carefully documented the various conflicts between what Piaget calls propositional logic and the actual logical system. He has summarized these conflicts in three recent essays (Ennis 1975, 1976, 1977).

I shall not undertake a detailed review of specific conflicts between Piaget's propositional logic and the real thing. Such a review would deal with technical questions that go beyond the scope of this book. In particular, such a review would presuppose a reasonably good acquaintance with symbolic logic. Since knowledge of symbolic logic is not a necessary requirement for most psychology studies, we shall forego a detailed analysis of the anomalies in Piaget's logic. I shall simply assure the reader that the anomalies are very real and direct interested persons to Ennis' work.

Fortunately, one can make some *general* statements about the technical shortcomings in Piaget's logic. What is more, it is also possible to say how such discrepancies affect the claim that concrete-operational children "cannot yet handle" propositional logic. There are three very general anomalies in Piaget's propositional logic that have been pointed out by Ennis. First, Piaget's logic is less parsimonious than the logician's. It incorporates many concepts that are redundant because they can be defined in terms of each other without a loss of meaning. In regular propositional logic, the complete system of sixteen propositional operations is *never* retained. All of these operations can be defined in terms of one or two other operations. For example, negation and conjunction can be used to define the other fourteen operations. For reasons of parsimony, therefore, a logician will reduce the operations in Table 6-1 to a single operation (nonconjunction or nondisjunction) or to, at most, a set of two operations (negation and conjunction or negation and disjunction). The other operations can always be constructed when they are needed. Piaget eschews economy and retains all sixteen.

A second anomaly is that the sorts of things that Piaget calls propositions are not the same things that logicians call propositions. As we saw earlier, regular propositional logic is concerned with abstract functions that become true or false when they take on certain interpretations. The theory itself deals entirely with the abstract functions and never considers concrete interpretations of these functions. Piaget's propositions, on the other hand, are more like interpreted propositional functions than abstract functions. In Ennis' words, Piaget's propositions cannot "stand alone" because they must always refer to some specific interpretation (a certain piece of metal in the floating bodies problem, a certain rod in the flexibility of rods problem, etc.). Since the logician's propositions can stand alone, they form the basis of an abstract calculus. One cannot found such a calculus on Piaget's propositions.

Third, the sixteen propositional operations are always completely independent of each other in regular logic but not in Piaget's logic. As an illustration, consider implication (Row 4, Table 6–1) and reverse implication (Row 3, Table 6–1). In regular propositional logic, the true/false/true/true pattern of outcomes is independent of the true/true/false/true pattern. This is because each pattern is associated with abstract functions that are assigned no specific interpretation. But in Piaget's logic the two patterns are not independent. Ennis has shown that whenever the implication pattern is present the reverse implication pattern cannot occur, and whenever the reverse implication pattern is present the implication pattern cannot occur. In general, Ennis has shown that when a certain pattern of true-false outcomes is present *other patterns can automatically be eliminated*. This is a consequence of the fact that Piaget's propositions are not abstract functions.

The unfortunate conclusion of the discrepancies between regular and Piagetian logic is that when Piaget says that concrete-operational children "cannot yet handle" propositional logic, he may be saying nothing at all. Or at least he may be saying nothing that we can put to a test, which in science is the same thing as saying nothing at all. A reader who knows some logic would naturally assume, upon encountering Piaget's claim for the first time, that it must mean that concrete-operational children cannot grasp the principles of propositional logic that appear in textbooks. But in view of discrepancies such as those we have noted, studying children's ability to understand regular propositional logic may not provide a definitive test of Piaget's claims. A definitive test would require that we study *his* version of propositional logic. But Piaget has never spelled out his version in any detail; all we know is some of the more obvious ways in which it differs from the usual version. Unfortunately, this suggests that Piaget's claim may, at present, be untestable. This is precisely the conclusion that Ennis has advanced: "No matter what the interpretation, I have concluded that the claim is either false, or untestable, or not about deductive logic" (1975, p. 39).

Implication reasoning. Logically speaking, none of the sixteen propositional operations is more important than the others. But, from a practical standpoint, some of them are known to play a more central role in human reasoning than others. When we use practical significance as our guide, the most important of the propositional operations are undoubtedly implication (Row 4, Table 6–1) and reverse implication (Row 3, Table 6–1). These two operations, which we shall see are really a single operation, are the heart of a process called *implication reasoning*. This process, in turn, is the key reasoning strategy underlying mathematics and science. Concerning mathematics, the remarks quoted earlier from Bertrand Russell make it evident that mathematics is basically concerned with what statements imply what other statements. Russell thought that mathematics could be even more concisely defined as "the class of all propositions of the form '*p* implies *q*,' ..." (1903, p. 3). Concerning science, implication reasoning forms the basis for all scientific laws. This is because scientific laws are statements of cause and effect, and cause-effect statements are, at bottom, statements of implication. Whenever we say "*A* causes *B*," what we are really saying, from a logical point of view, is "if *A* occurs, then *B* occurs also."

Now that we know that statements of implication are central in human reasoning, what do such statements say? To answer this question, we return to Table 6–1. Suppose that we again have two propositional functions *P* and *Q*. The meaning of the statement "*P* implies *Q*" may be found in Row 4. We see that this statement is only false when *P* is true and *Q* is false. Consequently, what the statement "*P* implies *Q*" is asserting is that *the truth of Q is contingent on the truth of P*. It tells us that if *P* is true, then *Q* must also be true. If it happens that *Q* is false when *P* is true, then the truth of *Q* does not depend on the truth of *P* and the statement that "*P* implies *Q*" is false. Since statements of implication assert a contingent relationship between two things, they are called *conditional* statements in everyday discourse. Reverse implication (Row 3, Table 6–1) is simply implication with the two propositions reversed. In other words, if we take "*P* implies *Q*" as our example of implication, then "*Q* implies *P*" automatically becomes our example of reverse implication. Both statements are saying the same thing; only the order of the propositions differs. In particular, the *relationship* being asserted (the truth of the second proposition depends on the truth of the first) is the same in both cases. This means that there is actually no difference between implication and reverse implication in everyday usage. Therefore, the term "implication" means both implication and reverse implication in what follows.

Since implication is so central in human thinking, there are reasons for wanting to known when children are capable of using and understanding this operation. Most of these reasons are educational. Mathematics and science comprise a major portion of the public school curriculum in industrial nations. If we wish to teach mathematics and science in such a way that pupils understand the relevant concepts rather than merely learn them by rote, it is necessary to acquaint them with the forms of logical reasoning on which these concepts are based. It is especially important to acquaint them with implication. But if we decided to teach propositional operations such as implication, when may we expect that children will be able to benefit from such instruction? On the one hand, there are educators (e.g., Suppes and Binford 1965) who believe that children in the early elementary grades can learn propositional logic. At the other extreme, there are adherents to Piaget's theory who believe that propositional logic should not be taught until junior high or high school. With such extreme differences of opinion, it is important to know when, precisely, children appear to understand propositional operations such as implication.

There is a long history of research on the development of implication reasoning dating back to the birth of the intelligence testing movement at the turn of the century. However, we are interested in a recent series of investigations, dating from the early 1960s, inspired by Piaget's claim that concrete-operational children "cannot yet handle" propositional logic. Everyone seems to agree that the starting point for this series of studies was a Stanford University doctoral dissertation by Hill (1961). The dissertation was supervised by Patrick Suppes, a renowned mathematical psychologist who, along with Ennis, has been one of the chief critics of Piaget's logic. Briefly stated, Hill's results showed that 6- and 8-year-olds were capable of a good deal more implication reasoning than the theory gives them credit for. This finding inspired a series of follow-up studies that is still continuing. The available literature now includes more than two dozen major investigations involving thousands of children and adolescents (e.g., Brainerd 1970, 1976d; Donaldson 1963; Ennis 1971; Ennis et al. 1969; Howell 1965; Kodroff and Roberge 1975; O'Brien and Shapiro 1968; Roberge 1970; Roberge and Paulus 1971; Shapiro and O'Brien 1970). By far the largest amount of data has been reported by Ennis and his associates. We begin by reviewing the general method used to study implication reasoning. We then examine the key findings which have emerged from these studies.

1. In everyday discourse, *if-then statements* are always statements of implication. For example, the statements, "If you punch me in the nose, then you will injure your knuckles," "If you study Greek, then you will be bored," and "If you eat hot pizza, then you will burn your mouth," are all implications. More generally, any statement of cause and effect, as in the case of a scientific law, is an implication. Statements of this sort are used to study the implication reasoning abilities of children and adolescents. The basic technique involves two steps. First, give the subject one or more statements of implication as premises. Second, determine whether or not the subject can deduce the correct conclusions from these premises. In the simplest possible case of problems of this genre, the subject is given the

statements "*P* implies *Q*" and "*P*" as premises. He is then expected to deduce the statement "*Q*" as a conclusion. For example, here is a sample problem from Hill's (1961) dissertation:

a. *Premise #1.* If this is Room 9, then it is the fourth grade, (*P* implies *Q*)
b. *Premise #2.* This is Room 9, (*P*)
c. *Conclusion.* This is the fourth grade. (*Q*)

In this problem, the subject is given Premise #1, then Premise #2, and finally is asked, "Is it the fourth grade?" Another example comes from a study of implication reasoning in first, second, and third graders by Kodroff and Roberge (1975):

a. *Premise #1.* If there is a knife, then there is a fork,
b. *Premise #2.* There is a knife,
c. *Conclusion.* There is a fork.

The testing procedure is the same as before—i.e., give the subject the two premises and then pose questions about the conclusion.

Problems of the preceding type are instances of the most fundamental rule of inference in propositional logic, the rule of *modus ponens*. Any statement of the form, "*P* implies *Q* and *P*; therefore, *Q*,*"* is an example of modus ponens. A slightly more difficult implication reasoning problem can be devised by giving the subject more than one implication statement as premises, and then determining whether correct conclusions are deduced. Such problems make use of the fact that implication is an asymmetrical-transitive relation. They have been used in several investigations (e.g., Brainerd 1970, 1976*d*; Ennis 1971). Here is a sample problem from Ennis (1971):

a. *Premise #1.* If the air weather report reads less than 10, then the ceiling is less than 1000 feet, (*P* implies *Q*)
b. *Premise #2.* If the ceiling is less than 1000 feet, then you may not fly out of this airport, (*Q* implies *R*)
c. *Premise #3.* The air weather report reads less than 10, (*P*)
d. *Conclusion.* You may not fly out of this airport. (*R*)

Here is another sample problem from Brainerd (1970):

a. *Premise #1.* If Jack washes the dishes, then his father will be very pleased.
b. *Premise #2.* If Jack's father is very pleased, then Jack gets 50¢.
c. *Premise #3.* Jack washes the dishes.
d. *Conclusion.* Jack gets 50¢.

In both examples the subject is given all three premises and then questions are posed about the conclusion.

In all of the above examples, the problems are designed to measure the extent to which subjects draw *correct* conclusions given one or more implications as premises. Problems of this sort are called, following Ennis (1971, 1975, 1976), *valid forms*. A second category of implication reasoning problems focuses on the extent to which subjects draw *incorrect* conclusions given one or more implications as premises. Problems falling in this category are termed, also following Ennis, *invalid forms*. The criterion of success on an invalid forms problem is that the subject *does not draw* some specific erroneous conclusion. We can construct invalid forms alternatives to each of the preceding valid forms problems. For example, the following is an invalid alternative to the first modus ponens example that has been used by Shapiro and O'Brien (1970):

a. *Premise #1.* If this is Room 9, then it is the fourth grade.
b. *Premise #2.* This is not Room 9.
c. *Erroneous Conclusion.* This is not the fourth grade.

Obviously, there could be a fourth-grade class in some room other than Room 9. The following is the invalid form for the second modus ponens problem mentioned above:

a. *Premise #1.* If there is a knife, then there is a fork.
b. *Premise #2.* There is not a knife.
c. *Erroneous Conclusion.* There is not a fork.

The testing procedure for invalid forms is the same as for their valid forms counterparts. In general, invalid forms are designed to assess an important reasoning error that is known as the *converse of the conditional error* in logic. Any statement of the form, "*P* implies *Q* and not-*P*; therefore, not-*Q*," is an example of the converse of the conditional error. This error is concerned with the fact that while "*P* implies *Q*" asserts a contingent relationship between the truth of *Q* and the truth of *P*, it does not assert a contingent relationship between the falsity of *Q* and the falsity of *P*.

The distinction between invalid forms and valid forms is an important one to bear in mind. The success rates for these two types of implication reasoning problems turn out to be quite different.

2. Research on implication reasoning has produced several findings about how various factors influence such reasoning that are of considerable educational interest. However, there are two critical findings that pertain to Piaget's claim that concrete-operational children "cannot yet handle" propositional logic. I state the conclusions at the outset and then review some sample findings that support them. First, when implication reasoning tests consist of valid forms problems, concrete-operational children pass them with flying colors. Even children whose ages fall within the second

half of the nominal range for preoperations (5- and 6-year-olds) perform exceptionally well on such tests. In general, when an elementary schooler is given "*P* implies *Q,* " and "*P,*" he almost always concludes "*Q*." Second, when implication reasoning tests consist entirely of invalid forms, concrete-operational children fail them across the board. But so does everyone else. Studies have consistently shown that children, adolescents, normal adults, and even college students fail invalid forms problems. Given the premises "*P* implies *Q*" and "not-*P*," almost everyone concludes "not-*Q*."

Studies by Ennis (1971), Kodroff and Roberge (1975), Paris (1973), and Taplin, Staudenmayer, and Taddonio (1974) will be used to illustrate the general trend of the findings on valid forms problems. In each of the latter three experiments, modus ponens problems ("*P* implies *Q* and *P*; therefore, *Q*") were studied. Kodroff and Roberge (1975) administered modus ponens problems to first, second, and third graders. First graders passed 77% of the problems, second graders passed 78% of the problems, and third graders passed 88% of the problems. Paris (1973) administered modus ponens problems to second, fifth, eighth, and eleventh graders. Overall, his subjects passed roughly 95% of the problems. Of special interest is the performance of the second graders. They passed roughly 90% of the problems. Finally Taplin, Staudenmayer, and Taddonio (1974) administered modus ponens problems to third, fifth, seventh, ninth, and eleventh graders. Overall, their subjects passed 87% of the problems. Third graders passed 78% of the problems. In short, no matter whose data you consider, modus ponens problems are very easy for children falling within the nominal age range for concrete operations.

Ennis (1971) studied the more difficult three-premise implication problems mentioned earlier ("*P* implies *Q* and *Q* implies *R* and *P*; therefore, *R*"). In view of the larger number of things that must be remembered, we would expect children to perform less well than on modus ponens problems. But performance was still surprisingly good. Ennis administered six of these three premise tests to first, second, and third grade children. Overall, they passed 55% of the problems. Roughly one-third of the children performed perfectly. Similar findings have been reported by Brainerd (1970). Brainerd administered three-premise problems resembling Ennis' to 8-year-olds. They passed roughly two-thirds of the problems.

The second conclusion, that concrete-operational children almost always fail invalid forms tests of implication reasoning ability, may be illustrated with data reported by Ennis (1971), Paris (1973), and Taplin, Staudenmayer, and Taddonio (1974). Tests of the converse of the conditional error ("*P* implies *Q* and not-*P*; therefore not-*Q*") were used in all these experiments. Ennis (1971) administered converse-of-the-conditional tests to first, second, and third graders. Overall, his subjects passed only about one-quarter of the problems. Paris (1973) administered converse-of-the-conditional tests to second, fifth, eighth, and eleventh graders. Overall, they passed only 7% of the problems. Taplin, Staudenmayer, and Taddonio (1974) administered converse-of-the-conditional tests to third, fifth, seventh, ninth, and eleventh graders. Overall, they passed 22% of the problems. No matter whose data you consider, it does not look as though children grasp invalid forms of implication reasoning.

It might be supposed that children's poor performance on invalid forms tests provides some support for Piaget's claims about the development of propositional logic. If we restrict ourselves to just invalid forms and forget about valid forms, it certainly appears that concrete-operational children "cannot yet handle" the propositional operation of implication. The problem is that no one else can either. When we confine ourselves to invalid forms, the vast majority of the subjects, regardless of how old they are, fail implication reasoning problems. For example, in Taplin, Staudenmayer, and Taddonio's (1974) experiment, the adolescent subjects (seventh, ninth, and eleventh graders) passed only about one-quarter of the invalid forms problems. The adolescent subjects in Paris' (1973) experiment (eighth and eleventh graders) performed even worse. They passed less than 5% of the invalid forms problems. Paris also administered his converse-of-the-conditional problems to a comparison sample of college students. They failed 95% of the problems! Other researchers (e.g., Wason and Johnson-Laird 1972) have repeatedly observed that even college-trained adults perform poorly on invalid forms tests of implication reasoning.

Other propositional operations. Although the largest single aggregate of studies is concerned with implication, there also has been extensive work done on other propositional operations. On the whole, this work tends to show that both of the conclusions advanced above for implication may also be extended to other operations. But, more important, studies of other propositional operations lead to a new conclusion as well. Regardless of whether one studies children, adolescents, or adults, there seem to be clear differences in the relative difficulty of the operations.

In this section, we examine findings on three additional operations: *conjunction* (Row 12, Table 6-1), *disjunction* (Row 2, Table 6-1), and *equivalence* (Row 8, Table 6-1). Although some studies of these three operations have also focused on implication (e.g., Paris 1973), most of them have not (e.g., Neimark 1970; Youniss, Furth, and Ross 1971). To illustrate the general trends, we begin by reconsidering a very comprehensive study by Paris (1973) that relied on the testing methods discussed earlier. We then turn to corroborative results obtained with some quite different procedures pioneered by Lyle E. Bourne of the University of Colorado (e.g., Bourne 1970; Bourne and O'Banion 1971; Haygood and Bourne 1965).

As I mentioned earlier, Paris (1973) administered modus ponens (valid and invalid) problems to second, fifth, eighth, and eleventh graders. He also administered tests of conjunction, disjunction, and equivalence. To see what the tests for these other three rules were like, let us take each in turn. From Row 12 of Table 6-1, we see that "conjunction" means that we have some compound proposition $P + Q$ which is true when both component propositions are true and is false otherwise. In everyday discourse, statements involving *and* (i.e., the " + " in $P + Q$ is "and") are statements of conjunction. An illustrative problem could be:

    a. *Premise #1.* Babe Ruth hit sixty home runs in a season and Roger Maris hit sixty home runs in a season.

    b. *Premise #2.* Babe Ruth hit sixty home runs in a season.

    c. *Conclusion.* Roger Maris hit sixty home runs in a season.

An invalid forms problem could be created by questioning the subject about the negation of the conclusion (i.e., Roger Maris did not hit sixty home runs in a season). From Row 2 of Table 6-1, we see that "disjunction" means that we have some compound proposition that is false when both component propositions are false and is true otherwise. In everyday discourse, statements involving the *inclusive use of or* (i.e., "and/or") are examples of disjunction. An illustrative problem could be:

    a. *Premise #1.* I have a full house or you have four of a kind.

    b. *Premise #2.* I have a full house.

    c. *Conclusion.* You do or do not have four of a kind.

This can be converted to an invalid forms problem by questioning the subject about only one of the two alternatives in the conclusion. Finally, we see from Row 8 of Table 6-1 that "equivalence" means that we have some compound proposition that is only true when the component propositions are either both true or both false. In everyday discourse, statements involving *if and only if* are examples of equivalence. An illustrative problem might be:

    a. *Premise #1.* You contract the flu if and only if you are exposed to the flu virus.

    b. *Premise #2.* You contract the flu.

    c. *Conclusion.* You are exposed to the flu virus.

This can be converted to an invalid forms problem by questioning the subject about the negation of the conclusion.

Consistent with the findings mentioned in the preceding section, invalid forms problems appear to be more difficult than valid forms problems. On conjunction problems, for example, Paris' second graders made many more errors on invalid forms than on valid forms. Thus, the following general conclusion seems to be in order: When taking a test for propositional operations, subjects of all ages normally find it much easier to decide that a correct conclusion is true than to decide that an incorrect conclusion is false. Since the valid-invalid forms distinction has already been discussed at some length for implication reasoning, we shall not discuss it any further. Instead, we shall concentrate on an entirely new finding. It seems that problems that tap certain propositional operations, regardless of whether the problems are valid or invalid forms, are more difficult than problems that tap other operations.

When valid and invalid forms tests for all the operations are lumped together, the following order of difficulty emerges from Paris' investigation. Conjunction problems were by far the easiest. Over all age levels and all problems, the subjects passed roughly 95% of the conjunction problems. Equivalence problems were next easiest. Over all age levels and all problems, the subjects passed roughly 80% of the equivalence problems. Disjunction problems were next in order of difficulty. Over all age levels and all problems, the subjects passed roughly 70% of the disjunction problems. The implication problems were the most difficult of all. Over all age levels and all problems, the subjects passed roughly 60% of the implication problems. Thus, the subjects in Paris' investigation generally performed well on all types of problems. (Note that the pass rate never dropped below 50% for any of the four operations being tested.) However, there were clear differences in the relative difficulty of the operations with the decline in accuracy between successive operations usually being about 10%.

The finding that there is an intrinsic order of difficulty underlying propositional operations has been repeatedly observed by other investigators. The best single source of corroborative evidence is a very large group of experiments that, for several years, has been coming out of Lyle E. Bourne's (e.g., 1967, 1968) laboratories. The subjects in most of these experiments have been college students. However, children and adolescents have also been studied on occasion. Bourne and his associates use a research paradigm that was originally introduced by Neisser and Weene (1962). We begin by outlining this paradigm. We then examine some illustrative findings.

In everything that has been said so far, we have assumed that the propositional functions P and Q in any compound proposition $P + Q$ are verbal statements such as "x crossed the Rubicon," "x is the tallest building in the world," and so on. But in Bourne's paradigm the component propositional functions are always *stimulus dimensions* of some sort. If there are two dimensions, P and Q, one value of each dimension is arbitrarily designated "correct" or "true" and all other values are arbitrarily designated "incorrect" or "false." The subject is presented with a series of concrete objects that take on different values of the two dimensions. Each object that the subject is shown takes on one and only one value of dimension P and takes on one and only one value of dimension Q. The subject is shown all possible combinations of the two dimensions. If there are two values of each dimension, there are four possible combinations; if there are three values of each dimension, there are nine possible combinations; etc. The subject is told that certain objects are "correct" or "true"—namely, those objects that correspond to the cells in Table 6-1 where the operation being studied is true. The subject is also told that certain other objects are "incorrect" or "false"—namely, those objects that correspond to the cells in Table 6-1 where the operation is false.

This description of the Bourne methodology sounds much more complicated than it actually is. It is nothing more than a variation of the class matrix problems discussed in Chapter 5. Suppose that our two dimensions are P = shape and Q = color. Suppose that there are two values of shape, circle and square, and that there are two values of color, blue and green. As test objects, we show our subjects a series of three-by-five-inch index cards. In the center of each card, a figure appears. The figure is either a circle or a square (but never both) and is either colored blue or colored green (but never both). This means that we have exactly four possible cards: (*a*) blue circle; (*b*) green circle; (*c*) blue square; (*d*) green square. Now, we designate one of the shapes as "true," say circle, and we designate one of the colors as "true," say blue. To study any one of the sixteen propositional operations, we proceed as follows. We show the subject the series of cards over and over again. Each time a card comes up that corresponds to a cell in Table 6-1 where the operation is true, we tell subjects that the card is correct. But when a card comes up that corresponds to any cell in Table 6-1 where the operation is false, we tell subjects that the card is incorrect. We say that subjects are using the operation when they always know whether a given card is correct or incorrect before we tell them.

The procedure just described can obviously be used to study any or all of the propositional operations. If we wished to study disjunction (Row 2, Table 6-1), we would tell the subject "incorrect" whenever card (*d*) came up and "correct" whenever any of the other cards came up. If we wished to study conjunction (Row 12, Table 6-1), we would say "correct" whenever card (*a*) came up and "incorrect" whenever any of the other cards came up. If we wished to study implication, we would say "incorrect" whenever card (*b*) came up and "correct" whenever any of the other cards came up. And so on for all the other operations.

Using this general procedure, Bourne and his associates (and investigators in other laboratories) have consistently found that propositional operations differ in their intrinsic difficulty. The most stable result, which has been replicated any number of times, is that propositional operations may be grouped into three broad classes of difficulty. The first or easiest class consists of affirmation, negation, affirmation of *P,* affirmation of *Q,* denial of *P,* and denial of *Q.* The second or intermediate class consists of conjunction, nonconjunction, disjunction, and nondisjunction. The third and most difficult class consists of the remaining six operations. For our purposes, the crucial thing to bear in mind is that this difficulty hierarchy is not confined to college students. It has also been observed in children and adolescents (e.g., Bourne and O'Banion 1971; King 1966; White and Lindquist 1974). As an illustration, we consider the results of an experiment by Bourne and O'Banion (1971).

Bourne and O'Banion administered conjunction, disjunction, implication, and equivalence problems to first, second, third, fifth, seventh, and ninth graders. They administered the same problems to a comparison sample of college students. The problems made use of four dimensions that could each take on three values: color (red, yellow, blue), size (small, medium, large), cardinal number (1, 2, 3), and shape (square, triangle, hexagon). The series of test objects were pictures projected on a screen. Each picture portrayed one and only one of the three values of each of the four dimensions. Bourne and O'Banion observed that conjunction tasks were easiest, disjunction tasks were next easiest, implication tasks were next easiest, and equivalence tasks were most difficult. All subjects, children as well as adolescents, performed very well on the conjunction and disjunction tasks. On conjunction tasks, the subjects performed perfectly after they had seen an average of only 4.2 pictures. On the disjunction tasks, the subjects performed perfectly after they had seen an average of only 7.3 pictures. But on the implication and equivalence problems, the subjects saw an average of 45.5 pictures and 51.2 pictures, respectively, before they performed perfectly. Thus, even the oldest subjects performed poorly on implication and equivalence. A crucial finding was that this order of difficulty held up for all the age levels studied. In particular, it was the same for concrete-operational subjects (first and third graders) and formal-operational subjects (fifth grade and above).

The findings we have considered on propositional operations other than implication raise some of the same questions about Piaget's views on propositional logic as the implication data did. It is clear that concrete-operational children can handle some propositional operations if we restrict ourselves to, say, the first two classes in Bourne's difficulty hierarchy. It is equally clear that concrete-operational children have great difficulty with other propositional operations—e.g., those in Bourne's third class. But adolescents and adults also do not do very well with these latter operations.

Summary. At first glance, Piaget seems to be saying some very straightforward things about the development of propositional logic. He *seems* to be saying that concrete-operational children cannot use the sixteen propositional operations while formal-operational children can. But this statement, as simple as it may appear, raises a hornet's nest of theoretical and empirical problems. On the theoretical side, a number of logicians, including Robert Ennis, Charles Parsons, and Patrick Suppes, have criticized Piaget's logic. Ennis, in particular, has scrupulously documented the major discrepancies between what Piaget calls propositional logic and the real thing. Since Piaget has never spelled out his own alternative logic in detail, it is possible that his claims about the development of propositional logic may be untestable.

On the empirical side, a large body of research dating back to the early 1960s shows beyond reasonable doubt that it is impossible to make blanket claims to the effect that below some specific age children "cannot yet handle" propositional logic. This research shows that any statements about the development of propositional logic will have to take account of two factors not explicitly discussed by Piaget. First, they will have to consider whether a propositional operation is being used to recognize valid or invalid conclusions. Children in the early elementary grades have very little trouble using even the more difficult operations (e.g., implication, equivalence) to recognize valid conclusions. But they are almost completely incapable of using certain operations to recognize invalid conclusions. Indeed, most humans *never* acquire the latter ability. Even college students routinely make, for example, the converse of the conditional error when confronted with an invalid form of modus ponens.

A second factor which must be taken into account is differences in intrinsic difficulty of the sixteen propositional operations. Regardless of whether the problems being administered are valid or invalid forms, some operations are always more difficult to use than others. It appears possible to group the operations into three classes of increasing difficulty. The two easiest classes, which include a total of ten of the sixteen operations, pose no great hardship for concrete-operational children. If we restrict ourselves to these particular operations, it would seem not unreasonable to conclude that concrete-operational children can use propositional logic. On the other hand, these same children perform poorly on tests for the remaining six operations. But this finding does not serve to separate the propositional logic ability of concrete-operational children from that of formal-operational children. It turns out that both adolescents and college students perform poorly on tests for these other six operations.

research on formal-operational schemes

Shortly after *The Growth of Logical Thinking* had been translated, follow-up studies making use of various formal-operational schemes tests were undertaken in some European laboratories (e.g., Lovell 1961; Lovell and Ogilvie 1961; Peluffo 1964). North American researchers soon followed. The amount of available data on these tests is now quite extensive, though not nearly so extensive as the data on propositional operations.

Although tests that Inhelder and Piaget (1958) used to investigate other formal-operational schemes have been administered in some studies (e.g., Berzonsky 1971; Saarni 1973; Tomlinson-Keasey 1972), the preponderance of replication research has been concerned with the proportionality and probability schemes. As we saw earlier, Piaget contends that these two schemes are very closely related. More explicitly, he has proposed (Piaget and Inhelder 1951) that the probability concept presupposes the ability to handle proportions. In the discussion that follows, we confine ourselves to replication research on the proportionality and probability schemes. Proportionality is considered first.

The proportionality scheme. Researchers outside Geneva have used two different procedures to study the development of the proportionality scheme. Interestingly, neither procedure is the same as Inhelder and Piaget's principal test for proportionality, the balance problem. The first method, borrowed from Piaget and Inhelder (1941), involves measuring subjects' understanding of volume concepts. The second method, originally introduced by Lunzer (1965), involves administering tests of verbal and numerical analogies. Since these two methods are quite different, the findings on each are reviewed separately.

1. In Piagetian theory, the concept of volume is said to belong to the formal-operational stage. Like the probability concept, the volume concept is supposed to call for the use of the proportionality scheme. This is because the volume concept supposedly requires that subjects be able to grasp the proportionate relationship that always obtains between the familiar Euclidean variables of length, width, and depth. Two specific techniques have been used to study the development of the volume concept. The first consists of administering conservation of volume tests which are similar to the conservation tests in Chapter 5. The second and, I think, more interesting technique focuses on subjects' grasp of the notions of "full" and "empty."

Conservation of volume tests have been administered to children and adolescents in several studies dating back to the early 1960s (e.g., Brainerd 1971; Brainerd and Allen 1971*b*; Elkind 1961; Hobbs 1973; Lunzer 1960*b*; Saarni 1973; Uzgiris 1964). There are two basic types of tests: (*a*) conservation of liquid volume relationships and (*b*) conservation of displaced volumes. Test (*a*) is the same as the quantity conservation test discussed in Chapter 5 except for the questions that the subject has to answer. On the quantity conservation test, the subject is asked, "Do these glasses contain the same amount of water," after the pouring transformation. On volume test (*a*), the subject is asked, "Does the water in each glass take up the same amount of space (or room)," after the pouring transformation. Subjects who answer affirmatively pass test (*a*). Test (*b*) is somewhat different. The subject is shown a glass approximately half filled with water, and a clay ball. The clay ball is dropped into the water, and the experimenter asks the subject to note how the water rises. The experimenter carefully marks the new water level with a rubber band or by drawing a line on the outside of the glass. After the water level has been marked, the clay ball is withdrawn from the glass and, of course, the water level falls. The experimenter then flattens the clay ball into a pancake. Subjects are asked to predict how high the water will rise if the pancake is now placed in the water. If subjects predict that the water will rise to exactly its previous level, then they pass the test. If subjects predict that the water will rise above or below its previous level, then they fail the test.

The results of replication research on conservation of volume consistently support Piaget's claim that the proportionality scheme does not appear until the formal-operational stage. Some selected findings will illustrate the general trend. Hobbs (1973) administered type (*a*) and (*b*) tests to 906 subjects between the ages of 10 and 18. The ages of the youngest subjects placed them in late concrete operations or early formal operations. Hobbs' subjects pass considerably less than 50% of the tests. Brainerd and Allen (1971*b*) administered type (*a*) and (*b*) tests to 10-year-olds. Their subjects passed less than one-quarter of the tests on the average. Brainerd (1971) administered type (*a*) and (*b*) tests to 72 third, sixth, and ninth graders (24 subjects per age level). The ages of the first group (8- to 9-year-old) placed them in the middle of the concrete-operational stage. A total of 52 subjects passed the type (*a*) tests. Only 6 of them were third graders. A total of 41 subjects passed the type (*b*) tests. Only 2 of them were third graders. Therefore, it seems that volume conservation tests are generally beyond the capacity of elementary schoolers.

The second method of studying the development of volume concepts was devised by Bruner and Kenney (1966). The procedure focuses on subjects' understanding of the words *full* and *empty*. To assess understanding of these words, Bruner and Kenney showed their subjects pairs of glasses containing different amounts of water. There were four different types of pairings: (*a*) two glasses of different heights and diameters that were both half filled with water; (*b*) two glasses of different heights and diameters that were both filled to the top with water; (*c*) two glasses of different heights and diameters both containing the same amount of water; (*d*) two glasses of the same height and diameter containing different amounts of water. Bruner and Kenney showed these four types of glasses to 160 children between the ages of 5 and 11. Each time subjects were shown a certain pair of glasses, they were asked which was fuller and which was emptier.

To perform correctly on all four types of problems, subjects must have some grasp of proportionality: "Take the notion of which of two identical glasses is the fuller: one that is a third full or one that is two-thirds full. To appreciate this proportion, one needs first to estimate the volume of the glass that is filled and relate it to the total volume, again a ratio'' (Bruner and Kenney 1966, p. 169). In line with the results mentioned above for volume conservation, Bruner and Kenney found that only the oldest subjects could pass their test. To the youngest subjects (5- and 6-year-olds), ''fuller'' and ''emptier'' meant the *amount of water* that a glass contained. If one glass contained more water than a second glass, the former was judged fuller and the latter emptier. To slightly older subjects (7- and 9-year-olds), ''fuller'' and ''emptier'' meant the *amount of empty space* that a glass contained. If one glass contained less empty space than a second glass, the former was judged fuller and the latter emptier. Only the oldest subjects (11-year-olds), understood that ''fuller'' and ''emptier'' judgments must be based on the amount of empty space in a glass relative to the total volume of the glass. Of course, these subjects' ages correspond to the nominal age for the onset of formal operations.

2. The second method of studying the development of the proportionality scheme originated with Lunzer (1965). Lunzer proposed that two general types of tests not used by Inhelder and Piaget (1958) are valid measures of the proportionality scheme, namely, *verbal analogies tests* and *numerical analogies tests*. Lunzer presented a detailed theoretical argument to support his claim that such tests are acceptable proportionality measures. Since the argument is rather complicated, we shall not go over it here. Instead, we simply consider the tests themselves and what sorts of findings have been obtained by administering them to children and adolescents.

The following four items, which resemble items found on standardized tests of intelligence, are examples of Lunzer's verbal analogies:

   a. Wheel/engine/hoot/four/horn is to car as bell is to bicycle.
   b. Oval/sphere/round/ring/diameter is to circle as cube is to square.
   c. Lion is to lair as set/burrow/dog is to rabbit/kennel/fox.
   d. Tank/army/soldiers/land is to regiment as air force is to airplane/air/squadron/airman.

Lunzer's numerical analogies items were modeled after items that one finds on standardized tests of mathematics achievement. On each item, the subject was given two series of numbers. There was always a simple arithmetical relationship between the corresponding items in each series. Specifically, each item in the second series could be obtained from the corresponding item in the first series by adding a constant, subtracting a constant, multiplying by a constant, or dividing by a constant. There were always certain numbers missing in the second series which the subject had to fill in. The following are illustrative numerical analogies used by Lunzer:

a. *Series #1:*   3   9   10   4
   Series #2:   1   7   8   ?
b. *Series #1:*   2   8   4   5
   Series #2:   6 24   12   ?
c. *Series #1:*   8 48   6   20
   Series #2:   2 12   1 1/2 ?
d. *Series #1:* 12   7   14   6
   Series #2: 18 10 1/2 21   ?

Lunzer administered his analogies to 153 subjects whose ages placed them from the middle of the concrete stage to the achievement phase of the formal stage. The results were remarkably consistent with Piaget's view that subjects do not understand proportionality until they reach the formal stage. On the verbal analogies test, subjects in the middle of concrete operations (9-year-olds) passed only 22% of the items on the average. The percentages of items passed for other age levels were 33% (10-year-olds), 51% (11-year-olds), 57% (12-year-olds), 67% (13-year-olds), 68% (14-year-olds), 77% (15-year-olds), 75% (16-year-olds), and 83% (17-year-olds). It is interesting to note that the age at which the subjects were first able to pass about half the items corresponds exactly to the nominal age for the onset of formal operations. On the numerical analogies test, subjects in the middle of the concrete-operational stage passed only 19% of the items. The percentages of items passed for other age levels were 23% (10-year-olds), 48% (11-year-olds), 46% (12-year-olds), 67% (13-year-olds), 63% (14-year-olds), 76% (15-year-olds), 76% (16-year-olds), 79% (17-year-olds). Once again, the age at which subjects were first able to pass about half the items corresponds to the nominal age for the onset of formal operations.

In a later experiment, Lovell (1968) replicated the general trend of Lunzer's (1965) results. While Lunzer administered both verbal and numerical analogies, Lovell administered only the latter. He also added some new items that tested subjects' understanding of geometrical analogies. The ages of the subjects tested ranged from 9 to 15 years. Like Lunzer, Lovell found that subjects whose ages placed them in the middle of the concrete-operational stage did not perform very well on analogies.

The probability scheme. While the replication data on volume concepts and analogical reasoning are very consistent with Piaget's hypothesis that proportionality is not understood until adolescence, the same cannot be said of the replication research on the probability scheme. The general trend of the research is simply stated: It appears that concrete-operational children, and perhaps preoperational children as well, may be capable of the sorts of responses that Piaget and Inhelder (1951) took as evidence of the probability scheme.

Our old friend the performance-competence problem cropped up again in three studies published during the 1960s (Davies 1965; Goldberg

1966; Yost, Siegel, and Andrews 1962). As usual, the investigators charged that Piaget and Inhelder's (1951) procedures for measuring subjects' understanding of probability concepts also measure a variety of extraneous skills. Consequently, the possibility arises that children's poor performance on the Piaget-Inhelder tests is due to the additional things they measure and not to an absence of probability concepts per se. In particular, it was suggested that failure on the Piaget-Inhelder tests may be attributable to excessive memory demands and language demands. When these two factors are eliminated, performance improves dramatically.

In these studies, several items were administered which presumably require that a subject be able to compute the ratio of "hits" and "misses" in a collection of objects. Subjects are shown two different sets of objects. Each set is comprised of two different types of elements. The total number of elements in the two sets is different. The subjects' task is to figure out which set affords the better chance of selecting a certain type of element on a random draw. To illustrate, suppose subjects are shown a set consisting of four blue poker chips and two white poker chips, and they are also shown a set consisting of six blue poker chips and twenty white poker chips. Subjects are asked which set they would be more likely to draw a blue chip from if they had to draw without looking (i.e., a random draw). To answer this question, subjects presumably must understand that the ratio 4/6 is larger than the ratio 6/26. According to Piaget and Inhelder (1951), concrete-operational children should select the *second* set because the absolute number of blue chips is greater. This is not what happens. Goldberg (1966) and Yost, Siegel, and Andrews (1962) observed that elementary schoolers almost always chose the correct set. What is more, preschoolers chose the correct set more often than one would expect by chance alone.

A more recent investigation by Chapman (1975) produced findings that resemble those of the three studies published during the 1960s. Chapman studied elementary schoolers. His tests made use of one of children's favorite candies, M&Ms. Chapman devised a series of fourteen problems that were similar to the poker chip test just described. At the beginning of each item, subjects were shown two glasses. Each glass contained a mixture of brown and yellow M&Ms. The total number of M&Ms in any given glass never exceeded twelve. Some of the specific mixtures that subjects had to compare were two brown/one yellow, eight brown/four yellow, and seven brown/five yellow. After subjects had been shown a given pair of glasses, they were asked which set of M&Ms afforded a better opportunity of drawing a candy of a specific color (brown or yellow) if they had to draw without looking. These problems were administered to first graders (late preoperational/early concrete-operational), third graders (middle concrete-operational), and fifth graders (late concrete-operational/early formal-operational). All age levels passed well over half the problems. The specific percentages of problems passed were 64% (first graders), 70% (third graders), and 87% (fifth graders). In short, by the time Chapman's subjects had reached the age level at which, according to Piaget, they are just beginning to grasp probability, they were already performing perfectly.

learning research

In Chapter 5, we discussed Piaget's theory of learning as it applied to the concrete-operational stage. We saw that Piaget admits that learning can influence concrete-operational contents such as conservation but that he places certain constraints on learning. There are two principal constraints. First, the subjects to be trained must have already acquired the cognitive structures of the stage to which the to-be-trained content belongs. Since we cannot directly measure cognitive structures, what this constraint actually says is that our subjects must possess a partial grasp of the to-be-trained content. Second, the procedures used to train contents must embody Piagetian laws of spontaneous cognitive development—i.e., active self-discovery. Although these constraints were discussed with reference to the concrete-operational stage, they apply to the formal-operational stage as well.

In the concluding section of Chapter 5, we saw that a large number of learning experiments have been conducted with concrete-operational contents. Unfortunately, data on learning formal-operational contents are as yet scarce. Only a handful of experiments have been published. However, the trend of the findings is, so far, consistent with the results of concrete-operational learning experiments. It appears that we can teach formal-operational contents to children who have not yet acquired formal-operational structures (i.e., to children who fail formal-operational tests across the board or whose ages place them well within the concrete-operational stage). It also appears that formal-operational contents can be taught without resorting to active self-discovery training. In fact, active self-discovery was not used in any of the experiments mentioned below.

Although a few formal-operational training experiments have been conducted with adolescents (e.g., Tomlinson-Keasey 1972), the experiments that we are most interested in are ones in which elementary schoolers were studied. Since the elementary school years correspond to the nominal age range for concrete operations, it should be difficult to teach formal-operational contents to elementary schoolers. Thus, elementary school samples provide a test of Piaget's hypothesis that learning does not influence formal-operational contents until formal structures have been acquired.

Each of the studies considered below was designed to train one or more of the specific problem solving skills used to measure formal operations in the *Growth of Logical Thinking*. To maintain consistency with earlier remarks, we group these experiments into two broad categories: (*a*) experiments in which the trained contents were used by Inhelder and Piaget (1958) to measure *propositional operations* and (*b*) experiments in which the trained contents were used by Inhelder and Piaget (1958) to measure *formal-operational schemes.*

Propositional operations training. Case (1974), Siegler, Liebert, and Liebert (1973), and Tomlinson-Keasey (1972) have reported experiments in which cognitive contents that Inhelder and Piaget associate with propositional operations have been trained. Since the subjects in the third experiment were adolescents and adults, we consider only the first two investigations.

Case (1974) trained his subjects on the flexibility of rods problems examined earlier in this chapter. On this problem, it will be recalled, the subject's task is to isolate all the various factors that determine how much a rod will bend when a weight is attached to it. Case's subjects were fifty-two children whose ages placed them from late preoperations to early concrete operations (6- and 8-year-olds). Case pretested his subjects for the ability to isolate variables on the flexibility of rods problem. His findings were consistent with those reported by Inhelder and Piaget (1958, Chap. 3). That is, his subjects performed poorly on the pretest. Next, a series of training trials was undertaken. The aim of the training was to teach the subjects how to isolate variables in several different situations. (According to Inhelder and Piaget, acquiring such knowledge requires a prior grasp of propositional operations.) The training trials were divided into four sessions spaced across four days. During each of the training sessions, the subject was taught how to isolate variables in a new situation (e.g., what factors determine how high two balls will bounce). Each situation was different from the pretest situation and different from the situations used in other training sessions. After the training had been completed, the flexibility of rods problem was readministered to determine whether the subjects' ability to isolate variables had improved. A new test modeled after the roulette wheel problem discussed earlier was also administered. The 6-year-olds did not make much progress. Hardly any of them could now isolate variables. However, the 8-year-olds learned very well. Roughly, three-quarters of the 8-year-olds showed marked improvement over their pretest performance. Many of them performed perfectly.

Siegler, Liebert, and Liebert (1973) trained their subjects on Inhelder and Piaget's oscillations of the pendulum problem. On this problem, it will be recalled, the subject's task is to discover which factors determine how rapidly the pendulum swings. There is only one determining factor, namely, the length of the pendulum. Siegler, Liebert, and Liebert's subjects were forty-six fifth-grade children. They pretested their subjects for the ability to solve the pendulum problem. Consistent with Inhelder and Piaget's (1958,

Chap. 4) findings, fifth graders performed poorly on the pretest. In particular, the subjects thought that irrelevant factors such as the weight of the pendulum or the height of its release point determined the rapidity of its oscillations. After the pretest, a series of training trials was administered. The subjects received two different types of training. The subjects were given *measurement training*. They were provided with a stopwatch which they could use to time the speed of the pendulum's oscillations. They were also given a data sheet on which the various factors they thought were relevant (length, weight, etc.) were listed. By using the stopwatch, they could determine whether each factor influenced the speed of the pendulum and they could then record the result on their data sheet. The subjects were also given *analogy training*. They were administered problems that were quite different than the pendulum problem but that, like the pendulum problem, involved only one relevant variable. For example, they were given four glasses of water. Two of the glasses were filled to the top, and two were half filled. One of the half-filled glasses contained hot water, and the other contained cold water. One of the full glasses contained hot water, and the other contained cold water. They were also given a thermometer. Their task was to determine what factors made the thermometer move. The answer, of course, was that only the temperature of the water is relevant.

As noted above, the performance of fifth graders who had not been given training was poor on the pendulum problem. In fact, only 8% discovered that the length of the pendulum is the only relevant variable. But subjects given training performed very well. Roughly two-thirds of Siegler, Liebert, and Liebert's fifth graders passed the pendulum test after they had been given measurement and analogy training.

Formal-operational schemes training. Two experiments by the writer provide evidence on the trainability of formal-operational schemes (Brainerd 1971; Brainerd and Allen 1971*b*). Both experiments were concerned with learning cognitive contents that Piaget associates with the proportionality scheme. The specific contents were volume conservation and density conservation.

Earlier, it was noted that Piaget uses the volume concept as one of his principal measures of the proportionality scheme. There is a closely related concept, density, that is also supposed to be a measure of the proportionality scheme. As most of us remember from high school physics, the density concept is defined in terms of the volume concept. Specifically, density is defined as weight per unit volume. Hence, Piaget reasons, if volume calls for the use of the proportionality scheme, then density must too.

The test for density, the density conservation problem, focuses on children's understanding of the fact that an object's ability to float (or sink) in water does not depend on its shape or its weight. The test begins like the second volume conservation test, volume test (*b*). The child is shown a clay ball and a container of water. The experimenter drops the clay ball into the water and asks the subject to note that it sinks to the bottom. The experimenter then withdraws the ball from the water and *changes its shape* by flattening it into a pancake. The subject is asked whether the clay will float now that it is "shaped like a raft." If the subject says no, the experimenter slices some clay off and asks the subject whether the raft will float now that it is "not so heavy as before." If the subject says no again, the experimenter continues to slice clay off until only a tiny piece is left. The subject is also asked whether the piece of clay could *ever* be made small enough so that it would float.

In the first experiment (Brainerd 1971), the density test just described and the two volume tests described earlier were administered to third, sixth, and ninth graders. A simple feedback procedure was used to train density conservation. On the test just described, the subjects were given feedback after each transformation of the piece of clay. That is, their predictions were confirmed or disconfirmed by placing the clay back in the water. After the experimenter had flattened the clay ball into a pancake and the subject had made his prediction, the clay was placed back in the water so that the subject could observe that shape was irrelevant. Similarly, each time the experimenter subtracted some clay and the subject made a prediction, the clay was placed back in the water so that the subject could observe that weight was irrelevant. The subjects were said to have learned the density concept if they concluded, after a series of feedback trials, that the clay could never be made small enough so that it would float. For our purposes, it is the learning of sixth graders (late concrete-operational) and third graders (middle concrete-operational) that is important. Both groups showed clear evidence of learning. Almost half (47%) of the third graders were judged to have learned density conservation. Moreover, *all* the sixth graders were judged to have learned density conservation.

Brainerd and Allen (1971*b*) replicated and extended these findings. They administered pretests for density and volume conservation to fifty-two fifth graders. In line with Piaget's claims about when the proportionality scheme emerges, they found that fifth graders initially performed rather poorly on these tests. A total of forty nonconserving subjects from the original sample of fifty-two was retained for the training phase of the experiment. Half the subjects were trained on density conservation via the feedback procedure just described. That is, the training session consisted of the experimenter performing various shape and weight transformations on a clay ball. Each time a particular transformation was made, the subject had to predict whether or not the clay would float. Following each prediction, feedback was provided by placing the clay in the water. Consistent with Brainerd's original findings, Brainerd and Allen found that this procedure produced a marked improvement in their subjects' density performance. In fact the procedure worked so well that there was no overlap between the density performances of trained subjects and untrained controls. Even the worst subject in the trained group performed better than the best subject in the untrained group. The effects of density training also transferred to volume conservation. After they had been trained on density, Brainerd and Allen's subjects performed much better on the volume tests than they had before the training sessions.

These two experiments certainly seem to suggest that one can train cognitive contents that, according to Piaget, call for the use of the formal-operational scheme of proportionality. Concerning Piaget's hypothesis that subjects must possess the structures for a given stage before they can learn contents from that stage, it is important to note that the subjects' ages in both experiments placed them within the concrete-operational stage. Also, the subjects showed no evidence of the trained contents on the pretests.

Synopsis

Piaget does not belong to the trouble-and-turmoil school of adolescence. He accentuates the positive features of this period rather than the negative ones. Formal operations first begin to appear during early adolescence. However, the achievement phase of the formal-operational stage is not attained until approximately age 15.

Features of formal-operational thought. Formal-operational intelligence differs from concrete-operational intelligence in three general ways. It is hypothetico-deductive, it is scientific, and it is reflective-abstractive. Formal operations are grouped into two categories: propositional (or combinatorial) operations and formal-operational schemes.

Hypothetico-deductive reasoning refers to any type of reasoning that transcends the confines of everyday experience and deals with things of which we have no direct experience. The distinguishing attribute of such reasoning is that it involves deducing conclusions from previously given premises. Language, which is much less important during earlier Piagetian stages, plays a central role in hypothetico-deductive reasoning. The most common examples of hypothetico-deductive reasoning occur in mathematics. Of these, Euclidean geometry is probably the best known. Mathematical examples illustrate a crucial weakness of hypothetico-deductive reasoning that is frequently overlooked: Our conclusions are true only if our premises are secure.

Scientific or "inductive" reasoning is also believed to emerge during the formal-operational stage. The quantitative laws of the physical sciences are widely regarded as the supreme illustrations of inductive reasoning. These laws are called inductive generalizations because they involve reasoning from specific facts to general principles. Piaget claims that, in problem-solving situations, adolescents behave like scientists do when they conduct research. First, adolescents formulate hypotheses. Next, they experiment. Finally, they arrive at inductive generalizations.

The reflective-abstractive aspect of formal operations is closely related to hypothetico-deductive and scientific reasoning, especially the former. It refers to the fact that the mental operations of this stage may operate on themselves. This process, which is usually called internal reflection, can produce new information. By comparison, the mental operations of the concrete stage are capable of operating on sensory information but not on themselves. Hence, concrete-operational children can only solve problems in which the underlying principle can be empirically demonstrated, while formal-operation subjects can solve problems in which the underlying principle must be deduced.

Transition from concrete to formal operations. Two specific changes signal the transition from concrete to formal operations: coordination of the two reversibility rules and the representation of potential actions. Concerning the former, Piaget maintains that concrete-operational children can solve problems that involve the application of either reversibility rule, but they cannot solve problems that require the simultaneous use of both. The coordination of the two reversibilities is said to produce the key mental structure of the formal-operational stage—the *INRC* group. This coordination is ostensibly achieved via reciprocal assimilation. Groups are simple mathematical systems that have four properties (closure, associativity, identity, inverse). There are many instances of groups that occur outside of mathematics in everyday life. Turning over two coins is a case in point. Piaget's *INRC* group is a special type of mathematical group. Specifically, an *INRC* group is a set of four reversibility operations in which each operation has special properties (I = identity operation, N = inverse operation, R = reciprocal operation, C = correlative operation).

The representation of potential actions helps intelligence become less concrete. While concrete-operational children are limited to representing actions that they are actually capable of performing, formal-operational subjects are not. This allows the latter to solve problems involving unseen factors such as friction.

Categories of formal operations. Propositional operations and formal-operational schemes are the two basic types of formal operations. Propositional operations are more abstract than formal-operational schemes. They are also closely related to the *INRC* group. Generally speaking, propositional operations are cognitive counterparts of the sixteen binary relations of ordinary propositional logic. Propositional logic is the logic of systems in which there are two (or more) variables that can take on either of two discrete values. Piaget endows the adolescent with the sixteen binary relations of propositional logic. However, the propositional operations of the formal-operational stage have three characteristics that propositional relations do not have. First, they are internalized actions. Second, they obey the two reversibility rules. Third, they are gathered together into a coherent structure. The structure underlying propositional operations is the *INRC* group. The system of sixteen propositional operations generates sixteen different *INRC* groups. Each group is generated by defining the *I* operation as one of the sixteen propositional operations.

The general advantage provided by propositional operations is that they allow formal-operational subjects to think in a manner that Piaget calls combinatorial. Combinatorial thinking is the sort of thinking involved in permutation and combination problems from algebra. Inhelder and Piaget used six different tests to study the development of propositional operations: angle of incidence versus angle of reflection problems, density problems, flexibility of rods problems, oscillation of pendulums problems, falling bodies problems, and magnitization problems. They proposed a three-stage model for the development of propositional operations. During Stage I, which corresponds to the second half of the preoperational period, subjects concentrate on momentary states, ignore transformations, and concentrate on perceptually salient features of tasks. During Stage II, which corresponds to the concrete-operational period, subjects fail to make use of abstract information, fail to generalize functional relationships among variables, and fail to see that given conclusions logically imply other conclusions. Stage III subjects (11- to 15-year-olds) solve propositional operations problems.

Formal-operational schemes are less abstract and more highly specialized than propositional operations. Piaget believes that formal-operational schemes are derived from propositional operations. For the most part, formal-operational schemes are representations of functional relationships in the physical environment. The most important of these schemes are proportionality, double reference, mechanical equilibrium, and probability. The proportionality scheme refers to subjects' understanding that the ratio of two quantities is equal to the ratio of two other quantities. Verbal and numerical analogies provide the simplest illustrations of the proportionality scheme. However, Inhelder and Piaget used a fulcrum problem as their chief proportionality test. They found that most subjects did not solve the fulcrum problem until age 11 or 12.

The scheme of double reference is concerned with systems in which the effects of one variable can be either canceled or enhanced by the operation of some other variable. Relativistic motion provides an illustration. Subjects' grasp of relativistic motion is tested by a problem in which a snail and a board move independently of each other. Piaget reports that the snail problem is not solved until the formal-operational stage. The scheme of mechanical equilibrium is concerned with Newton's action-reaction principle. It is studied with a hydraulic press problem that is a miniaturized version of the presses used to raise and lower automobiles in service stations. The probability scheme refers to the fact that some events happen by chance and are not governed by natural laws. Piaget says that the probability scheme depends on the proportionality scheme. A three-stage model of probability development is proposed. During Stage I (preoperations), subjects fail to see that there is any distinction between chance events and events governed by natural laws. During Stage II (concrete operations), subjects recognize this distinction, but they do not yet understand the quantitative laws governing the behavior of chance events. During Stage III (11- to 15 years old), the quantitative laws of probability are understood.

Replication research. Replication research on formal operations may be divided into research on propositional operations, formal-operational schemes, and learning. Concerning propositional operations, many logicians have criticized Piaget for bad logic. Although most of these criticisms have been haphazard, the errors and idiosyncracies in Piaget's propositional logic have been meticulously catalogued by Robert Ennis. Piaget's logic suffers from three salient shortcomings. First, it is nonparsimonious. Second, his definition of "proposition" does not square with the correct definition. Third, propositional operations are not independent of each other. In view of these anomalies, some investigators have concluded that Piaget's statement that subjects cannot handle proportional logic until they reach the formal-operational stage is either false or untestable.

By far the largest amount of research on propositional operations has dealt with implication reasoning. Implication reasoning tests make use of "if-then" problems. Most of the problems administered in studies conducted to date have been modus ponens problems (*P* implies *Q* and *P*; therefore, *Q*) and transitivity of implication problems (*P* implies *Q*, *Q* implies *R*, and *P*; therefore, *R*). Both valid and invalid forms of implication reasoning problems have been administered. A valid forms problem measures subjects' ability to draw a correct conclusion, and an invalid forms problem measures their ability to avoid drawing incorrect conclusions. Two critical findings have emerged from experiments on implication reasoning. First, when implication reasoning problems are valid forms, even concrete-operational children can solve them. Second, when implication reasoning problems are invalid forms, both concrete-operational and formal-operational children fail to solve them.

Research on propositional operations other than implication reveals a clear difficulty order. Conjunction problems are easier then disjunction problems and disjunction problems are easier than equivalence problems. These studies also show that valid forms are easier than invalid forms with propositional operations other than implication. Some studies have administered verbal reasoning problems, while others make use of concrete stimuli. An important conclusion that emerges from this research is that it is impossible to make blanket claims about when children can handle propositional logic. It appears that concrete-operational children are capable of using conjunction, disjunction, and implication but perhaps not equivalence.

Most of the replication research on formal-operational schemes has been concerned with the proportionality and probability schemes. Some of the proportionality studies focus on the development of volume concepts, while others focus on verbal and numerical analogies. Two conservation concepts, conservation of liquid volume and conservation of displaced volume, have been used to study the development of volume concepts. Consistent with Piagetian theory, it has been routinely observed that volume conservation tests are not passed prior to adolescence. Bruner and Kenney's (1966) test for relative fullness is another procedure for measuring the volume concept. The relative fullness test, like volume conservation tests, is not pased prior to adolescence. The same picture emerges from studies of verbal and numerical analogies. On the whole, therefore, the available data are consistent with Piaget's hypothesis that proportionality concepts appear during adolescence.

The replication data on probability concepts have failed to confirm Piaget's predictions. It appears that concrete-operational children are capable of solving the problems that Piaget and Inhelder used to measure the probability scheme. In four experiments, the subjects were administered tests in which their task was to predict the likelihood of certain events in various collections of objects—e.g., the probability of drawing a blue chip from a set of four blues and two whites and a set of six blues and twenty whites. Children in the late preoperational to early concrete-operational age range seem to perform quite well on such tests.

A few learning experiments have been conducted on formal-operational concepts. Although the data are not yet extensive, they are consistent with the findings of learning experiments on concrete-operational concepts. It appears that children who fall within the age range for concrete operations and/or who have failed formal-operational tests can be taught formal-operational concepts. There is no evidence that active self-discovery training must be used if learning is to occur.

Supplementary Readings

1. BART, "A Generalization of Piaget's Logical-Mathematical Model for the Stage of Formal Operations" (1971). Bart's paper is one of the few formal analyses of propositional operations and the *INRC* group published in English. The paper concentrates on the relationship between the *INRC* group and propositional operations. It also presents some generalizations of Piaget's model.

2. BUDDEN, *The Fascination of Groups* (1972). It is extremely difficult to recommend a textbook on group theory for the beginning reader. This is because the theory of groups is, as Sir Arthur Stanley Eddington once observed, "usually associated with the strictest logical treatment." I can, however, recommend Budden's test without reservation. It is eminently readable and presupposes no mathematics beyond high school algebra. There is considerable material on the *INRC* group, especially in Chapter 11.

3. ENNIS, "Children's Ability to Handle Piaget's Propositional Logic: A Conceptual Critique" (1975). "An Alternative to Piaget's Conceptualization of Logical Competence" (1976). These papers are Ennis' two major contributions on the subject of propositional operations. The first paper spells out the various idiosyncracies in Piaget's logic, and reviews empirical evidence bearing on the hypothesis that concrete-operational children "cannot yet handle" propositional logic. A new formulation that eliminates the weakness in Piaget's logic is presented in the second paper.

4. LUNZER, "Problems of Formal Reasoning in Test Situations" (1965). Although Lunzer's paper is now somewhat dated, it is, in my view, still one of the best research-oriented discussions of the formal-operational stage. Propositional operations and the *INRC* group are both discussed. Special emphasis is placed on the use of verbal and numerical analogies. A detailed rationale is presented to support the claim that such tests are valid measures of formal operations.

5. NEIMARK, "Intellectual Development During Adolescence" (1975). Neimark's chapter is a comprehensive and wide-ranging review of research on adolescent intelligence. A large portion of it deals with research on formal operations.

6. SIEGLER, "The Origins of Scientific Reasoning" (1978). Siegler's chapter contains a review of both recent research on scientific reasoning and earlier work. Siegler also describes a new program of research and discusses its relevance to the study of scientific reasoning.

chapter 7

Piaget on Education

Since its inception, the scientific study of intelligence has been more intimately connected with the theory and practice of education than most other areas of basic psychological research. There are historical reasons for this relationship that date back to the birth of the modern intelligence testing movement at the turn of the century. Leading intelligence theorists such as Burt (e.g., 1949), Cattell (e.g., 1963), Guilford (e.g., 1967), and Spearman (e.g., 1927) have relied almost entirely upon data generated by standardized tests of intelligence. These are the so-called "IQ tests" administered to almost every school child in North America and Western Europe. These tests, of which the two most frequently used are the Stanford-Binet (e.g., Terman 1960) and the Wechsler (e.g., Wechsler 1967) are commonly thought to be tests simply of intelligence. But that is not all they measure. They also measure educational aptitude.

All of today's tests of intelligence are lineal descendants of some tests first devised by the father of intelligence testing, Alfred Binet. To understand why these tests are measures of educational aptitude, it is necessary to understand what led Alfred Binet to construct them in the first place. In 1904, the French Minister of Public Instruction had become concerned about the problem of so-called "backward children" in Paris public schools. The problem was this. It had been known for some time that certain children, who were physically indistinguishable from their classmates, did not derive much benefit from the public school curriculum. These "backward" children were usually not identified until they had already been in school for several years. Obviously, it would be helpful if such children could be identified earlier and placed in special classes as soon as possible. To this end, the minister struck a committee, to which Binet was eventually appointed, that was charged with studying the question of how to diagnose backwardness. Binet, in collaboration with Théodore Simon, wrote a series of tests for this purpose. The tests, which were of varying levels of difficulty, were first administered to Paris school children in 1904. The complete series of tests was published in 1905. The tests underwent several revisions between 1905 and 1911, the year of Binet's death. To quantify children's performance on the tests, Binet and Simon computed a ratio in which the number of items that a child passed was divided by his chronological age. This ratio, called the *intelligence quotient* or "IQ," proved to be an excellent predictor of classroom performance. When the tests were administered to groups of backward and normal children, the intelligence quotient was invariably much higher for the latter.

The Binet-Simon tests were a resounding success. To a large extent, their success was insured by the fact that, in addition to predicting school performance, they were easily administered and did not make use of any costly apparatus. The tests were soon translated into English by Sir Cyril Burt in Great Britain and by Louis Terman in the United States. Of course, they have undergone many revisions over the years (e.g., Terman 1916; Terman and Merrill 1937, 1960). But the chief practical reason for their existence has continued to be the prediction of school achievement. As I noted earlier, modern theories of intelligence, for better or for worse, have been built on data from these tests. This fact guarantees a close relationship between the psychology of intelligence and education. Since standardized intelligence test scores are excellent predictors of school achievement, any theory which attempts to explain these scores is, in some sense, also a theory of education.

Piaget's theory differs from other approaches to intelligence in that it makes essentially no use of findings generated by standardized tests. Apart from Piaget's early contact with such tests while an assistant in Binet's laboratories, his work has not been much influenced by them. He has preferred to rely instead on the more flexible clinical method. This lack of reliance on standardized intelligence tests has meant that there is not the same degree of prima facie overlap between Piaget's theory and education as there is in the case of other theories. Nevertheless, the close historical tie between education and the psychology of intelligence has led many educators to ask what the principal implications of Piaget's theory are for education. A large number of papers and books on this subject are now available (e.g., Flavell 1963, Chap. 11; Furth 1970; Kamii 1973*a*; Lunzer 1960*b*; Schwebel and Raph 1973; Sigel 1969; Wickens 1973). Piaget has even entered the lists himself with a recent book (Piaget 1970*e*).

In this chapter, we conclude our survey of Piaget's theory with a brief look as some of the theory's most obvious consequences for teaching. Although the theory has implications for instruction at all age levels, most of the work on educational applications has been confined to the preschool level. We begin with an overview of some of the general instructional guidelines that educators have derived from the theory. We then review some illustrative Piaget-oriented curricula.

Some General Principles of Instruction

Educators discovered Piaget's theory rather more recently than psychologists did. Although considerable work has been done on sieving out the theory's educational implications from the rest of its claims, educators are, at present, still in the process of deciding what the basic issues are. Consequently, there is much disagreement among the experts about whether this or that pedagogical prescription follows from the theory. A few educators have devoted their careers to sorting out these disagreements. The work of Constance Kamii (e.g., 1970, 1972, 1973*a*, 1973*b*), for example, comes to mind. Kamii has written on the educational applications of Piaget's theory from a number of different perspectives. She has also been a leader in developing new Piaget-oriented curricula.

If the question of how Piaget's theory applies to education remains controversial, much of the controversy stems from the fact that Piaget has been extremely cautious about spelling out the educational ramifications of this theory. Although he has written many papers on education dating back to the 1930s (e.g., Piaget 1935), they deal in generalities rather than in specifics. The following remark, which leaves a definite impression of giving with the right hand and taking away with the left, is typical: "I am convinced that what we have found can be of use in the field of education, in going beyond learning theory, for instance, and suggesting other methods of learning. I think this is basic. But I am not a pedagogue myself, and I don't have any advice to give educators. All we can do is provide some facts. Still, I think educators can find many new educational methods" (quoted from Evans 1973, p. 51).

Although the subject of educational applications of Piaget continues to generate lively debate in the technical educational literature, there are some general instructional recommendations that all the experts seem to agree on. It is these particular recommendations that will concern us in this section. For convenience, they may be grouped into three broad categories: (*a*) recommendations about the *sequencing* of curriculum material; (*b*) recommendations about the *content* of curriculum material; (*c*) recommendations about the *methodology* of teaching. Category (*a*) is concerned with when certain topics should be introduced, given that we wish to introduce them at all. Category (*b*) is concerned with what specific topics should be part of the curriculum. Category (*c*) is concerned with the strategies that teachers should adopt when dealing with children.

curriculum sequencing

Are there any inherent limitations on what we can teach children of a given age level? This is a question that we have already encountered in one form in Chapter 5, namely, the question of readiness to learn. One can imagine a continuum of possible answers to this question. At one extreme, there would be strong antireadiness statements asserting that, if only we do things right, we can teach children of just about any age just about any material we wish. Answers of this sort would tend to emphasize the role of the environment in learning. The North American learning tradition (e.g., Gagné 1965; Skinner 1954, 1958) leans toward this end of the continuum. At the other extreme, there would be strong proreadiness statements asserting that, no matter what we do, we cannot teach children anything until they are ready to learn it. Answers of this sort are usually associated with a more maturational outlook on education that dates back to Rousseau (e.g., cf. Brainerd 1977c). Piaget's theory, as we saw earlier, leans toward the readiness end of the continuum.

Most commentaries on the educational implications of Piaget's theory stress children's readiness to learn as a prime criterion in deciding when to introduce certain subjects (e.g., Kamii 1973a; Sigel 1969; Sinclair and Kamii 1970). The following remarks by Sigel, for example, are fairly typical:

> That development proceeds in an orderly invariant sequence is another principle relevant for the educator. Knowledge of the sequence of stages and their behavior indices as expressed in language and thought provide the educator with the criteria upon which to gauge the "readiness" of the child to assimilate material. The *sequence* is the crucial question, here, not the particular age at which particular cognitive behaviors appear. Since teaching strategy and curriculum are dependent on the educator's awareness of the child's capacity to deal with material, it is necessary for the teacher to identify the child's level of cognitive functioning. The matching of curriculum and teaching strategy to the intellectual level of the child is a tricky issue. It is easy to confuse the child's manifest level of cognitive competence with his "true" understanding. [1969, pp. 470-71]

From these remarks as well as from the general Piagetian emphasis on readiness, at least four specific sequencing prescriptions appear to follow. First and most important, we should not try to teach children material that is clearly beyond their present stage of cognitive development. A case in point is provided by arithmetic instruction. All the basic concepts of arithmetic—number, addition, subtraction, etc.—are supposed to be achievements of the concrete-operational stage. Instruction in these concepts comprises just slightly less than half the curriculum in the early elementary grades. But in these same grades most classes will contain a mixture of preoperational, transitional, and concrete-operational pupils. According to the theory, only the last two groups may be said to be "ready" to begin learning arithmetic. Preoperational children presumably will not derive much benefit from arithmetic instruction because they do not yet possess the cognitive structures necessary to assimilate the relevant information. One must admit that it is difficult to imagine a child who does not conserve number making much progress with addition or subtraction.

A second sequencing prescription is that teachers should avoid trying to *accelerate* their pupils' progress through the material on a given subject. Since the speed of pupils' progress is frequently used as an index of how well they are learning, teachers often strive to speed up learning as much as possible. But Piagetian theory cautions the teacher that *thorough mastery* of a subject over the widest possible range of situations is a much better criterion of learning than sheer speed. On the question of acceleration versus mastery, the Piagetian message is again one of readiness. You cannot speed up mother nature, so why bother to try? The following observations by Kamii illustrate this view:

> A third characteristic of Piaget's interactionism and constructivism is the view that this construction is the same for all children in all cultures. The educational implication of the universality of the developmental sequence is that, if we want learning to be permanent and solid enough to permit cognitive development throughout the child's life, we must (1) let the child go from one stage after another of being "wrong" rather than expect him to reason logically like an adult, and (2) allow for a certain slowness in the developmental progress. [1973*a*, p. 225][1]

Clearly, patience is an important virtue in a Piagetian curriculum.

The third sequencing recommendation states that we should try, where possible, to teach children new concepts in the same order that these concepts emerge during spontaneous cognitive development. A curriculum that incorporates this principle is usually called a *developmentally based* curriculum. Piaget's normative studies of the preoperational and concrete-operational stages provide extensive information about the order of spontaneous concept development. Educators may draw on these studies when attempting to devise developmentally based curricula. For example, consider arithmetic instruction. Since the advent of the so-called "new math," arithmetic curricula have included a substantial amount of material

---

[1] From *Piaget in the Classroom,* edited by Milton Schwebel and Jane Raph, © 1973 by Basic Books, Inc., Publishers, New York, and Routledge & Kegan, Ltd., London.

on classification (e.g., Brainerd 1976*e*). The research on classification examined in Chapter 5 (e.g., Inhelder and Piaget 1964) contains some definite suggestions about the order in which children should be taught classificatory concepts: First, teach them how to classify collections of objects exhaustively; next, teach them how to classify collections of objects simultaneously according to two or more criteria; finally, teach them the quantitative relationship between subordinate classes and superordinate classes. Sigel has noted that similar suggestions about the order in which geometric concepts are taught can also be derived from Piaget's studies: "Children pay attention to the topological nature of a surface before they attend to its metric characteristics. This suggests, then, that a curriculum for Euclidean geometry might proceed as follows: topological, projective, metric" (1969, p. 485).

The fourth prescription is implied by the ones we have just discussed. From the standpoint of current educational practice, it is by far the most revolutionary of the four. In a Piagetian curriculum, teaching is always a two-step process of *diagnosis followed by instruction* in the concepts for which the child is ready. Teachers in Piaget-inspired programs must be equal parts diagnostician and instructor, whereas they are primarily the latter in traditional programs. If a developmentally based curriculum is to work, it is critical to identify each pupil's present cognitive stage. Moreover, a single global diagnosis for each child ("preoperational," "transitional," "concrete-operational") is not sufficient. For any given child, the current stage of classificatory development may be different from the current stage of relational development, and both may be different from the current stage of spatial development. Thus, separate diagnoses must be undertaken in each area in which the child is to receive instruction. Once the stage has been defined in a given area, the teacher can orchestrate the instructional material accordingly. The long-term implication of the diagnostic prescription is that teacher training programs of university colleges of education must be prepared to train diagnostic skills as well as pedagogical skills.

The fact that Piagetian curricula require careful specification of each pupil's stage in each area of instruction poses two important difficulties that have tended to cool the enthusiasm of professional educators for such curricula. First, if we are to undertake the diagnosis of cognitive stages on a large scale, then we shall need a catalogue of reliable and valid instruments that teachers can be trained to use in the classroom. In particular, since we are talking primarily about elementary schoolers, we need standardized tests for concrete-operational contents such as relations, classification, number, space, socialized language, and so on. Although good progress has been made in constructing standardized tests of certain concrete-operational contents (e.g., Goldschmid and Bentler 1968), this is the exception rather than the rule. There are deep disagreements in the technical literature about how to construct valid tests of concrete-operational contents. The chances that these disagreements will soon be resolved do not appear promising.

A second problem posed by the diagnostic emphasis is sheer cost. Piaget-oriented curricula are quite personalized. Compared with the sorts of classrooms in which you and I were educated, Piagetian classrooms involve highly individualized programs of instruction. In fact, theoretically there would be a separate program tailored to the developmental level of each student. While everyone would no doubt concede that such personalization would be nice, even desirable, it would be tremendously costly in contrast to traditional curricula. The cost differential stems from the fact that personalized programs presuppose low student-teacher ratios. Some educators have even suggested that a true Piagetian curriculum would require one teacher for every pupil! While this sounds a bit far-fetched, everyone seems to agree that Piagetian curricula would require student-teacher ratios of no more than 10 to 1. The cost increase that this would engender may be approximated by considering that normal student-teacher ratios in North American elementary schools are between 25 to 1 and 30 to 1.

curriculum content

During the first few elementary grades, the curriculum is devoted almost entirely to two subjects—basic mathematical skills and basic linguistic skills. With the exception of his very first book (Piaget 1926*a*), Piaget's studies of children's intelligence have not been directly concerned with the development of language. Hence, it is difficult to find many concrete suggestions in his writings for the linguistic half of elementary school curricula. But his writings abound with suggestions for the mathematical half. Virtually all of Piaget's work on the concrete-operational stage deals with cognitive contents that may be loosely termed "mathematical" because they are quantitative. This fact has led educators to formulate a number of recommendations about specific items that might be taught to children if we wished to do so. Examples of items that presumably could be taught but are not much emphasized at present include seriation (Inhelder and Piaget 1964; Piaget 1952*a*), transitive inference (Piaget 1952*a*; Piaget, Inhelder, and Szeminska 1960), ordinal number (Piaget 1952*a*), multiple classification (Inhelder and Piaget 1964), and class inclusion (Inhelder and Piaget 1964). I mention these particular items because each is known to be closely related to certain arithmetic skills (Brainerd 1977*b*). More generally, we may say that there is a large group of concepts belonging to the elementary logic of relations and classes that, though rarely taught nowadays, could be included in elementary school curricula if we wished to do so.

Another content recommendation that regularly appears in educationally oriented discussions of Piaget (e.g., Flavell 1963; Sigel 1969) deals with geometry. Most readers will no doubt remember that they did not receive any systematic training in geometry until grade ten, at which time they received a year of plane geometry. Piaget's research on spatial development (Piaget and Inhelder 1956; Piaget, Inhelder, and Szeminska 1960) indicates that we could begin teaching geometry long before high school. As we saw in Chapter 5, topological ideas are acquired during the preoperational stage. Since most children are preoperational when they begin school, geometry instruction could be initiated in kindergarten or first grade so long as it is confined to topological notions such as proximity, open-closed, etc. While topology instruction is taking place, our teacher-diagnostician is constantly measuring the child's level of development in the spatial area. As the child's manifest level of spatial operations draws closer and closer to true concrete operations, projective concepts such as rotation and perspective are introduced. Euclidean concepts such as distance and measurement are added at the same time. If the timetable that Piaget has reported for spatial development is correct, geometry instruction would focus mainly on topology through grade two. It would then concentrate on projective and Euclidean contents in grades three through six. This means that the average child would be introduced to most of the geometric concepts now reserved for high school before entering junior high.

Following the above suggestions, there is a clear trend toward teaching geometry in the elementary grades. Many standardized elementary mathematics programs (e.g., Eicholz 1969) now include units on topological, projective, and Euclidean concepts. Although the practice of teaching geometry to elementary schoolers has been growing in recent years, it is by no means the rule as yet.

One can also formulate some surprisingly detailed hypotheses about the specific things that children should be taught to get them to learn a particular concept. An excellent example is afforded by the concept of cardinal number, which plays a very important role in modern arithmetic curricula. The concept of cardinal number refers to subjects' understanding of the precise conditions under which two classes do and do not contain the same number of elements. We saw in Chapters 4 and 5 that children do not possess the concept of cardinal number at the time they enter elementary school. When asked to judge the relative numerousness of the elements of two classes, they routinely base their judgments on incorrect information. Explicitly, they tend to rely on spatial cues such as how much space classes occupy (classes occupying larger amounts of space are usually judged more numerous than classes occupying smaller amounts of space) and how densely their elements are packed (classes whose elements are closely packed are usually judged more numerous than classes whose elements are loosely grouped). These facts lead to some clear recommendations concerning what children should be taught as part of a program designed to induce the concept of cardinal number. First, they must be shown that their natural tendency to depend on spatial cues should be given up. Second, after children's dependency on spatial cues has been reduced, they may be taught how to use operations such as counting and correspondence as bases for inferring the relative numerousness of two classes.

Materials. Further content recommendations are concerned with the nature of the *materials* that are used to teach subjects such as arithmetic to elementary schoolers. Generally speaking, these materials should always have two properties: (*a*) they should be *concrete* rather than abstract and (*b*) they should be objects that can be manipulated. Concerning property (*a*), one of the central themes of Chapters 5 and 6 was that children do not grasp concepts at an abstract linguistic level until they have reached the formal-operational stage. It would seem to follow that teaching children concepts by simply explaining them verbally or by using symbols (as in the case of mathematical expressions) is unlikely to produce good learning. On this point, it was observed in an early educational analysis of Piaget's theory that:

> There is a transition between children's preoperational thinking at kindergarten age and some of their thinking in terms of propositions when the pupils leave elementary school at twelve years or so. It seems to me that in general this transition in children's thinking is not recognized by present educational practice in the United States. Teachers with whom I have been in contact have not seemed to be much aware that there is such a change taking place and I would say that most instruction above the kindergarten takes place on what one might call the formal level. As an unfortunate consequence of this fact many students never understand the intent of instruction and become dissatisfied with school by the time they are fourteen or sixteen. [Karplus 1964, p. 113]

The alternative to teaching elementary schoolers at "the formal level" is to teach them at the concrete level. This implies two specific recommendations about teaching materials. The first concerns textbooks. Children's textbooks should, insofar as possible, be simply and attractively illustrated. They should, in advertising jargon, be attention grabbers. Every important concept should be illustrated with several pictures rather than with words or with other abstract symbols. This particular recommendation has already been put into practice. Although children's textbooks were still rather drab at the time Karplus wrote, this is no longer the case. One has only to glance through, for example, the textbooks that are now used to teach arithmetic (e.g., Eicholz 1969) to see that they are colorfully and profusely illustrated. The second recommendation concerns teachers rather than textbooks. Whenever it is feasible, teachers should avoid illustrating and explaining concepts on a purely verbal level. There is a tremendous temptation simply to "lecture" to children. Although teachers must make use of language to communicate with children, language is not the medium in which concrete-operational subjects learn new concepts. They learn through concrete demonstrations. Hence, teachers should strive to illustrate their verbal presentations with many concrete demonstrations. According to Piaget, concrete-operational children will learn far more from a few simple demonstrations than from hours of lecturing.

Concerning property (*b*), manipulability, concrete demonstration materials may be said to fall into two general groups. First, there are materials that children cannot actually manipulate for themselves. Items of this sort include pictures in books, films, recordings, and any demonstration apparatus that only the teacher is allowed to use (e.g., a tape recorder or a slide projector). All of these materials have the advantage of being concrete rather than abstract. But none of them requires active involvement on the part of the child. Such materials may be contrasted with objects that children can manipulate. If we were teaching children classification, for example, some manipulative materials might consist of sets of a dozen or so objects that the child could sort into various classes. If we were teaching geometry, some manipulative materials might consist of devices such as strings and straight edges which can be used to construct circles, triangles, rectangles, etc. If we were teaching arithmetic, some manipulative materials might consist of devices for measuring simple physical quantities such as length (e.g., a ruler) and weight (e.g., a pan balance).

Materials that children can manipulate for themselves play an absolutely fundamental role in any Piaget-inspired curriculum. One of the most important aspects of Piaget's theory is that thought is said to be based on action. Thinking operations are defined as internalized actions rather than internalized language or internalized percepts. If thinking is ultimately action-based, it would seem that the best possible learning would be the kind that results when children do things for themselves. In particular, this learning should be better than the kind that results when children are *told* something or the kind that results when children are *shown* something. Consider classification, for example. Children presumably learn more about classification from sorting collections of objects for themselves than from either being told how to sort collections or observing someone else sorting collections.

teaching methods

At the present time, the single richest source of Piaget-based instructional directives is the area of teaching methodology. Lists of teaching dos and don'ts are routinely included in most essays on Piagetian educational applications (e.g., Duckworth 1964; Kamii 1973a; Sinclair and Kamii 1970). Although specific dos and don'ts vary from one author to another, a few underlying themes can be discerned. There are three themes, in particular, that occur repeatedly. First, the teacher is asked to bear in mind the central role that children play in their own learning and to try to make learning experiences as active as possible. Second, the teacher is encouraged to adopt pedagogical strategies designed to make children aware of conflicts and inconsistencies in their beliefs. Third, it is argued that teachers should make use of the child's peers as teachers in their own right. We examine each of these themes in turn.

Self-discovery methods. It is virtually impossible to find a discussion of Piagetian educational applications that does not exhort teachers, occasionally with almost religious fervor, to adopt active learning strategies. In the Piagetian view of learning, it will be remembered, learning procedures should ideally satisfy two conditions. They should be securely grounded in spontaneous (outside the laboratory) laws of cognitive development, and they should stress the subjects' active self-discovery of whatever it is they are supposed to learn. Active self-discovery learning is emphasized because it is believed that "*active discovery* is what happens in development" (Sinclair 1973, p. 58). It follows from this assumption that the best teaching strategies are those in which the teacher tries to make the child himself "the mainspring of his development, in that it is his own activity on the environment or his own active reactions that make progress" (Sinclair 1973, p. 58).

The usual way of introducing this first theme is by contrasting active self-discovery teaching with what are said to be more traditional methods in which teaching "is a matter of presenting the material to be learned and reinforcing the correct answers that the learner gives back to the teacher" (Kamii 1973a, p. 200). The following remarks about self-discovery learning by Duckworth, who has translated many of Piaget's works, are widely quoted by educators. Duckworth's observations also illustrate the missionary zeal that frequently accompanies the advocacy of self-discovery:

> As far as education is concerned, the chief outcome of this theory of intellectual development is a plea that children be allowed to do their own learning. ... You cannot further understanding in a child simply by talking to him. Good pedagogy must involve presenting the child with situations in which he himself experiments, in the broadest sense of the term—trying things out to see what happens, manipulating symbols, posing questions and seeking his own answers, reconciling what he finds one time with what he finds at another, comparing his findings with those of other children. ... [1964, p. 2]

Educators frequently express concern with the efficiency of the self-discovery method. It is sometimes suggested that the method requires more time to teach children *less* than traditional methods. However, advocates of Piagetian curricula assure teachers that "the child learns more through direct experience, and that he learns even more if this experience is discovered rather than being offered" (Kamii 1973a, p. 207). When children learn by self-discovery, the results are supposed to be qualitatively *and quantitatively* superior to traditional instruction. To produce these results, teachers are cautioned that they must not fall prey to false forms of self-discovery in which discovery "means to discover what the teacher wants to have discovered" (Kamii 1973a, p. 200). This would be tantamount to acceleration which, as we have already seen, is not favorably viewed in Piaget-inspired teaching. Perhaps the best illustration of false self-discovery teaching occurs when the so-called "Socratic method" is used. This method has been widely employed in elementary arithmetic since the late 1950s (e.g., see Johnson 1966). The heart of the method consists of posing leading questions to children of the form "Do you believe that ...," "Do you suppose it is true that ...," and so on. What is undoubtedly the most famous illustration of the method appears in Plato's *The Meno*, where Socrates uses it to cause an illiterate street urchin to discover the Pythagorean theorem. Teaching the Pythagorean theorem to someone who can neither read nor write is what I would call acceleration. More generally, the Socratic method suffers from two faults in the eyes of Piagetian educators. First, it leads children inexorably to the conclusion that the teacher has in mind from the beginning. Second, the method is heavily verbal and, therefore, is more appropriate for adolescents than children.

Several excellent illustrations of true active self-discovery teaching occur in a recent series of learning experiments by three of Piaget's co-workers (Inhelder, Sinclair, and Bovet 1974). The experiments were designed to teach various conservation principles to children who did not yet understand them. We consider the particular method that the authors used to train the quantity conservation principle (Inhelder, Sinclair, and Bovet 1974, Chap. 1). It will be recalled that quantity conservation refers to children's understanding of the fact that two quantities of liquid remain equal when one of them is poured into containers of different sizes and shapes. A group of children was first identified who failed the usual tests for quantity conservation discussed in Chapter 5. To train the concept, the authors used an apparatus consisting of six glass containers of different widths into which liquid could be poured. Subjects manipulated this apparatus during the training sessions. The manipulations consisted of pouring an initial quantity of water into each of the different containers. Before each pouring, subjects were asked to note whether the height and width of the liquid changed. After some pourings, the experimenter posed questions such as "Is there still the same amount of water in this container as before you poured it?" But the experimenter *never* told subjects whether any of their answers were correct or incorrect. This general procedure satisfies three conditions that are deemed to be essential in true self-discovery learning. First, learning is *active*. Note that it is the *subject* and not the experimenter who manipulates the training apparatus. This means that subjects are actively involved in their learning rather than simply being observers. Second, the experimenter does not lead subjects to some predetermined conclusion. The subjects can make any inferences they care to about the rules governing the apparatus. Third, the experimenter does not provide reinforcement by confirming or disconfirming the subjects' answers to the various questions.

Conflict teaching. A second theme in discussions of how Piagetian teachers should instruct their pupils is the advocacy of what I shall call *conflict teaching*. Conflict teaching consists of getting children to learn something new by confronting them with major inconsistencies in some of the beliefs they currently hold. Of course, this strategy must conform to the active self-discovery principles just examined. Specifically, when children are being confronted with inconsistencies and conflicting information, the teacher must rigorously avoid the temptation to tell them what is right and what is wrong. Children must discover for themselves. Sigel gives the following summary of the philosophy of conflict teaching:

> A major thrust of a teaching strategy is to confront the child with the illogical nature of his point of view. The reason for confrontation is that it is a necessary and sufficient requirement for cognitive growth. The shift from egocentric to sociocentric thought comes about through confrontation with the animate and inanimate environment. These forces impinge on the child, inducing disequilibrium. The child strives to reconcile the discrepancies and evolves new processes by which to adapt to the new situations. [1969, p. 473]

The theoretical rationale for conflict teaching may be traced back to the equilibration process. Up to this point, we have repeatedly seen that good Piagetian instruction conforms to the natural laws of spontaneous cognitive development. The most important of these laws is equilibration. As we discussed in Chapter 2, this is the mechanism by which the cognitive structures of one level evolve into those of the next level. It will be remembered that equilibration is a *disequilibrium* process. Children at a given stage of development possess a certain set of cognitive structures. They exercise the structures by using them to assimilate incoming information. Some of the incoming information can be processed by the structures, but the rest cannot. This discrepancy between what these children can assimilate and what they *should* assimilate engenders an internal imbalance in their cognitive structures. This internal imbalance causes the structures to undergo three changes. First, they broaden in scope so as to handle a greater range of information. Second, they become more thoroughly differentiated from each other. Third, they become more tightly integrated and interdependent. The latter process is known as reciprocal assimilation.

Numerous illustrations of conflict instruction may be found in learning experiments designed to teach children concrete-operational cognitive contents. One example may be found in a conservation training experiment by Botvin and Murray (1975). Children were pretested for their grasp of four conservation principles (weight, quantity, number, and mass). A group of seventeen children who failed tests for all four principles were trained as follows. Each child, which we shall hereafter call the observer, was taken to a small room. The observer was seated ten feet away from a group of five children that we shall hereafter call the working group. The observer was asked to watch the working group carefully. The working group was composed of three children who understood all four conservation principles and two children who did not. While the observer was watching, the experimenter administered several conservation tests to the working group. He asked the children in the working group to discuss their answers to his questions and arrive at a single consensual response that they all agreed was true. The observer watched the debate. It was hoped that, as a result of seeing the debate, observers would notice some of the inconsistencies in their own beliefs about conservation. This, in turn, might generate internal disequilibrium and structural change. It is important to note that the experimenter did not specifically point out any of these inconsistencies. Observers had to notice them for themselves. Thus, in Genevan terms, the procedure involved self-discovery instruction.

Peer teaching. The third and final thread running through essays on Piagetian teaching methodology is an emphasis on making use of children to teach each other. This particular theme is rooted in some of Piaget's earliest writings. Although he has not done so lately, Piaget once laid considerable stress on children's interactions with their peers as a source of cognitive development. This peer interaction emphasis is most clearly evident in *The Language and Thought of the Child.* Piaget proposed in this work that peer interactions were essential if children were to make the transition from egocentric uses of language to communicative ones. Piagetian educators have observed that if it is indeed true that peer interactions are necessary in the transition from one stage to the next, then the classroom is an excellent environment in which to provide these interactions. Kamii (1973a) sums up the theoretical rationale for providing such interactions in the classroom:

> Piaget believed strongly that for intellectual development the cooperation among children is as important as the child's cooperation with adults. Without the opportunity to see the relativity of perspectives, the child remains prisoner of his own naturally egocentric point of view. A clash of convictions among children can readily cause an awareness of different points of view. Other children at similar cognitive levels can often help the child more than the adult can to move out of his egocentricity. [p. 200]

How are we to foster this "clash of convictions" in the classroom? The basic teaching strategy seems to involve the use of what we could call committee work. Rather than work on homework problems solitarily, children are assigned to small discussion groups. The members of the group discuss and debate various possible solutions and arrive at consensual answers. As with the Supreme Court, there may also be minority opinions. Since the members of the group are peers and the teacher is excluded from the group, there is less likelihood that debate will be restricted and that certain answers will be considered automatically correct just because they come from certain people.

In our earlier examination of self-discovery instruction, we saw that there is a danger that teachers will adopt methods which look like self-discovery but actually are not. There are similar dangers with the peer interaction strategy of committee work. Again, Kamii sums up the possible pitfalls:

> Teachers and teacher trainers often advocate committee work and discussions among pupils. However, current theories do not have a clear rationale for deliberately setting up the classroom to encourage children of similar cognitive ability to exchange their views. In practice, social interactions among children are *allowed* more than they are expressly *encouraged* as a means of actively involving children in juxtaposing different points of view. [1973a, p. 200]

An illustration of committee work in the Piagetian mold comes from another conservation learning experiment by Murray (1972). Murray administered pretests for six different conservation principles to 108 children. On the basis of their pretest performance, the children were assigned to two categories: (*a*) subjects who understood none or few of the principles and (*b*) subjects who understood all of the principles. A committee work procedure was then instituted to teach the subjects in category (*a*) to conserve. Murray divided his subjects into committees consisting of three children each, one child from category (*a*) and two children from category (*b*). The training session consisted of having an experimenter administer several conservation tests to each committee. The children in each committee were told that they could not respond individually to the experimenter's questions. They were told that they must discuss their responses and formulate a single consensual answer to each of the experimenter's questions. The experimenter did not, at any time, comment on the answers or suggest that some were more accurate than others. He also did not enter into the children's discussions. Thus, to the extent that nonconservers learned how to conserve as a result of such experiences, they learned through a "clash of convictions" with their peers. Incidentally, this proved to be a very effective training procedure.

Illustrative Piagetian Curricula

To summarize the general instructional principles reviewed up to this point, it might be useful to construct another continuum. Various philosophies of education are arranged along this particular continuum. At one extreme are found philosophies that we shall call *interventionist*. At the other extreme are found philosophies that we shall call *horticultural*.

The interventionist extreme is distinguished by an emphasis on achieving precisely defined instructional goals that are externally imposed. It is also distinguished by an absence of child-centeredness. On the issues of sequencing, content, and teaching methodology, interventionists take positions that are quite different from those we have discussed. Concerning sequencing, there is a prima facie presumption that, in the absence of evidence to the contrary, we can teach most children just about anything at just about any time we wish to teach it to them. The secret of good teaching, according to this view, lies in adopting the right instructional technology for each topic, not in the child's stage of cognitive development. It is held that cognitive development sets only very broad and vague limits on what can be taught. Moreover, these limits are not believed to be sufficiently precise to justify expending large amounts of time and effort on diagnosing developmental levels. Concerning content, the emphasis is on teaching pupils the sorts of things that parents and educational experts believe are essential for success in the adult world of work. That is, the emphasis is on specific skills that have concrete occupational payoffs rather than on promoting general intellectual growth. Concerning methodology, the construction of teaching strategies is *pragmatic* rather than theoretical. A "good" teaching method is one that works rather than one that is derived from some theory of cognitive development. A teaching method is said to work only to the extent it can be shown to produce clear improvements in target skills. One interesting result of this pragmatic approach to teaching is that it is entirely possible that we might end up using wildly different methods to teach different things. For example, we might find ourselves using structured reinforcement procedures, complete with teaching machines, to teach reading and small discussion groups to teach arithmetic. The apparent inconsistency should not bother us as long as the methods being used are the ones that work the best for each topic.

It is doubtful whether the extreme interventionist philosophy is operating in any school system anywhere. I think most experts would agree that the curricula found in schools for retarded and emotionally disturbed children (e.g., token economies) are the closest available approximations to the interventionist extreme. Piaget-oriented educators routinely charge that the educational philosophy that has tended to predominate in North American schools inclines toward the interventionist end of our continuum. But little proof is provided for this assertion.

The horticultural end of the continuum is clearly child-centered rather than parent- or teacher-centered. On questions of content, sequencing, and methodology, the emphasis is on permitting children to learn what they want to learn when they want to learn it and in the manner they choose to learn it. I call this philosophy "horticultural" largely because of an experience I once had in a school for gifted children. I was conducting a study dealing with gifted children's ability to learn advanced mathematical and logical concepts. Of all the children who took part in the study, there was one particular pupil who seemed head and shoulders above the others. (He eventually graduated from high school at age 10 and received a Ph.D. at age 18.) I asked the teacher how she went about teaching this prodigy. Surprised that I should ask a question whose answer was so obvious, she replied, "I water him and he grows." As she saw it, her role as a teacher consisted of tending the plants in her garden and watching them grow of their own accord. One derives the same general impression from the writings of most child-centered educators. The basic assumption seems to be that children's minds, if planted in fertile soil, will grow quite naturally on their own. Some readers may recall that this educational philosophy was first popularized by Rousseau.

As was the case for the interventionist extreme, it is doubtful that any school system anywhere was ever guided by pure horticulturalism. One possible exception might be A. S. Neill's famous Summerhill School (see Neill 1960). However, as the preceding remarks suggest, the schools that usually provide the closest approximations to pure horticulturalism are those for the gifted. With gifted children it seems silly to adopt any other policy than one that allows them to learn what they want when they want and how they want. It should be obvious from our earlier discussion of Piagetian educational principles that this sort of instruction leans toward the horticultural end of our continuum.

With these remarks as a background, we turn to some attempts to construct and test experimental curricula that conform to Piagetian guidelines. It is remarkable, I think, that relatively few such projects have been undertaken in comparison to the number of papers and books that have been written espousing Piaget-based instruction. No doubt this disparity may be explained, at least in part, on the ground that it is much easier to set forth instructional guidelines than it is to figure out how to put them into operation in a classroom and how to evaluate the results. Fortunately, the number of available projects, though small, is still adequate to reveal some general trends.

We shall briefly examine four Piaget-inspired curriculum projects: (*a*) Celia Lavatelli's Early Childhood Curriculum (e.g., Lavatelli 1970, 1971); (*b*) David Weikart's Open Framework Program (e.g., Weikart 1973; Weikart et al. 1971); (*c*) the University of Wisconsin's Piagetian Preschool Education Program (e.g., Bingham-Newman 1974; Bingham-Newman, Saunders and Hooper 1974); (*d*) Constance Kamii's Piaget for Early Education Program (e.g., Kamii and DeVries 1974). For the most part, educators who have been in the forefront of Piagetian curriculum development have concentrated on evolving their own unique interpretations of how the theory should be put to work in the classroom. There has been little interest in comparing and contrasting different experimental projects. One notable exception to this rule is Frank H. Hooper of the University of Wisconsin's Research and Development Center for Cognitive Learning. Although Hooper has been actively involved in developing his own curriculum ideas, he has also written the only definitive reviews of other Piagetian curriculum projects (e.g., Hooper and DeFrain 1974; Lawton and Hooper 1977). Each of the four projects just mentioned is examined at length in Hooper's reviews. Most of the points raised about these projects below also appear in Hooper's reviews.

Although each of the four projects has its own unique and special features, all of them share one fundamental characteristic. They are all *preschool* programs—i.e., they are all designed for children at the preoperational stage. The reason that Piagetian curriculum projects have so far been restricted to the preschool level is quite simple. It is difficult and expensive to experiment at the elementary, junior high, and high school levels. At these latter three levels, there are definite instructional goals set down by local school boards, state and provincial departments of education, and parent-teacher organizations. It is an extremely difficult proposition to convince these various authorities that established instructional objectives should be altered merely for the sake of testing some new ideas. The task is made even more difficult by the fact that there are no guarantees that the results will not be calamitous. By comparison with elementary, junior high, and high school programs, preschool curricula have traditionally been more flexible and experimental. There has always been a sense that preschools should set the stage for what is to come rather than attempt to inculcate specific skills. Since the objectives of preschool education are vaguely defined, it is much easier to introduce innovative programs merely for the sake of trying them out. What is more, I think most educators feel that any Piagetian curriculum approach will have to prove itself at the preschool level before there will be any chance of introducing it at more advanced levels.

Below, we review some of the specific features of each of the four projects. We also consider some evaluation data on each. The projects are reviewed in their approximate historical order—the Lavatelli and Weikart programs have been around the longest. It is interesting to note that the historical ordering of the programs is the reverse of their order of ideological purity. The Lavatelli and Weikert projects might be called ''liberal'' Piaget-inspired programs. While both programs focus on Piagetian cognitive contents, they do not adhere rigidly to all of the guidelines we have discussed. In the Wisconsin and Kamii projects, on the other hand, there has been a concerted effort to ground every detail in Piagetian theory.

early childhood
curriculum

Lavatelli's Early Childhood Curriculum seeks to give children systematic exposure to several key concrete-operational cognitive contents. It is claimed that such exposure should make for a more efficient transition from the preoperational stage to the concrete-operational stage. The specific contents that children are exposed to are divided into five categories, namely, number, space, classification, seriation, and measurement.

Lavatelli has developed and tested a kit that contains materials for teaching contents in these categories. The kit, a manual for its use, and a complete description of the Early Childhood Curriculum are available from American Science and Engineering of Boston for about $300. The program's main emphasis is on learning through active interactions with concrete objects. A case in point is provided by the following example of a Lavatelli procedure for teaching conservation of number:

> Using toys and pennies for example a child may on a perceptual level state that there are more toys in a long row than there are pennies to buy these toys when an identical amount of pennies is placed in a pile near the row of toys. Moving the pennies one-to-one beside each toy may cause the child to reconsider; now there is one penny for each toy. After piling up the pennies again he can now realize that for each toy there is still a penny despite the perceptual difference. His thinking has been challenged by operating on real materials in an enjoyable activity. [Lavatelli 1970, p. 4]

The use of discussion groups is recommended as a fruitful teaching strategy. Lavatelli suggests that, for each of the five categories, the teacher should organize small working groups of five or six children. The children in each group can then work together on the exercises for a given content. It is recommended that children participate in such working groups several times per week and that the exercises for each content be repeated several times. In addition to being grounded in Piagetian theory, the working group technique also has an economic advantage. It reduces the number of Lavatelli kits that a school must purchase.

By comparison to some of the programs we shall consider, the teacher plays a very active role in the Lavatelli curriculum. The teacher, not the child, is primarily responsible for structuring each day's work. The teacher is charged with carefully selecting exercises that emphasize the correct components of each content and deemphasize the incorrect components. The teacher is supposed to avoid introducing exercises that encourage children to make incorrect responses. There is, in effect, a right way and a wrong way to learn concrete-operational contents in the Early Childhood Curriculum. An illustration is provided by the earlier number conservation example. Piaget's (e.g., 1952a) studies show that an important difference between the preoperational and concrete-operational concepts of cardinal equivalence is that preoperational children think that spatial cues (e.g., length, density) are reliable guides to the relative numerousness of two sets. But concrete-operational children know that spatial cues do not always give the correct answer. Hence, when working with preoperational children, one should select number exercises that underscore the fact that spatial cues are not infallible guides to number judgment. Since preoperational children already depend too much on spatial cues, one should avoid selecting exercises in which spatial cues provide correct answers.

There are some evaluation data available on the effectiveness of the Early Childhood Curriculum. Before publication, the program was used in a pilot project at the University of Illinois and in some public school kindergartens in Missouri. The main evaluation procedure consisted of examining children's scores on standardized tests of intelligence and on a battery of Piagetian concrete-operational tests. The children who participated were given both types of tests at the beginning of the program. Several months later, after completion of the program, the tests were re-administered. Lavatelli (1970) reported that at the second testing both standardized intelligence test scores and Piaget test scores were higher than in the beginning. But this does not tell us very much. In particular, it does not tell us that the Early Childhood Curriculum produces greater gains than more traditional programs. The problem is that children's scores on such tests increase *spontaneously* during the preschool and kindergarten years. For example, other things being equal, kindergartener's scores on a conservation test will be higher in June than when they entered kindergarten in September. This will happen even if they receive *no* instruction during the intervening months. Therefore, if we wish to prove that the Early Childhood Curriculum produces more substantial gains than traditional preschool programs, we would have to compare the amount of improvement observed in children receiving the curriculum to the corresponding amount of improvement observed for children receiving some other curriculum.

As mentioned above, a central aim of the Lavatelli program is to prepare the way for the transition from preoperations to concrete operations. This is done by teaching children the components of key contents such as classification, seriation, etc. But some more orthodox Piagetian educators (e.g., Kamii and DeVries 1974) criticize this practice on the grounds that it is tantamount to acceleration. That is, instead of merely preparing the way for concrete operations, the Early Childhood Curriculum seeks to accelerate children's stages of cognitive development. As we saw earlier, the ideal Piagetian curriculum eschews acceleration and concentrates on thorough mastery.

the open framework program

The distinguishing feature of Weikart's Open Framework Program is that it concentrates on a single type of concrete-operational content: classification. Weikart believes that the classification skills studied by Inhelder and Piaget (1964) are absolutely fundamental to the learning of such familiar subjects as reading and arithmetic. Consequently, he has evolved a curriculum for teaching children all of the classificatory skills we examined in Chapter 5 and some others as well. In all, children are instructed on eleven different skills. There are separate exercises for each. The curriculum is sequential in that the skills are introduced in the approximate order in which children acquire them spontaneously. The specific skills are:

1. Identify objects that do not belong to some given set.
2. Identify objects that are the same in any way.
3. Identify objects that are the same in some given way.
4. Identify objects that are not the same.
5. Be able to state specific ways in which objects are the same and different.
6. Group objects into sets using internally generated criteria.
7. Classify all the members of a group of objects into a single set.
8. Exhaustively sort all the members of a group of objects into two mutually exclusive categories.
9. Sort and resort groups of objects according to different criteria. Be able to resort the group when new objects are added to it.
10. Be able to solve class inclusion problems. That is, be able to recognize subordinate classes of a given class and understand that the elements of the subordinate class are always less numerous than the elements of the class to which it belongs.
11. Be able to group sets of objects together to form hierarchical systems of classes. For example, group roses and tulips together to form flowers, then group flowers and trees together to form plants, and so on.

In the course of arranging exercises for each of these eleven skills, Open Framework teachers are asked to follow four general guidelines. First, at the beginning of an exercise, try to control the specific materials and activities. In particular, try to focus on materials that facilitate comparing, combining, and sorting objects. Second, although the teacher *trys* to control materials and exercises, children should not be discouraged from choosing materials and exercises of their own. Third, the teacher observes the children's activities and poses questions. The questions are designed to encourage the children to expand their activities in correct directions. Fourth, at the end of each day the teacher evaluates the children's classificatory activities. Attention is given both to the materials they have been using and to specific uses made of them. This evaluation is used to plan the next day's activities.

From this description, it is apparent that the Open Framework teacher plays an active role in controlling the daily content of the curriculum. However, the teacher seems to exert less control than in the Lavatelli program. Explicitly, there seems to be less of an emphasis on the "right" and "wrong" ways to learn classificatory skills. The third guideline, for example, allows children to choose their own materials and exercises if they wish to do so. There is no explicit recommendation in the Open Framework Program that teachers should rigorously avoid all exercises that might reinforce preoperational rather than concrete-operational classificatory behavior.

Weikart (1973) has reported an extensive evaluation of the Open Framework Program. Unlike Lavatelli's evaluation, Weikert's included comparison groups of children enrolled in non-Piagetian programs. The Open Framework Program was compared to both an experimental curriculum that leaned toward the interventionist end of our continuum of educational philosophies and a program that leaned toward the horticultural end. The interventionist curriculum was a reinforcement-based program that focused on traditional subjects such as arithmetic and language. The horticultural curriculum was a child-centered program that focused on social and personality development. All the programs were part of a single experimental project. The programs were administered to three separate groups of 3- and 4-year-old retardates. Each child attended five half-day classes per week. In addition, each child was given an individual ninety-minute tutorial session once per week in his home. The measures of curriculum effectiveness, which were administered both before and after the program, included such things as standardized intelligence tests, teacher ratings, and ratings by outside experts.

To his surprise, Weikart found that all three programs worked equally well. All of them produced excellent gains in the various measures of curriculum effectiveness. This led Weikart to advance a conclusion that poses some problems for educators who wish to revamp curricula along more child-centered lines. Weikart concluded that the crucial factor making for curriculum success was that all the children were enrolled in an experimental project in which the teaching staff was well-motivated and conscientious. If the curriculum program is such that it requires teachers to work hard and be committed to what they are doing, it makes little difference which specific curriculum program they are using. This seems to suggest that the critical factor in insuring the success of a curriculum is the teacher rather than the child or the content of the curriculum.

Like all Piaget-inspired programs, the Open Framework Program stresses learning through active encounters with concrete materials. It differs from Lavatelli's program, as we have seen, in that it seems to be more child-centered and less teacher-centered. But some Piagetian educators have raised the same criticism of Weikart's program as of Lavatelli's—i.e., they believe all the guided instruction in classification skills is tantamount to acceleration. The standard reply is that these exercises are only designed to make the transition to concrete operations smoother, not to speed it up.

the Piagetian Preschool Education Program

The Lavetelli and Weikart programs are clearly Piaget-inspired in that they rely on active learning strategies and expose pupils to concrete-operational contents. But there is no attempt to make every detail of either program adhere to Piagetian theory. This fact greatly displeases educators of a more orthodox turn of mind. In the view of such people, the Lavatelli and Weikart programs are unacceptably liberal translations of Piaget. The program that we now take up, the University of Wisconsin's Piagetian Preschool Education Program, attempts to provide a more literal translation.

The Piagetian Preschool Education Program was designed for use with 3-, 4-, and 5-year-olds. At the outset, the ostensive aim of the project was to discover whether a program constructed along more or less orthodox Piagetian lines could facilitate intellectual and social development in pre-schoolers. At first glance, the program resembled Lavatelli's in that it emphasized several concrete-operational content areas and made use of small-group instruction. The specific content areas covered were number, seriation, classification, space, time, and measurement. A total of 100 specific curriculum items and twenty-eight weeks of lesson plans were devised by the authors. From its inception, the project was guided by nine goals. These were summarized by one of the authors, Bingham-Newman (1974), in a doctoral dissertation written after the project had been in operation for three years:[2]

> The following principles furnished the framework for the Piagetian Preschool Program (PPEP):
> 1. More than the mere accumulation of facts, intelligence is the incorporation of the given data of experiences into an organized framework. It involves the individual's ability to organize and adapt through the reciprocal processes of assimilation and accommodation to various aspects of the environment.
> 2. Intelligence is developed through interaction between the environment and the organism. Timing and quality in an environment are important factors for an evolving intellect.
> 3. Growth of intelligence enhances functioning in all areas of psychological development, including affective, cognitive, and psychomotor development.
> 4. Learning is an active process, subordinate to development, which involves manipulative and exploratory interaction with the environment in the search for alternative actions and properties applicable to objects and events. This involves both mental and physical activity.
> 5. Each stage in the development of intelligence is characterized by the presence or absence of specific cognitive operations—children think about the world very differently than adults. They make different interpretations and draw different conclusions from given events than adults do.
> 6. There is an invariant sequence of development through the major periods of cognitive growth: sensori-motor, preoperational, concrete operational, and formal operations and the within stage sub-sequences associated with the various concept domains. Each individual moves through the sequence at his own pace.
> 7. Language helps to focus on concepts and to retrieve them. It does not *in itself* build concepts.

[2]Ann Bingham-Newman (unpublished Doctoral dissertation, University of Wisconsin, 1974), pp. 53–55.

8. Intellectual growth is fostered by social interaction with peers and adults as well as by interaction with the physical environment.

9. Autonomy with cooperation, rather than simple obedience to authority, contributes to the child's intellectual and moral development. [Bingham-Newman 1974, pp. 53-55]

The "theoretical purity" of the Wisconsin project is evident from the fact that most of the principles of Piaget-based instruction discussed earlier in this chapter may also be found in Bingham-Newman's list. In the actual classroom activities, the emphasis was on getting children to discover concepts on their own. But there was no attempt to teach the concepts directly. Most exercises focused on interacting with physical objects and interacting with peers rather than interacting with teachers. Children were free to select their own activities and respond in their own way. In other words, little or no stress was placed on the "right" and "wrong" methods of learning concepts. Teachers were not charged with avoiding activities that might lead to incorrect responses.

Like Weikart's Open Framework Program, the Piagetian Preschool Education Program has been subjected to careful evaluation. The principal measures of curriculum success were children's performance on tests for concrete-operational contents. Other measures included two standardized tests of intelligence (Peabody Picture Vocabulary and the Raven Matrices). Children who attended the Piagetian Preschool Education Program from 1971 to 1973 were compared to a group of children attending a traditional preschool during the same period. Also, children who attended the Piagetian preschool from 1972 to 1974 were compared to a group of children attending a traditional preschool during the same period. The results were remarkably similar to Weikart's findings. On the one hand, the children in the Piagetian Preschool Educational Program showed excellent improvement on the various measures. Hence, the Piagetian curriculum was "effective" to the extent that it produced clear gains on these measures. But there was no evidence that it was more effective than traditional curricula. When the test performances of children in the Piagetian and traditional groups were compared, virtually all of the comparisons showed no differences between the groups. In fact, those few comparisons which revealed differences tended to favor the traditional group!

Piaget for early education

We turn now to the last and most orthodox our experimental applications of Piaget. This particular application is the work of Constance Kamii of the University of Illinois. Unfortunately, for our purposes, Kamii's project is not yet completed. Her curriculum apparently is still in the development and evaluation phase. Hence, it is impossible to be as specific about Kamii's work as we were with the first three projects. However, some its general features may be noted.

Perhaps the easiest way to discuss Kamii's views is to do it the way she does—by contrasting them with those of other authors. Kamii strenuously objects to programs such as Lavatelli's and Weikart's. Although several specific criticisms are raised, the general objection is lack of ideological purity. Weikart's curriculum is said to be based on gross distortions of Piagetian theory. It is also criticized for being overly concerned with children's language and with accelerating the natural process of cognitive development. Lavatelli's curriculum is said to contain fewer distortions than Weikart's. However, Lavatelli is also criticized for being overly concerned with language. As a remedy for the Weikart and Lavatelli programs, Kamii recommends seven principles to guide the true Piagetian preschool. First, encourage children to be independent and curious. Second, encourage children to interact with each other. Third, encourage equality between children and teacher. Fourth, try to teach things with reference to children's play activities. Fifth, encourage children to give "wrong" answers as well as "right" answers. Sixth, adapt teaching methods to fit the particular subject being taught. Seventh, teach content as well as process. The first few principles on this list also appear on our earlier list of guidelines for the Piagetian Preschool Education Project.

Kamii opposes both narrow curriculum objectives and attempts to train specific concrete-operational contents in the classroom. Concerning curriculum objectives, she prefers broadly and vaguely defined goals. These may be divided into two categories, short-term and long-term. Short-term goals include promoting curiosity, encouraging children to be alert, getting children to pose interesting questions, and encouraging children to notice similarities and differences. Long-range goals include general personality development, general intellectual development, and the facilitation of autonomous systems of values. It should be obvious that these goals are indeed broad and vague by comparison to the other curricula we have considered.

Although the above statements make a fine show of orthodoxy, many readers may be wondering what *specific things* Kamii recommends that teachers should teach. The answer is that there are no specific recommendations. Kamii says that it is inappropriate to construct a "cookbook" curriculum like Lavetelli and Weikart have done. Daily lesson plans and predetermined exercise items are said to be antithetical to the true Piagetian approach. Rather than serving as an administrator of a curriculum devised by someone else, the Kamii teacher makes up the curriculum as she goes along. The teacher's job is "to create an environment and an atmosphere conducive to learning; to provide materials, suggest activities, and assess what is going on inside the child's head from

moment to moment; to respond to children in terms of the kind of knowledge involved; and to help the child extend his ideas" (Kamii and DeVries
1974; pp. 64–65).

epilogue

To conclude this discussion of Piaget-inspired curricula, it is
important to observe that none of the evaluation findings discussed above
seems sufficiently positive to warrant a rush toward revamping existing
curricula along Piagetian lines. While there are some positive findings, there
does not seem to be any evidence that would convince a prudent reader that
the lofty claims made by the developers of Piagetian curricula are true.
There appears to be no proof of either short-term or long-term superiority
in Piaget-instructed children. For the only two programs on which detailed
comparisons with more traditional curricula have been made, there is no
evidence of differential curriculum effects. There is a suggestion that the
teacher, not the curriculum being administered, is what makes the big
difference. To me, this suggests that we might do well to spend less time
arguing educational doctrines and more time developing highly motivated
teachers.

Synopsis

Historically, the psychology of intelligence has been closely tied to educational practice. This is due, in part, to the fact that most theories of intelligence have been built on data generated by standardized tests of intelligence.
These tests were originally devised to predict educational achievement and,
to this day, children's scores on them are strongly correlated with their
classroom performance. Although Piaget's theory is not based on such
tests, there has been an inevitable tendency to wonder what the theory's
instructional recommendations are. When speaking of education, Piaget
has preferred to talk in generalities rather than spell out concrete proposals.

Despite Piaget's unwillingness to deal in specifics, educators believe
that three types of recommendations follow from the theory: recommendations about the sequencing of curriculum material; recommendations about
curriculum content; recommendations about teaching methods. Sequencing
recommendations are concerned with the order in which certain topics
should be introduced to children. There are four general recommendations.
First, never teach things that are clearly above the child's present stage of
cognitive development. Second, avoid attempts to accelerate and concentrate instead on thorough mastery of each topic. Third, try to teach children
concepts in the same order in which they acquire them spontaneously. A

wealth of evidence about the order in which children spontaneously acquire mathematics-related concepts can be found in Piaget's normative research. Fourth, teaching is a two-step process in which instruction is preceded by diagnosis of children's cognitive-developmental stages. The fourth recommendation is problematical. There are few standardized tests available that would permit teachers to diagnose stages of classificatory development, spatial development, and so on.

During the first few elementary grades, the curriculum is devoted chiefly to mathematics and language. Piaget's writings contain many suggestions about the former. For example, there are mathematics-related skills that are not now taught but that could be if we wished to do so. These include seriation, transitive inference, ordinal number, multiple classification, and class inclusion. Another content recommendation is that many geometric ideas could be introduced during elementary school rather than waiting until high school. Topological contents could be taught during the early elementary grades, while projective and Euclidean contents could be taught during the later grades.

Two general recommendations about teaching materials seem to follow from the theory. First, materials should be concrete rather than abstract. Second, they should be action-based rather than passive. The first recommendation follows from the distinction between concrete- and formal-operational intelligence. If children do not grasp concepts at an abstract or symbolic level, it makes little sense to rely on verbal explanations to convey ideas. Instead, concepts should be simply and attractively illustrated in children's textbooks. Also, teachers should avoid the tendency to lecture to children and concentrate on concrete demonstrations. The second recommendation about teaching materials means that they should be manipulable. That is, they should require active involvement on the part of the child rather than passive observation. Since thought is based on action in Piaget's theory, manipulable teaching materials are fundamental to any Piaget-inspired program.

The largest single group of Piagetian educational recommendations are in the area of teaching methodology. Many lists of dos and don'ts are available. There are three items, in particular, that seem to appear on every list. First, teachers are constantly exhorted to use active learning strategies. This recommendation follows from the fact that children play a central role in their own cognitive development in Piagetian theory. Second, teachers are also encouraged to adopt strategies designed to make children aware of the conflicts and inconsistencies in their beliefs. The rationale for this proposal is that conflict promotes equilibration. Third, teachers are asked to make use of the child's peers as teachers. The rationale for this proposal appears in some of Piaget's earliest work, in which he stressed the role of peer influences in the transition from egocentric to socialized language.

Educational philosophies may be assigned positions on some simple conceptual dimensions. One of these is the interventionist (or teacher-centered) versus horticultural (or child-centered) continuum. Extreme interventionism emphasizes precisely defined instructional goals that are externally imposed. There is no consideration of children's stages of cognitive development. On the whole, interventionist curricula are pragmatically based rather than theoretically based. Extreme horticulturalism is child-centered. Emphasis is placed on what the child wants to learn when he wants to learn it. Interventionist-oriented curricula tend to predominate in schools for the retarded, while the horticultural outlook is influential in programs for the gifted. Piaget-oriented programs clearly incline toward the horticultural end of the continuum.

Experimental curricula. Although a large number of essays have been written about the merits of Piaget-based instruction, very few programs have actually been worked out and put into operation. There are four major programs: Lavatelli's Early Childhood Curriculum; Weikart's Open Framework Program; the University of Wisconsin's Piagetian Preschool Education Program; and Kamii's Piaget for Early Education Program. All four of these experimental curricula are for preschoolers rather than elementary schoolers.

Lavatelli's Early Childhood Curriculum is focused on five types of concrete-operational contents—number, space, classification, seriation, and measurement. The basic idea is to give preschool children systematic instruction in each of these areas. The underlying assumption is that such instruction will help smooth the way for the transition from pre-operations to concrete operations. Weikart's Open Framework Program is focused on one specific type of concrete-operational content, classification. Weikart believes that classificatory skills are especially important for reading and arithmetic. In all, children are exposed to eleven different classificatory contents. The contents are introduced in the same order that children are assumed to acquire them spontaneously.

The Lavatelli and Weikart programs have been criticized for being insufficiently orthodox. Although they are definitely Piaget-inspired in the sense that they deal with concrete-operational contents and make use of active teaching strategies, it is also true that no attempt has been made to ground every aspect of the programs in Piagetian theory. The authors of the other two programs have attempted to adhere more closely to the theory. The Piagetian Preschool Education Program is based on nine instructional guidelines. Like the Lavatelli and Weikart curricula, pupils are exposed to contents from the concrete-operational level. However, the emphasis is on getting children to discover these contents by themselves. Most instructional activities consist of manipulating concrete objects and interacting with other children. The Piaget for Early Education project is more difficult to describe than the other three projects. This is because the program is not yet completely evolved and because its author, like Piaget, prefers to speak in terms of general principles. These principles are concerned, for the most part, with fostering the growth of global behavioral capacities such as curiosity, socialization, and independence. No explicit mention is made of the tangible educational goals normally associated with classroom instruction. Daily lesson plans and other features of "cookbook" curricula are viewed as inconsistent with the true Piaget approach to teaching.

On the whole, one is forced to conclude that Piaget-oriented educators have failed to establish a case for restructuring traditional curricula along Piagetian lines. The evaluation data on the aforementioned projects have failed to show any differences between Piagetian instruction and other curricula. There is good reason to believe that it is the characteristics of teachers, not those of curricula and their associated educational philosophies, that are most crucial.

Supplementary Readings

1. ELKIND, *Child Development and Education: A Piagetian Perspective* (1976). Elkind's book is an elementary introduction to several basic educational questions from the Piagetian point of view. The book also contains an overview of basic Piagetian concepts.
2. LAWTON AND HOOPER, "Developmental Theory in the Early Childhood Classroom: An Analysis of Piagetian Inspired Principles and Programs". (1977). This reading provides a general introduction to Piaget-based preschool projects. The basic principles that underlie these projects are examined, and the four curricula summarized earlier in the present chapter are reviewed.
3. SCHWEBEL AND RAPH, *Piaget in the Classroom* (1973). Schwebel and Raph's book appears to be the most important collection of essays on Piagetian applications to education that is available at present. There are chapters by most of the prominent workers in this area. Of special interest are chapters by one of Piaget's chief collaborators, Hermina Sinclair, and by Kamii. Taken together, these papers give the orthodox Piagetian stances on most of the questions discussed in the present chapter.
4. SIGEL, "The Piagetian System and the World of Education". (1969). This essay is a wide-ranging introduction to the problem of what Piaget has to say to educators. The paper has routinely cited by authors of subsequent papers on the same theme and, hence, may be viewed as a classic in the field.
5. SZEMINSKA, "The Evolution of Thought: Some Applications of Research Findings to Educational Practice". (1965). This paper is one of the earliest discussions of Piaget and education by one of Piaget's coworkers. It is instructive to compare Szeminska's proposals to later proposals in Readings 3 and 4.

References

ACHENBACH, T.M., and WEISZ, J.R. 1975. A longitudinal study of developmental synchrony between conceptual identity, seriation, and transitivity of color, number, and length. *Child Development* 46: 840–48.

AHR, P.R., and YOUNISS, J. 1970. Reasons for failure on the class inclusion problem. *Child Development* 41: 131–43.

ALLEN, L.R. 1970. Scalogram analysis of classificatory behavior. *Journal of Research in Science Teaching* 5: 43–45.

ALMY, M., CHITTENDEN, E., and MILLER, P. 1966. *Young children's thinking.* New York: Columbia University Press.

ANDERSON, P. W. 1972. More is different. *Science* 177: 393–96.

ANNETT, M. 1959. The classification of instances of four common class concepts by children and adults. *British Journal of Educational Psychology* 29: 223–36.

BANDURA, A. 1969. Social learning theory of identificatory processes. In *Handbook of socialization theory and research*, D.A. Goslin, ed. Chicago: Rand McNally.

———, and WALTERS, R. 1963. *Social learning and personality development.* New York: Holt, Rinehart and Winston.

BARON, J., LAWSON, G., and SIEGEL, L.S. 1975. Effects of training and set size on children's judgments of number and length. *Developmental Psychology* 11: 583–88.

BART, W.M. 1971. A generalization of Piaget's logical-mathematical model for the stage of formal operations. *Journal of Mathematical Psychology* 8: 539–53.

BEARISON, D.J. 1969. Role of measurement operations in the acquisition of conservation. *Developmental Psychology* 1: 653–60.

BEILIN, H. 1964. Perceptual-cognitive conflict in the development of an invariant area concept. *Journal of Experimental Child Psychology* 1: 208–26.

299

———— . 1965. Learning and operational convergence in logical thought development. *Journal of Experimental Child Psychology* 2: 317–39.

———— . 1966. Feedback and infralogical strategies in invariant area conceptualization. *Journal of Experimental Child Psychology* 3: 267–78.

———— . 1971*a*. Developmental stages and developmental processes. In *Measurement and Piaget,* ed. D.R. Green, M.P. Ford, and G.B. Flamer. New York: McGraw-Hill.

———— . 1971*b*. The training and acquisition of logical operations. In *Piagetian cognitive-developmental research in mathematics education*, ed. M.F. Rosskopf, L.P. Steffe, and S. Taback. Washington, D.C.: National Council of Teachers of Mathematics.

————,KAGAN, J., and RABINOWITZ, R. 1966. Effects of verbal and perceptual training on water level representation. *Child Development* 37: 317–29.

BELL, C.R. 1954. Additional data on animistic thinking. *Scientific Monthly*, 79: 67–69.

BERZONSKY, M.D. 1971. Interdependence of Inhelder and Piaget's model of logical thinking. *Developmental Psychology* 4: 469–76.

BETH, E.W., and PIAGET, J. 1966. *Mathematical epistemology and psychology.* Dordrecht, The Netherlands: Reidel.

BIJOU, S.W. 1975. Development in the preschool years: A functional analysis. *American Psychologist* 30: 829–37.

BINGHAM-NEWMAN, A.M. 1974. Development of logical operations abilities in early childhood: A longitudinal comparison of the effects of two preschool settings. Doctoral dissertation, University of Wisconsin.

BINGHAM-NEWMAN, A.M., and HOOPER, F.H. 1974. Classification and seriation instruction and logical task performance in the preschool. *American Educational Research Journal* 11: 379–93.

———— . 1975. The search for the woozle circa 1975: Some comments on Brainerd's observations. *American Educational Research Journal* 12: 379–87.

BINGHAM-NEWMAN, A.M., SAUNDERS, R.A., and HOOPER, F.H. 1974. A longitudinal comparison of an experimental Piagetian preschool program. Hatch Research Project No. 142-1769, University of Wisconsin.

BLANCHARD, J.L. 1975. Identity and reversibility rules: Their order of emergence and effect on conservation acquisition. Honors thesis, University of Alberta.

BORKE, H. 1971. Interpersonal perception of young children: Egocentrism or empathy? *Developmental Psychology* 5: 263–69.

———— . 1972. Chandler and Greenspan's "ersatz egocentrism": A rejoinder. *Developmental Psychology* 7: 107–9.

———— . 1973. The development of empathy in Chinese and American children between three and six years of age: A cross-cultural study. *Developmental Psychology* 9: 102–8.

———— . 1975. Piaget's mountains revisited: Changes in the egocentric landscape. *Developmental Psychology* 11: 240-43.

———— . 1977. Piaget's view of social interaction and the theoretical construct of empathy. In *Alternatives to Piaget: Critical essays on the theory*, ed. L.S. Siegel and C.J. Brainerd. New York: Academic Press.

BOTVIN, G.J., and MURRAY, F.B. 1975. The efficacy of peer modeling and social conflict in the acquisition of conservation. *Child Development* 46: 796–99.

BOURNE, L.E. 1967. Learning and the utilization of conceptual rules. In *Memory and the structure of concepts*, ed. B. Kleinmutz. New York: Wiley.

_____. 1968. Concept attainment. In *Verbal behavior and general behavior theory*, ed. T.R. Dixon and D.L. Horton. Englewood Cliffs, N.J.: Prentice-Hall.

_____. 1970 Knowing and using concepts. *Psychological Review* 77: 546–56.

BOURNE, L.E., and O'BANION, K. 1971. Conceptual rule learning and chronological age. *Developmental Psychology* 5: 525–34.

BOWER, T.G.R. 1966. The visual world of infants. *Scientific American* 215: 80–92.

_____. 1967. The development of object-permanence: Some studies of existence constancy. *Perception & Psychophysics* 2: 411–18.

_____. 1971. The object world of the infant. *Scientific American* 225: 30–47.

_____. 1974. *Development in infancy*. San Francisco: W.H. Freeman.

BOWER, T.G.R., BROUGHTON, J.M., and MOORE, M.K. 1970. The coordination of visual and tactual input in infants. *Perception & Psychophysics* 8: 51–53.

_____. 1971. Development of the object concept as manifested in changes in the tracking behavior of infants between 7 and 20 weeks of age. *Journal of Experimental Child Psychology* 11: 182–93.

BOWER, T.G.R, and PATERSON, J.G. 1972. Stages in the development of the object concept. *Cognition* 1: 47-55.

_____. 1973. The separation of place, movement, and object in the world of the infant. *Journal of Experimental Child Psychology* 15: 161–68.

BOWER, T.G.R., and WISHART, J.G. 1972. The effects of motor skill on object permanence. *Cognition* 1: 165–72.

BRAINE, M.D.S. 1959. The ontogeny of certain logical operations: Piaget's formulation examined by nonverbal methods. *Psychological Monographs* 73, no. 5 (Whole no. 475).

_____. 1962. Piaget on reasoning: A methodological critique and alternative proposals. In Thought in the young child, ed. W. Kessen and C. Kuhlman. *Monographs of the Society for Research in Child Development* 27, no. 2 (Whole no. 83).

BRAINERD, C.J. 1970. The development of the formal operations of implication-reasoning and proportionality in children and adolescents. Doctoral dissertation, Michigan State University.

_____. 1971. The development of the proportionality scheme in children and adolescents. *Developmental Psychology* 5: 469–76.

_____. 1972a. Reinforcement and reversibility in quantity conservation acquisition. *Psychonomic Science* 27: 114–16.

_____. 1972b. The age-stage issue in conservation acquisition. *Psychonomic Science* 29: 115–17.

_____. 1973a. Order of acquisition of transitivity, conservation, and class inclusion of length and weight. *Developmental Psychology* 8: 105–16.

_____. 1973b. Neo Piagetian training experiments revisited: Is there any support for the cognitive developmental stage hypotheses? *Cognition* 2: 349–70.

_____. 1973c. The origins of number concepts. *Scientific American* 228 (3): 101–9.

_____. 1973d. Mathematical and behavioral foundations of number. *Journal of General Psychology* 88: 221–81.

_____ . 1974*a*. Training and transfer of transitivity, conservation, and class inclusion of length. *Child Development* 45: 324–34.

_____ . 1974*b*. Inducing ordinal and cardinal representations of the first five natural numbers. *Journal of Experimental Child Psychology* 18: 520–34.

_____ . 1975*a*. Structures-of-the-whole and elementary education. *American Educational Research Journal* 12: 369–78.

_____ . 1975*b*. Rejoinder to Bingham-Newman and Hooper. *American Educational Research Journal* 12: 389–94.

_____ . 1976*a*. "Stage," "structure," and developmental theory. In *The psychology of the twentieth century*, ed. G. Steiner, vol. 7. Munich: Kindler.

_____ . 1976*b*. Does prior knowledge of the compensation rule increase susceptibility to conservation training? *Developmental Psychology* 12: 1–5.

_____ . 1976*c*. Analysis and synthesis of existing research on children's ordinal and cardinal number concepts. In *Number and measurement*, ed. R.A. Lesh. Columbus, Ohio: ERIC.

_____ . 1976*d*. On the validity of propositional logic as a model for adolescent intelligence. *Interchange* 7: 40–45.

_____ . 1976*e*. Concerning Macnamara's analysis of Piaget's theory of number. *Child Development* 47: 893–96.

_____ . 1977*a*. Feedback, rule knowledge, and conservation learning. *Child Development* 48: in press.

_____ . 1977*b*. *The origins of the number concept.* New York: Praeger.

_____ . 1977*c*. Learning research and Piagetian theory. In *Alternatives to Piaget: Critical essays on the theory*, ed. L.S. Siegel and C.J. Brainerd. New York: Academic Press.

_____ . 1977*d*. Effects of spatial cues on children's cardinal number judgments. *Developmental Psychology* 13: in press.

_____ . 1977*e*. Cognitive development and concept learning: An interpretative review. *Psychological Bulletin* 84: in press.

BRAINERD, C. J., AND ALLEN, T.W. 1971*a*. Experimental inductions of the conservation of "first-order" quantitative invariants. *Psychological Bulletin* 75: 128–44.

_____ . 1971*b*. Training and generalization of density conservation: Effects of feedback and consecutive similar stimuli. *Child Development* 42: 693–704.

BRAINERD, C.J., and BRAINERD, S.H. 1972. Order of acquisition of number and liquid quantity conservation. *Child Development* 43: 1401–5.

BRAINERD, C. J., AND FRASER, M. 1974. A further test of the ordinal theory of number development. *Journal of Genetic Psychology* 125: 141–52.

BRAINERD, C. J., AND HOOPER, F. H. 1975. A methodological analysis of developmental studies of identity conservation and equivalence conservation. *Psychological Bulletin* 82: 725–37.

BRAINERD, C. J., AND KASZOR, P. 1974. An analysis of two proposed sources of children's class inclusion errors. *Developmental Psychology* 10: 633–43.

BRAINERD, C. J., AND VANDEN HEUVEL, K. 1974. Development of geometric imagery in five- to eight-year-olds. *Genetic Psychology Monographs* 98: 89–143.

BROWN, I. 1973. A study of object permanence. Honors thesis, University of Edinburgh.

BROWNELL, W. A. 1928. The development of children's number ideas in the primary grades. *Supplementary Education Monographs*, no. 35.

_____ . 1941. *Arithmetic in grades I and II.* Durham, N. C.: Duke University Press.

BRUNER, J. S. 1964. The course of cognitive growth. *American Psychologist* 19: 1–15.

———. 1966. On the conservation of liquids. In *Studies in cognitive growth*, ed. J. S. Bruner, R. R. Olver, and P. M. Greenfield. New York: John Wiley.

BRUNER, J. S., AND KENNEY, H. J. 1966. On relational concepts. In *Studies in cognitive growth*, ed. J. S. Bruner, R. R. Olver, and P. M. Greenfield. New York: John Wiley.

BRUNER, J. S.; OLVER, R. R.; AND GREENFIELD, P. M., eds. 1966. *Studies in cognitive growth*. New York: John Wiley.

BRYANT, P. E. 1974. *Perception and understanding in young children*. London: Methuen.

BRYANT, P. E., AND TRABASSO, T. 1971. Transitive inference and memory in young children. *Nature* 232: 456–58.

BUCHER, B., AND SCHNEIDER, R. R. 1973. Acquisition and generalization of conservation by pre-schoolers using operant training. *Journal of Experimental Child Psychology* 16: 187–204.

BUDDEN, F. J. 1972. *The fascination of groups*. Cambridge, England: Cambridge University Press.

BURT, C. 1949. The structure of the mind: A review of the results of factor analysis. *British Journal of Educational Psychology* 19: 100–111, 176–99.

CALHOUN, L. G. 1971. Number conservation in very young children. *Child Development* 42: 561–72.

CASE, R. 1974. Structures and strictures: Some functional limitations on the course of cognitive growth. *Cognitive Psychology* 6: 544–73.

CATTELL, R. B. 1963. Theory of fluid and crystallized intelligence. *Journal of Educational Psychology* 54: 1–22.

CAZDEN, C. B. 1970. The situation: A neglected source of social class differences in language use. *Journal of Social Issues* 26: 35–60.

CHANDLER, M. J. AND GREENSPAN, S. 1972. Ersatz egocentrism: A reply to H. Borke. *Developmental Psychology* 7: 104–6.

CHAPMAN, R. H. 1975. The development of children's understanding of proportions. *Child Development* 46: 141–48.

CHITTENDEN, E. A. 1964. The development of certain logical abilities and the child's concepts of substance and weight: An examination of Piaget's theory. Doctoral dissertation, Columbia University.

COHEN, L. B. AND SALAPATEK, P. 1976. *Infant Perception*. 2 vols. New York: Academic Press.

COPI, I. 1961. *Introduction to logic*. New York: Macmillan.

CORMAN, H. H., AND ESCALONA, S. K. 1969. Stages of sensorimotor development: A replication study. *Merrill-Palmer Quarterly* 15: 351–61.

COWAN, P. A. 1967. The link between cognitive structure and social structure. Paper read at Society for Research in Child Development, New York, March 1967.

CRANNELL, C. N. 1954. Responses of college students to a questionnaire on animistic thinking. *Scientific Monthly* 78: 54–56.

CRONBACH, L. J. 1957. The two disciplines of scientific psychology. *American Psychologist* 12: 671–84.

CROWELL, D. H., AND DOLE, A. A. 1957. Animism and college students. *Journal of Educational Research*, 50: 391–95.

CURCIO, F., KATTEF, E., LEVINE, D., AND ROBBINS, O. 1977. Compensation and susceptibility to conservation training. *Developmental Psychology* 7: 259–65.

DAVIES, C. M. 1965. Development of the probability concept in children. *Child Development* 36: 779–88.

DÉCARIE, T. G. 1965. *Intelligence and affectivity in early childhood.* New York: International Universities Press.

DE LONG, H. 1970. *A profile of mathematical logic.* Reading, Mass.: Addison-Wesley.

DENNIS, W. 1938. Historical notes on child animism. *Psychological Review* 45: 257–66.

DENNIS, W., AND MALLINGER, B. 1949. Animism and related tendencies in senescence. *Journal of Gerontology* 4: 218–21.

DENNY, N. W. , ZEYTINOGLU, S., AND SELZER, S. C. 1977. Conservation training in four-year-olds. *Journal of Experimental Child Psychology*, in press.

DE VRIES, R. 1969. Constancy of generic identity in the years three to six. *Monographs of the Society for Research in Child Development* 34, no. 3 (Whole no. 127).

DODWELL, P. C. 1963. Children's understanding of spatial concepts. *Canadian Journal of Psychology* 17: 191–205.

DONALDSON, M. 1963. *A study of children's thinking.* London: Tavistock.

DOUGLASS, H. R. 1925. The development of number concepts in children of preschool and kindergarten ages. *Journal of Experimental Psychology* 8: 443–70.

DUCKWORTH, E. 1964. Piaget rediscovered. In *Piaget rediscovered*, ed. R. E. Ripple and V. N. Rockcastle. Ithaca, N. Y.: Cornell University Press.

EICHOLZ, R. E. 1969. *Elementary school mathematics.* Reading, Mass.: Addison-Wesley.

ELKIND, D. 1961. Children's discovery of the conservation of mass, weight, and volume: Piaget replication study II. *Journal of Genetic Psychology* 98: 219–27.

———. 1967a. Piaget's conservation problems. *Child Development* 38: 15–27.

———. 1967b. Egocentrism in adolescence. *Child Development* 38: 1025–34.

———. 1976. *Child development and education: A Piagetian perspective.* New York: Oxford University Press.

ELKIND, D., AND SCHOENFELD, E. 1972. Identity and equivalence conservation at two age levels. *Developmental Psychology* 6: 529–33.

EMRICK, J. A. 1968. The acquisition and transfer of conservation skills by four-year-old children. Doctoral dissertation, University of California at Los Angeles.

ENNIS, R. H. 1969. *Ordinary logic.* Englewood Cliffs, N. J.: Prentice-Hall.

———. 1971. Conditional logic and primary children. *Interchange* 2: 126–32.

———. 1975. Children's ability to handle Piaget's propositional logic: A conceptual critique. *Review of Educational Research* 45: 1–41.

———. 1976. An alternative to Piaget's conceptualization of logical competence. *Child Development* 47: 903–19.

———. 1977. Conceptualization of children's logical competence: Piaget's propositional logic and alternative proposals. In *Alternatives to Piaget: Critical essays on the theory,* ed. L. S. Siegel and C. J. Brainerd. New York: Academic Press.

ENNIS, R. H., FINKELSTEIN, M., SMITH, E., AND WILSON, N. 1969. *Conditional logic and children*. Ithaca, N. Y.: Cornell Critical Thinking Readiness Project.

ERIKSON, E. H. 1963. *Childhood and society*. New York: Norton.

―――. 1968. *Identity: Youth and crisis*. New York: Norton.

EVANS, W. F., AND GRATCH, G. 1972. The stage IV error in Piaget's theory of object concept development: Difficulties in object conceptualization or spatial localization? *Child Development* 43: 682–88.

FANTZ, R. L. 1961. The origin of form perception. *Scientific American* 204: 66–72.

FERGUSON, G. A. 1954. On learning and human ability. *Canadian Journal of Psychology* 8: 95–112.

FISCHBEIN, E., PAMPU, L., AND MANZAT, I. 1970. Comparison of ratios and the chance concept in children. *Child Development* 41: 37–89.

FLAVELL, J.H. 1963. *The developmental psychology of Jean Piaget*. Princeton, N.J.: Van Nostrand.

―――. 1970. Concept development. In *Carmichael's manual of child psychology*, ed. P.H. Mussen. New York: John Wiley.

―――. 1971. Stage-related properties of cognitive development. *Cognitive Psychology* 2: 421–53.

FLAVELL, J.H., BOTKIN, P.T., FRY, C.L., WRIGHT, J.W., AND JARVIS, P.E. 1968. *The development of role-taking and communication skills*. New York: John Wiley.

FLAVELL, J.H., AND WOHLWILL, J.F. 1969. Formal and functional aspects of cognitive development. In *Studies in cognitive development*, ed. D. Elkind and J.H. Flavell. New York: Oxford University Press.

FURTH, H.G. 1968. Piaget's theory of knowledge: The nature of representation and interiorization. *Psychological Review* 75: 143–54.

―――. 1969. *Piaget and knowledge*. Englewood Cliffs, N.J.: Prentice-Hall.

―――. 1970. *Piaget for teachers*. Englewood Cliffs, N.J.: Prentice-Hall.

GAGNÉ, R.M. 1965. *The conditions of learning*. New York: Holt, Rinehart and Winston.

GARVEY, C., AND HOGAN, R. 1973. Social speech and social interaction: Egocentrism revisited. *Child Development* 44: 562–68.

GELMAN, R. 1972. The nature and development of early number concepts. In *Advances in child development and behavior*, ed. H.W. Reese, vol. 7. New York: Academic Press.

GELMAN, R., AND WEINBERG, D.H. 1972. The relationship between liquid conservation and compensation. *Child Development* 43: 371–83.

GIBSON, E.J., AND WALK, R.D. 1960. The "visual cliff." *Scientific American* 202: 64–71.

GLASER, R., AND RESNICK, L.B. 1972. Instructional psychology. In *Annual review of psychology*, ed. P.H. Mussen and M. Rosenzweig. Palo Alto, Calif.: Annual Reviews.

GLUCKSBERG, S., AND KRAUSS, R.M. 1967. Studies of the development of interpersonal communication. Paper read at Society for Research in Child Development, New York, March.

GOLDBERG, S. 1966. Probability judgments by preschool children: Task conditions and performance. *Child Development* 37: 157–67.

GOLDSCHMID, M.L. 1968. Role of experience in the acquisition of conservation. *Proceedings of the American Psychological Association* 76: 361–62.

―――――, AND BENTLER, P.M. 1968. The dimensions and measurement of conservation. *Child Development* 39: 787–802.

GONCHAR, A.J. 1975. A study of the nature and development of the natural number concept: Initial and supplementary analyses. Technical Report no. 340. Madison, Wis.: Research and Development Center for Cognitive Learning, University of Wisconsin.

GRATCH, G.A. 1972. A study of the relative dominance of vision and touch in six-month-old infants. *Child Development* 43: 615–23.

GRATCH, G., APPEL, K.J., EVANS, W.F., L COMPTE, G.K., AND WRIGHT, N.A. 1974. Piaget's stage IV object concept error: Evidence of forgetting or object conception? *Child Development* 45: 71–77.

GRATCH, G., AND LANDERS, W.F. 1971. Stage IV of Piaget's theory of infants' object concepts: A longitudinal study. *Child Development* 42: 359–72.

GRUEN, G.E., AND VORE, D.A. 1972. Development of conservation in normal and retarded children. *Developmental Psychology* 6: 146–57.

GUILFORD, J.P. 1967. *The nature of human intelligence.* New York: McGraw-Hill.

HALFORD, G.S., AND FULLERTON, T.J. 1970. A discrimination task which induces conservation of number. *Child Development* 41: 205–13.

HAMEL, B.R. 1971. On the conservation of liquids. *Human Development* 14: 39–46.

HAMEL, B.R., AND RIKSEN, B.O.M. 1973. Identity, reversibility, rule instruction, and conservation. *Developmental Psychology* 9: 66–72.

HAMEL, B.R., VAN DER VEER, M.A.A., AND WESTERHOF, R. 1972. Identity, language-activation training and conversation. *British Journal of Educational Psychology* 42: 186–91.

HARRIS, P.L. 1971. Examination and search in infants. *British Journal of Psychology* 62: 469–73.

―――――. 1973. Perseverative errors in search by young children. *Child Development* 44: 28–33.

―――――. 1974. Perseverative search at a visibly empty place by young children. *Journal of Experimental Child Psychology* 18: 535–42.

―――――. 1975. Development of search and object permanence during infancy. *Psychological Bulletin* 82: 332–44.

HAYGOOD, R.C., AND BOURNE, L.E. 1965. Attribute and rule-learning aspects of conceptual behavior. *Psychological Review* 72: 175–95.

HILL, S.A. 1961. A study of the logical abilities of children. Doctoral dissertation, Stanford University.

HOBBS, E.D. 1973. Adolescents' concepts of physical quantity. *Developmental Psychology* 9: 431.

HOOPER, F.H., AND DE FRAIN, J. 1974. The search for a distinctly Piagetian contribution to education. Technical Report no. 500. Madison, Wis.: Research and Development Center for Cognitive Learning, University of Wisconsin.

HOOPER, F.H., SIPPLE, T.S., GOLDMAN, J.A., AND SWINTON, S.S. 1974. A cross-sectional investigation of children's classificatory abilities. Technical Report no. 295. Madison, Wis.: Research and Development Center for Cognitive Learning, University of Wisconsin.

HOWELL, E.N. 1965. Recognition of selected inference patterns by secondary school mathematics students. Doctoral dissertation, University of Wisconsin.

INHELDER, B. 1972. Information processing tendencies in recent experiments in cognitive learning. In *Information processing in children*, ed. S. Farnham-Diggory. New York: Academic Press.

INHELDER, B., BOVET, M., SINCLAIR, H., and SMOCK, C.D. 1966. On cognitive development. *American Psychologist* 21: 160–64.

INHELDER, B., and PIAGET, J. 1958. *The growth of logical thinking from childhood to adolescence.* New York: Basic Books.

———. 1959. *La genese des structures logiques élémentaires, classifications et sériations.* Neuchâtel and Paris: Delachaux et Niestlé.

———. 1964. *The early growth of logic in the child.* London: Routledge & Kegan Paul.

INHELDER, B., and SINCLAIR, H. 1969. Learning cognitive structures. In *Trends and issues in developmental psychology*, ed. P.H. Mussen, J. Langer, and M. Covington. New York: Holt, Rinehart & Winston.

INHELDER, B., SINCLAIR, H., and BOVET, M. 1974. *Learning and the development of cognition.* Cambridge, Mass.: Harvard University Press.

JENNINGS, J.R. 1970. The effect of verbal and pictorial presentation on class-inclusion competence and performance. *Psychonomic Science* 20: 357–58.

JOHNSON, D.A. 1966. *The new mathematics in our schools.* New York: Macmillan.

JOHNSON, E.C., and JOSEY, C.C. 1931-32. A note on the development forms of children as described by Piaget. *Journal of Abnormal and Social Psychology* 26: 338–39.

KAMII, C. 1970. Piaget's theory and specific instruction: A response to Bereiter and Kohlberg. *Interchange* 1: 33–39.

———. 1972. An application of Piaget's theory to the conceptualization of a preschool curriculum. In *The preschool in action*, ed. R.K. Parker. Boston: Allyn & Bacon.

———. 1973a. Pedagogical principles derived from Piaget's theory: Relevance from educational practice. In *Piaget in the classroom*, ed. M. Schwebel and J. Raph. New York: Basic Books.

———. 1973b. Piaget's interactionism and the process of teaching young children. In *Piaget in the classroom*, ed. M. Schwebel and J. Raph. New York: Basic Books.

KAMII, C., and DE VRIES, R. 1974. Piaget for early education program. In *The preschool in action*, ed. R.K. Parker. 2nd ed. Boston: Allyn & Bacon.

KARPLUS, R. 1964. The science curriculum improvement study. In *Piaget rediscovered*, ed. R.E. Ripple and V.N. Rockcastle, Ithaca, N.Y.: Cornell University Press.

KESSEN, W. 1962. "Stage" and "structure" in the study of children. In Thought in the young child, ed. W. Kessen and C. Kuhlman. *Monographs of the Society for Research in Child Development* 27, no. 2 (Whole no. 83).

KING, W. 1966. A developmental study of rule learning. *Journal of Experimental Child Psychology* 4: 217–31.

KING, W.H. 1961. Studies of children's scientific concepts and interests: I. The development of scientific concepts in children. *British Journal of Educational Psychology* 31: 1–20.

KLAHR, D., and WALLACE, J.G. 1972. Class inclusion processes. In *information processing in children*, ed. S. Farnham-Diggory. New York: Academic Press.

KODROFF, J.K., and ROBERGE, J.J. 1975. Developmental analysis of the conditional reasoning abilities of primary-grade children. *Developmental Psychology* 11: 21–28.

KOFSKY, E. 1966. A scalogram study of classificatory development. *Child Development* 37: 191–204.

KOHLBERG, L., YAEGER, J., and HJERTHOLM, E. 1968. The development of private speech: Four studies and a review of theories. *Child Development* 39: 691–736.

KOHNSTAMM, G.A. 1967. *Piaget's analysis of class-inclusion: Right or wrong?* The Hague: Mouton.

KOOISTRA, W.H. 1965. Developmental trends in the attainment of conservation, transitivity, and relativism in the thinking of children: A replication and extension of Piaget's ontogenetic formulations. Doctoral dissertation, Wayne State University.

KRAMER, J.A., HILL, K.T., and COHEN, L.B. 1975. Infant's development of object permanence: A refined methodology and new evidence for Piaget's hypothesized ordinality. *Child Development* 46: 149–55.

LANDERS, W.F. 1971. Effects of differential experience on infants in a Piagetian stage IV object-concept task. *Developmental Psychology* 5: 48–54.

LARSEN, G.Y., and FLAVELL, J.H. 1970. Verbal factors in compensation performance and the relationship between conservation and compensation. *Child Development* 41: 965–77.

LAURENDEAU, M., and PINARD, A. 1962. *Causal thinking in the child.* New York: International Universities Press.

––––––. 1970. *The development of the concept of space in the child.* New York: International Universities Press.

LAVATELLI, C.S. 1970. *Early childhood curriculum, a Piagetian program.* Boston: American Science & Engineering.

––––––. 1971. *Piaget's theory applied to an early childhood curriculum.* Boston: American Science & Engineering.

LAWSON, G., BARON, J., and SIEGEL, L.S. 1974. The role of number and length cues in children's quantitative judgments. *Child Development* 45: 731–36.

LAWTON, J.T., and HOOPER, F.H. 1977. Developmental theory in the early childhood classroom: An analysis of Piagetian inspired principles and programs. In *Alternatives to Piaget: Critical essays on the theory,* ed. L.S. Siegel and C.J. Brainerd. New York: Academic Press.

LESH, R.A., ed. 1976. *Number and measurement.* Columbus, Ohio: ERIC.

LLOYD, B.B 1971. Studies of conservation with Yoruba children of differing ages and experience. *Child Development* 42: 415–28.

LOOFT, W.R. 1972. Egocentrism and social interaction across the life span. *Psychological Bulletin* 78: 73–92.

LOOFT, W.R., and BARTZ, W.H. 1969. Animism revived. *Psychological Bulletin* 71: 1–19.

LOOFT, W.R., and CHARLES, D.C. 1969. Modification of the life concept in children. *Developmental Psychology* 1: 445.

LOVELL, K. 1959. A follow-up study of some aspects of the work of Piaget and Inhelder on the child's conception of space. *British Journal of Educational Psychology* 29: 104–17.

––––––. 1961. A follow-up study of Inhelder and Piaget's *The growth of logical thinking. British Journal of Psychology* 52: 143–53.

_____ . 1968. Some recent studies in cognitive and language development. *Merrill-Palmer Quarterly* 14: 123–38.

_____, HEALEY, D., and ROWLAND, A.D. 1962. Growth of some geometrical concepts. *Child Development* 33: 751–67.

LOVELL, K., MITCHELL, B., and EVERETT, I.R. 1962. An experimental study of the growth of some logical structures. *British Journal of Psychology* 53: 175–88.

LOVELL, K., and OGILVIE, E. 1961. The growth of the concept of volume in junior school children. *Journal of Child Psychology and Psychiatry* 2: 118–26.

LOWRIE, D.E. 1954. Additional data on animistic thinking. *Scientific Monthly* 79: 69–70.

LUNZER, E.A. 1960*a*. Some points of Piagetian theory in light of experimental criticism. *Journal of Child Psychology and Psychiatry* 1: 191–202.

_____ . 1960*b* *Recent studies in Britain based on the work of Jean Piaget*. London: National Foundation for Educational Research in England and Wales.

_____ . 1965. Problems of formal reasoning in test situations. In European research in cognitive development, ed. P.H. Mussen. *Monographs of the Society for Research in Child Development* 30, no. 2 (Whole no. 100).

MCCARTHY, D. 1930. *The language development of the preschool child*. Minneapolis, Minn.: University of Minnesota Press.

_____ . 1954. Language development in children. In *Manual of child psychology*, ed. L. Carmichael. New York: John Wiley.

MCGRAW, M.B. 1940. Neural maturation as exemplified in achievement of bladder control. *Journal of Pediatrics* 16: 580–89.

MCLELLAN, J.A., and DEWEY, J.D. 1896. *The psychology of number and its application to methods of teaching arithmetic*. New York: Appleton.

MEAD, G.H. 1934. *Mind, self, and society*. Chicago: University of Chicago Press.

MEHLER, J., and BEVER, T.G. 1967. Cognitive capacity of very young children. *Science* 158: 141–42.

MILLER, D., COHEN, L.B., and HILL, K.T. 1970. A methodological investigation of Piaget's theory of object concept development in the sensory-motor period. *Journal of Experimental Child Psychology* 9: 59–85.

MILLER, N.E., and DOLLARD, J. 1941. *Social learning and imitation*. New Haven: Conn.: Yale University Press.

MOWRER, O.H. 1960. *Learning theory and the symbolic processes*. New York: John Wiley.

MURRAY, F.B. 1972. Acquisition of conservation through social interaction. *Developmental Psychology* 6: 1–6.

MURRAY, F.B., and JOHNSON, P.C. 1969. Reversibility in nonconservation of weight. *Psychonomic Science* 16: 285–86.

MURRAY, J.P., and YOUNISS, J. 1968. Achievement of inferential transitivity and its relation to serial ordering. *Child Development* 39: 1259–68.

NEILL, A.S. 1960. *Summerhill: A radical approach to child rearing*. New York: Hart.

NEIMARK, E.D. 1970. Development of the comprehension of logical connectives: Understanding of "or." *Psychonomic Science* 21: 217–19.

NEIMARK, E.D. 1975. Intellectual development during adolescence. *Review of child development research,* ed. F.D. Horowitz. Chicago: University of Chicago Press.

NEISSER, U., and WEENE, P. 1962. Hierarchies in concept attainment. *Journal of Experimental Psychology* 64: 640–45.

NEWMAN, J.R. 1956. *World of mathematics.* Vol. 3. New York: Simon & Schuster.

O'BRIEN, T., and SHAPIRO, B. 1968. The development of logical thinking in children. *American Educational Research Journal* 5: 531–41.

PARIS, S.G. 1973. Comprehension of language connectives and propositional logical relationships. *Journal of Experimental Child Psychology* 16: 278–91.

PARSONS, C. 1960. Inhelder and Piaget's *The growth of logical thinking*, II: A logician's viewpoint. *British Journal of Psychology* 51: 75–84.

PAYNE, J.N. 1976. Review of research on fractions. In *Number and measurement,* ed. R.A. Lesh. Columbus, Ohio: ERIC.

PELUFFO, N. 1964. La nozioni di conservazione del volume e le operazioni di combinazione come induce di sviluppo del pensuro operatorio in soggetti appartenenti fisici e socioculturali diversi. *Revista di Psicolozia Sociale* 2–3: 99–132.

PETERSON, G.W., HOOPER, F.H., WANSKA, S., and DeFRAIN, J. 1975. An investigation of instructional transfer effects for conservation, transitive inference, and class inclusion reasoning in kindergarten and first grade children. Technical Report no. 368. Madison, Wis.: Research and Development Center for Cognitive Learning, University of Wisconsin.

PIAGET, J. 1962a. *The language and thought of the child.* London: Kegan Paul.

————. 1926b. *Judgment and reasoning in the child.* New York: Harcourt & Brace.

————. 1929. *The child's conception of the world.* New York: Harcourt & Brace.

————. 1930. *The child's conception of physical causality.* London: Kegan Paul.

————. 1932. *The moral judgment of the child.* London: Kegan Paul.

————. 1935. Education et instruction. *Encyclopédie Francaise,* vol. 15.

————. 1942. *Classes, relations et nombre.* Paris: Vrin.

————. 1946a. *Le développement de la notion de temps chez l'enfant.* Paris: Presses Universitaires de France.

————. 1946b. *Les notions de mouvement et de vitesse chez l'enfant.* Paris: Presses Universitaires de France.

————. 1949. *Traité de logique.* Paris: Colin.

————. 1950. *The psychology of intelligence.* New York: International Universities Press.

————. 1951. *Play, dreams, and imitation in childhood.* New York: Norton.

————. 1952a. *The child's conception of number.* New York: Humanities.

————. 1952b. *The origins of intelligence in children.* New York: International Universities Press.

————. 1953. *Logic and psychology.* Manchester, England: University of Manchester Press.

————. 1954. *The construction of reality in the child.* New York: Basic Books.

————. 1960. The general problems of psychobiological development in children. In *Discussions on child development,* ed. J.M. Tanner and B. Inhelder, vol. 4. London: Tavistock.

————. 1962. Comments on Vygotsky's critical remarks concerning *The language and thought of the child* and *Judgment and reasoning in the child.* In L.S. Vygotsky, *Thought and language.* Cambridge, Mass.: M.I.T. Press.

————. 1967a. *Six psychological studies.* New York: Random House.

_____ . 1967*b*. *Biology and knowledge.* Chicago: University of Chicago Press.

_____ . 1968. *On the development of memory and identity.* Worcester, Mass.: Clark University Press.

_____ . 1969. *The mechanisms of perception.* London: Routledge & Kegan Paul.

_____ . 1970*a*. *Structuralism.* New York: Basic Books.

_____ . 1970*b*. Piaget's theory. In *Carmichael's manual of child psychology,* ed. P.H. Mussen. New York: John Wiley.

_____ . 1970*c*. *Genetic epistemology.* New York: Columbia University Press.

_____ . 1970*d*. A conversation with Jean Piaget. *Psychology Today* 3(212): 25–32.

_____ . 1970*e*. *Science of education and the psychology of the child.* New York: Orion.

_____ . 1971*a*. *The child's conception of movement and speed.* New York: Basic Books.

_____ . 1971*b*. *The child's conception of time.* New York: Basic Books.

_____ . 1972. *Essai de logique opératoire.* Paris: Dunod.

_____ . 1973. *The child and reality.* New York: Grossman.

PIAGET, J., AND INHELDER, B. 1941. *Le développement des quantités chez l'enfant.* Neuchatel: Delachaux et Niestlé.

_____ . 1948. *La représentation de l'espace chez l'enfant.* Paris: Presses Universitaires de France.

_____ . 1951. *La genese de l'idée de hazard chez l'enfant.* Paris: Presses Universitaires de France.

_____ . 1956. *The child's conception of space.* London: Routledge & Kegan Paul.

_____ . 1969. *The psychology of the child.* New York: Basic Books.

_____ . 1972 *Mental imagery in the child.* New York: Basic Books.

_____ . 1973. *Memory and intelligence.* New York: Basic Books.

_____ , AND SZEMINSKA, A. 1948. *La géométrie spontanée de l'enfant.* Paris: Presses Universitaires de France.

_____ . 1960. *The child's conception of geometry.* New York: Harper.

PIAGET, J., AND SZEMINSKA, A. 1941. *La genese du nombre chez l'enfant.* Neuchâtel: Delachaux et Niestlé.

PUFALL, P.B., AND SHAW, R.E. 1972. Precocious thoughts on number: The long and the short of it. *Developmental Psychology* 7: 62–69.

PUFALL, P.B., SHAW, R.E., AND SYRDAL-LASKY, A. 1973. Development of number conservation: An examination of some predictions from Piaget's stage analysis and equilibration model. *Child Development* 44: 21–27.

QUINE, W.V.O. 1951. *Mathematical logic.* Cambridge, Mass.: Harvard University Press.

RICCIUTI, H.N. 1965. Object grouping and selective ordering behavior in infants 12 to 24 months old. *Merrill-Palmer Quarterly* 11: 129–48.

RICCIUTI, H.N., AND JOHNSON, L.J. 1965. Developmental changes in categorizing behavior from infancy to the early pre-school years. Paper read at Society for Research in Child Development, Minneapolis, Minnesota, March 1965.

RILEY, C.A., AND TRABASSO, T. 1974. Comparatives, logical structures, and encoding in a transitive inference task. *Journal of Experimental Child Psychology* 17: 187–203.

ROBERGE, J.J. 1970. A study of children's abilities to reason with basic principles of deductive reasoning. *American Educational Research Journal* 7: 538-95.

ROBERGE, J.J., AND PAULUS, D.H. 1971. Developmental patterns for children's class and conditional reasoning abilities. *Developmental Psychology* 4: 191-200.

ROODIN, M.L., AND GRUEN, G.E. 1970. The role of memory in making transitive judgments. *Journal of Experimental Child Psychology* 10: 264-75.

ROSENTHAL, T.L., AND ZIMMERMAN, B.J. 1972. Modeling by exemplification and instruction in training conservation. *Developmental Psychology* 6: 392-401.

ROTHENBERG, B., AND COURTNEY, R. 1968. Conservation of number in very young children: A replication of and a comparison with Mehler and Bever's study. *Journal of Psychology* 70: 205-12.

RUBIN, K.H., AND MAIONI, T.L. 1975. Play preference and its relationship to egocentrism, popularity, and classification skills in preschoolers. *Merrill-Palmer Quarterly* 21: 171-79.

RUSSELL, B. *Foundations of geometry.* 1897. Cambridge, England: Cambridge University Press.

———. 1903. *The principles of mathematics.* Cambridge, England: Cambridge University Press.

———. 1948. *A history of western philosophy.* New York: Simon and Schuster.

———. 1956. Mathematics and the metaphysicians. In *World of mathematics,* ed. New York: Simon and Schuster.

RUSSELL, R.W. 1940. Studies in animism: II. The development of animism. *Journal of Genetic Psychology* 56: 353-66.

———. 1942. Studies in animism: V. Animism in older children. *Journal of Genetic Psychology* 60: 329-35.

RUSSELL, R.W., AND DENNIS, W. 1939. Studies in animism: I. A standardized procedure for the investigation of animism. *Journal of Genetic Psychology* 55: 389-400.

RYOTI, D.E. 1972. Student responses to equivalent inference schemes in class and conditional logic. Doctoral dissertation, University of Illinois.

SAARNI, C.I. 1973. Piagetian operations and field independence in children's problem-solving performance. *Child Development* 44: 338-45.

SCHWEBEL, M., AND RAPH, J. 1973. *Piaget in the classroom.* New York: Basic Books.

SHAPIRO, B.J., AND O'BRIEN, T.C. 1970. Logical thinking in children ages six through thirteen. *Child Development* 41: 823-29.

SHEPPARD, J.L. 1973. A study of the development of operational thought. Doctoral dissertation, University of Newcastle.

SIEGEL, L.S. 1971a. The sequence of development of certain number concepts in preschool children. *Developmental Psychology* 5: 357-61.

———. 1971b. The development of certain number concepts. *Developmental Psychology* 5: 362-63.

———. 1974. Development of number concepts: Order and correspondence operations and the role of length cues. *Developmental Psychology* 10: 907-12.

SIEGLER, R.S. 1978. The Origin of scientific reasoning. *Children's thinking: what develops?* ed. R.S. Siegler. Hillsdale, N.J.: Erlbaum.

SIEGLER, R.S., AND LIEBERT, R.M. 1972. Effects of presenting relevant rules and complete feedback on the conservation of liquid quantity task. *Developmental Psychology* 7: 133-38.

SIEGLER, R.S., LIEBERT, D.E., and LIEBERT, R.M. 1973. Inhelder and Piaget's pendulum problem: Teaching preadolescents to act as scientists. *Developmental Psychology* 9: 97–101.

SIGEL, I.E. 1969. The Piagetian system and the world of education. In *Studies in cognitive development,* ed. D. Elkind and J.H. Flavell. New York: Oxford University Press.

SIGEL, I.E., AND MERMELSTEIN, E. 1966. Effects of nonschooling on Piagetian tasks of conservation. Unpublished manuscript, Merrill-Palmer Institute.

SILVERMAN, I.W., AND GEIRINGER, E. 1973. Dyadic interaction and conservation induction: A test of Piaget's equilibration model. *Child Development* 44: 815–20.

SIMMONS, A.J., AND GOSS, A.E. 1957. Animistic responses as a function of sentence contexts and instructions. *Journal of Genetic Psychology* 91: 181–89.

SINCLAIR, H. 1973. Recent Piagetian research in learning studies. In *Piaget in the classroom,* ed. New York: Basic Books.

SINCLAIR, H., AND KAMII, C. 1970. Some implications of Piaget's theory for teaching young children. *School Review* 78: 169–83.

SKINNER, B.F. 1938. *The behavior of organisms.* New York: Appleton-Century.

_____ . 1954. The science of education and the art of teaching. *Harvard Educational Review* 24: 86–97.

_____ . 1958. Teaching machines. *Science* 128: 969–77.

_____ . 1974. *About behaviorism.* New York: Knopf.

SMEDSLUND, J. 1959. Apprentisage des notions de la conservation et de la transitivité du poids. *Etudes d'épistémologie génétique* 9: 3–13.

_____ . 1963. The effect of observation on children's representation of the spatial orientation of a water surface. *Journal of Genetic Psychology* 102: 195–201.

SMITH, M.E. 1935. A study of some factors influencing the development of the sentence in preschool children. *Journal of Genetic Psychology* 46: 182–212.

SMITHER, S.J., SMILEY, S.S., AND REES, R. 1974. The use of perceptual cues for number judgment by young children. *Child Development* 45: 693–99.

SPEARMAN, C. 1927. *The abilities of man.* New York: Macmillan.

STEVENSON, H.W. 1970. Learning in children. In *Carmichael's manual of child psychology,* ed. P.H. Mussen. New York: John Wiley.

SULLIVAN, H.S. 1940. *Conceptions of modern psychiatry.* New York: Norton.

SUPPES, P., AND BINFORD, F. 1965. Experimental teaching of mathematical logic in the elementary school. *The Arithmetic Teacher* 12: 187–95.

SZEMINSKA, A. 1965. The evolution of thought: Some applications of research findings to educational practice. In European research in cognitive development, ed. P.H. Mussen. *Monographs of the Society for Research in Child Development* 30, no. 2 (Whole no. 100).

TANNER, J.M., AND INHELDER, B. 1960. *Discussions on child development.* Vol. 4. London: Tavistock.

TAPLIN, J.E., STAUDENMAYER, H., AND TADDONIO, J.L. 1974. Developmental changes in conditional reasoning: Logical or linguistic? *Journal of Experimental Child Psychology* 17: 360–73.

TERMAN, L.M. 1916. *The measurement of intelligence.* Boston: Houghton-Mifflin.

TERMAN, L.M., AND MERRILL, M. 1937. *Measuring intelligence.* Boston: Houghton-Mifflin.

———— . 1960. *Stanford-Binet intelligence scale.* Boston: Houghton-Mifflin.

THOMAS, H., JAMISON, W., AND HUMMEL, D.D. 1973. Observation is insufficient for discovering that the surface of still water is invariably horizontal. *Science* 181: 173–74.

THURSTONE, L.L. 1928. The absolute zero in intelligence measurement. *Psychological Review* 35: 175–97.

TOMLINSON-KEASEY, C. 1972. Formal operations in females from eleven to fifty-four years of age. *Developmental Psychology* 6: 364.

TONIOLO, T., AND HOOPER, F.H. 1975. Micro-analysis of logical reasoning relationships: Conservation and transitivity. Technical Report no. 326. Madison, Wis.: Research and Development Center for Cognitive Learning, University of Wisconsin, 1975.

UZGIRIS, I.C. 1964. Situational generality of conservation. *Child Development* 35: 831–41.

URGIRIS, I.C., AND HUNT, J. McV. 1974. *Toward ordinal scales of psychological development in infancy.* Urbana, Ill.: University of Illinois Press.

VOEKS, V. 1954. Sources of apparent animism in students. *Scientific Monthly* 79: 406–7.

WASON, P.C., AND JOHNSON-LAIRD, P.N. 1972. *Psychology of reasoning.* Cambridge, Mass.: Harvard University Press.

WEBB, R.A., MASSAR, B.M., AND NADOLNY, T. 1972. Information and strategy in young children's search for hidden objects. *Child Development* 43: 91–104.

WECHSLER, D. 1967. *Wechsler preschool and primary scale of intelligence.* New York: Psychological Corporation.

WEIKART, D.P. 1973. Development of effective preschool programs: A report on the results of the High/Scope-Ypsilanti preschool projects. Paper presented at the High/Scope Educational Research Foundation Conference, Ann Arbor, Michigan.

WEIKART, D.P., ROGERS, L., ADCOCK, C., AND McCLELLAND, D. 1971. *The cognitively oriented curriculum: A framework for preschool teachers.* Urbana, Ill.: University of Illinois Press.

WEINREB, N., AND BRAINERD, C.J. 1975. A developmental study of Piaget's groupement model of the emergence of speed and time concepts. *Child Development* 46: 176–85.

WEIR, R. 1962. *Language in the crib.* The Hague: Mouton.

WHITE, B.L. 1969. The initial coordination of sensorimotor schemas in human infants—Piaget's ideas and the role of experience. In *Studies in cognitive development,* ed. D. Elkind and J.H. Flavell. New York: Oxford University Press.

WHITE, R.M., AND LINDQUIST, D. 1974. Transfer from conceptual rule problems to a truth-table-sorting task. *Developmental Psychology* 10: 155–62.

WICKENS, D. 1973. Piagetian theory as a model for open systems of education. In *Piaget in the classroom,* ed. M. Schwebel and J. Raph. New York: Basic Books.

WINER, G.A. 1968. Induced set and acquisition of number conservation. *Child Development* 39: 195–205.

———— . 1974. An analysis of verbal facilitation of class-inclusion reasoning. *Child Development* 45: 224–27.

WINER, G.A., AND KRONBERG, D.D. 1974. Children's responses to verbally and pictorially presented class-inclusion items and to a task of number conservation. *Journal of Genetic Psychology* 125: 141–52.

WOHLWILL, J.F. 1959. Un essai d'apprentissage dans le domaine de la conservation du nombre. *Etudes d'épistémologie génétique* 9: 125–35.

_____ . 1968. Responses to class-inclusion questions with verbally and pictorially presented items. *Child Development* 39: 449–65.

YOST, P., SIEGEL, A., AND ANDREWS, J. 1962. Nonverbal probability judgments by young children. *Child Development* 33: 769–80.

YOUNISS, J. 1971. Classificatory schemes in relation to class inclusion before and after training. *Human Development* 14: 171–83.

YOUNISS, J., FURTH, H.G., AND ROSS, B.M. 1971. Logical symbol use in deaf and hearing children and adolescents. *Developmental Psychology* 5: 511–17.

YOUNISS, J., AND MURRAY, J.P. 1970. Transitive inferences with nontransitive solutions controlled. *Developmental Psychology* 2: 169–75.

ZIMMERMAN, B.J., AND ROSENTHAL, T.L. 1974. Observational learning of rule-governed behavior by children. *Psychological Bulletin* 81: 29–42.

ZIMILES, H. 1966. The development of conservation and differentiation of number. *Monographs of the Society for Research in Child Development* 31, no. 6 (Whole no. 108).

Index

Index